# KAPLAN

# GRE*

## ALL-IN-ONE

## TEST PREP PLUS
## GRADUATE
## SCHOOL
## ADMISSIONS

# KAPLAN
# GRE*
## ALL-IN-ONE

## TEST PREP PLUS GRADUATE SCHOOL ADMISSIONS

BY JOSE FERREIRA, GRETCHEN VANESSELSTYN, AND THE STAFF OF KAPLAN EDUCATIONAL CENTERS

**Bantam Doubleday Dell**

* GRE is a registered trademark of the Educational Testing Service, which is not affiliated with this product.

Published by
Bantam Doubleday Dell Publishing Group, Inc.
1540 Broadway, New York, NY 10036

Cartoons reprinted by permission of the *Wall Street Journal*, Cartoon Features Syndicate, R. Chast, Chronicle Features, Universal Press Syndicate

"American Radical Historians On Their Heritage," by Aileen S. Kraditor, *Past and Present*, No. 56, August 1972. Reprinted by permission of *Past and Present*.

"Art and Experience in Classical Greece," by J.J. Pollitt, © Cambridge University Press, 1972. Reproduced with the permission of Cambridge University Press.

"A Unified Theory of Elementary Particles and Forces," by Howard Georgi, *Scientific American*, April 1991. Reprinted with permission from Technology Review, copyright © *Scientific American, Inc.*, V. 244.4. Reprinted by permission.

Special thanks to:
Glenn Maciag, Larry Kunofsky, Robert Greenberg,
Margot Shapiro, Janeann Britt, Pat Johnston, Eric Goodman,
Laura Barnes, Gary Krist, Scott Prentzas, Rob Levy, David Stuart, Robert Reiss, Amparo Graf,
Amy Sgarro, Donna Ratajczak

Manufactured in the United States of America
Published Simultaneously in Canada

April 1996

10 9 8 7 6 5 4 3 2 1

ISSN: 1084–9130
ISBN: 0–385–31627–5

# CONTENTS

# PREFACE

CALVIN AND HOBBES copyright Waterson. Reprinted with permission of UNIVERSAL PRESS SYNDICATE. All rights reserved.

Y ou've probably heard the good news: According to recent surveys, Americans with a graduate degree earn, on average, 35 to 50 percent more than do those with just a bachelor's degree. No, that's not a misprint: 35 to 50 percent more.

Maybe that's one reason why there are more people than ever in the United States taking the GRE and applying to graduate schools. In fact, the number of GRE takers has virtually *doubled* in the last decade. No, that's not a misprint either. Only around 293,000 took the test back in 1987, but it's estimated that the number of test takers will climb to half a million by 1997. GRE test-giving may very well be the growth industry of the 1990s.

But what do these remarkable statistics mean for you, the prospective grad school applicant? Well, they mean that while the rewards of advanced study are lucrative, the competition for getting into a good graduate school is as keen as it's ever been. There are a lot of people out there thinking about going to graduate school. Meanwhile, the variety of graduate programs offered by graduate institutions is also growing. And the degree to which they're all keeping pace with the dizzying changes in technology varies widely as well.

That's why, now more than ever, you've got to find a graduate school with a program that's exactly right for you. And not only do you have to find that school, you've got to get into it—at a time when there are more people than ever pounding on the grad school door.

And that's where Kaplan comes in. We at Kaplan have had decades of experience getting people into great grad schools, and one thing we've learned is that *you've got to have a comprehensive strategy*. You can't approach graduate school admission in a casual, piecemeal way. If you want to maximize your likelihood of success, you've got to take advantage of *every* opportunity at your disposal to strengthen your application. Getting the highest possible GRE score is only part of the battle; all other elements of your application have to be maximized as well, so that they add up to a coherent statement of purpose.

That's the philosophy behind this Kaplan guide. In the various sections of this book, we'll show you how to orchestrate everything from recommendations to personal statements to the GRE itself, so that your application becomes a powerful marketing tool for yourself. In our Admissions section, Kaplan's expert in grad school admissions will take you step-by-step through the entire application process—whether to apply, where to apply, when to apply, how to apply, and (last but certainly not least) how to afford it once you're in. Then, in our GRE section, we'll tackle that critical element in your application (and in your efforts for financial aid)—your GRE score. We'll give you a quick course in the legendary Kaplan GRE strategies and techniques. Then, we'll give you a Practice Test to prepare for the real thing, complete with diagnostic software and full strategic explanations for every question.

Throughout the book, moreover, we'll be showing you how to *take control* of the entire application process. Remember, while every element of your application is an opportunity to present yourself in a favorable light, it's also an opportunity to screw up. But if you're in control, you won't make foolish mistakes. We'll show you how to avoid the common pitfalls and make your application stand out from the crowd.

And there's another factor to keep in mind—the test can be taken in the traditional way (on paper) or it can be taken on computer. We'll discuss the advantages and disadvantages of taking the GRE on computer so you can decide which way is best for you.

So don't worry about all those other people who are also applying to graduate school. By following the advice in this book, you'll find the perfect graduate school for you.

# A MESSAGE FROM ALL OF US AT KAPLAN

Welcome to Kaplan. You are preparing for the GRE with the nation's leader in test preparation. Each year, Kaplan raises students' scores through its courses, books, videos, online services, and digital products. We spend millions of dollars annually on research and development to ensure that our materials set the standards for the industry and reflect even the most minor test changes. With more than 160 centers and 750 satellite locations across the United States and abroad, Kaplan prepares more than 150,000 students each year for college and graduate admissions tests, professional licensing, and language exams. Kaplan is a wholly-owned subsidiary of The Washington Post Company, which also owns *Newsweek* magazine.

Kaplan remains at the forefront of test preparation because of the outstanding team of professionals who create and deliver our products and services. Thanks to all of those who made this book—and your score improvement—possible.

Best of luck with the GRE!

# A MESSAGE FROM
# ALL OF US AT KAPLAN

# HOW TO USE THIS BOOK

*GRE All-In-One: Test Prep Plus Graduate School Admissions* is more than just your normal test-prep guide. True, because your GRE score is the most important statistic that you can still do something about (it's too late to change that D in Geology 101, unfortunately), the bulk of this book is devoted to test prep. But grad schools base their admissions decisions on far more than just the GRE. In fact, there are a host of other parts of your application that can make or break your candidacy. So, to give you the very best odds, we've enlisted the help of an admissions expert to lead you through the part of the application process beyond the GRE.

This all-in-one guide, in other words, is just what the name implies, a test prep guide and an admissions guide—all in one.

Here's how to use the various components of this book:

## STEP ONE: READ THE ADMISSIONS SECTION

In this section, Kaplan's own grad school admissions experts will give you an overview of the entire application process. We'll outline a sensible, step-by-step plan to make your application as strong a sales pitch for yourself as it can be. Along the way, moreover, we've included checklists and schedules to keep you on track. We've also isolated certain key points for special emphasis in the outside margins:

**Action Steps**
Things you can do now to get a leg up on the competition

**Red Flags**
"Musts to avoid," classic errors that admissions people may use as an excuse to reject your application

**Bare Facts**
The sometimes harsh truths of grad school admission—important things to keep in mind when developing your application strategy

## STEP TWO: READ THE GRE SECTION

Kaplan's live GRE course has been famous for decades. In this section, we've distilled the main techniques and approaches from our course in a clear, easy-to-grasp format. We'll introduce you to the mysteries of the GRE and show you how to take control of the test-taking experience on all levels:

### Level One: Test Content
Here's where you'll learn specific methods and strategies for every kind of question you're likely to see on the test.

### Level Two: Test Expertise
In addition to the item-specific techniques, you also have to learn how to pace yourself over the entire section, choosing which questions to answer and which to guess on. You should also know how the peculiarities of a standardized test can sometimes be used to your advantage. This is where you'll learn these skills.

### Level Three: Test Mentality
Finally, you'll learn how to execute all of what you've learned with the proper test mentality, so you know exactly what you should be doing at every moment on test day.

And in this GRE section, too, we've distilled the most important points in easy-to-read side-bars in the outer margins.

## STEP THREE: TAKE KAPLAN'S GRE PRACTICE TEST—ON PAPER OR ON COMPUTER

Having trained in the Kaplan methods, you should now use the Practice Test—a timed, simulated GRE—as a test run for the real thing. You can take the test on paper, or you can take the same test on computer (as many GRE takers currently do). Even if you take the test on paper, though, you'll want to enter your answers on Kaplan's unique GRE Digital Test Booklet software afterwards, in order to take advantage of our advanced on-line diagnostics.

Kaplan's GRE Digital Test Booklet allows you to take the Practice Test under enforced time conditions and have the computer record and analyze your timing, confidence level, use of elimination strategies, and answer-changing habits. Each of these areas is analyzed by question-type, so that you can learn, for instance, whether you can recognize typical wrong choices on Logical Reasoning questions but not on Reading Comp.

Naturally, the software will also analyze your overall performance by question-type and content area, provide concise explanations for each question, and give you a score for the exam. (We're working on the updated version that will also do your laundry while you study . . .)

## STEP FOUR: USE THE PRINTED STRATEGIC EXPLANATIONS

Explanations for every question on the test will enable you to understand your mistakes, so that you don't make them again on test day. Try not to confine yourself to the explanations for the questions you've gotten wrong. Instead, read all of the explanations—to reinforce good habits and to sharpen your skills so that you can get the right answer even faster and more reliably next time.

## STEP FIVE: REVIEW TO SHORE UP WEAK POINTS

Go back to the GRE section and review the topics in which your performance was weak. Read the Last-Minute Tips to make sure you're in top shape on test day. And finally, review the Admissions section to make sure that you've done everything you can to strengthen the rest of your grad school application.

Follow these five steps, and you can be confident that your application to grad school will be as strong as it can be.

# GRADUATE SCHOOL ADMISSIONS

## BY GRETCHEN VANESSELSTYN

# CHAPTER 1

# WHY SHOULD I GO TO GRADUATE SCHOOL?

**W**hat kind of job would you like to have in two years? In five years? In ten years? You probably know more about your own career and lifestyle aspirations than you think. Are you interested in teaching on the college level? Does a career in academia appeal to you? Do you hope to conduct research in the sciences? Would a graduate degree help you advance in your current career? A "yes" answer to any of these questions probably means that, like it or not, graduate school will be part of your future. A master's degree is a prerequisite for most teaching positions, and almost all academic work is done by people with doctoral degrees—in some cases, even a few years of postdoctoral work. In many fields, such as primary and secondary school teaching and nursing, people with graduate training earn higher salaries. In short, if you've already made your career decision, grad school may be part of the larger picture, and your next step is to find a school where you'll be happy, a place that fits your needs and your goals. The following chapters should help you to make and solidify your decisions.

But what if grad school isn't part of your clear path to success in a chosen career? What if you're just thinking about it because it sounds interesting or exciting? Many aspiring grad students feel this way. Not everyone is motivated by a desire to teach college courses or conduct advanced scientific research, to make more money or advance in their profession. Many college students find that they want to continue in a certain field or begin work in a new field from a sheer love of learning. The title "professional student" might be exactly what you want. The idea of graduate study for its own sake is familiar to most admissions people, and a strong interest in a field that is not tied to a particular career goal won't be viewed as flaky or immature. If you fall into this group, you'll want to pay particular attention to the next few sections as we explore what the life of a grad student is really like, as well as different opportunities for study and potential careers.

There are many different reasons for going to graduate school. Not everyone falls into the broad categories outlined above, and, whatever your particular needs and goals, you're not alone. Thousands of other potential graduate students are wrestling with the same issues.

## WHAT ARE THE OPPORTUNITIES?

☞ IN THE SAME BOAT

You're not alone. Thousands of people are applying to graduate schools along with you. Many share your fears and concerns about the admissions process.

As more and more companies and institutions need employees with graduate degrees, more people choose to maximize their earning power and marketability by attending graduate school. As a result, many universities are accepting more graduate students than ever and diversifying the fields of study in which they offer degree programs. At the same time, a minor panic about a potential lack of professors in the humanities and science departments of graduate schools has caused many universities to admit fewer students, while seeking younger faculty members in order to prevent this trend from emptying their classrooms of capable teaching staff. Although all these trends may have some bearing on the admissions policies of various universities, none is so sweeping or powerful that it is likely to have more than a minimal effect on your individual admission opportunities.

Because graduate education encompasses so many different fields, it is difficult to make generalizations about admissions opportunities. One thing is certain: No matter how obscure your field, there are programs that offer opportunities for study, and it's likely that you'll find one that meets your needs. Not everyone is interested in the top five schools. Major academic breakthroughs take place every year at small universities, and many people, especially those who would find it impossible to relocate, find programs close to home that are not only convenient but also meet their academic needs. What's most important to know is that, with the large number of programs available, there's probably one that's right for you, but you may have to do a little work to find it.

## WHAT DO ACADEMICS REALLY DO ANYWAY?

Perhaps you don't want to become an academic. You might be pursuing graduate study because you want to be a psychologist, a scientist, a teacher, or an engineer. If so, please bear with us for a moment and don't skip to the next section; you might learn a thing or two that will be useful.

The world of academia is very similar to the university life that you experienced in college, yet there are some significant differences. Most people in academia focus on a few major activities: They teach a class or two, conduct research of their own, and seek publication in journals in their fields. You may have heard the expression "publish or perish," which has some validity in academia. Much of an academic's reputation—and by the same token, the reputation of his or her department and university—hinges on publication of experimental results or other information in journals, as well as larger pieces and books on issues in the field. As an academic, you will almost always be occupied with reading the literature in the field, writing abstracts, seeking grants, and talking with colleagues. If your ideal job is one that you can leave at 5 PM and return to at 9 AM without thinking in between, academia is definitely not for you. If a life of deadlines, books, papers, and reading and writing sounds great, then you're on the right track.

If your interests lie in hands-on research in the sciences, anthropology, archaeology, psychology, or other disciplines, then you can count on a great deal of field work as you explore and test hypotheses. Scientists spend much of their time in laboratories, carrying out experiments or supervising students, or at on-site experimental areas. You may be relieved to hear that not all academics sit in their cramped offices all day. Many fields allow you to get your hands dirty, and if you find this appealing, you'll want to look into this type of career.

The best way to experience what your life really will be like in your chosen career is to spend time with a sociolinguist, an ethnobotanist, a Spencerian scholar, a psychometrician, or whatever professional is relevant in your case. Ideally, you should try to spend at least a day at work with someone in your field, observing both the interesting and the more tedious and mundane parts of their workday. If you know more than one person in the field, even better; you can spend two days or a week. The best way to avoid unrealistic expectations is to explore the various aspects of your field and potential career early on.

## WILL YOU BE HAPPY?

Think about it. There are many different aspects to your life: where you live, whom you live with, where you study, what you study, where you work, whom you work with, what you do all day, how

> ☞ **THE RIGHT FIT**
>
> Whether you want to study William Blake's illuminated texts, 14th century masonry architecture, or the mating habits of capybaras, you will be able to find a program that fits your needs. But it will take a little effort on your part to find the perfect school for you.

> 🖎 **A DAY IN THE LIFE . . .**
>
> If you are entering grad school to pursue a specific career, first make sure that the career is right for you. Spend a work day with a professional in your chosen field.

much leisure time you have, and so on. So many different factors add up to make your life as pleasant or miserable as it is today, so as you make decisions about your future, you'll have to consider all of the same factors. Should you move to Indiana or New York City just because the best graduate program in your field is there? Will you accept that teaching assistantship even though it makes you nervous to speak in front of groups? Can you learn to get along with that brilliant but annoying thesis advisor?

Everyone's life is a balance of different factors, and you will probably have to make some compromises. A good way to organize your thoughts and decisions is to make a list of factors, such as home, work, school, spouse, kids, parents, climate, personal idiosyncrasies, hobbies, likes, and dislikes. Prioritize your list, marking factors that are essential, important, and not so important. This method of organization may help you to see where your real priorities lie. Again, very few people can have everything that they want, but with thorough research, you should be able to find your niche in the grad school world without making too many sacrifices or compromising your personal happiness.

Will you really be happy in grad school? If so, read on.

## 👍 WHAT MAKES YOU YOU?

To help you think more coherently about graduate school and your future, make a list of factors that are important to you and determine where your priorities lie.

# CHAPTER 2

# WHERE TO APPLY

The question of where you should apply is usually a two-part question. First: What schools should you consider, regardless of your chances? And second: Which of these schools can you actually get into? Let's begin with the first question:

## WHAT SCHOOLS SHOULD YOU CONSIDER?

Once you've made the decision to pursue graduate studies, the decision about where to go to graduate school shouldn't be taken lightly. It will have a major influence over your daily life for the next several years and will influence your academic and career paths for years to come. Many students allow themselves to be influenced by a professor or mentor, then find that they're unhappy in a certain program because of its location, workload, cost, or some unforeseen factor. With all those scary things said, remember: This is for your own good! Some hard work today will help to ensure that you'll be happy in your choice tomorrow. Let's take a look at some of the factors that you'll need to consider when choosing a school. They aren't presented in order of importance because only you can determine that order, and if you went through the exercise of determining your priorities in the last chapter, then these may be old hat by now.

### Reputation

Although it may seem obvious that everyone will want to go to the school that offers the best program in a certain field, that's not always true. How many people apply to a given program certainly increases application pressure, which makes it more likely that the program will accept only the most qualified candidates. If you don't feel prepared to compete with students of the highest caliber, you may want to consider a program with a less exalted reputation.

Of course, you'll still want to make sure that the program fits your needs and goals. Does the school have knowledgeable faculty

> ☞ **FACTORS TO CONSIDER WHEN CHOOSING A SCHOOL**
>
> - Reputation
> - Curriculum choices
> - Workload
> - Location
> - Cost

> ☞ **MOUNT EVEREST ISN'T FOR EVERY CLIMBER**
>
> The most prestigious school in your chosen field may not necessarily be the best one for you. Make sure every school that you apply to fits your specific needs and goals.

in your field? Is the field new to the university? (This scenario has its ups and downs. An emerging department often has more enthusiasm than one with a more jaded faculty. Yet new departments don't always get the funding or support from the university accorded by more established departments.)

In some fields, such as law and medicine, it can be difficult to secure a good position if you don't attend one of the top ten law or medical schools. This situation isn't necessarily true in academia or the sciences, but if you're primarily considering schools below the first two tiers, you should consult with people in your field about job prospects for applicants from less distinguished programs.

As a rule of thumb, you should attend the school with the best reputation at which you are accepted. This general rule, however, only applies when you've made a careful analysis of the possibilities and have applied only to schools where you would actually consider going.

### Curriculum Choices

One of the most interesting and complicated parts of your decision will revolve around curriculum. By its nature, graduate study is very specialized. Although in a doctoral program you'll probably have at least two years of course work, which will help you narrow your interests before beginning work on your doctoral thesis, you need to have a good idea of what you'd like to study before choosing a university. For example, schools may offer degree programs in Arts Administration but not in the more specialized field of Arts Management. A school with a reputation for a great Engineering department may not offer a degree in Industrial Engineering. An interest in psychology may attract you to a program, but you may then find that they do not offer a degree in Counseling Psychology, your particular interest. Departmental offerings are varied, and the only way to avoid being surprised or disappointed is to check out graduate school guides and university catalogs carefully and early.

Another important consideration with regard to curriculum is program prerequisites. You may find a program that sounds perfect for you, only to discover that it requires a one-year internship before application, an advanced biology class that you didn't take as an undergrad, or 40 credits in Dramatic Literature. These scenarios underscore the necessity to start your research into graduate programs as early as possible. You may determine that you need to delay your plans while you get some work experience or catch up with some extra coursework. This problem is particularly acute for people who seek to enter a field that is different from their undergraduate concentration.

Although transferring is not unheard of at the graduate level, it's very important to keep curricular considerations foremost in your mind when choosing a program. By doing so, you'll avoid many of the traps that new grad students fall into and make your academic life much easier.

### Workloads

A factor that is very important to most students is the amount of work they'll be doing on a day-to-day basis, especially if they plan to work while studying or have family or other personal considerations. Unfortunately, this is one area that is difficult to research. Unlike such factors as cost and curriculum, workload is not included in rankings of universities, and most students are reluctant to ask a professor or admissions officer, "So how much homework will I have? Will I be able to keep up?" Don't be afraid to ask; these are valid questions and important concerns.

Many students prefer a flexible program that allows them to work on papers throughout a semester (rather than a program that requires only end-of-term exams, which determine students' entire grades). Other students prefer lots of time for independent study. Questions about class schedules and syllabi are perfectly valid, and you can usually get a good idea about how much work a class will require by talking with the professor. But your most valuable resource will probably be students who are currently enrolled in the programs that you're interested in; they can give you a good idea of what their workload is like, and most will probably be willing to talk your ear off. Grad students have a reputation for being single-mindedly interested in their work.

### Location and size

The location of the school that you choose is a very personal decision, and you know best about your own concerns. If you elect not to relocate, you may need to make some compromises because most people, unless they live in large urban centers, don't have a lot of local schools to choose from. If you are free to relocate, though, you should think about the type of location you prefer, taking into consideration such factors as climate and environment. Many universities are isolated from the larger community; others are fully integrated in the life of a town or city. You probably have fairly firm opinions about whether you prefer a rural, suburban, or urban setting, especially if you relocated to go to college. Grad school can be a great time to change locations, but you should be sure that you'll be happy with the change that you decide to make. Definitely visit the schools that you're interested in, and, as you narrow down your

> ### 📖 WHAT AM I GETTING MYSELF INTO?
>
> Don't be reluctant to ask admissions officers, professors, or students about the nature of the work that is expected of graduate students in your program of interest.

> ### ☞ YOU COULDN'T PAY ME TO LIVE THERE
>
> Ask yourself: Do I prefer to go to school in a large or small city, the suburbs, or a rural area? Whatever the answer, it's a good idea to visit the schools that you're serious about attending.

list, plan to spend at least a few days in the area to get a feel for the people and places.

Size constitutes another factor that may influence your life as a grad student. Large universities, especially state-sponsored ones, often have a larger range of course and degree offerings, which may appeal to students with obscure interests and those who are interested in being part of a large academic community. Smaller institutions tend to have fewer students in each concentration, which may mean more individual attention and a feeling of closeness.

### Cost

Although you'll most likely receive some form of financial aid, you will want to consider the cost of the different universities to which you are applying. Cost per credit is usually a good way to compare tuition rates, because the number of credits taken in a semester vary and, therefore, listings by cost-per-year may be deceptive. One caveat: It often happens that some universities offer a course for three credits and others offer the same course for four, depending on their registration policy. Therefore, always make sure that you are comparing apples with apples when evaluating the cost of a given program.

State-and city-sponsored universities often have lower tuition rates than do private universities, and many of them are among the top ten schools in certain curriculum areas. Most offer even lower rates for in-state residents, and some potential grad students go so far as to move to a state a year or two before entering school to establish residency and receive lower tuition.

When considering cost, you'll also want to think about the cost of living in the area where you'll be going to school. A $10,000 per year stipend will go considerably farther toward covering your living expenses in Mississippi than in Connecticut. Housing is very expensive in many cities, and reduced cost of tuition may not always mean that you'll save money overall. There are several books that provide statistics on the cost of living in various cities and regions. They can give you an idea of the financial situation in various communities.

You'll learn more about paying for graduate school in later chapters, but for now, put cost on your list of factors to consider.

### A final note

As we mentioned at the beginning of this section, there are as many factors to consider when choosing a grad school as there are reasons to go to grad school, and you're sure to have some needs and desires that we haven't specifically mentioned here. What's most important is that you decide what's important to you and keep your

☞ **MONEY MATTERS**

When calculating the cost of graduate education, consider:
• tuition rates
• cost of living
• the likelihood of receiving financial aid

☞ **RULE OF THUMB**

When grappling with the important task of finding the right program for yourself, decide what's important to you and keep your priorities in mind while assessing all of the schools on your list.

priorities straight. That way, you'll be prepared to recognize the perfect program for you when it comes along, and you'll avoid the old grad student moan, "Why didn't I think of that six months ago? Now I'm stuck with this climate" or "this department head" or "this insane workload" or "this enormous tuition bill" or "this (insert your biggest gripe here)."

## WHERE CAN YOU GET IN?

Let's now turn to the second question, "Where Can I Get In?" Now that you've developed your dream list of schools meeting all the criteria mentioned above, it's time to get realistic.

### Assessing your chances

Whether you'll be admitted to a given program isn't necessarily the mystery that some people may lead you to believe. Chances are that when that stack of letters from colleges arrived five, ten, or twenty years ago, you had a very good idea of which were acceptances and which rejections, whether you were prepared to admit it or not. The trick? Knowing where you stand with regard to the various factors that programs consider when making admissions decisions. There are always surprises, but, overall, the admissions process is more systematic than you may think.

An important first step is to take a hard look at yourself. A good way to get a sense of how graduate schools will perceive you is to make up a fact sheet with your GRE scores (or projected scores), overall GPA, and GPA in your major (and minor, if applicable). Outside activities, work experience, internships, and so forth will contribute to the "holistic" score that admissions people will use to evaluate you, but let's stick with the raw data for now.

The next step is to find a current source of information about graduate programs. There are several guides published every year that provide rankings of schools, along with data about acceptance rates for given years, median GPA and GRE scores, as well as reputation rankings done by students, professors, and prominent people in the field. Your best bet is to find a guide that gives these statistics separately rather than reporting a holistic score because many institutions consider one aspect to be more important than another, and a holistic score doesn't give you that kind of information. The school of your dreams may not care very much about your lousy GPA, but it might be very interested in your excellent GRE score. It's better for you to be sure what the school cares about.

How do you and the schools that you're interested in match up?

---

☞ **NUMBERS COUNT**

To get a sense of your numerical profile, make a list of your:
• GRE score
• overall GPA
• GPA in your major

---

☞ **HOW DO YOU MEASURE UP?**

Put your GRE score and GPA alongside the median numbers of schools that interest you. The comparison will give you a good idea of where you stand, but remember that schools don't just look at their applicants' numbers.

Be honest with yourself! The best way to gauge whether a school is right for you is to compare your numbers to theirs. And remember that you needn't hit the nail on the head. Median means right in the middle, so some applicants do better or worse than the GRE score or GPA cited. And, remember all those other factors that add up to make you a desirable applicant. Comparing numbers is merely a good way to get a preliminary estimate of your compatibility with the schools of your choice.

### "Safe" schools

Now that you have some idea of where you fall in the applicant pool, you can begin to make decisions about your application strategy. Lots of students waste time and money with the scatter-gun approach; don't become one of them!

No matter what your circumstances, it's wise to choose at least one school that is likely to accept you. Make sure it's one that fits your academic goals and your economic circumstances. This isn't to say that every student should apply to a lowest-tier school. For you, a safe school may be a second- or third-tier school. Once you have a good idea of how your application stacks up, you'll know what "safety" is for you. If your GRE scores and GPA are well above a school's median scores, and you don't anticipate any problems with other parts of your record or application, you've probably found a safe school.

The next question to ask yourself is: Would I actually go there? Think back to the last section, "What Schools Should You Consider?" You have a good idea of what you need to be happy, so you'll need to think about the schools you're interested in with those terms in mind. If your safe school (or schools) satisfies most of your needs, if you can imagine yourself having a happy and productive academic career there, then go for it.

What if you can't find a safe school that appeals to you? There's a chance that you're being too choosy; perhaps you should reevaluate your needs and desires. Maybe you're judging yourself too harshly: Go back and take another look at some rankings charts and do the statistics again.

Maybe you're very committed to one or two programs, or perhaps graduate school for you means a certain program at a particular school. In this case, it doesn't make sense to pick a safety, because you wouldn't go there anyway. If you're confident in your ability to get into your chosen program, go ahead and apply! If there's a reasonable doubt that you'll be admitted, you should probably arrange an interview with an admissions official or member of your prospective department and ask them for a frank evaluation of your poten-

> ☞ **SAFETY FIRST**
>
> You should apply to at least one school that is virtually certain to accept you. Make sure that it's a school that you would actually attend.

tial. Perhaps they can suggest ways of improving your chances: a year's work experience, additional preparation for standardized tests, or more coursework.

Picking a safe school is like finding the bottom line: Once you've decided how low you'll go, there's nowhere to go but up! The bulk of your list should be made up of reasonable schools, ones that you would be happy to attend and that are likely to accept you. Keep in mind that, if you've made an accurate assessment of your potential, one of these is probably the school you'll attend, so pick them wisely.

### "Wishful-thinking" schools

Reach high and apply to one or two very competitive, number-one slot programs. Yes, yes, you should try to avoid unreasonable expectations and carefully evaluate your potential so that you won't be disappointed, but you may be surprised! Some people tend to underestimate their potential and apply only to "sure thing" schools, which often leads to disappointment when they end up at one of these schools and discover that it doesn't provide the degree of academic challenge they want. Just as with safe schools, this doesn't mean that everyone should apply to the top one or two schools in the field. Your "wishful-thinking" school may be on the first, second, or third tier.

The same caveat applies when choosing a "wishful-thinking" school as when choosing a "safe" school: Would you actually go there? Don't make the mistake that many potential grad students make of applying to a top school "just to see if I can get in." Why bother? You're just wasting time and money. Instead, choose one or two schools that seem somewhat beyond your grasp, schools that you would happily attend. The top school in the field may not be ideal for you anyway, if it would mean a sacrifice in terms of curriculum choice, location, cost, or other consideration important to you. Use good judgment and don't let your thinking be clouded by the ivory tower effect. In addition, evaluate your potential to succeed in your chosen program. If you got in, would you be able to keep up? Granted, you want grad school to challenge you, but remember the workload consideration that we discussed in the "What Schools Should You Consider?" section. You don't want to be so swamped that you can't cope!

With all of these considerations in mind, try to choose an appropriate wishful thinking school. Follow your dreams, but use your head as well.

☞ **GO FOR IT!**

Apply to one or two very competitive schools. You might be pleasantly surprised.

☞ **A BASIC APPLICATION STRATEGY**

• apply to at least one "safe" school
• apply to one or two "wishful-thinking" schools
• apply to several schools between these extremes
• don't apply to too many schools

### Avoiding application overkill

There are lots of grad schools out there, and unless your field is very obscure, you'll have plenty of departments and programs to choose from. You'll have lots of room to explore, but don't think that you must apply to every suitable program or even to every one that strikes your fancy. Sending out lots and lots of applications in the hope that at least a few schools will accept you is overkill.

So how do you avoid overkill?

1. Know yourself: Who are you and what do you want?
2. Know the schools: What do they want?
3. How do you match up with the schools?

The better you can answer these questions, the better equipped you are to choose the grad schools that you should apply to. Once you have the answers, you can make educated decisions. If it makes sense within your set of guidelines, choose one or two safety schools. With the same guidelines in mind, choose one or two "wishful-thinking" schools. The rest of your list should consist of schools that are likely to accept you and that are appealing in terms of location, cost, curriculum, degree of challenge, and all the other factors that you deem most important to your academic career.

With all that in mind, how many schools should you apply to? Unless you have your heart set on one or two specific programs, you should submit somewhere between three and seven applications, depending on your individual needs. Fewer than three? If you don't have a particular commitment, you may want to consider a wider range of schools. More than seven? Go back to the drawing board and narrow down your list; you probably need to get a better idea of which programs match up with your needs. You can use the Application List at the end of this chapter to write down the schools that you want to send applications to.

No one can decide for you where you should go to grad school, though some people may try! Your most valuable tools are self-knowledge and the information you have accumulated in your research of the different opportunities available to you. Once you're confident that you know enough about your potential and the opportunities that are available, you have almost as much information as the admissions people have. That will help to assure that you won't underestimate yourself or reach too high. By following the strategies discussed in this section, you'll be able to pick a variety of schools that seem right for you and then wait for the acceptances to come rolling in.

# Application List

You should apply to between three and seven schools, depending on your individual needs. Your list should break down into the three categories discussed in this chapter:

### "Wishful-Thinking" Schools

1.
2.

### "In-Between" Schools

1.
2.
3.
4.
5.

### "Safe" Schools

1.
2.

# CHAPTER 3

# WHEN TO APPLY

With the explosion in the number of graduate school applications in the 1990's, the issue of when to apply for admission has become very important.

## OPTING FOR EARLY ADMISSIONS

Some schools offer early admissions for students who are certain that they want to attend a particular program. Through this system, applicants apply to one program several months earlier than the regular application deadline, and the school informs these students of their decision a month or two after receiving the application. This is an exclusive arrangement: Graduate schools expect students to apply to only one program for early admission. Most programs adopt stricter admissions standards for students considered for early admission, but you will want to contact the program in question for more information about their procedures. The decision of whether to offer early admissions as an option is primarily that of the university, though it can be decided on a program-by-program basis. If you think you might be interested in pursuing early admission, find out as soon as possible whether your desired program offers this option.

So your dream school offers early admissions? Should you give it a try? Well, there are some decided advantages. If you're sure that a certain program is right for you, you can alleviate much of the tension of waiting to hear about your admission decision. If you're accepted, you avoid spending the time and money involved in filing a number of different applications. You give yourself more time to plan financial and living arrangements.

> ☞ **ADVANTAGES OF EARLY ADMISSIONS**
>
> • you don't have to wait around so long to find out if you're in
> • you don't spend time and money filing a lot of applications
> • you have more time to plan how to pay for grad school

☞ DISADVANTAGES OF
EARLY ADMISSION

• if accepted, you are obliged
to attend
• you may discover more suitable program later
• the earliness of the deadline
may force you to submit a less-
polished or less-complete
application, unless you begin
to plan your application extra-
early.

What are the drawbacks to early admissions? If you're accepted
to a program under early admissions, you have an obligation to
attend that program, and, while regulations surrounding this situation vary from school to school, it is more or less compulsory.
This is fine if it's your dream school, but what if you've found
something better in the meantime? Early admissions is really only
for those who are absolutely sure of what they want, and if you're
afraid that it might limit your possibilities in a way that makes you
uncomfortable, consider regular admissions instead.

If you apply for early admission and are not accepted, most programs will reconsider your application in the normal applicant
pool. Don't be discouraged right away, but don't count on getting
in either! No matter how sure you are of your chances for early
admission, you should always have a few back-up schools ready so
you don't find yourself with a rejection letter from your dream
school the day before regular applications are due to the other
schools that you have in mind.

Early admissions can be a dream for some and a nightmare for
others, so you should carefully consider this decision—when you
apply can be as important as where you apply!

## SETTING UP AN APPLICATION SCHEDULE

There are perfect times to begin and end the application process,
and some people are able to move smoothly from step to step on
the road to grad school admissions. Ideally, if you are an undergraduate, you should begin the process the summer before your
senior year. If you have graduated, you should begin a year before
you plan to enter school, preferably in summer.

But honestly, who makes decisions about their life in neat,
packaged time slots? Don't worry if the following schedule doesn't
exactly meet your needs. You may just have to rush things a little
more than some of your colleagues, or you may have several extra
months to think and explore possibilities. Keep in mind, though,
that a few dates are written in stone, and you should find out what
they are as early as possible and incorporate them into your own
personal application schedule, which should include the following
dates:

• Standardized test registration deadlines.
• Transcript deadlines. Some schools send out transcripts only
    on particular dates, so check with your records office to find

out when you have to make requests.

- Letters of recommendation. Be sure to give your recommendation writers plenty of time!
- Application deadlines. Some schools allow you to apply as late as the summer before classes begin, but we recommend that you submit your application as early as possible to ensure that you get a fair and comprehensive review.
- Financial aid forms. Federal and state programs have definite deadlines, and you should also check deadlines from individual universities and independent sources of aid.

The following "seasonal" schedule is organized to help you understand how to proceed through the admissions process. Within each section, you have plenty of room to move around, but the order of the sections is pretty crucial.

*Summer*
- Start thinking about your personal statement. Write drafts, talk it over with friends and colleagues. This should help you define and solidify your goals while you still have time to explore different options.
- Research! Browse through university catalogs and collect information on different grants and loans. Devise a system for keeping track of this information and create your own graduate school library.
- Consider registering for the October GRE. Scores from this test are mailed in November, which will give you plenty of time to submit your scores with your application, rather than mailing them later. Test takers for other dates risk missing application deadlines.
- Research your options for test preparation. How do you feel about standardized tests? Did you prep for the SAT or ACT? How did you do? Should you take a live Kaplan course? Take the test included in this book—and use the software—to give you a good idea of where you stand with regard to the GRE.

*Summer or Early Fall*
- If you are an undergraduate, meet with faculty at your school to discuss your personal statement and possible graduate programs. If you aren't currently in school, go back to your undergrad institution or seek out people who are acquainted with your field; talk with them about your interests and goals.
- Ask for recommendations. Make sure that your recommendation writers know enough about you to write a meaningful letter. Discuss your personal and academic goals with them; help them get to know you well enough to write excellent recom-

> ## 👍 LADIES AND GENTLEMEN, START YOUR ENGINES!
>
> You should begin the application process a year before you plan to enter graduate school.

mendations. Once your recommendation writers have agreed to write a recommendation, let them know when deadlines will be, so you can avoid any timing conflicts. Somehow recommendation writers all tend to go on vacation at awkward times. It's up to you to avoid this catastrophe.

*Late Fall*
- Take the GRE.
- Request applications from schools.
- Request institutional, state, and federal financial aid materials from school aid office.
- Request information on independent grants and loans.
- Order transcripts from your undergraduate institution(s).

*Winter*
- Fill out applications. Mail them as early as possible.
- Fill out financial aid applications. Mail these early as well.
- Make sure your recommendation writers have the appropriate forms and directions for mailing. Remind them of deadline dates.

*Spring*
- Sit back and wait. Some programs may inform you of their decision shortly after they receive your application; others may make you wait several months. This is also a crucial time to solidify your financial plans as offers of aid begin to roll in (with any luck.)

Again, the timing described here is necessarily quite rough, and you needn't follow it exactly. The most important thing for you to do is make yourself aware of strict deadlines well in advance, so that you'll be able to give your application plenty of quality time.

## AVOIDING THE LAST-MINUTE CRUSH

Are you one of those people who believes that you work best under pressure? Do you tend to leave things until the last possible moment? Are you hopelessly disorganized? Well, if any of these apply to you, you'll have to change your ways when it comes to grad school applications. Regardless of when you make your decision to go to grad school, the very worst thing you can do is wait until the last minute. Remember, this isn't a college term paper, which depends only on you and the functioning of your typewriter or printer.

Your grad school application is made up of many different pieces, including some that need outside attention, such as transcripts and

### 👍 MARK YOUR CALENDAR

Keep track of the deadlines for the GRE, admissions applications, financial aid forms, and other materials. Submit everything on time; missing a deadline may be fatal to your admissions chances.

recommendations. Each piece of the application that is beyond your control is one more disaster waiting to happen. You need to be prepared for the worst, and you need plenty of time to patch up mistakes if and when things go wrong. Besides, do you really do your best work under pressure? Probably not.

Trust us on this one; plan ahead, using the guidelines we discussed in the last section. Read program catalogs on the bus. Make inquiry calls on your lunch hour. Write a quick draft of your personal statement before you go to bed every night for a week. Don't type all those long tedious data sheets at the same time because you're sure to make a mistake. The key is to remain calm and spread out the work. If the process is gradual and relaxed, it will be much less painful, and each piece of your application will get the attention that it needs and deserves.

> ### To Avoid Catastrophe
>
> • Plan ahead.
> • Spread out the work.
> • Give yourself plenty of time to complete each facet of the application.
> • Don't wait until the last minute.

# CHAPTER 4

# How To Apply

After you have made the decision to apply to graduate school and have decided where and when to apply, your first move is to order the application forms from the various schools you've chosen. This can be done by mail, but the quickest way is just to call the admissions offices around July and get put on their mailing lists. Once the applications begin arriving you'll notice one thing quickly. No two applications are exactly alike. Some require one recommendation, others two or three. Some ask you to write one essay or personal statement, and others may ask for two or even three. Some have very detailed forms requiring extensive background information; others are satisfied with your name and address and little else.

Despite these differences, most applications follow a general pattern with variations on the same kinds of questions. So read this chapter with the understanding that, although not all of it is relevant to all parts of every application, these guidelines will be valuable for just about any graduate school application that you'll encounter.

> ☞ JUST LIKE
> SNOWFLAKES . . .
>
> No two graduate school applications are exactly alike, but most ask for the same kind of information and look for the same qualities in the applicant. You won't be writing 10 different applications so much as 10 variations on a single application.

## UNDERSTANDING HOW SCHOOLS MAKE THEIR ADMISSIONS DECISION

A helpful step in the application process is to understand how graduate schools make their admissions decisions. What are admissions officers looking for in an applicant? In this next section, we'll help you get inside the mind of an admissions officer, which should give you some ideas about the best way to present yourself in your application.

**What factors are taken into consideration?**

Admissions officers will look at a number of factors when considering your application. Foremost among these factors are: your grade point average (GPA), the reputation of your undergraduate college, your course choices, and your GRE scores.

*Your GPA*

Your undergraduate grade point average is among the most important factors that schools consider. Indeed, many otherwise excellent applications are rejected because of poor undergrad grades. And this makes sense, doesn't it? After all, admissions officers and professors want students to do well in grad school, to be able to keep up with the workload, and to excel if possible. If you couldn't get decent grades in college, why should they believe that you'll do any better in grad school? Using the GPA is one of the easiest ways for institutions to make distinctions between students, and, if yours is low, you should expect that the number of opportunities available to you will be smaller because of it. On the other hand, if your GPA is high, then your application has one important thing going for it already.

With all that said, let's look into the idea of GPA a little more deeply. Admissions personnel who are skilled and knowledgeable (most of them are) understand that numbers can't be considered true measures of human potential. Yes, numbers make it easy to limit an application pool: A school may decide that no one below 2.0 or 2.5 (or whatever) will be considered for admission. But there are so many factors that determine a student's grades that accurate comparisons can't really be made without a thorough transcript review. Because of this, admissions people are trained to look at student transcripts with a somewhat holistic approach. What this means to you is that the poor grades for those two courses you took outside your major may be ignored and that rough semester freshman year may be forgiven. A careful look at your transcript will help an application reader to view your GPA in an appropriate light. In addition, readers for certain programs will essentially ignore grades outside your major (if your major is appropriate to your planned course of study, that is), which is a relief to many students.

What if your grades really aren't an accurate measure of your potential? Maybe personal circumstances affected your performance for one or more semesters, or some other factors influenced your record in a negative way. Maybe you've been out of school for a while and you feel that your work habits have improved after a few years in the work force. Although admissions people aren't interested in feeble excuses, some legitimate cases can be made by applicants for admissions people to ignore undergraduate grades, or at least to take them with a grain of salt. If this situation applies to you, ask the admissions office how they deal with extenuating circumstances such as yours. Often it makes sense to include a letter with your application that explains your situation, but some schools make it a policy to ignore any extraneous materials—it's better to call and

> ☞ **MAKING THE GRADE**
>
> Grade Point Average (GPA) is a crucial criterion in the admissions process. Grades that you earned in your major, if your major is related to your planned course of study, are more important than grades from other courses.

make sure. Another way to incorporate pertinent information about your record in your application is to include it in your personal statement, particularly if the circumstances have something to do with your reasons for applying to grad school or your academic or career goals.

Grades aren't everything, and not everyone will look at your GPA in the same way, but almost every program to which you apply will consider your grades important.

*Reputation of Your Undergraduate College*

Admissions officers are keenly interested in your background, and one of the most important parts of your academic past is your undergraduate institution. This doesn't mean, though, that you have no chance of getting into a top grad program if you didn't go to an Ivy League or top-tier school. Admissions people know better than anyone that lesser-known schools often have leading departments and a degree from these schools in certain fields is considered to be top-notch, even if the institution itself is not of the highest rank. In addition, an excellent record from a good school is often looked upon with more favor than a mediocre record from an excellent school. Consistency and hard work, rather than brilliance, are often considered to be the definitive characteristics of the graduate student, and a solid undergrad record shows that you'll probably excel in advanced studies as well.

What if you went to a top school and did very well? Will you get credit for it? Yes, certainly. Admissions people understand that a 3.5 GPA in a very difficult field at a very challenging school means more than the same 3.5 in a less rigorous program.

The reputation of your undergraduate college probably won't make or break you, but it casts a certain light on your grades and academic record, helping admissions people to compare applications accurately and make fair decisions.

*Your Course Choices*

As we mentioned earlier, an A is not an A is not an A, necessarily. Application readers usually take a good look at your transcript and make an evaluation based on your grades in your major subject or subjects, then look at the rest of your grades with all of these factors in mind. Most schools have a numbering system that they explain in transcript mailings, which allows readers to determine the level of difficulty and/or workload of a given course. For example, 100 level courses may be considered to be basic, whereas 400 level courses are very advanced. By using this kind of system, readers can tell whether that anthropology class was a breeze-through for

## ☞ UNUSUAL CIRCUMSTANCES

If there are compelling reasons why your GPA is low, explain those reasons somewhere in your application. Be aware that feeble excuses will do more harm than good.

## ☞ IVY LEAGUE BLUES

The reputation of your undergraduate school affects how admission officers interpret your academic record. But making top grades at a good school is generally seen as more indicative of success at the graduate level than making average grades at a top school.

## ☞ THE HARD ROAD TO SUCCESS

Admissions officers look closely at the difficulty and scope of your undergraduate courses. Your academic record will look more impressive to them if you've taken challenging courses and made good grades in them.

🖐 **BRAVE NEW WORLD**

If you are planning to enter a graduate field that is not related to your undergraduate major, make sure that you've taken the necessary prerequisite courses. Admissions officers will look closely at your grades in those courses.

you, or a real academic challenge, which will help them to view your A or your C in the appropriate light. In general, schools are looking for applicants who chose a relatively challenging course load, students who have demonstrated an interest in learning and who have been academically successful in their chosen courses.

In addition, the appropriateness of your chosen curriculum is evaluated: If your major isn't directly related to your proposed graduate field, do you at least have the necessary prerequisites? Does your record show excellent performance in core or basic classes in your new field? It's often difficult, but not impossible, for students to change fields from undergraduate to graduate work without some transitional coursework.

You're probably well aware by now that your undergraduate record says a great deal about you, and this can be an advantage or a disadvantage, depending on your past. Your grades, the school you went to, and the choices you made about your coursework all make up a large part of your academic background for better or for worse, and you can be sure that each of these factors will be considered in the review of your application.

*Your Standardized Test Scores*

The importance of test scores to admissions officers varies widely from program to program. How your scores are weighed doesn't depend on the quality of the program: Many top-tier schools don't place much importance on scores, whereas many less prestigious schools believe scores to be very important, and vice versa. The best way to find out about a school's attitude toward test scores is to ask. The university policy on test scores will probably appear in the catalog, but you should probably get a more exact idea by speaking to admissions people on the phone or in person.

☞ **EYE OF THE BEHOLDER**

Different schools treat standardized test scores differently. The best way to find out a school's attitude toward them is to ask.

The GRE General Test is typically required for entrance into North American graduate schools, and some programs require that you take one or more GRE Subject Tests as well, tests that determine your knowledge and expertise in a specific field. We'll give you more information about the GRE Subject Tests at the end of the Test Prep section.

In addition to, or in lieu of, the GRE, some schools require the Miller Analogies Test (MAT), a mental ability test of 100 problems in analogy form. You can find out more about the MAT by calling The Psychological Corporation at (512) 921-8803.

Almost all schools ask students for whom English is not a native language to take the Test of English as a Foreign Language (TOEFL). To find out more about TOEFL, call ETS at (609) 951-1100.

No matter where you go, it will help significantly to get a great score on the GRE. Many programs are particularly interested in one or two of the three areas that the GRE tests: Math, Verbal, and Analytical. Engineering, math, and science programs will look for a high math score, English and humanities programs for a high verbal score. Programs with a particular interest in students' critical thinking skills, whether math- or verbal-based, will look for a high analytical score.

You'll learn much more about the GRE in the test prep section of this book, so we won't go into any further detail here. For now, all you need to know is that almost all schools will consider your standardized test scores to be an important part of your application as a whole.

### How each factor is weighed

Some admissions officers may be willing to sit down with you and explain the mathematical equations that they use in determining an applicant's eligibility, combining GRE score with GPA with a holistic assessment of activities, school reputation, and curriculum choice factored in. Yet even if you do get your hands on the mystical formula used by one specific school, there's still no guarantee that you'll be accepted to that school, and the formula certainly can't be transferred to cover any other institution's admissions policies.

So what do you do, just throw your application at the wall and hope that it sticks? Well, it's a little more concrete than that. You can look at median test scores and GPAs required by different programs. You can talk with admissions people to get an idea of their views on the importance of different factors; often you'll get some important revelations, if not precise formulas.

Most admissions officers consider certain factors to be primary: usually undergraduate grades, recommendations, and standardized test scores. These three factors, along with an interview (usually optional) are considered more or less equally, and review of them forms the bulk of the decision process. Secondary factors—such as the essay, extracurricular activities, and work experience—help to form the rest of the general picture of you as an applicant. Although you'll probably never know exactly what "score" your application gets, you can be pretty sure that the different factors will be balanced more or less in this fashion.

## DEVELOPING A BASIC APPLICATION STRATEGY

A key part of your approach to getting into the graduate school of your choice is to develop a basic application strategy so you can present yourself in the best light.

---

**👍 TOP OF THE CHARTS**

Scoring high on the GRE will help you get into the graduate program of your choice. Preparation is the key to GRE success.

---

**☞ THE TOP THREE ADMISSIONS FACTORS**

The most important factors in the admissions process are:
• your undergraduate grades
• your standardized test scores
• your recommendations

---

**☞ FILLING IN THE PICTURE**

Admissions officers also look closely at:
• your work experience
• your essay
• your extracurricular activities

## YOU LOOK MAH-H-H-VELOUS

You can improve your chances of being admitted to the graduate school of your choice by enhancing the presentation of your personal data.

## SELL YOURSELF

Devise a plan to create an image of yourself that will stick in the minds of admissions officers. Remember to:
• present facts concisely
• double check to make sure facts don't conflict
• exclude any useless, unnecessary facts

## WHAT THEY WANT

Graduate schools want you to tell them why they should accept you into their program. Taken together, the elements of your application should answer this question.

### Your application as a marketing tool

Okay, it's time to face some facts. Lots of people want to go to the same schools that you're interested in. Lots of them have the same GPA and the same GRE scores that you do. You're all literate and articulate, so the essay and interview balance out. How will you help your application to stand out from the crowd? The raw facts that you have to present can't be tweaked. You can't magically raise your GPA or get two years of work experience in a month and a half. And there comes a time when you need to take an honest look at what you've got. You can't enhance the data, but what you can and should do to improve your chances is to enhance the presentation of that data.

When a company sets out to market a product, they sit down and look at the key features of the product: what does it do, what does it look like, how will it help the consumer, what's its appeal? Marketers then boil down the image to a few key selling points and structure their entire campaign around those points. You don't see a soda campaign with billboards that say "Drink our colorful Pop because it's blue!" and TV spots that say "Gee, Soy Pop is extra-nutritious!" and radio ads saying "Our Pop saves lives—we make donations to charities!" No, you're bombarded for weeks on end with the same slogan: "Pop's the Best!"

Granted, you won't need a slogan or a jingle, but you will need to condense all the information about you into a clear, concise package. Face it, application readers really don't want to get to know you on a personal level; they don't have time to be interested in your likes and dislikes. If you can tell them exactly what to think about you, you'll make their job much easier, which makes them happy and improves your chances for acceptance. Are you convinced? (See what a little marketing can do?)

So how do you begin? Well, marketing yourself doesn't mean that you have to lie, or even embellish; it just means that you have to make a tight and coherent presentation of the facts. Everything adds up in a good marketing campaign. There are no scattered pieces, no information that seems extraneous or unnecessary. "Our floor wax is strong, tough, and powerful! Oh, and it comes in an attractive bottle." Marketing copy is never weak or wishy-washy. You'll never read an ad that says "So our odor-preventing shoe insoles are pretty decent, and that's why you should probably consider buying them." This doesn't mean that you need to present yourself as one-dimensional: You're not just a physics whiz or a Dickens freak, you're a well-rounded human being. But there are certain key points that can be distilled from your experience, your characteristics, and your goals, and those are the points that you'll capitalize on as you create your image.

Almost all application forms have a certain tone, one that's comforting and accepting. Why would you like to come to our school, they seem to be asking. Well, yes, they really want an answer to that question, but what's even more important—the subtext for the whole application process—is a bigger question: Why should we want to accept you? This is the question that your application will answer, and, with some good marketing, your answer will be clear, concise, coherent, and strong.

**What self do you want to portray?**

So how do you develop an image? First of all, it should fit; it should feel natural. Don't bother to try to sell yourself as something you're not:  It'll be uncomfortable for you, and it probably won't work. Application readers are trained to see through smoke screens, and any dog-and-pony show without some substance behind it will be quickly exposed as a sham. Besides, part of what readers do when they evaluate your application is form an image of you from the various parts of your application. Your job is to help them, not hinder them. Remember, that's what will make them happy.

Let's try an example. Cindy wants to pursue a doctorate in Molecular Biology at a pretty tough school. Her grades for her first two years as an undergrad are pretty weak, but after her transfer to a different school, her grades rose dramatically for her junior and senior years. She was a biology major, and her grades in science courses were As and high Bs. Cindy's GRE scores are just okay. Math is pretty high; analytical is about average; but her verbal score is significantly below average. Cindy has been out of school for three years, working in a biological research lab. During this time, she has gained a great deal of experience in her field, which has brought her to the decision to pursue a graduate degree in order to enhance her career options.

How should Cindy sell herself? Well, her greatest strengths seem to lie in her real-world experience and the expertise and knowledge that she has gained in the last three years. Therefore, she has certain qualities that distinguish her from a student fresh out of college. Cindy should include information about her job in her essay, pointing out different research projects that she's worked on, publications her work has appeared in, and other aspects of her job that are relevant to her potential as a scientist. She should seek recommendations from her superiors at work and make sure that they understand why she is applying to grad school, so that the information they provide in their letters will enhance her image as well.

Although Cindy's grades and math GREs will be okay selling

> **THE REAL YOU**
>
> Don't try to make yourself sound like someone you're not. Your application will sound forced, and admissions officers can sniff out most attempts at deception.

> **DON'T BE JUST ANOTHER FACE IN THE CROWD**
>
> In your application, focus on what you think makes you stand out, what makes you better prepared for graduate school than other applicants. Accentuate your strong points.

### 👍 GET A THEME

Start thinking early about what theme you want your application to convey. Decide what your real purpose is in applying to grad school and make sure that this sense of purpose comes through in all aspects of your application.

For instance, is it your goal to teach at the college level? If so, give your entire application a teaching theme. Become a volunteer for a local tutoring service to demonstrate your interest in teaching (and make sure to list that activity on your application form); ask the head of the same organization to write a recommendation for you; use the personal statement to discuss your involvement in the organization. All of these efforts will give your application coherence and a sense of purpose—and help it stick in the minds of the admissions officers.

points, she will probably do better to focus on her experience because it separates her from the crowd, makes her stand out. Work experience on its own isn't one of the top three most important application characteristics, but, by working it into her essay and recommendations, Cindy can capitalize on it to such a degree that readers may choose to pay less attention to the weaker features of her application. She is a scientist, a person who is deeply involved in her field and wants to gain additional knowledge and expertise. Can you picture Cindy? She has a clear, coherent image, one that readers can understand and grasp quickly.

So where do your strong points lie? Are your grades excellent? Maybe you should sell yourself as a stellar student, one who is fascinated by the academic process, dedicated to a field for the love of learning. Maybe you've done independent writing or research that can tie in to this studious image. If so, sell yourself as a self-starter, an independent thinker, a potential Einstein.

But there's nothing special about me, you may be saying right about now. Get a hold of yourself. Reread the last section if you want. You don't have to be a cartoon character, Super Student or Academic Woman. Developing a strategy for your application just means emphasizing your strengths and downplaying your weaknesses in such a way that application readers can, after a quick read-through, understand something about who you are, why you're going to grad school, and why their grad school should accept you.

## MAXIMIZING THE VARIOUS PARTS OF YOUR APPLICATION

Now let's look at how you should approach the specific parts of your application.

### Essays

Essays play an important role in the admissions process because they give admissions officers a more complete picture of who you are. Essays give you an opportunity to make your true self leap out from the pages of your application.

*What do they want from me?*

The Statement of Purpose. These four ominous words bring a shiver to the spine of many a potential grad student. The easy answer? Don't let the statement be a stumbling block! Instead, think of it as an opportunity to show admissions officers what you're made of. What they really want to know is why you want to go to grad

### 👍 APPLICATION BASICS

Whatever strategy you choose, make sure your application conveys:
• who you are
• why you want to go to grad school
• why the program you're applying to should accept you

school, *their* grad school in particular. Start early. Go over your goals and aspirations, defining them as clearly as possible, writing drafts, talking to students and teachers, making everyone you know read it, until you can give a short lecture on your ideal future in your sleep.

Then give some thought to how your goals and dreams will fit into grad school. How will you accomplish them? How will they change the world? (Or at least the world of academia.) Remember, essay readers want to get a clear picture of who you are, but they also want to be able to picture you in your desired program. What will grad school do for you? What will you do for grad school? Answer these questions in a clear, concise manner, and you've got the basis for a decent essay.

Some applications will have a series of questions for you to respond to, some of which require critical thinking or creative interpretation. The key advice for these questions is to answer the question they're asking. If they want to know what you think the president of the United States will be like in the year 2078, don't write an essay about the puppy you got for your birthday when you were ten (unless there's some bizarre connection). For the specific-question type of essay, make your answer clear, concise, and on-topic. They're not so interested in your past or even your future in these essays; they want to get a general idea about your thinking and writing skills.

Most applications have the generic personal statement type of essay. It's the kind of question that gives you little clue as to what they'd like to hear, no matter how many times you scrutinize each word. What are some of the things that readers are looking for in an essay? Honestly, there are no specific "musts" for an application essay, which makes your job easier and more difficult at the same time. The typical personal statement includes some information about the writer, her goals and interests, her reasons for pursuing a graduate degree in a specific field and her background and experience in the field or in related areas. Some essays include personal information about the writer, especially information that pertains to career goals and major topics of interest. Autobiographical or personal information is not necessary (unless specifically requested in the question), but it often allows the writer to describe his goals more accurately and concisely, within a clear context.

Overall, you can't go wrong in a personal statement by giving readers a good idea of what you'd like to do with your life and why. A description of the circumstances surrounding your motivation and background is usually a good idea as well. If you can keep on topic, stay organized, and answer the question they're asking, you

☞ **THE RIGHT STUFF**

Application essays should be viewed as an opportunity for you to show admissions officers what you're really made of.

☞ **HOW TO HANDLE SPECIFIC-QUESTION ESSAYS**

If an application asks you to answer a specific question, answer the question clearly and concisely and don't stray from the topic at hand.

📖 **PERSONAL STATEMENT TIPS**

In your personal statement, you can include:
• what you'd like to do with your life
• why you want to pursue a graduate degree
• background and experience in your field of study
• personal history that's relevant to your career goals or field of study

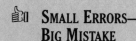

## SMALL ERRORS— BIG MISTAKE

Once you've finished your essay, get other people to read it. Cajole an editing whiz to read it and make corrections. Type your final draft and proofread it carefully. Make sure it's perfect—THAT MEANS NO TYPOS!

## STAND OUT FROM THE CROWD

In writing your essay, try to be distinctive rather than merely comprehensive.

can write a good personal statement. If you want to go beyond "good," keep reading.

Did we forget to mention essay appearance? Make it neat. Type it (or print it out, if you use a computer). Type it again if there's one little mistake. Remember what we said about having lots of people read your statement? Preferably at least one of those people should be a near-expert in grammar, spelling, and usage. Even the most literate pre-grad student can make mistakes, and you can't be too careful. Sure, application readers will probably forgive you one or two little mistakes, but why give them any chance to turn you down? Make sure that your essay is as perfect as it can be.

### Making Your Essay Distinctive

So now you know some of the qualities of a good essay, one that won't be dismissed by even the most critical reader. But what if you want or need a *great* essay? Almost everyone applying to grad school can write a clear essay in a pleasing style—how else would you have made it through college? You're competing against your peer group, and there's no reason to believe that your statement will be better than anyone else's just because it's yours. Depending on the amount of time you have and the amount of effort you're willing to put in, you can write an essay that will stand out from the crowd.

One of the first mistakes that students make is in thinking that "thorough" and "comprehensive" are good qualities for a personal statement. This will make me stand out, they think, because the reader will really get to know me. I'm so lovable that he or she can't possibly turn me down. Ahem. Such applicants try to include as much information about their lives as possible, from hobbies and interests to reminiscences about childhood vacations and detailed plans for their education, career, and retirement. Not a good idea. This is how those bloated 15-page essays you hear about are created, and no application reader in his right mind will wade through that much material. So how do you decide what to include? There's only one sheet of paper, and they don't really want you to write much more than that. First, get rid of the idea of "comprehensive" and focus more on "distinctive."

How do you make your essay distinctive? Think back to what we said about marketing. Remember, you're selling yourself with your application, and the statement is where you have the most room to say exactly what you want, to put your past and future into a clear, tight package that shows who you are. From a marketing perspective, this is your real chance to customize your application, to make your big presentation of yourself. If you haven't sat down to think about your most marketable qualities, do it now. Take a look at the various features of your background, your grades, your test scores, your academic and non-academic past. Flip back to the "Application Strategy" section and give it a try, then come and join us in the next paragraph.

This is not the time to be blasé. Unless they ask for it, you don't have to include any particular information, so why dwell on your weak points? A strong essay about how much you learned from your independent study with a local veterinarian and how the experience and knowledge you gained inspired you to become a vet will give readers what they want—a quick image of who you are, and how you got that way, and why you want to go to their school. By the same token, a description of the first article you read in a computer publication, how it made you want to pursue a degree in educational technology, and the pride you felt when your first article was published in the same magazine would give the reader a good idea of your background and goals, while giving you a chance to show off at the same time. One of the best ways to be distinctive is to sell your image briefly and accurately, including real-life examples to back up your points.

"Distinctive" just means that your essay should answer the questions that admissions officers think about while reading essays: What's different about this applicant? Why should we pick this applicant over others? Authentic enthusiasm can be a plus, and writing about parts of your life or career that are really interesting or relevant is helpful. Sometimes an interesting approach to the essay itself is a good idea, but check out the caveats in the next section. As a rule, stay away from the generic, such as: "I first realized that I wanted to go into forestry when I was four years old and my grandpa helped me plant a tree. As I grew, so did my interest in trees and forests. In high school, I planted lots of trees. In college, my interest in forests was reinforced by my botany teacher." Almost anything that works harder than the average chronological history essay will probably get a little extra attention from jaded essay readers, so take advantage of this opportunity.

*Is being creative worth the risk?*

Many myths surround the idea of creativity in the personal statement. Everyone seems to know someone who filled out his whole application to Harvard in crayon, but they can't seem to remember whether he got in. The idea that anything that wakes up an application reader is a good thing is rampant on many campuses, yet this idea, too, seems unfounded. Creativity is definitely a risk, but it may be one that you're willing to take.

What do we mean by creativity? Creative essays usually fall into

---

### 📖 HOW TO WRITE A DISTINCTIVE ESSAY

• Create a quick image of who you are and why you want to go to grad school.
• Sell your image briefly and accurately.
• Include real-life examples to support your points.
• Make sure your enthusiasm for your field of study shines through.

---

### 👎 ESSAY NO-NOS

1. Don't dwell on your weak points.
2. Don't employ dull chronological histories.
3. Don't disregard length limitations (one page or so should suffice)
4. Don't lie in your essay—or in any part of your application.

two categories: dangerous and not-so-dangerous. Dangerous attempts at creativity are ones that will probably be looked upon as flippant or obnoxious. In other words, no crayon. No write-it-on-a-balloon-so-they-have-to-blow-it-up-to-read-it. Really. They hate that. Probably the most dangerous way to be creative in your essay or in your application in general is to lie. No. No. No. Very bad idea. Not only is an application a legal document that you sign your name to, there's a very good chance that schools will find out that you're lying, and even if they don't seek prosecution, they definitely won't accept you. Okay, lecture over. What else is dangerous? Any attempt at eliciting an emotional response from an essay reader, especially sympathy, is a mistake. It won't work, and you'll look like a fool for trying.

Not-so-dangerous types of creativity may seem a little tame to you, but we tend to take the better-safe-than-sorry approach. If you're willing to go out on a limb, then do it, but don't expect universal acceptance of your zany scheme. Creative inclusion of anecdotes is okay, and sometimes very appropriate, but don't go too far afield. The same is true of humor. One, maybe two, jokes might be tolerated, but this isn't a comedy sketch. Depending on your field and the schools you're applying to, some literary creativity may be appreciated, but only if it's done really, really well.

In general, anything that's not typed on nice, plain, white paper is out. Essay readers aren't easily amused. Within the constraints of the typed page, verse is almost always inappropriate, as is the stream-of-consciousness approach. Yes, grad schools want you to be inventive, creative, excited about life and about learning, but not in the personal statement.

Again, this is not to say that interesting prose is uncalled for or that your essay must be in five-paragraph form with introduction, body, and conclusion. But consider yourself warned: Many readers are conservative, jaded, and overworked enough to ignore or even resent any attempts on your part to entertain them. With this in mind, choose your own path to the perfect essay. If you're not sure if you've made a bad decision, your many readers should be able to help you. If you think that your essay is reasonably conservative, but your readers are fainting in the aisles, take another look.

## Recommendations

*Whom should you choose?*

As we mentioned earlier, recommendations are one of the top three things that application readers look at, along with grades and test scores. That's a big chunk of your application, and it may seem to lie beyond your control. You may think that you can't do anything about recommendations except hope for the best. Wrong, wrong, wrong. Although you can't actually write the recommendations yourself (don't even think about it), you can have a great deal of influence over how accurate and persuasive they are. As with every other piece of your application, though, getting good recommendations will take both legwork and headwork.

Most schools require two or three letters of recommendation, and, if you're still in college and you've done pretty well, the process of choosing recommenders may be one of narrowing down a number of prospects. (If this doesn't describe your situation, be patient. We'll get to you later in this section.) You may want to make a list of potential recommendation writers to refer to as you go through the decision process.

What are the qualities of a good recommendation writer? First of all, it's probably obvious that you should choose someone who likes you, who thinks you're good at what you do. This doesn't mean that you have to be intimate pals, but sworn enemies don't often write good recommendations. It helps if the person is a good writer so that he or she can clearly express an opinion about you. Poor writing skills on the part of a recommendation writer probably won't reflect badly on you, but an incoherent assessment of you won't help you much either.

Most, if not all, of your recommendations for academic programs should come from professors or other academic faculty. Understandably, admissions officers like to hear good things about you from someone who has worked with lots of students. That way, presumably, your recommendation writer can make an accurate (and favorable) comparison of your credentials with those of other students. It helps if at least one recommendation writer is familiar with the field you hope to enter, as he or she will have a good idea of your potential to succeed in that field. A professor with whom you have studied and worked on an internship or mentorship basis is often an excellent choice, because he or she can give a picture of you in more than one frame of reference.

If your field is nonacademic, at least one recommendation from a professional in the field is usually a good idea. If you've done an internship or work project outside school, you probably know people who can make a fair assessment of your potential as well or better than your undergraduate professors can. You may want to advise nonacademic recommendation writers to describe their credentials in their letter, especially if they work in nontraditional fields.

Does your cousin's wife's hairdresser live next-door to a prize-winning architect? Did you once brush up against a best-selling author

### 👍 TAKE CONTROL

You can influence how accurate and persuasive your recommendations are.

### ☞ QUALITIES OF A GOOD RECOMMENDER

The best recommendation writers will be those who:
• like you
• know you well enough to provide a credible opinion
• have familiarity with your chosen field
• write well

### 👍 MAKE A LIST, CHECK IT TWICE . . .

Make a list of potential recommendation writers at the beginning of the application process. Narrow down your list as your needs become clearer.

at a cocktail party? Have you thought about asking these people for a recommendation to graduate school? Well, it's not necessarily a bad idea, but it will require much more work on your part. If you have access to a person who is well-known and well-respected in your field or a similar field, it may be good for your potential career to get to know them, if you can do so without interrupting their life. If you're lucky enough to hit it off, you may be able to meet to discuss your goals and possibly ask for a recommendation. Of course, if this should happen, you'll have to present your potential recommendation writer with materials that will help him or her get to know you and your work, as we'll explain in the next section. In general, if you can get a thorough, meaningful recommendation from a famous person, go ahead. What if you've never met the person, but Aunt Millie can ask him to write you a letter anyway? Forget it. A form letter from a famous person will carry no more weight than a form letter from Aunt Millie herself in the eyes of the intelligent application reader.

What if you've been out of school for a few years and haven't kept in touch with your professors? The first thing you should do is call or write the admissions offices of the schools to which you're applying. Don't assume that it's okay to send fewer letters than required or to substitute other kinds of information for recommendation letters. Most schools have specific policies on this subject, and you'll feel better knowing that you're not just winging it.

Most likely, schools will allow you to submit recommendations from employers and colleagues in your field or from other people with knowledge about your background, skills, and goals. Some schools may ask you to take more courses and seek recommendations from the professors under whom you study. Other schools may waive the requirement or allow you to substitute other types of information. Remember, it's best to be sure what the school wants.

If you haven't been out of school for very long, there's a good chance that professors with whom you worked closely will remember you and be happy to meet with you to discuss your goals and, perhaps, to write a recommendation. Contact these people by mail or phone and, if they seem amiable, set up an appointment to speak with them. Don't be shy; you may be more memorable than you realize.

One more important topic on the subject of recommendations for students who have been out of school: credentials files. Did you create one as an undergrad and forget about it? If so, give your undergrad career placement office a call. Many schools keep recommendation letters and other materials on file for students who don't go on to grad school right away. If you're an undergrad, you may want to take advantage of this service; look into it. If you've been out of school, search your memory bank: Were you on the ball as a college student? If so, you may be in luck.

So you've narrowed your list of potential recommendation writers down to several choices, all of whom are people who could probably write you a good letter. Play with your list a little and try different groupings. Three professors from your undergrad major department will probably have similar things to say about you. Why not include someone from another field who knows lots about your thinking and writing skills? It's not always easy to form a perfectly balanced selection of recommendation writers, and it's more important that each one be good than that they balance one another. Just try not to have three carbon-copies of the same letter because it may make you seem a little one-sided.

Now you've made your selections. You have three or four firm choices and a few back-up choices. How do you ensure that you get good, on-target letters of recommendation? Read on.

### Asking for recommendations

No matter how well you know a person, it's not always easy to ask them for something, especially for a letter that says nice things about you. Do you fear that a potential recommendation writer will say, "Me? Recommend you?" and walk away laughing? Don't worry: If you've thought to ask this person for a recommendation, lots of other students over the years have probably done so as well. Most professors write several recommendations a year, so it's old hat to them. If the person you're asking isn't a professor, things are a little different and you may need to make them aware of the recommendation procedure (we'll get more into that later). In any case, most people will probably be flattered that you've asked them and will be likely to at least consider writing you a letter.

There are two fundamental rules of asking for recommendations: ask early and ask nicely. As soon as you decide to go to grad school, you should start sizing up potential recommendation writers and letting them know that you may ask them for a recommendation. This will give them plenty of time to get to know you better and to think about what to say in their letter. Once they've agreed, let them know about deadlines well in advance to avoid potential scheduling conflicts. The more time they have, the better the job they'll do recommending you. As for asking nicely, we hope that will come naturally to you. All this means is that you should let the person know you think highly of their opinion and you'd be happy and honored if they would consider writing you a letter of recommendation. You don't have to get down on one knee, just be polite.

> ### 📖 BALANCING ACT
>
> If possible, try to find recommendation writers from different parts of your life. Recommendations from people who know different things about you will draw a more complete picture of you.

> ### 📖 CARDINAL RULES OF ASKING FOR RECOMMENDATIONS
>
> 1. Ask early.
> 2. Ask nicely.

*Making Sure Your Recommendation Writers Know What They Need To Know*

Once the person has agreed to consider writing a letter for you, arrange an appointment to discuss your background and goals for your future. Many students don't bother with this, even though it's the most crucial step to getting a great recommendation. By failing to take this step, you might end up with mediocre, vague recommendations in your admissions file. Of course, you won't let this happen to you. Some recommendation writers accustomed to uninterested students may be surprised that you asked, but they'll be willing to schedule an appointment with you. Most will realize that it's not easy to write a good letter about someone you hardly know, and they'll be happy to have this opportunity to get some more information about you.

You should bring with you copies of appropriate documentation, such as your transcript, papers that you've written, your résumé or curriculum vitae, your personal statement, and/or a sheet of bullet points that you plan to feature in your application and essay. These "leave-behinds" will go a long way toward making sure that your recommendation writers say relevant things about your good points and your background. You should also supply recommendation writers with the appropriate form or forms, as well as stamped, addressed envelopes and a copy of your home address and telephone number.

Keep the appointment relatively brief; you're already taking up enough of their time. Give your recommendation writers a good idea of why you want to go to graduate school and your reasons for interest in particular programs. Play up your good points, of course, but be reasonably humble. If you have a very specific "marketing" image that you're trying to project, let your recommendation writers in on it because they may want to focus on some of the same points that you're trying to stress. It's often a good idea to explain to recommendation writers why you chose them, because it will give them an idea of the perspective from which you would like them to write. You may want to discuss your Statement of Purpose with your recommendation writers, but don't take up their time with the finer points of style and structure. Save that favor for someone else. Above all, don't tell your recommendation writers what to write! Don't even give them the impression that you're doing so! Recommendation writers tend to resent any attempts at manipulation, and they may, as a consequence, refuse to write your letter.

One last issue with regard to recommendations is confidentiality. You'll need to decide whether or not to waive your right to read letters written about you, and you should discuss this issue with your recommenders from the outset. Many writers will only write confidential letters, and, unless you have serious reservations, it's usually wise to waive this right.

The biggest favor that you can do for those who consent to write you letters of recommendation is to give them appropriate material about which to write. No matter how well you think they may know you, all letter-writers appreciate having something to sink their teeth into, and strong, relevant letters are just what readers are looking for.

After you've received confirmation from schools that your application is complete, write a thank-you letter to each person who wrote a recommendation for you. It's a nice way to express your appreciation, and people tend to remember these details, which may help you in the future.

**The interview**

Preliminary meetings with department personnel conducted while you make your decision about grad school can be considered "interviews," even though it may seem as though you're the one asking all the questions. For these informal meetings, it's important to be alert, interested, and articulate. Interviewers will be interested in your knowledge of the field and your reasons for interest in their program, but their main function will be to dispense information to you.

The admissions interview is a different kind of meeting, one that puts a little more pressure on you. Most graduate programs don't require admissions interviews, but almost all admissions offices and departments are willing to meet with interested students. Should you arrange an interview if it's not required? It really depends on you. If the thought of personal interviews terrifies you, and you'd rather have your teeth drilled (without painkillers) than answer questions about yourself, skip it and let your application speak for itself. If your interpersonal skills are polished, however, and you're interested in talking about your field with admissions or departmental personnel, you may want to consider arranging an interview, especially if your application could use an edge above the competition.

Most graduate school interviewers will ask you about the same kinds of things that you'll discuss in your personal statement: your background, goals, and interests. Some interviewers may ask provocative questions about controversial issues in order to assess your thinking and reasoning skills, but this usually only occurs in required interviews.

**☞ WAIVE IT GOOD-BYE**

As a general rule, it's better to waive your right to read letters of recommendation. Admissions officers place greater trust in recommendations written in confidence.

**☞ FACE TO FACE**

Most admissions offices and departments are willing to schedule interviews with prospective students.

☞ **INTERVIEW TIPS**

• Practice with friends beforehand
• Dress appropriately
• Be prepared to discuss the facts in your personal statement
• Use the interview to flesh out your application and to impress the interviewer

As for any interview, you should think about questions that may be asked and prepare answers. Practice with a friend or relative so that you'll feel comfortable when the time comes. Overall, think of your interview as an extended conversation, an opportunity to inform and possibly impress someone, a chance to talk about yourself and your interests. For most graduate programs, an interview makes up a very small part of the decision process, so see what you can learn from the experience while you make the best impression possible.

# CHAPTER 5

# FINANCIAL AID

To this point, we've discussed the main issues concerning the graduate school admissions process. Now let's talk about one of the most important aspects of graduate school—paying for it.

## WHEN TO APPLY FOR FINANCIAL AID

If there's a set of deadlines that you can't afford to miss, it's the ones for financial aid. If you're thinking about skipping this section for one reason or another, think again. If you think you won't need financial aid or won't be eligible for it, keep reading—you'll probably be pleasantly surprised.

First of all, almost all graduate students require some form of financial aid at some point in their academic career, and, rather than bankrupt yourself in the first year or so, you should work out a financial plan from the very beginning. Second, the category of financial aid is a broad one, encompassing both need-based and merit-based aid. That means that, if your record is good enough, you don't necessarily have to need the money in order to get it.

There are two favors you can do for yourself with regard to financial aid: Get as much information as you can and get it early. There's plenty available, but competition, especially for popular fellowships and assistantships, is often tough, so it's important to research the possibilities carefully and apply early. As soon as you've made the decision to go to grad school, even before you know which schools you'll be applying to, you can begin to collect information about outside sources of financial aid. As soon as you know where you'll be applying, you should get information about aid sources from the financial aid office and from the individual departments you'll apply to.

On the graduate level, the administration of aid is often handled by the department rather than by the university, so you'll want to find out as soon as possible whom you'll be dealing with. What's even more confusing is that some schools won't let you apply for aid

---

☞ **DOLLARS AND SENSE**

Even if you don't think you can qualify for financial aid, you should explore all of the possibilities anyway. Some types of aid are not based on your financial situation and may not require you to repay the money.

👍 **DIGGING FOR GOLD**

The best approach to financial aid is to research the possibilities carefully and to apply early.

👍 **FUND YOUR FUTURE**

KapLoan, The Kaplan Student Loan Information Program, can help you get information and guidance about educational loans for grad school. For more information, call 1–800–KAP–1057.

unless you've been admitted, whereas others require you to apply for aid at the same time that you apply for admission. Again, it's just a matter of being organized and getting information as early as possible.

## HOW TO APPLY FOR FINANCIAL AID

Just when you thought you couldn't possibly type your social security number on one more form, it's time to apply for financial aid. This process is probably more boring than anything you'll ever do in your life, but just remember that the end result of your hard work will, most likely, be money for grad school.

Just as with admissions applications, it's important to fill out forms neatly and accurately, to make sure you've filled out every piece with the same complete information, and to keep good records (and photocopies) of the forms you've sent and where you've sent them. As with any bureaucracy, financial aid offices occasionally lose a form or two, and it's up to you to make sure that your records are complete. By the same token, don't be shy about following up on applications if you don't hear from aid sources within a reasonable period of time.

One important thing to remember about financial aid: Federal regulations often change from year to year, and the requirements for independent aid sources change frequently as well. Don't ever say to yourself, "Well, this pamphlet from 1986 probably has accurate information." Get this year's information and make sure it's up to date.

The Free Application for Federal Student Aid (FAFSA), which was created by and is processed by the U. S. Department of Education, is required for any student applying for any type of federal aid. This form is due in May, and you must fill it out every year that you apply for or plan to continue to receive federal aid. You can get a copy at your financial aid office. You can also get information about federal financial aid programs by calling the Federal Student Aid Information Center at (800) 433-3243 from 8 AM to 7 PM (Central Time).

In addition to the basic form required for each program, most schools and independent aid sources require one of the two official forms that allow them to determine the amount of aid you'll need. There are other approved forms used by some schools, but the most popular ones required is the Financial Aid Form (FAF), which you may be familiar with from undergrad aid applications. The FAF is available at any financial aid office or from the College Scholarship Service (CSS). In addition, you'll probably have to supply schools

---

👍 **GOOD HOUSEKEEPING**

Fill out all financial aid forms neatly, accurately, and completely. Keep copies of everything that you mail out and record when you sent in the forms.

---

☞ **UNCLE SAM WANTS YOU . . . TO FILL OUT HIS FORM**

If you plan on applying for any type of federal financial aid, you must submit the Free Application for Federal Student Aid (FAFSA).

---

and aid programs with copies of your tax returns and financial aid transcripts from your undergrad institution.

## ALL ABOUT AID

### What's "need-based aid?"

Most federal- and state-provided aid are based on student need. Some independent and university-based aid is distributed on a need basis as well. As you skim through listings of grants and loans, the most common terms you'll see are "need-based" and "merit-based." So what does that really mean? For almost all financial aid purposes, need is defined as the cost of your education—which includes books, tuition, room and board, and other living expenses while you're in school—minus your financial resources. Resources, according to financial aid people, include your savings and money you will earn while a student, and, depending on your situation, may include the earnings and savings of your spouse or parents. Any gap between your potential expenses and your potential resources is your potential need. Therefore, need-based aid is designed to fill all or part of that gap, thus enabling you to go to grad school even if you can't cover all the expenses. Need-based aid comes in several different forms, which we'll get to a little later.

### What about "merit-based aid?"

Eligibility for merit-based aid is primarily decided by your undergraduate GPA and your GRE scores, though other factors may be taken into consideration by certain programs. Individual universities and departments often offer merit-based aid, as do foundations and other independent sources. Some merit-based scholarships require fairly elaborate applications, including essays and sometimes an interview. Although merit-based aid programs are often very competitive, it's usually worth the trouble of applying because many grants and fellowships will completely cover your tuition and your living expenses. That's not a bad deal for a few extra hours of work.

### A note on the GRE and merit-based aid

As we mentioned above, besides using the GRE as a tool to guide admissions, schools also use it as a means of determining merit-based aid eligibility. Outside providers of merit-based aid, such as foundations that award grants and fellowships, also use GRE scores as a measure of an applicant's merit. Decisions about candidates for

☞ **THE TWO CATEGORIES OF FINANCIAL AID**

There are two main types of financial aid:
• need-based
• merit-based

☞ **BROTHER, CAN YOU SPARE A DIME?**

Most types of financial aid depend on the financial needs of students. Need is determined by comparing the cost of the student's education with his or her financial resources.

☞ **CREAM OF THE CROP**

Some financial aid is merit-based, which means that you can receive scholarships and grants on the basis of your academic achievement and other factors. Your GPA and GRE score are important factors in qualifying for merit-based financial aid.

teaching and research assistantships can also be partly based on GRE scores. Because of heavy competition for fellowships, as well as university-directed scholarships and assistantships, many programs establish cutoff points for GRE scores to limit the application pool. This may not seem fair to students with excellent credentials despite low GRE scores, but these programs argue that establishing strict standards is the only way that they can make aid decisions. GRE scores have no influence on the results of a student's application for need-based aid.

### Targeted Aid

Certain aid programs sponsored by the federal government and independent foundations target specific student populations. Some targeted aid goes to students pursuing degrees in specific fields, such as education or the sciences. Other targeted aid depends on who you are. These programs seek to fund students from groups that are underrepresented in certain fields, usually women or people from minority groups.

## WHAT TYPES OF AID ARE AVAILABLE TO ME?

Financial aid falls into three major categories: fellowships and grants, assistantships and other work opportunities, and loans.

### Fellowships and grants

These two terms are often used interchangeably, though they have very different connotations and meanings in the graduate school world. Both types of aid are almost always outright gifts, which don't require repayment or service on the part of the recipient. Both usually cover tuition and some, if not all, of a student's living expenses. The difference between the two lies in the criteria for awarding the aid. Grants are usually based on student need, though they often target students who need aid in specific fields. The selection of students for fellowships is usually based on merit in a particular field and has nothing to do with student need.

Fellowships are often limited to doctoral and post-doctoral students, though there are some that specifically target Master's students in particular fields. Most fellowship programs are highly competitive and are designed to attract students with excellent academic records. Grants are almost always limited in scope, and, if you fall into a particular category of student, certain grant programs will be interested in hearing from you. Portable fellowships and grants are offered by independent donors or organizations and can be applied

☞ **THEY'RE GRE-A-A-A-T!!!**

Your GRE scores are important beyond admissions. They are often used to determine who should receive merit-based scholarships and fellowships and who should get teaching and research assistantships.

☞ **TYPES OF FINANCIAL AID**

The three categories of financial aid are:
• fellowships and grants
• assistantships and other work opportunities
• loans

at any university. Several different guides to portable fellowships can be found in your financial aid office or public library. Institutional fellowships and grants are awarded through specific university programs. The financial aid offices of the schools to which you are applying can give you information on any available institutional fellowships.

### Sources Of Fellowship And Grant Aid

*Federal grants*

Federal aid is administered by a variety of different agencies, and the types and amounts of aid granted by different programs vary considerably. Some of the government agencies that provide aid for graduate study are the National Aeronautics and Space Administration, the National Institutes of Health, and the National Science Foundation. For a complete list and more information, write the Fellowship Office of the National Research Council at 2101 Constitution Avenue, Washington, D. C. 20418 or call (202) 334-2872.

Students in the arts, humanities, and social sciences can seek grants from the U. S. Department of Education's Jacob Javits Fellowship Program. Jacob Javits Fellows receive up to $6,000 toward tuition and as much as $10,000 as a stipend. To request an application, write: Director, Jacob Javits Fellowship Program, U. S. Department of Education, 400 Maryland Avenue, SW, ROB-3, Washington, D. C. 20202-5251 or call (202) 708-9415.

Another good resource for information about federal and other sources of fellowship and grant aid is the Publications Office of the National Science Foundation. Their number is (202) 357-7861.

*State grants*

Many states provide grant money to help state residents attend graduate school. In some states, a resident must attend grad school in-state to be eligible, but other states allow students to "travel" with their grants. What's a state resident? Generally, to qualify as a legal resident you must have lived in a state for at least 12 months before enrolling, though some states require longer periods of residence to qualify. Contact your state scholarship office; you can get the address and phone number from any guidance office or from your public library.

*Institutional grants*

In order to attract excellent students to their programs, universities use their own funds and those of donors and alumni to offer fellowships and grants. Many students choose to attend a certain uni-

---

**☞ FREE MONEY**

Students who receive grants and fellowships usually do not have to repay the money or do any work.

---

**☞ CASH COWS**

Sources for grants and fellowships include:
- the federal government
- state governments
- institutions
- corporations
- foundations

versity because they've been offered a particularly desirable fellowship. It's wise to find out what kinds of programs are available at the schools you're interested in as early as possible.

### Corporate grants

Many corporations offer tuition assistance for their employees when they take courses or pursue a degree on a part-time basis, particularly if their field of study relates to their job. If you're interested in finding out more about these programs, speak with your supervisor at work or with someone in the human resources department of your company. Guidebooks that describe corporate tuition assistance programs are also available at your bookstore or library.

### Foundation grants

Various independent foundations—such as the Ford, Howard Hughes, and Spencer foundations—provide grants and fellowships for graduate study in many different fields. A good source of information about foundation assistance is: The Foundation Center, 79 Fifth Avenue, 8th Floor, New York, NY 10003-3050, phone number (212) 620-4230. The Center has several publications on the subject of foundation assistance, as well as a data bank service.

## ASSISTANTSHIPS

☞ **YOUR ASSISTANTSHIP HAS COME IN**

Assistantships may be the most desirable form of financial aid. You can receive money for working as a graduate assistant and gain invaluable experience teaching or conducting research in your field.

☞ **ON-THE-JOB TRAINING**

Teaching assistants perform a variety of tasks, from reading students' papers to leading seminar groups to tutoring individuals.

Probably the most prevalent, and one of the most desirable, forms of financial aid is assistantships. Most assistantships are granted on a merit basis, though need may be taken into account by some institutions. Students who serve as graduate assistants receive aid in the form of a paycheck and, in some cases, tuition reduction or waiver. In return, the students work, usually on a part-time basis, for the institution or department. Assistantships are a particularly desirable form of aid for students because they allow students to earn money for school while gaining valuable work experience, usually in their chosen field of study.

There are several different types of assistantships, and not every program will offer all of them. Usually you should seek information about available positions when applying, though the consideration process usually won't begin until after you've been accepted into a program.

One of the more popular and desirable positions is that of teaching assistant. If your undergraduate institution was large and had a grad school attached to it, you probably knew several TAs, the people who assisted your professors, read your papers, and, perhaps, led seminar groups or small tutoring sessions. Teaching assistants perform all of these tasks, and more, in exchange for a salary and, often, tuition remission or reduction. It's not an easy job, but competition for these places is usually tough because the experience gained by TAs is considered very desirable by most employers.

Research assistants, common in the sciences but also prevalent in other fields, oversee laboratories and assist professors on projects. Research assistants are connected with a specific professor, a mentor, and much of their work involves carrying out experiments or analyzing data for the professor's major research. Most RAs tailor their dissertations to correspond with those of their mentors (thus, they need to make the decision about whether to work with a certain mentor carefully.) This arrangement allows these students to incorporate their own academic work with the research they complete for their mentor. Most research assistants are appointed after their first year of graduate school, which gives them the opportunity to explore different aspects of the field and to seek an appropriate mentor relationship. Competition for these spots, like that for TA positions, is usually quite tough.

Administrative assistantships give graduate students the opportunity to earn money and, sometimes, tuition reduction or remission in exchange for support and administrative services. These jobs aren't as glamorous or sought-after as TA or RA positions, but many students find that they also aren't very intellectually challenging, which leaves them more time to pursue their studies than would a more demanding position. If you decide to pursue an AA position, you should consider contacting the office of the department you'll be studying in, or a department in a similar field. Working with professors and other academic staff in your field on a colleague basis can sometimes help you make contacts that would otherwise be difficult to make, which may lead to future mentorships.

Residence assistants usually receive free room and board, as well as a stipend or small salary. These assistants commonly live in undergraduate dorms and have responsibility for the well-being of groups of students. These positions are desirable for students who need assistance with living expenses but can't afford to take much time from their studies. Experience gained as a Residence Assistant looks good to potential employers in the fields of education, counseling, and social work, as well as other fields where a strong background in human relations is desirable.

Work-study programs allow students to take jobs outside the university, usually jobs in the community that are relevant to the student's field. Although work-study positions are granted on a need

## ☞ RESEARCH WHIZZES

Research assistants help a specific professor carry out experiments or analyze data for the professor's research projects.

## ☞ OFFICE WORK

Administrative assistants perform clerical duties, usually for the department in which he or she is studying.

basis, applicants must fulfill certain requirements established by the federal government, which pays more than half the student's wages under most programs. You can find out more about work-study programs from your university's financial aid office.

### Loans

Many graduate students, despite generous support from other aid programs, have to take a loan at some point in their academic careers, and if this looks like a necessity for you, don't panic. Student loans are designed to be low-interest and relatively hassle-free, so try to look upon them as an investment in your education. One of the most important things to remember is not to borrow more than you need! Don't arrange for a loan until you have a clear idea of the outcome of all your other applications for aid. Once you've put a package together, you can then sit down with a financial aid counselor to assess whether a loan will be necessary and what kind of loan will meet your needs. We'll describe some different loan programs here, but this certainly isn't a complete list. To help assess how to finance your graduate studies, call KapLoan, The Kaplan Student Loan Information Program, at (800) KAP–1057.

- **Perkins Student Loans** are need-based loans administered through university financial aid programs. Ninety percent of Perkins loan funds come from the federal government and 10 percent from your school or institution. You can borrow up to $5,000 per year to a maximum of $30,000 at 5 percent interest. The amount that a student can borrow through Perkins Loans, however, is determined by the school sponsoring the loan, so you'll need to get their exact numbers from the financial aid office. Nearly all graduate students with financial need are eligible for these low-interest loans, and you can get an application through your institution's financial aid office.
- **Federal Subsidized Stafford Loans,** which used to be called Guaranteed Student Loans, are available through independent banks and savings institutions. Through these loans, which are subsidized by the federal government, you can borrow up to $8,500 per year, up to a total of $65,500, at a variable interest rate that is set in July of each year. You need not repay Subsidized Stafford Loans until you've finished school. You can get information about these loans, which are based on need, through any bank. You can also get basic information from the Financial Aid Services Hotline at (800) 642-6234.
- **Federal Unsubsidized Stafford Loans,** which which aren't quite as desirable as Perkins or Subsidized Stafford Loans. Many students, however, find that they adequately cover gaps in their

funding, allowing them to attend school. The interest rate on the Unsubsidized Stafford Loan is set at the 91-day Treasury Bill rate plus 2.5 percent, with an 8.5 percent cap, the same rate as the Subsidized Stafford Loan. The interest on the unsubsidized loan either must be paid or accrues while you are in school. You must first apply for a Subsidized Stafford Loan before you apply for an Unsubsidized Stafford Loan. You can borrow up to $18,500 in an Unsubsidized Stafford Loan minus any amount borrowed in Subsidized Stafford Loan for that academic period. For more information, contact your financial aid office or a participating bank.

## FINANCIAL AID—IT'S NOT REALLY SO BAD

As you've seen, there are many different types of financial aid, and, with all those possibilities, you're bound to find a package that's right for you. Remember, "free money" isn't necessarily your best bet, because some financial aid opportunities will give you the chance to get valuable work experience. If you really need to look for a silver lining, think about how good your credit rating will be when you repay your student loan on time! Be calm, organized, and on time, and you'll breeze through the financial aid process without too much personal strife.

## CONCLUSION

We hope that this section on graduate school admissions has made you realize that there's a lot more to getting into grad school than just taking the GRE. A strong application requires substantial planning and a great deal of time and effort on your part. If you're not prepared to make that kind of commitment, maybe you should look at how committed you are to going to graduate school in the first place.

But if you're prepared to make an effort to follow the above advice, you can be sure that you'll be putting forward the best possible case for yourself. And for most of you, your grad school experience and the work in your field will be your reward. Good luck.

# THE GRE

## BY JOSE FERREIRA

# CHAPTER 1

# AN INTRODUCTION TO THE GRE

This test preparation section will explain more than just a few basic strategies. It will cover practically everything that's ever on the GRE.

No kidding.

We can do this because we don't explain questions in isolation or focus on particular problems. Instead, we explain the underlying principles behind all of the questions on the GRE. What a particular question is *really* testing. We give you the big picture.

One of the keys to getting the big picture is knowing how the test is constructed. Why should you care how the GRE is constructed? Because if you understand the difficulties that ETS has when they make this test, you'll understand what it is you have to do to overcome it. As someone famous once said, "Know thine enemy." And you need to know firsthand the way this test is put together if you want to take it apart.

## THE SECRET CODE

There is a sort of unwritten formula at the heart of the GRE. First, there's psychometrics, a peculiar kind of science used to write standardized tests. Also, ETS bases its questions on a certain body of knowledge, which doesn't change. ETS tests the same concepts in every GRE. The useful thinking skills and shortcuts that succeed on one exam—the exam that you're signing up to take, for instance— have already succeeded and will continue to succeed, time and time again.

> **BE PREPARED**
>
> You can't really study for the GRE, but you can *prepare* for it.

> **U2 CAN HAVE THE EDGE**
>
> More than 400,000 people take the GRE each year. By reading the following chapters, you'll learn the underlying principles of GRE questions and acquire test strategies that will help increase your score.

## THE GAME

If you're like the authors of this book, you weren't too crazy about the idea of taking the SAT back in high school. It seemed unfair that one's entire future—where we went to college and where that took us afterwards—would be based on our performance on an unfeeling exam one dreary Saturday morning. Some of us weren't too crazy about our GPAs, which we could no longer do much about.

There are a great many people who think of these exams as cruel exercises in futility, as the oppressive instruments of a faceless societal machine. People who think this way usually don't do very well on these tests.

The key discovery that people who ace standardized tests have made, though, is that fighting the machine doesn't hurt it. If that's what you choose to do, you will just bloody your hands. So, instead, they choose to think of the test as a game. Not an instrument of punishment, but an opportunity for reward. And like any game, if you play it enough times, you begin to get really good at it.

## PLAY THE GAME

You may think that the GRE isn't fair or decent, but that attitude won't help you get into graduate school. Many things in the world aren't fair or decent; survivors manage to overcome them.

None of the GRE experts who work at Kaplan were *born* acing the GRE. No one is. That's because these tests do not measure innate skills; they measure *acquired* skills. People who are good at standardized tests are, quite simply, people who've already acquired the necessary skills. Maybe they acquired them in math class, or by reading a lot, or by studying logic in college, or perhaps the easiest way—in one of Kaplan's GRE classes. But they have, perhaps without realizing it, acquired the skills that bring success on tests like the GRE. And if *you* haven't, you have nothing whatsoever to feel bad about. You simply must acquire them now.

## SAME PROBLEMS—BUT DIFFERENT

We know it sounds incredible, but it's true: The test makers use the same problems on every GRE; only the words and the numbers change. They test the exact same principles over and over. Let's give you an example (time to dust off your algebra):

This is a type of math problem known as a Quantitative

Comparison. Look familiar? These are also on the SAT. Your job is to pick (A) if the term in Column A is bigger, (B) if the term in Column B is bigger, (C) if they're equal, or (D) if there is not enough information given to solve the problem.

| COLUMN A | COLUMN B |
|---|---|
| $2x^2 = 32$ | |
| x | 4 |

Most people answer (C), that they're equal. They divide both sides of the equation by 2 and then take the square root of both sides.

Wrong.

The answer isn't (C), because x doesn't have to be 4. It could be 4 *or* -4. Both work. If you just solve for 4 you'll get this problem—and every one like it—wrong. ETS figures that if you get burned here, you'll get burned again next time. Only next time it won't be $2x^2 = 32$; it will be $y^2 = 36$ or $s^4 = 81$

The concepts that are tested on any particular GRE—Pythagorean triangles, simple logic, word relationships, and so forth—are the underlying concepts at the heart of *every* GRE.

Basically, every GRE is exactly the same as every other one administered that year. In fact, the GREs being given today are extremely similar to those given a decade ago. For instance, most of the math problems you are going to get on the test that you've signed up for are just superficially different from the math problems that have been on every other GRE. To guarantee scores that are almost perfectly consistent, ETS writes tests that are almost perfectly consistent.

## WHY DON'T THEY JUST START TESTING SOMETHING NEW?

If ETS started testing different principles, they would have to compromise score consistency. Even when they make very minor changes in test structure or content, they do so between school years, introducing the revisions into the October administration, so that everyone who takes the exam that school year has the same kind of test. That's important, because it means that Kaplan knows what every GRE is going to look like, before it's administered.

ETS makes these minor changes only after testing them exhaustively. This process is called *norming,* which means taking a normal

### OLD FAITHFUL

The GRE tests the same principles over and over. Every GRE is virtually the same as every other one because the tests must be consistent from year to year to yield dependable results.

test and a changed test and administering them to a random group of students. As long as the group is large enough for the purposes of statistical validity and the students get consistent scores from one test to the next, then the revised test is just as valid and consistent as any other GRE.

That may sound technical, but norming is actually quite an easy process. We do it at Kaplan all the time—for the tests that we write for our students. The test at the back of this book, for instance, is a normed exam.

## THEY LIKE THEIR TEST

Another major reason they don't re-work most or all of the GRE is that they think it's really a pretty good test. (We know what you're thinking. . . .) To be more specific, they feel that the GRE tests what it's designed to test: various fundamental concepts of algebra, geometry, verbal ability, reasoning ability, and so on. The way ETS figures it, so what if people learn all those principles and get better at the test? That doesn't mean the test is rotten. Quite the opposite: To improve your score you have to learn a lot of important things.

## LET THEM THINK THAT

What do you care if it's a good test or not? If ETS and the Graduate School Admissions Council want you to learn a bunch of simple concepts and improve your vocabulary, why fight it?

We don't think any of Kaplan's students, after they took the GRE, ever said to themselves, "Now that it's all over, I just wish I hadn't learned all that damn vocabulary!" Let's face it, none of us would mind being able to read dense, confusing material better and faster. Or being more logical and analytical thinkers. Or improving our vocabulary.

All those things are good things, and they translate into success on test day. So grin and bear it—we'll do what we can to help. And the first step is taking a close look at the set-up of this test that ETS thinks so much of.

> ### RECOGNIZE WHAT YOU CAN'T CHANGE
>
> Your opinion of the test doesn't matter. Your score on it does.

## THE SECTIONS

The paper-and-pencil GRE consists of six scored 30-minute sections, one for each of its three measure types: Verbal, Quantitative (Math), and Analytical (Logic). That's two Verbal, two Math, and two Logic, with a 10 to 15 minute break halfway through. (We'll discuss the computerized GRE, known as the CAT, near the end of the test prep section.)

In addition to these six sections, the test will include one 30-minute, unscored *experimental* section, which will probably look just like any other section of one of the three measures above. ETS uses this section to pre-test the questions that will show up on the scored sections of future GREs.

The big thing about the experimental section is that it's unscored. If you could figure out which of your sections was experimental on test day, you could skip it entirely, draw big smiley-faces on that column of your answer grid, play connect the dots, or whatever you like, and your score would be exactly the same.

Naturally, then, many people try hard to figure out which section is experimental. But because ETS really wants you to try hard on it, they keep you guessing. All you will know is that you have three sections of one measure type and only two each of the others.

Furthermore, trying to figure out which section is experimental can be dangerous to your health—or your test score, at any rate. That's because you could be wrong, and it's not worth the risk of losing big points if you goof. Besides, it's doubtful that taking a 30-minute nap during a section will help you anyway; it may actually lower your score if you can't get your brain clicking again when the next section begins.

Plus, if everyone were to figure out which section was experimental and skip it, then ETS wouldn't be able to write these tests. And we wouldn't want that, now, would we?

## SCORING

Each of the three measures described above yields a scaled score within a range of 200 to 800. You cannot score higher than 800 on any one measure, no matter how hard you try! Similarly, it's impossible (again, no matter how hard you try) to have a score lower than 200 on any of the three measures. Scaled scores are much like the old scores that you received if you took the SAT, the major difference being the addition of a score for the Analytical measure, which isn't tested on the SAT.

But you don't *only* receive scaled scores. You will also receive a percentile rank, which will place your performance relative to those of a large sample population of other GRE takers. Percentile scores tell graduate schools just what your scaled scores are worth. For instance, if everyone always got very good scaled scores, universities

## WHAT'S A PERCENTILE?

The percentile figure tells you how many other test takers scored at or below your level. In other words, a percentile figure of 80 means than 80% did as well or worse than you did and that only 20% did better.

## MEASURE FOR MEASURE

Your percentile rank is the most important result from your GRE. It tells graduate schools how you stack up against other test takers.

## MAKING THE CUT

Research the graduate schools that you're interested in to find out what level of scores they're looking for. You'll have to aim higher than their minimum scores to impress them.

would still be able to differentiate candidates by their percentile score.

Percentile ranks match up with scaled scores differently, depending on the measure. Let's imagine that our founder, Stanley H. Kaplan, were to take the GRE this year. He would (no doubt) get a perfect 800 on each measure type, but that would translate into different percentile ranks. In Verbal, he'd be scoring above 99% of the population, so that would be his percentile rank. But in the Math and Logic sections, many other people will score very high as well. Difficult as these sections may seem, so many people score so well on them that high-scaled scores are no big deal. Mr. Kaplan's percentile rank for Math, even if he doesn't miss a single question, would be only in the 96th percentile. So many other people are scoring that high in Math that no one can score above the 96th percentile! Similarly, his Logic percentile would just be 98th.

What this means is that it's pretty easy to get good scaled scores on the GRE and much harder to get good percentile ranks. A Math score of 600, for example, is actually not all that good; if you are applying to science or engineering programs, it would be a handicap at most schools. Even a score of 700 in Math is relatively low for many very selective programs—after all, it's only 79th or 80th percentile.

The relative frequency of high-scaled scores means that universities pay great attention to percentile rank. What you need to realize is that scores that seemed good to you when you took the SAT might not be all that good on the GRE. It's important that you do some real research into the programs you're thinking about. Many schools have cut-off scores below which they don't even consider applicants. But be careful! If a school tells you they look for applicants scoring 600 average per section, that doesn't mean they think those are good scores. 600 may be the baseline. You owe it to yourself to find out what kinds of scores *impress* the schools you're interested in and work hard until you get those scores. You can definitely get there if you want to and if you work hard enough. We see it every day.

A final note about percentile rank: The sample population that you are compared against in order to determine your percentile is not everyone else who takes the test the same day as you do. ETS doesn't want to penalize an unlucky candidate who takes the GRE on a date when everyone else happens to be a rocket scientist. So they compare your performance with those of a random three-year population of recent GRE test takers. Your score will not in any way be affected by the other people who take the exam on the same day as you. We often tell our students, "Your only competition in this classroom is yourself."

## THE KAPLAN THREE-LEVEL MASTER PLAN

To give your best performance on the GRE, you'll need to have the right kind of approach for the entire test as a whole. We've developed a plan to help you, which we call (cleverly enough) "The Kaplan Three-Level Master Plan for the GRE." You should use this plan as your guide to preparing for and taking the GRE. The three levels of the plan are: Test Content, Test Mechanics, and Test Mentality.

### Level 1: Test Content

In the first part of the test prep section, we'll talk about how to deal with individual short verbal questions, reading passages, math problems, logic games, and logical reasoning questions. For success on the GRE, you'll need to understand how to work through each of these question-types. What's the difference between Antonym and Analogy questions? What are the best ways of handling each? What's a Sentence Completion and how do I approach it? How should I read a Reading Comprehension passage and what should I focus on? What's the best way to approach the Math section? Is there a secret to Logic Games? How do I solve Logical Reasoning questions? Our instruction in Level 1 will provide you with all of the information, strategies, and techniques you'll need to answer these questions and more.

### Level 2: Test Mechanics

Next, we'll move up the ladder from individual question-types to a discussion of how to complete each section within the specified time limit. We'll reveal the test mechanics that will help you to use the strategies you learned in Level 1—and the time to use them.

### Level 3: Test Mentality

On this final level, we'll help you pull everything you've learned together. By combining the question strategies and test mechanics, you'll be in control of the entire test experience. With good test mentality, you can have everything at your fingertips—from building good bridges to gridding techniques, from sequencing game strategies to pacing methods. We'll also outline all of the subtle attitudinal factors that will help you perform your absolute best on test day.

Understanding the three levels, and how they interrelate, is the first step in taking control of the GRE. We'll start, in the next chapter, with Level 1, Test Content.

# CHAPTER 2

# TEST CONTENT

In this chapter, which makes up the bulk of the GRE section, we'll give you the nuts and bolts of GRE preparation—the strategies and techniques for each of the individual question-types on the test. For each of the multiple choice sections—Verbal, Quantitative, and Analytical—we'll present you with the following:

- **Directions and General Information**
  The specific directions for each section will help introduce you to the question-types. We'll also give you some ground rules for each question-type.

- **Basic Principles**
  These are the general rules-of-thumb that you need to follow to succeed on this section.

- **Common Question-Types**
  Certain types of questions appear again and again on each section. Here's where we'll show you what these question-types are and how best to deal with each one.

- **The Kaplan Approach**
  This is a step-by-step way of organizing your work on every question in the section. The Kaplan Approach will allow you to orchestrate all of the individual strategies and techniques into a flexible, powerful *modus operandi*.

Now let's begin with an important part of the GRE, the Verbal Section.

# A. VERBAL

Here's the deal on the Verbal section:

Two sections
30 minutes per section
38 questions in each section

The chart below shows which question numbers correspond to each question-type, how much time you should spend on each question-type, and in what order you should answer each question type.

| | SENTENCE COMPLETION | ANALOGIES | READING COMPREHENSION | ANTONYMS |
|---|---|---|---|---|
| Question Numbers | 1-7 | 8-16 | 17-27 | 28-38 |
| Time per Question | 30-45 seconds | 30-45 seconds | > 1 minute | 30 seconds |
| When you should do them | 1st | 2nd | 4th | 3rd |

Sentence Completions, Analogies, and Antonyms are called short verbal questions. Every section of a short verbal question-type goes from easiest to hardest, where the first few are easiest and the last few are hardest. Reading Comp, however, doesn't follow this pattern.

There are two basic things that the Verbal section tests: your vocabulary and your ability to read a particular kind of passage quickly and efficiently. You may have asked yourself: How is what we covered earlier about test construction going to help us in the GRE verbal sections? Well, just like the math questions, which are the same from test to test (just with different numbers), the verbal questions are the same (just with different words). Have you ever heard the expression, "That's an SAT word"? It's a commonly used phrase among high school students, and it refers to any member of a very particular class of prefixed and suffixed words derived from Latin or Greek. For instance, "profligate" is a great SAT word. It's also a great GRE word.

## VOCABULARY—THE MOST BASIC PRINCIPLE FOR VERBAL SUCCESS

Many of the same kinds of words that would commonly show up on the SAT are likely candidates for the GRE as well. Because the same company, ETS, writes both tests, it's cheaper and easier for them to write similar tests, and it means they're testing the same kinds of skills (which they like to do).

The GRE tests the same kinds of words over and over again. (Remember: For ETS, consistency is key.) We'll call these words "GRE words," and we're going to make a point of including them in the rest of this chapter. That way, you can get a feel for what they look and sound like, and you can see them used in context. So if you see a word in this book that's unfamiliar, take a moment to look it up in the dictionary and re-read the sentence with the word's definition in mind. Learning words in context is one of the best ways for the brain to retain their meanings. (At least, that's what our cognitive scientists tell us!)

The GRE words used in this chapter will appear in boldface, like **this.** Look 'em up while you read. We'll give you an example of what we mean by "the same kinds of words over and over again."

The words in the box below all mean nearly the same thing. They all have something to do with the concept of criticism, a concept often tested on the GRE. The GRE that you take could well test you on one of these words or one of the other synonyms for "criticize." A great way to prepare for GRE Vocabulary, then, is to learn which word concepts are tested most frequently and learn all those words.

> **IT'S DÉJÀ VU ALL OVER AGAIN**
>
> The same kinds of vocabulary words that you saw on the SAT may well appear on your GRE.

> **CONTEXT IS KEY**
>
> Learning words in context is a good way to retain their meanings.

```
CRITICIZE
chastise
deride/derisive
derogate
lambaste
oppugn
pillory
rebuke
remonstrate
calumny
diatribe
harangue
```

On the test, you might, for instance, see an ANTONYM question like this:

REMONSTRATE:
(A) show
(B) atone
(C) vouchsafe
(D) laud
(E) undo

Or an ANALOGY question that looks something like this:

VITUPERATE : DISPARAGE ::
(A) profligate : bilk
(B) equivocate : reduce
(C) parody : excuse
(D) lie : prevaricate
(E) brave : succeed

There are many such families of word synonyms whose members appear frequently on the GRE. We'll run across more as we proceed.

## WORD FREQUENCY

The best way to prepare for the Vocabulary section is to learn the word concepts that are tested most frequently on the GRE.

## A LITTLE KNOWLEDGE IS NOT A DANGEROUS THING

You don't have to know the exact meaning of a word to get the right answer on a GRE vocabulary question.

## WHAT YOU NEED TO KNOW

The GRE does not test whether you know exactly what a particular word means. If you only have an idea what the word means, you will get just as many points for that question as you will if you know the precise dictionary definition of the word. That's because ETS isn't interested in finding out whether you're a walking dictionary. They want to see if you have a broad and diverse (but, of course, classically-based) vocabulary.

## 20% X 500 > 100% X 50

This means, simply, that it's better to know 20 percent of the definition of 500 words than it is to know the exact definition of 50. Or, more generally put, it's better to know a little bit about a lot of words than to know a lot about just a few. In fact, it's a lot better. And it's a lot easier.

## THESAURUS > DICTIONARY

You see, "criticize" is not the only family of synonyms whose members appear frequently on the GRE. There are plenty of others. And lists of synonyms are much easier to learn than lots of words in isolation. So don't learn words with a dictionary; learn them with a thesaurus. Make synonym index cards based on the common families of GRE words (listed at the end of this chapter) and **peruse** those lists periodically. It's like weight-lifting for vocabulary. Pretty soon you will start to see results.

If you think this might be **fallacious,** then check this out:

The words in the box below all have something to do with the idea of falsehood. Their precise meanings vary: **erroneous** means "incorrect," whereas **mendacious** means "lying." But unless you are shooting for a very high verbal score (720 or higher) you don't need to know the exact meanings of these words. You will most likely get the question right if you simply know that these words have something to do with the idea of falsehood.

| FALSE | |
|---|---|
| apocryphal | guile _sly_ |
| dissemble | mendacious/ |
| duplicity | mendacity |
| equivocate | prevaricate |
| equivocation | prevarication _deviate from truth_ |
| erroneous | specious |
| ersatz | spurious |
| fallacious | |

_words uncertainty disguise? misleading ranging_

The way that you should use a list like this is to look it over once or twice a week for 30 seconds every week until the test. If you don't have much time until the exam date, look over your lists more frequently. Then, by test day, you should have a rough idea what most of the words on your lists mean. If you get an antonym question such as:

HONESTY:  (A) displeasure (B) mendacity
(C) disrepute (D) resolution (E) failure

you might not know exactly what "**mendacity**" means, but you'll know that it's "one of those FALSE words," which will be enough to get the question right. Your subconscious mind has done most of the work for you!

It might be **vexatious** to learn word meanings the slow way, but you'll be amazed how easy and **facile** vocabulary-building can be when you do it this way. Here are some more word families:

| ANNOY | BEGINNER | FOUL |
|---|---|---|
| aggravate | acolyte | festering |
| irritate | neophyte | fetid |
| perturb | novice | fulsome |
| vex | proselyte | invidious |
| irk | tyro | noisome |

You may not know exactly what **invidious** means, but if you study the last list, pretty soon you will know that it refers to something FOUL.

We're now going to give you a lot of common GRE words grouped together by meaning. This isn't high-stress learning. All you have to do is make flash cards from these lists and look over your cards a few times a week from now until test day. You'll find that your subconscious mind does much of the work for you.

CAUTION: The categories in which these words are listed are general and should not be understood as the exact definitions of the words.

## DIFFICULT TO UNDERSTAND

abstruse
arcane
enigmatic
esoteric
inscrutable
obscure
opaque
rarefied
recondite
turbid

## DEBAUCHED/ DEBAUCHERY

bacchanalian
depraved
dissipated
iniquity
libertine
libidinous
licentious
reprobate
ribald
salacious
sordid
turpitude

## CRITICIZE/CRITICISM

aspersion
belittle
berate
calumny
castigate
decry
defamation
deride/derisive
diatribe
disparage
excoriate
gainsay
harangue
impugn
inveigh
lambaste
obloquy
objurgate
opprobrium
pillory
remonstrate
rebuke
reprehend
reprove
revile
vituperate

## PRAISE

accolade
aggrandize
encomium
eulogize
extol
laud/laudatory
venerate/veneration

## FALSEHOOD

apocryphal
dissemble
duplicity
equivocate
equivocation
erroneous
ersatz
fallacious
guile
mendacious/mendacity
prevaricate
prevarication
specious
spurious

## BITING (AS IN WIT OR TEMPERAMENT)

acerbic
acidulous
acrimonious
asperity
caustic
mordant
mordacious
trenchant

## RENDER USELESS/ WEAKEN

enervate
obviate
stultify
undermine
vitiate

---

### BUILD YOUR VOCABULARY

Make flash cards from these lists and look over your cards a few times a week from now until test day.

## HARMFUL
- baleful
- baneful
- deleterious
- inimical
- injurious
- insidious
- minatory
- perfidious
- pernicious

---

### ALL IN THE FAMILY

Lists of synonyms are easier to learn than long lists of unrelated words.

---

## TIMID/TIMIDITY
- craven
- diffident
- pusillanimous
- recreant
- timorous
- trepidation

## STUBBORN
- froward
- implacable
- inexorable
- intractable
- intransigent
- obdurate
- obstinate
- pertinaceous
- recalcitrant
- refractory
- renitent
- untoward

## BEGINNING/YOUNG
- burgeoning
- callow
- inchoate
- incipient
- nascent

## OVERBLOWN/WORDY
- bombastic
- circumlocution
- garrulous
- grandiloquent
- loquacious
- periphrastic
- prolix
- turgid

## HOSTILE/ONE WHO IS HOSTILE
- antithetic
- churlish
- curmudgeon
- irascible
- malevolent
- misanthropic
- truculent
- vindictive

## CLICHÉED/BORING
- banal
- fatuous
- hackneyed
- insipid
- mundane
- pedestrian
- platitude
- prosaic
- quotidian
- trite

## THE TOP 100

While we're at it, here, gathered together for easy reference, are the 100 difficult words that appear most frequently on the GRE. You will notice that a number of these words are also in the preceding lists of near synonyms.

1.  Equivocal/ Equivocate/ Equivocation—ambiguous, open to two interpretations *false*
2.  Tractable (Intractable)—obedient, yielding
3.  Placate (Implacable)—to soothe or pacify
4.  Miser—person who is extremely stingy
5.  Engender—to produce, cause, bring out
6.  Dogma(tic)(tism)(tist)—rigidly fixed in opinion, opinionated
7.  Garrulous (Garrulity)—very talkative
8.  Homogeneous (Homogenize)—composed of identical parts
9.  Laconic—using few words
10. Quiescence (Quiescent)—inactivity, stillness
11. Anomalous—irregular or deviating from the norm
12. Venerate(-ion)—to respect
13. Assuage—to make less severe, ease, relieve
14. Misanthrope (-ic)—person who hates human beings
15. Digress(ive)—to turn aside; to stray from the main point
16. Corroborate(-ion)—to confirm, verify
17. Buttress—to reinforce or support
18. Antipathy—dislike, hostility, extreme opposition or aversion
19. Disabuse—to free from error or misconception
20. Feigned (Unfeigned)—pretended
21. Banal(ity)—trite and overly common
22. Desiccate(-ion)—to dry completely, dehydrate
23. Diatribe—bitter verbal attack
24. Pedant(ic)(ry)—uninspired, boring academic
25. Guile(less)—trickery, deception
26. Eulogy (-ize)—high praise, often in public
27. Fawn(ing)—to flatter excessively, seek the favor of
28. Aberrant/Aberration—different from the usual or normal
29. Heresy/Heretic(al)—an act opposed to established religious orthodoxy
30. Obdurate—stubborn
31. Prevaricate(-ion)—to lie, evade the truth

32. Embellish(ment)—to ornament; make attractive with decoration or details; add details to a statement
33. Pragmatic/Pragmatism—practical; moved by facts rather than abstract ideals
34. Precipitate—to cause to happen; to throw down from a height
35. Proximity—nearness
36. Profundity—depth (usually depth of thought)
37. Adulterate—to corrupt or make impure
38. Sanction—permission, support; law; penalty
39. Ameliorate(-ion)—to make better, improve
40. Anachronism/Anachronistic—something chronologically inappropriate
41. Vindictive—spiteful, vengeful, unforgiving
42. Propitiate—to win over, appease
43. Aver—to declare to be true, affirm
44. Burgeon(-ing)—to sprout or flourish
45. Commensurate—proportional
46. Mitigate/Mitigation—to soften, or make milder
47. Culpability—guilt, responsibility for wrong
48. Specious(ness)—having a false appearance of truth; showy
49. Turpitude—inherent baseness, depravity
50. Diffident/Diffidence—shy, lacking confidence
51. Repudiate—to reject as having no authority
52. Discrete—individually distinct; consisting of unconnected elements
53. Obviate—to make unnecessary; to anticipate and prevent
54. Dissemble—to pretend, disguise one's motives
55. Implacable—inflexible, incapable of being pleased
56. Emulate—to copy, imitate
57. Complaisance/Complaisant—disposition to please or comply
58. Enervate—to weaken, sap strength from
59. Latency—the condition of present but hidden
60. Erudite(ition)—learned, scholarly
61. Espouse—to support of advocate; to marry
62. Florid(ness)—gaudy, extremely ornate; ruddy, flushed
63. Occlude—to shut, block
64. Harangue—a ranting writing or speech; lecture
65. Hieroglyph(ic)—pictorial character
66. Iconoclast—one who attacks traditional beliefs
67. Impervious—impossible to penetrate; incapable of being pleased
68. Efficacy/Efficacious—effectiveness, efficiency
69. Inchoate—imperfectly formed or formulated
70. Loquacity/Loquacious—talkative

71. Irascible(-ity)—easily angered
72. Ephemeral—momentary, transient, fleeting
73. Laudable(-atory)—deserving of praise
74. Insipid—bland, lacking flavor; lacking excitement
75. Magnanimity/Magnanimous—generosity
76. Precarious(ly)—uncertain
77. Endemic—belonging to a particular area; inherent
78. Mollify—to calm or make less severe
79. Rarefy/Rarefaction—to make thinner, purer, or more refined
80. Disinterest(ed)(edness)—unbiased; not interested
81. Foster—to nourish, cultivate, promote
82. Perennial—present throughout the years; persistent
83. Malevolent—ill-willed; causing evil or harm to others
84. Defer(ence)—to show respect or politeness in a submissive way
85. Precursor(y)—forerunner, predecessor
86. Lucid—clear and easily understood
87. Probity—honesty, high-mindedness
88. Abscond—to depart secretly
89. Propensity—inclination, tendency
90. Audacious—bold, daring, fearless
91. Wheedle—to influence or entice by flattery
92. Prudent—careful, cautious
93. Mundane—worldly; commonplace
94. Diffuse—widely spread out
95. Aggrandize—to make larger or greater in power
96. Decimate—to reduce drastically; to destroy a large part of
97. Succinct—terse, brief, concise
98. Enigma(tic)—puzzling, inexplicable
99. Unfettered—free, unrestrained
100. Ascetic—self-denying, abstinent, austere

## ROOTS

You knew that this dreaded word from grade school was going to come up sooner or later. Because GRE words are so heavily drawn from Latin and Greek, roots can be extremely useful, both in deciphering words with obscure meanings and in guessing intelligently.

Use the Kaplan Root List in the back of this book to pick up the most valuable GRE roots. Target these words in your vocabulary prep. Learn a few new roots a day, familiarizing yourself with the meaning.

> **GOTTA DIG YOUR ROOTS**
>
> The more roots you know, the better you'll be at deciphering perplexing words on the GRE and at coming up with smart guesses.

## LEARNING VOCABULARY

In review, the three best ways (in no particular order) to improve your GRE vocabulary are:

1. Learning words in context
2. Learning families of words
3. Deciphering words by their roots

A broader vocabulary will serve you well on all four verbal question-types on the GRE. Now let's look at the verbal question-type that you should tackle first.

# 1. SENTENCE COMPLETIONS

The directions for this section look like this:

> Directions: Each sentence below has one or two blanks indicating that something has been omitted. Beneath the sentence are five lettered words or sets of words. Choose the word or set of words for each blank that best fits the meaning of the sentence as a whole.

Like all short verbal questions, Sentence Completion questions go from easy to hard, which means:

- You can trust your gut feeling on the easier (first few) questions.

- You should be wary of first impulses on the hardest questions. Approach them systematically, using the Kaplan strategies.

- You should never spend a great deal of time on questions 6 and 7: You're least likely to get them right, and they're only worth one point each.

---

### IT GETS HARDER AS YOU GO ALONG

Sentence completion questions, like analogy and antonym questions, go from easiest to hardest. The first few are the easiest, and the last few are the hardest.

---

## THE FOUR BASIC PRINCIPLES OF SENTENCE COMPLETION

**1. Every clue is right in front of you.**

Each sentence contains a few crucial clues that determine the answer. In order for a sentence to be used on the GRE, the answer must already be in the sentence. Elements *in the sentence* limit the possible answer, and finding these elements will guide you to the correct answer.

For example, could the following sentence be on the GRE?

> The student thought the test was quite _____.
> (A) long    (B) unpleasant  (C) predictable
> (D) ridiculous  (E) indelible

No. Because nothing in the sentence tells us which word to choose, it would be a terrible test question.

---

### FILL IN THE BLANK

When working through a sentence completion question:
• look for clues in the sentence
• focus on what's directly implied
• pay attention to the meanings of the words

---

Now let's change the sentence to get a question that *could* be answered:

> Since the student knew the form and content of the questions in advance, the test was quite _____for her.
> (A) long        (B) unpleasant (C) predictable
> (D) ridiculous  (E) indelible

What are the important clues in this question? Well, the word *since* is a great structural clue. It indicates that the missing word follows logically from part of the sentence. Specifically, the missing word must follow from "knew the form and content . . . in advance." That means the test was predictable.

## 2. Look for what's directly implied and expect clichés.

We're not dealing with poetry here. These sentences aren't excerpted from the works of Toni Morrison or William Faulkner. The correct answer is the one most directly implied by the meanings of the words in the sentence.

## 3. Don't imagine strange scenarios.

Read the sentence literally, not imaginatively. Pay attention to the meaning of the words, not associations or feelings that you have.

## 4. Look for structural roadsigns

Structural roadsigns, such as *since,* are keywords that will point you to the right answer. The missing words in sentence completions will usually have either a same as or opposite relationship from other words in the sentence. Keywords, such as "and" or "but," will tell you which it is.

On the GRE, a semicolon by itself always connects two closely related clauses. If a semicolon is followed by another roadsign, then that roadsign determines the direction. Just like on the highway, there are roadsigns on the GRE that tell you to go ahead and that tell you to take a detour.

"Straight Ahead" signs are used to make one part of the sentence support or elaborate another part. They continue the sentence in the same direction. The positive or negative charge of what follows is not changed by these clues. Straight ahead clues include: *and, similarly, in addition, since, also, thus, because, ; (semicolon)*, and *likewise*.

---

### FULL STEAM AHEAD

"Straight ahead" roadsigns—such as *because, thus,* and *consequently*—continue the sentence in the same direction.

---

"Detour" signs change the direction of the sentence. They make one part of the sentence contradict or qualify another part. The positive or negative charge of an answer is changed by these clues. Detour signs include: *but, despite, yet, however, unless, rather, although, while, unfortunately,* and *nonetheless.*

In the following examples, test drive your knowledge of sentence completion road signs by finding the right answers (in the parentheses):

1. The winning argument was_____*and* persuasive. (cogent, flawed)

2. The winning argument was_____*but* persuasive. (cogent, flawed)

3. The play's script lacked depth and maturity; *likewise,* the acting was altogether_____. (sublime, amateurish)

4. The populace_____the introduction of the new taxes, *since* they had voted for them overwhelmingly. (applauded, despised)

5. *Despite* your impressive qualifications, I am_____to offer you a position with our firm. (unable, willing)

6. Scientists have claimed that the dinosaurs became extinct in a single, dramatic event; *yet* new evidence suggests a_____decline. (headlong, gradual)

7. The first wave of avant-gardists elicited_____from the general population, *while* the second was completely ignored. (indifference, shock)

By concentrating on the roadsigns, wasn't it easy to find your way through the question and arrive at the right answer?

## HARD TO STARBOARD

"Detour" signs—such as *but, however,* and *on the other hand*—change the direction of the sentence.

## ANSWERS TO THE ROADSIGN QUESTIONS

1. cogent
2. flawed
3. amateurish
4. applauded
5. unable
6. gradual
7. shock

## THE KAPLAN FOUR-STEP APPROACH TO SENTENCE COMPLETIONS

Now that you have the basics, here's how to combine skills.

1. **Read the sentence strategically, using your knowledge of scope and structure to see where the sentence is heading.**
2. **In your own words, anticipate its answer.**
3. **Look for answers close in meaning to yours and eliminate tempting wrong answers using the clues.**
4. **Read your choice back into the sentence to make sure it fits.**

## USING KAPLAN'S FOUR-STEP APPROACH

Try the following sentence completion questions using the Kaplan Four-step Approach. These are more difficult, but you should be able to do them. Time yourself: You only have 30-45 seconds to do each question.

1. The yearly financial statement of a large corporation may seem_____at first, but the persistent reader soon finds its pages of facts and figures easy to decipher.
   (A) bewildering
   (B) surprising
   (C) inviting
   (D) misguided
   (E) uncoordinated

2. Usually the press secretary's replies are terse, if not downright_____, but this afternoon his responses to our questions were remarkably comprehensive, almost _____.
   (A) rude . . . concise
   (B) curt . . . verbose
   (C) long-winded . . . effusive
   (D) enigmatic . . . taciturn
   (E) lucid . . . helpful

3. Organic farming is more labor intensive and thus initially more _____, but its long-term costs may be less than those of conventional farming.
   (A) uncommon
   (B) stylish
   (C) restrained
   (D) expensive
   (E) difficult

4.  Unfortunately, there are some among us who equate tolerance with immorality; they feel that the _____ of moral values in a permissive society is not only likely, but _____.

(A) decline . . . possible
(B) upsurge . . . predictable
(C) disappearance . . . desirable
(D) improvement . . . commendable
(E) deterioration . . . inevitable

<table>
</table>

**ANSWERS TO THE SENTENCE COMPLETION QUESTIONS**

1. A
2. B
3. D
4. E

Think about how you went about solving these sentence completion questions. You should use the same approach when you encounter sentence completion questions on the GRE.

Now let's move to the question-type that you should tackle second in the verbal section: Analogies.

# 2. ANALOGIES

The directions in this section look like this:

**Directions:** In each of the following questions, a related pair of words or phrases is followed by five lettered pairs of words or phrases. Select the lettered pair that best expresses a relationship similar to that expressed in the original pair.

Like all short verbal questions, analogy questions go from easy to hard, which means:

- You should trust your gut feeling on the easier (first few) questions.

- You should be wary of first impulses on the hardest questions. Approach them systematically, using the Kaplan strategies.

- You should never spend a great deal of time on questions 14-16: You're least likely to get them right, and they're only worth one point each.

## THE FOUR BASIC PRINCIPLES OF ANALOGIES

**1. Every analogy question consists of two words, called the stem pair, that are separated by a colon.**

Below the stem pair are five answer choices. That means Analogy questions look like this:

> MAP : ATLAS ::
> (A) key : lock
> (B) street : sign
> (C) ingredient : cookbook
> (D) word : dictionary
> (E) theory : hypothesis

**2. There will always be a logical and necessary relationship between the words in the stem pair.**

You express this relationship by making a short sentence that we call *the bridge*. A bridge is whatever simple sentence you come up with to relate the two words. Your goals when you build your bridge should be to keep it as short and as clear as possible.

A weak bridge expresses a relationship that isn't necessary or direct. For the sample analogy question above, weak bridges include:

---

## WHAT'S A STEM PAIR?

Analogy questions consists of two words—the stem pair—that are separated by a colon. Stem pairs look like this:

PREPARATION : SUCCESS

---

## WHAT'S A BRIDGE?

A bridge is a short sentence that connects the two words in the stem pair. You should always make a bridge before you look at the answer choices.

- Some MAPS are put in ATLASES.
- A MAP is usually smaller than an ATLAS.
- MAPS and ATLASES have to do with geography.
- A MAP is a page in an ATLAS.

You know you have a weak bridge if it contains such words as "usually," "can," "might," or "sometimes."

A strong bridge expresses a logical and necessary relationship. For the analogy above, strong bridges include:

- MAPS are what an ATLAS contains.
- MAPS are the unit of reference in an ATLAS.
- An ATLAS collects and organizes MAPS.

Strong bridges express a definite relationship and can contain an unequivocal word, such as "always," "never," or "must."

The best bridge is a strong bridge that fits exactly one answer choice.

**3. Always try to make a bridge *before* looking at the answer choices.**

Because the test is so consistent, ETS uses certain kinds of bridges over and over on the GRE. We call these bridges the five classic bridges. You don't have to memorize them, but exposing yourself to them now will give you a feel for the sort of bridge that will get you the right answer. Try to answer these questions as you go through them.

1. The **Definition** bridge ("is always" or "is never")

   PLATITUDE : TRITE ::
   (A) riddle : unsolvable
   (B) axiom : geometric
   (C) omen : portentous
   (D) syllogism : wise
   (E) circumlocution : concise

2. The **Function/Purpose** bridge

   AIRPLANE : HANGAR ::
   (A) music : orchestra
   (B) money : vault
   (C) finger : hand
   (D) tree : farm
   (E) insect : ecosystem

> ### WHAT MAKES A STRONG BRIDGE?
>
> You might think that the words TRUMPET and JAZZ have a strong bridge. Don't be fooled. You can play many things on trumpets other than jazz, such as fanfares and taps. You can also play jazz on things other than trumpets. TRUMPET and INSTRUMENT do have a strong bridge. A trumpet is a type of instrument. This is always true—it's a strong, definite relationship.

> ### THE FIVE CLASSIC BRIDGES
>
> 1. Definition
> 2. Function/Purpose
> 3. Lack
> 4. Characteristic action/items
> 5. Degree

3. The **Lack** bridge

   LUCID : OBSCURITY ::
   (A) ambiguous : doubt
   (B) provident : planning
   (C) furtive : legality
   (D) economical : extravagance
   (E) secure : violence

4. The **Characteristic Actions/Items** bridge

   PIROUETTE : DANCER ::
   (A) sonnet : poet
   (B) music : orchestra
   (C) building : architect
   (D) parry : fencer
   (E) dress : seamstress

5. The **Degree** (often going to an extreme) bridge

   ATTENTIVE : RAPT ::
   (A) loyal : unscrupulous
   (B) critical : derisive
   (C) inventive : innovative
   (D) jealous : envious
   (E) kind : considerate

### ANSWERS TO THE FIVE CLASSIC BRIDGES DRILL

1. C
2. B
3. D
4. D
5. B

So there you have them, the five classic bridges. Keep them in mind as you practice for the GRE.

**4. Don't fall for Analogies of Type.**

Analogies of Type are pairs of words that are not related to each other but only to a third word.

For instance, it may seem as though there is a strong relationship between RING : NECKLACE; they're both types of jewelry. But this type of relationship will never be a correct answer choice on the GRE. If you see an answer choice like this—where the two words are not directly related to one another but only to a third word (like "jewelry)— you can always eliminate it.

Now that you have a grasp of the Basic Principles of Analogies, let's take a look at the Kaplan Approach to Solving Analogy questions.

# THE KAPLAN FOUR-STEP APPROACH TO ANALOGIES

1. **Find a strong bridge between the stem words.**

2. **Plug the answer choices into the bridge.**
   Be flexible: Sometimes it's easier to use the second word first.

3. **Adjust the bridge as necessary.**
   You want your bridge to be simple and somewhat general, but if more than one answer choice fits into your bridge, it was too general. Make it a little more specific and try those answer choices again.

4. **If stuck, eliminate all answer choices with weak bridges.**
   If two choices have the same bridge—for example, (A) TRUMPET : INSTRUMENT or (B) SCREWDRIVER : TOOL—eliminate them both. Try to work backwards from remaining choices to stem pair and make your best guess.

---

## USING THE KAPLAN FOUR-STEP APPROACH

Let's try an example to learn how to use the four-step approach.
   What if you encounter the following question:

> AIMLESS : DIRECTION ::
> (A) enthusiastic : motivation
> (B) wary : trust
> (C) unhealthy : happiness
> (D) lazy : effort
> (E) silly : adventure

For this question, a good bridge is: "Someone *aimless* lacks *direction.*" Now plug that into the answer choices. Only choice (B) fits. If you were stuck, you should have eliminated choices (A), (C), and (E), because their bridges are weak. Remember: If an answer choice has a weak bridge it cannot be correct, because no stem pair that you'll find on the GRE will ever have a weak bridge. To be correct, an answer choice must have a strong, clear relationship.

If you can't build a good bridge because you don't know the definition of one or both stem words, all is not lost. Even when you can't figure out the bridge for the words in the stem pair, you can guess intelligently by eliminating answer choices. In the following questions, there are no stem words. How are you supposed to do

## TICK, TOCK, TICK, TOCK . . .

Don't waste valuable time reading the directions on test day. Learn them now.

them, you ask? Well, do you remember the scene in *Star Wars* when Obi Wan Kenobi is teaching Luke Skywalker about the Force? He put that helmet on Luke's head so that Luke can't see when the little robot tries to zap him. This entire scene was actually just a clever (if subtle) metaphor for what it's like to do an analogy when you don't know what the stem words mean.

Take a look at the following sets of answer choices and eliminate all choices that have a weak bridge. Also, if two choices in the same problem have the same bridge, you can eliminate them both (because if one of them were correct the other would have to be also).

1. _ _ _ _ : _ _ _ _ ::
   (A) terrible : appall
   (B) sinister : doubt
   (C) trivial : defend
   (D) irksome : annoy
   (E) noble : admire

## ANSWERS TO THE ANSWER CHOICE ELIMINATION DRILL

(1) Eliminate A and D because they have the same bridge. Eliminate B and C because they have weak bridges.
(2) Eliminate B, D, and E because they have weak bridges.
(3) Eliminate B, C, D, and E because they have weak bridges.
(4) Eliminate B and C because they have the same bridge. Eliminate E because it has a weak bridge.

2. _ _ _ _ : _ _ _ _ ::
   (A) enlist : draft
   (B) hire : promote
   (C) resign : quit
   (D) pacify : mollify
   (E) endanger : enlighten

3. _ _ _ _ : _ _ _ _ ::
   (A) congratulate : success
   (B) amputate : crime
   (C) annotate : consultation
   (D) deface : falsehood
   (E) cogitate : habit

4. _ _ _ _ : _ _ _ _ ::
   (A) tepid : hot
   (B) lackluster : lackadaisical
   (C) ordinary : banal
   (D) perfunctory : routine
   (E) unique : popular

Now let's turn to the third verbal question-type that you should answer: Antonyms.

# 3. ANTONYMS

The directions for this section will look like this:

> **Directions:** Each question below consists of a word printed in capital letters, followed by five lettered words or phrases. Choose the lettered word or phrase that is most nearly **opposite** in meaning to the word in capital letters.
>
> Since some of the questions require you to distinguish fine shades of meaning, be sure to consider all the choices before deciding which one is best.

As with all short verbal questions, Antonym questions go from easy to hard, which means:

- You can trust your gut feeling on the easier (first few) questions.

- You should be wary of first impulses on the hardest questions. Approach them systematically, using the Kaplan strategies.

- You shouldn't spend a great deal of time agonizing over questions 36-38. You're least likely to get them right, and they're only worth one point each. Antonym questions go in order of difficulty. Here is a general rule of thumb:

> 28-30 are EASY antonyms
> 31-35 are MEDIUM antonyms
> 36-38 are DIFFICULT antonyms

## THE SEVEN BASIC PRINCIPLES OF ANTONYMS

**1. Think of a context in which you've heard the word before.**

For example, you might be able to figure out the meaning of the italicized words in the following phrases from their context: "*travesty* of justice," "crimes and *misdemeanors*," "*mitigating* circumstances," and "*abject* poverty."

**2. Look at word roots, stems, and suffixes.**

Even if you don't know what "benediction" means, its prefix (*bene*, which means good) tells you that its opposite is likely to be something bad. Perhaps the answer will begin with *mal*, as in *malefaction*.

### 3. Use your knowledge of another Romance Language.

For example, you might guess at the meaning of credulous from the Italian, *creder;* moratorium from the French, *morte;* and mundane from the Spanish, *mundo.*

### 4. Use the positive or negative charges of the words to help you.

Mark up your test booklet with little + signs for words with positive connotations, − signs for those with negative connotations, and = signs for neutral words. This strategy can work wonders. For instance:

$$\overset{-}{\text{PERDITION}} : \overset{-}{\text{(A) deterrent}} \overset{=}{\text{(B) rearrangement}}$$

$$\overset{=}{\text{(C) reflection}} \overset{+}{\text{(D) salvation}} \overset{-}{\text{(E) rejection}}$$

### 5. Eliminate any answer choices that do not have a clear opposite.

For instance, in the sample problem above, neither choice (B) nor choice (C) has a clear and obvious opposite. They are unlikely to be correct.

### 6. On the last few antonyms, watch out for trick choices and eliminate them.

For instance, if you come across:

CEDE : (A) make sense of   (B) fail

(C) get ahead of   (D) flow out of   (E) retain

you should eliminate B, C, and D. Why? Because "cede" will remind some people of "succeed," they will pick B. It will remind others of "recede," as in "receding hairline" or "receding tide," so they will pick C or D. ETS never rewards people for goofing up. No one ever "lucks" into the right answer on the GRE by making a mistake.

### 7. Never leave an answer blank on the GRE.
When in doubt, guess!

Now that you've got a grasp of the Basic Principles of Antonyms, let's look at the Kaplan Approach to solving Antonym questions.

## THE KAPLAN FOUR-STEP APPROACH TO ANTONYMS

1. Define the root word.
2. Reverse it by thinking about the word's opposite.
3. Now go to the answer choices and find the opposite, that is, the choice that matches your preconceived notion of the choice.
4. If stuck, eliminate any choices you can and guess among those remaining.

## USING KAPLAN'S FOUR-STEP APPROACH

Now let's put this approach to the test. Suppose you encounter "LOITER" in an antonym question:

*Step One:* Ask yourself what LOITER means. Write a definition below:

_____

_____

*Step Two:* Think about LOITER's *opposite.*

The opposite of LOITER is _____

*Step Three:* Choose the answers that best matches your reversal of the original word.

LOITER: (A) change direction (B) move purposefully (C) inch forward (D) clean up (E) amble

What's the *opposite* of the choice you picked? Does that match the meaning of the original word?

The opposite of "move purposefully" is "stand around," or "loiter."

*Step Four:* If you get stuck, eliminate choices and guess.
(A) change direction and (D) clean up seem to be unlikely choices and can be eliminated.

# 4. READING COMPREHENSION

## WHERE DO THE PASSAGES COME FROM?

Topics for the Reading Comp passages come from:
• the Social Sciences
• the Natural Sciences
• the Humanities

Reading Comprehension is the only question-type that appears on all major standardized tests, and the reason isn't too surprising. No matter what academic area you pursue, you'll have to make sense of some dense, unfamiliar material. The topics for GRE Reading Comp passages are taken from three areas: Social Sciences, Natural Sciences, and Humanities.

These passages tend to be wordy and dull, and you may find yourself wondering where the test makers get them (probably from the same source as computer installation manuals). Well, actually, the test makers go out and collect the most boring and confusing essays available, then chop them up beyond all recognition or coherence. The people behind the GRE know that you'll have to read passages—and many more of them—like these in graduate school, so they choose test material accordingly. In a way, Reading Comp is the most realistic of all the question-types on the test. And right now is a good time to start shoring up your critical reading skills, both for the test and for future study in your field.

## FORMAT AND DIRECTIONS

## A WIN-WIN OPPORTUNITY

Read the newspaper daily, either just in the weeks before the test or as part of your permanent routine. You'll have practice overcoming the hurdle of reading unfamiliar or difficult material, and as a bonus you'll sound intelligent and connected during interviews.

The directions in this section look like this:

> <u>Directions:</u> Each passage in this group is followed by several questions. After reading the passage, choose the best response to each question. Your replies are to be based on what is <u>stated</u> or <u>implied</u> in the passage.

There are two Reading Comp passages—one long and one short—in each of the two Verbal sections, for a total of four passages. There are 11 Reading Comp questions for each pair of passages in the Verbal section, for a total of 22 questions. Unlike the questions in other GRE sections, the questions for these passages do **NOT** appear in order of difficulty.

Before you even begin the Reading Comp section, you should learn these three general strategies:

1. Do all of the short Verbal questions, including Antonyms, before Reading Comprehension. Short Verbal questions take less time than do Reading Comp questions but are worth just as much each.

2. You'll have two Reading Comp passages per Verbal section—one long (around 60 lines, 7 questions) and one short (around 20 lines, 4 questions). Leave about 15 minutes per section for Reading Comprehension, using about 9 or 10 minutes for the long passage and 5 or 6 minutes for the short one.

3. Do the passages in a section in any order you want. Many students find that they do shorter passages relatively faster, probably because there's more text per question to read in the long passage. The short passages, however, can be very dense and, therefore, time-consuming. Check over the two passages and do first whichever has a topic that is more familiar to you.

## THE SEVEN BASIC PRINCIPLES OF READING COMPREHENSION

To improve your Reading Comp skills, you'll need a lot of practice—and patience. You may not see dramatic improvement after only one drill. But with ongoing practice, the Seven Basic Principles will help to increase your skill and confidence on this section by test day. After reviewing the following principles, you'll find your first opportunity to apply them by working on a sample passage. And later, on the practice test, you'll have an opportunity to master these skills.

### 1. Pay special attention to the first third of the passage.

The first third of a Reading Comp passage usually introduces its topic and scope, the author's main idea or primary purpose, and the author's tone. It almost always hints at the structure that the passage will follow. Let's take a closer look at these important elements of a Reading Comp passage.

*Topic and Scope*

Topic and scope are both objective terms. That means they include no specific reference to the author's point of view. The difference between them is that the topic is broader; the scope narrows the topic. Scope is particularly important because the answer choices (often many) that depart from it will always be wrong. The broad topic of "The Battle of Gettysburg," for example, would be a lot to cover in 450 words. So if we encountered this passage, we should ask ourselves, "What aspect of the battle does the author take

---

**READING COMPREHENSION GENERAL STRATEGIES**

• Do the Reading Comp section after answering the short Verbal questions.
• Plan to spend about 15 minutes on Reading Comp questions.
• Pick whichever passage you want to do first . . . or second.

---

**COME ON AND ZOOM, ZOOM, ZOOM-A-ZOOM**

As you read the first third of the passage, try to zoom in on the main idea of the passage by first getting a sense of the general topic, then pinning down the scope of the passage, and finally zeroing in on the author's purpose in writing the passage.

up?"—and, because of length limitations, it's likely to be a pretty small chunk. Whatever that chunk is—the pre-battle scouting, how the battle was fought—that will be the passage's scope. Answer choices that deal with anything outside of this narrowly-defined chunk will be wrong.

*Author's Purpose*

The distinction between topic and scope ties into another important issue: the author's purpose. In writing the passage, the author has deliberately chosen to narrow the scope by including certain aspects of the broader topic and excluding others. Why the author makes those choices gives us an important clue as to why the passage is being written in the first place. From the objective and broadly stated topic (for instance, a passage's topic might be "solving world hunger") you zoom in on the also objective but narrower scope ("a new technology for solving world hunger"), and the scope quickly leads you to the author's subjective purpose ("the author is writing in order to describe a new technology and its promising uses"). The author's purpose is what turns into the author's main idea, which will be discussed at greater length in the next principle.

So don't just "read" the passage; instead, try to do the following three things:
1. Identify the topic.
2. Narrow it down to the precise scope that the author includes.
3. Make a hypothesis about why the author is writing and where he or she is going with it.

*Structure and Tone*

In their efforts to understand what the author says, test takers often ignore the less glamorous but important structural side of the passage—namely, how the author says it. One of the keys to success on this section is to understand not only the passage's purpose but also the structure of each passage. Why? Simply because the questions at the end of the passage ask both what the author says AND how he or she says it. Here's a list of the classic GRE passage structures:

- Passages arguing a position (often a social sciences passage)
- Passages discussing something specific within a field of study (for instance, a passage about Shakespearean sonnets in literature)
- Passages explaining some significant new findings or research (often a science passage)

Most passages that you'll encounter will feature one of these classic structures, or a variation thereof. You've most likely seen these structures at work in passages before, even if unconsciously. Your job is to actively seek them out as you begin to read a passage. Usually, the structure is announced within the first third of the passage. Let these classic structures act as a "jump start" in your search for the passage's "big picture" and purpose.

As for "how" the author makes his or her point, try to note the author's position within these structures, usually indicated by the author's tone. For example, in passages that explain some significant new findings or research structure, the author is likely to be clinical in description. In passages that argue a position, the opinion could be the author's, in which case the author's tone may be opinionated or argumentative. On the other hand, the author could simply be describing the strongly-held opinions of someone else. In the latter case the author's writing style would be more descriptive, factual, even-handed. His or her method may involve mere storytelling or the simple relaying of information, which is altogether different from the former case.

Notice the difference in tone between the two types of authors (argumentative vs. descriptive). Correct answer choices for a question about the main idea would, in the former case, use such verbs as "argue for," "propose," or "demonstrate," whereas correct choices for the same type of question in the latter case would use such verbs as "describe" or "discuss." Correct answers are always consistent with the author's tone, so noting the author's tone is a good way to understand the passage.

## 2. Focus on the main idea.

Every passage boils down to one big idea. Your job is to cut though the fancy wording and focus on this big idea. Very often, the main idea will be presented in the first third of the passage, but occasionally the author will build up to it gradually, in which case you may not have a firm idea of it.

In any case, the main idea always appears somewhere in the passage, and when it does, you must take note of it. For one thing, the purpose of everything else in the passage will be to support this idea. Furthermore, many of the questions—not only "main idea" questions but all kinds of questions—are easier to handle when you have the main idea in the forefront of your mind. Always look for choices that sound consistent with the main idea. Wrong choices often sound inconsistent with it.

---

### CLASSIC PASSAGE STRUCTURES

GRE Reading Comp passages usually either:
• argue a position
• discuss a specific subject
• explain new findings or research

---

### DON'T BE TONE DEAF

The author's tone—ranging from argumentative and opinionated to descriptive and clinical—can provide a clue about how to answer Reading Comp questions.

---

### WHAT'S THE BIG IDEA?

You should always keep the main idea in mind, even when answering questions that don't explicitly ask for it. Correct answers on even the detail questions tend to echo the main idea in one way or another.

### 3. Get the gist of each paragraph.

It will come as no surprise to you that the paragraph is the main structural unit of any passage. After you've read the first third of the passage carefully, you need to find the gist, or general purpose, of each paragraph and then try to relate each paragraph back to the passage as a whole. To find the gist of each paragraph, ask yourself:

- Why did the author include this paragraph?
- What shift did the author have in mind when moving on to this paragraph?
- What bearing does this paragraph have on the author's main idea?

### 4. Don't obsess over details.

There are differences between the reading skills required in an academic environment and those that are useful on standardized tests. In school, you probably read to memorize information for an exam. But this isn't the type of reading that's good for racking up points on the GRE Reading Comprehension section. On the test, you'll need to read for short-term retention. When you finish the questions on a certain passage, that passage is over, gone, done with. Go ahead, forget everything about it!

What's more, there's no need to waste your time memorizing details. The passage will always be right there in front of you. You always have the option to find any details if a particular question requires you to do so. If you have a good sense of a passage's structure and paragraph topics, then you should have no problem navigating back through the text.

### 5. Attack the passages, don't just read them.

Remember when you took the SAT? Like some of us, did you celebrate when you finally finished the passage and then treat the questions as afterthoughts? If so, we suggest that you readjust your thinking. Remember: You get no points for just getting through the passage.

When we read most materials, a newspaper, for example, we start with the first sentence and read the article straight through.

The words wash over us and are the only things we hear in our minds. This is typical of a passive approach to reading, and this approach won't cut it on the GRE.

To do well on this test you'll need to do more than just read the words on the page. You'll need to read actively. Active reading involves keeping your mind working at all times, while trying to anticipate where the author's points are leading. It means thinking

---

### IT AIN'T GOING NOWHERE

You don't have to memorize or understand every little thing as you read the passage. Remember, you can always refer back to the passage to clarify the meaning of any specific detail.

about what you're reading as you read it. It means paraphrasing the complicated-sounding ideas and jargon. It means asking yourself questions as you read:

- What's the author's main point here?
- What's the purpose of this paragraph? of this sentence?

While reading actively you keep a running commentary in your mind. You may want to jot down notes in the margin or underline. When you read actively, you don't absorb the passage, you attack it!

### 6. Beware of classic wrong answer choices.

Knowing the most common wrong answer-types can help you to eliminate wrong choices quickly, which can save you a lot of time. Of course, ideally, you want to have prephrased an answer choice in your mind before looking at the choices. When that technique doesn't work, you'll have to go to the choices and eliminate the bad ones to find the correct one. If this happens, you should always be on the lookout for choices that:

- contradict the facts or the main idea
- distort or twist the facts or the main idea
- mention true points not relevant to the question (often from the wrong paragraph)
- raise a topic that's never mentioned in the passage
- sound off the wall or have the wrong tone

Being sensitive to these classic wrong choices will make it that much easier to zero in on the correct choice quickly and efficiently.

### 7. Use outside knowledge carefully.

You can answer all the questions correctly even if you don't know anything about the topics covered in the passages. Everything you'll need to answer every question is included in the passages themselves. However, as always, you have to be able to make basic inferences and extract relevant details from the texts.

Using outside knowledge that you may have about a particular topic can be beneficial to your cause, but watch out! Outside knowledge can also mess up your thinking. If you use your knowledge of a topic to help you understand the author's points, then you're taking advantage of your knowledge in a useful way. However, if you use your own knowledge to answer the questions, then you may run into trouble because the questions test your understanding of the

---

**ATTACK THE PASSAGE**

You can be an active reader by:
- thinking about what you're reading
- paraphrasing the complicated parts
- asking yourself questions about the passage
- jotting down notes or underlining important words

---

**IT'S ALL THERE**

Everything you need to answer Reading Comp questions is in the passage.

## DON'T BE A KNOW-IT-ALL

Use your own knowledge to help you to understand the passages, but remember that questions often begin: "According to the author . . ."

## THE SEVEN BASIC PRINCIPLES OF READING COMPREHENSION

1. Read the first third of the passage very carefully.
2. Focus on the main idea.
3. Get the gist of each paragraph.
4. Don't obsess over details.
5. Attack the passages, don't just read them.
6. Beware of classic wrong answer choices.
7. Use outside knowledge carefully.

author's points, not your previous understanding or personal point of view on the topic.

So the best approach is to use your own knowledge and experience to help you to comprehend the passages, but be careful not to let it interfere with answering the questions correctly.

## READING COMPREHENSION TEST RUN

Here's a chance to familiarize yourself with a short Reading Comp passage and questions. You'll have more opportunities to practice later, under timed conditions. For now, we want you to take the time to read actively, to give the Seven Principles a test run.

> **Directions:** Each passage in this group is followed by questions based on its content. After reading a passage, choose the best answer to each question. Answer all questions following a passage on the basis of what is stated or implied in that passage.

Migration of animal populations from one region to another is called faunal interchange. Concentrations of species across regional boundaries vary, however, prompting zoologists to classify routes along which (5) penetrations of new regions occur.

A corridor, like the vast stretch of land from Alaska to the southeastern United States, is equivalent to a path of least resistance. Relative ease of migration often results in the presence of related species along the entire length of (10) a corridor; bear populations, unknown in South America, occur throughout the North American corridor. A desert or other barrier creates a filter route, allowing only a segment of a faunal group to pass. A sweepstakes route presents so formidable a barrier that penetration is (15) unlikely. It differs from other routes, which may be crossed by species with sufficient adaptive capability. As the name suggests, negotiation of a sweepstakes route depends almost exclusively on chance, rather than on physical attributes and adaptability.

1. It can be inferred from the passage that studies of faunal interchange would probably
   (A) fail to explain how similar species can inhabit widely separated areas
   (B) be unreliable because of the difficulty of observing long-range migrations
   (C) focus most directly on the seasonal movements of a species within a specific geographic region
   (D) concentrate on correlating the migratory patterns of species that are biologically dissimilar
   (E) help to explain how present-day distributions of animal populations might have arisen

2. The author's primary purpose is to show that the classification of migratory routes
   (A) is based on the probability that migration will occur along a given route
   (B) reflects the important role played by chance in the distribution of most species
   (C) is unreliable because further study is needed
   (D) is too arbitrary, because the regional boundaries cited by zoologists frequently change
   (E) is based primarily on geographic and climatic differences between adjoining regions

3. The author's description of the distribution of bear populations (lines 8-11) suggests which of the following conclusions?
   I. The distribution patterns of most other North American faunal species populations are probably identical to those of bears
   II. There are relatively few barriers to faunal interchange in North America
   III. The geographic area that links North America to South America would probably be classified as either a filter or a sweepstakes route
   (A) I only
   (B) II only
   (C) III only
   (D) I and II only
   (E) II and III only

4. According to the passage, in order to negotiate a sweepstakes route an animal species
   (A) has to spend at least part of the year in a desert environment
   (B) is obliged to move long distances in short periods of time
   (C) must sacrifice many of its young to wandering pastures
   (D) must have the capacity to adapt to a very wide variety of climates
   (E) does not need to possess any special physical capabilities

**How Did You Do?**

Were you able to zoom in from the broad topic (migration) to the scope (classification of migration routes)? Did the author's tone and purpose become clear, then, as explanatory rather than argumentative? And were you able to focus on the correct answers and not get distracted by outside knowledge or misleading details? You'll be able to assess your performance and skills as you review the next section, where we'll explore the strategies for dealing with the three question-types and how these strategies apply to the above questions.

## THE THREE COMMON READING COMP QUESTION-TYPES

We find it useful to break the Reading Comp section down into the three main question-types that accompany each passage: Global, Explicit Detail, and Inference. Most test takers find Explicit Detail questions to be the easiest type in the Reading Comp section, because they're the most concrete. Unlike inferences, which hide somewhere between the lines, explicit details sit out in the open—in the lines themselves. For this reason, we suggest placing Explicit Detail questions high on your list of priorities, above Inference questions but below Global questions, when choosing the order in which you tackle the questions. Let's look at each of these question-types more closely, using the sample questions you just dealt with for illustration.

### 1. Global Questions

*Description:* A Global question will ask you to sum up the author's overall intentions, ideas, or passage structure. It's basically a question whose scope is the entire passage. Global questions account for 25 to 30 percent of all Reading Comp questions. Question 2 in the preceding sample is a Global question because it asks you to identify the author's primary purpose.

*Strategy:* In general, any Global question choice that grabs onto a small detail—or zeroes in on the content of only one paragraph—will be wrong. Often, scanning the verbs in the Global question choices is a good way to take a first cut at the question. The verbs must agree with the author's tone and the way in which he or she structures the passage, so scanning the verbs and adjectives can narrow down the options quickly. The correct answer must be consistent with the overall tone and structure of the passage, whereas common wrong-answer choices associated with this type of question are those that are too broad or narrow in scope and those that are inconsistent with the author's tone. You'll often find Global questions at the beginning of question sets, and often one of the wrong choices will play on some side issue discussed at the tail end of the passage.

*Strategy Applied:* Take a closer look at the Global question, number 2 in the sample. You've already articulated the passage's topic (migration), scope (the classification of migration routes), and tone (explanatory). The author mentions three different classifications of migration routes—corridors, filter routes, and sweepstakes routes. And what distinguishes one kind of route from another? The likelihood of migration, from the most likely (corridors, with no barriers to migration) to least likely (sweepstakes routes, with barriers that species can cross only by chance). So the author's primary purpose here is to show how the classifications are defined according to how likely migration is along each type of route. That should have led you directly to choice (A).

A scan of verbs and adjectives is enough to eliminate choices (C) and (D); both imply that the author is making judgments about the classification, but the tone of the passage is objective and explanatory. Meanwhile, (B) focuses too much on one part of the passage—the explanation of sweepstakes routes—where the role of chance is mentioned only in relation to that one classification. And (E) is a distortion, because the author nowhere mentions climatic and geographic differences between adjoining regions.

*Related Global Question-Types*

## Main Idea And Primary Purpose Questions

The two main types of Global questions are Main Idea and Primary Purpose questions. We discussed these types a little earlier, noting that main idea and purpose are inextricably linked, because the author's purpose is to convey his or her main idea. The format

---

**GLOBAL QUESTIONS AT A GLANCE**

- 25 to 30 percent of Reading Comp questions
- sums up author's overall intentions or passage structure
- nouns and verbs must be consistent with the author's tone and the passage's scope
- Main Idea and Primary Purpose, Title, Structure, and Tone questions are related

for these question types are pretty self-evident:

> Which one of the following best expresses the main
> idea of the passage?

> *or*

> The author's primary purpose is to . . .

### Title Questions

A very similar form of Global question is one that's looking for a title that best fits the passage. A title, in effect, is the main idea summed up in a brief, catchy way. This question may look like this:

> Which of the following titles best describes the con-
> tent of the passage as a whole?

Be sure not to go with a choice that aptly describes only the latter half of the passage; a valid title, much like a main idea and primary purpose, must cover the entire passage.

### Structure Questions

Another type of Global question is one that asks you to recognize a passage's overall structure. Here's what this type of question might sound like:

> Which of the following best describes the organiza-
> tion of the passage?

Answer choices to this kind of Global question are usually worded very generally; they force you to recognize the broad layout of the passage as opposed to the specific content. For example, here are a few possible ways that a passage could be organized:

> A hypothesis is stated and then analyzed.
> A proposal is evaluated and alternatives are explored.
> A viewpoint is set forth and then subsequently defended.

When choosing among these choices, literally ask yourself: "Was there a hypothesis here? Was there an evaluation of a proposal or a defense of a viewpoint"? These terms may all sound similar but in fact, they're very different things. Learn to recognize the difference between a proposal, a viewpoint, and so on. Try to keep a constant eye on what the author is doing as well as what the author is saying, and you'll have an easier time with this type of question.

## Tone Questions

Finally, one last type of Global question is the Tone question, which asks you to evaluate the style of the writing or how the author sounds. Is the author passionate, fiery, neutral, angry, hostile, opinionated, low-key? Here's an example:

> The author's tone in the passage can best be characterized as . . .

Make sure not to confuse the nature of the content with the tone in which the author presents the ideas: A social science passage based on trends in this century's grisliest murders may be presented in a cool, detached, strictly informative way. Once again, it's up to you to separate what the author says from how he or she says it.

## 2. Explicit Detail Questions

*Description:* The second major category of Reading Comprehension questions is the Explicit Detail question. As the name implies, an Explicit Detail question is one whose answer can be directly pinpointed and found in the text. This type makes up roughly 20 to 30 percent of the Reading Comp questions. Question 4 in the sample above is an Explicit Detail question because it asks you to go back to the passage and examine the description of a sweepstakes route.

*Strategy:* Often, these questions provide very direct clues as to where an answer may be found, such as a line reference or some text that links up with the passage structure. (Just be careful with line references; they'll bring you to the right area, but usually the actual answer will be found in the lines immediately before or after the referenced line.) Detail questions are usually related to the main idea, and correct choices tend to be related to major points.

Now, you may recall that we advised you to skim over details in Reading Comp passages in favor of focusing on the big idea, topic, and scope. But now here's a question-type that's specifically concerned with details, so what's the deal? The fact is, most of the details that appear in a typical passage aren't tested in the questions. Of the few that are, you'll either:

- Remember them from your reading
- Be given a line reference to bring you right to them
- Simply have to find them on your own in order to track down the answer.

### EXPLICIT DETAIL ALERT

Key phrases in the question stem include:
- According to the passage/author . . .
- The author states that . . .
- The author mentions which one of the following as . . .

### EXPLICIT DETAIL QUESTIONS AT A GLANCE

- 20 to 30 percent of Reading Comp questions
- answers can be found in the text
- sometimes includes line references to help you locate the relevant material
- are concrete and, therefore, the easiest Reading Comp question type for most people

97

In the third case, if your understanding of the purpose of each paragraph is in the forefront of your mind, it shouldn't take long at all to locate the details in question and then choose an answer. And if even that fails, as a last resort you have the option of putting that question aside and returning to it if and when you have the time later to search through the passage. The point is, even with the existence of this question-type, the winning strategy is still to note the purpose of details in each paragraph's argument but not to attempt to memorize the details themselves.

*Strategy Applied:* Take a closer look at the Explicit Detail question in the sample, question 4. When an Explicit Detail question directs you to a specific place in the passage, as question 4 does to the discussion of sweepstakes routes, your first job is to go right to that spot in the passage and reread it. And if you do that here, you read that negotiation of a sweepstakes route depends "almost entirely on chance, rather than on physical attributes and adaptability." The discounting of physical attributes here should have led you directly to choice (E).

Choice (A)'s mention of a desert environment sinks that choice, because the desert was mentioned by the author in the discussion of filter routes. As for the other choices, "short periods of time," "wandering pastures," and "a wide variety of climates" aren't mentioned in the passage with regard to sweepstakes routes.

## 3. Inference Questions

*Description:* An inference is something that is almost certainly true, based on the passage. Inferences require you to "read between the lines." Questions 1 and 3 in the preceding sample are Inference questions. Question 1 specifically asks you what can be "inferred from the passage" and question 3 asks you to glean possible conclusions based on what is presented.

*Strategy:* The answer to an inference question is something that the author strongly implies or hints at but does not state directly. Furthermore, the right answer, if denied, will contradict or significantly weaken the passage.

Extracting valid inferences from Reading Comp passages requires the ability to recognize that information in the passage can be expressed in different ways. The ability to bridge the gap between the way information is presented in the passage and the way it's presented in the correct answer choice is vital. In fact, inference questions often boil down to an exercise in translation.

---

### A GOOD INFERENCE

• stays in line with the gist of the passage
• stays in line with the author's tone
• stays in line with the author's point of view
• stays within the scope of the passage and its main idea
• is neither denied by, nor irrelevant to, the ideas stated in the passage
• always makes more sense than its opposite

---

*Strategy Applied:* Take a closer look at the sample Inference questions, numbers 1 and 3. Question 1 asks you to select a possible application of the migration study, based only on what you know from the passage. Because the different concentrations of animals prompted the zoologists to classify the migration routes in the first place (line 5), it would make sense that the migration study would help explain how these different concentrations, or distributions, would have arisen. So choice (E) is correct.

Choice (A) contradicts the purpose of the passage, which we discussed for question 2, and unless we're told in the passage that the study was a failure (which we are not), we can't guess that it would be one. Choice (B) is outside of the passage's scope because the passage never touches on the reliability of the study or on any difficulties in observing long-range migrations. The answer must be based on the passage. Choices (C) and (D) are misleading distortions. The study does focus on movements of species, but there's no mention of a seasonal influence, and the study does focus on route comparisons but not on species comparisons.

Question 3 asks you to look back to the passage for the example of the bears and decide what conclusion(s) could be drawn based on this example. We read that bear populations occur throughout North America because North America is a "path of least resistance," meaning there are relatively few barriers. The bears did not continue to migrate further south, however, because they're "unknown in South America." This suggests that South America is either a filter or a sweepstakes route. Nowhere are the bears compared with other species, because the focus isn't the bears but the routes. So option I can be eliminated, and options II and III are accurate. This should have led you, then, to choice (E).

## THE KAPLAN THREE-STEP APPROACH TO READING COMPREHENSION

Now that you've got the basics of GRE Reading Comp under your belt, you'll want to learn our three-step approach that allows you to orchestrate them all into a single modus operandi for the questions.

1. Attack the First Third of the Passage.
2. Read the Rest of the Passage.
3. Do the Questions in an Efficient Order.

### 1. Attack the First Third of the Passage.
As outlined in the Basic Principles section, read the first part of the passage with care, in order to determine the main idea and purpose

(via the zooming-in process we talked about earlier). Two caveats, however: First, in some passages, the author's main idea won't become clear until the end of a passage. Second, occasionally a passage won't include a main idea, which itself is a strong hint that the passage is more of a descriptive, storytelling type of passage, with an even-handed tone and no strong opinions. Bottom line: Don't panic if you can't immediately pin down the author's main idea and purpose. Read on.

**2. Read the Rest of the Passage.**
Do so as we described in the Basic Principles section above, making sure to take note of paragraph topics, location of details, etc.

**3. Do the Questions in an Efficient Order.**
Quickly scan the question stems for Global questions, specifically Main Idea or Primary Purpose questions. Doing these questions first will often help you solidify your conception of the author's main idea and purpose, and you're more likely to answer them correctly now, while the passage is still fresh in your mind.

If there are any other Global types, such as questions regarding the author's overall tone or the organization of the passage, you may benefit from seeking out and handling those next. Explicit Detail questions, especially those with references, are good candidates to tackle after that. Many test takers benefit from leaving the more difficult Inference questions for last.

This, of course, is only a rough order based on question-type. You may want to revise this order to account for the difficulty level of each individual question. For example, on any given passage, some Inference questions may actually be easier than some Explicit Detail questions. So, for each question, quickly ask yourself: Can I answer this question quickly? Shop around—tackle the questions that you think will get you quick points first, and leave the others for later on. This reinforces the all-important GRE Mindset—your conscious decision to take control of the test.

## USING THE KAPLAN THREE-STEP APPROACH

Now let's try the three-step approach on another actual GRE-strength Reading Comp passage. For the time being, we've just included the question-stems of the questions attached to this passage, since you don't want to get into individual choices until later.

Directions: Each passage in this group is followed by several questions. After reading the passage, choose the best response to each question. Your replies are to be based on what is <u>stated</u> or <u>implied</u> in the passage.

Although there have been many third-party movements in U.S. history, no third-party candidate has ever been elected president. And except for the Republican Party, which gained prominence when the Whigs were
(5) declining in the 1850s, no third party has ever achieved national major-party status.

The basic factors that have shaped the U.S. political system account for both the frequency and the weakness of peripheral party movements. Chief among these are
(10) the size and widely varying social and economic features of the country. Different interests and voting blocs predominate in various regions, resulting in an electorate that is fragmented geographically. This heterogeneity is heightened by a federal structure that requires major parties
(15) to find support at the state and local levels in different regions. To take one example, the Democratic Party in the mid-twentieth century drew support simultaneously from Blacks in the North and White segregationists in the South.
(20) The U.S. electoral system intensifies the difficulties of smaller groups. This system, in which the candidate with the highest vote is the "winner who takes it all"—with no provision for proportional representation, as in many countries—rewards broad-based political strategies that
(25) avoid alienating the mainstream voting population, and, conversely, sharply penalizes parties with more restricted support, whose voters may be left unrepresented.

The nondoctrinal character of U.S. politics has meant that new issues tend to be ignored initially by major parties.
(30) Rather, issues such as opposition to immigration, the abolition of slavery, and the rights of workers and farmers frequently gain entry to the political arena through the creation of a third party. Thus, while mainstream voters have usually viewed certain issues as divisive or threatening,
(35) a dedicated minority has often been instrumental in placing them on the national agenda. Indeed, nearly every major national dilemma has sparked some sort of third-party movement. More ephemeral questions, fringe issues such as vegetarianism and prohibitionism, and highly ideological
(40) programs such as Socialism and Populism, have also

frequently served as seeds for third-party movements.

Ironically, certain elements that help to give birth to third-party movements also contribute to their failure to thrive. Parties based on narrow or short-term appeals (45) remain isolated or fade rather rapidly. Parties that raise more salient issues and attract more widespread support face limits of a different kind. Long before a third party might begin to emerge as a truly major political force, major parties will attempt to capture the significant (50) minority of voters that are represented. The Democratic Party thus pirated much of the platform of the Populists in 1896, and, in subsequent decades, in the eras of Wilson and Roosevelt, sponsored progressive and social welfare programs that relentlessly undercut the influence (55) of the Socialists.

1. According to the passage, a major factor responsible for the rise of third parties in the U.S. is the

2. The author cites all of the following as contributing to the weakness of third parties EXCEPT:

3. It can be inferred that which of the following have contributed to the "nondoctrinal character of U.S. politics" (line 28)?

4. It can be inferred from the passage that the probable attitudes of many voters in the general population to the ideas initially put forth by a third party could best be described as

5. It can be inferred that the Republican Party was successful in establishing itself as a major party because

6. The author's description of the U.S. electoral system suggests that it

7. The author of this passage is concerned primarily with

### 1. Attack the First Third of the Passage.

The first few sentences introduce the topic: Third-party movements. The scope, as you recall, is the specific angle the author takes on the topic, and this seems to be the factors hindering the success of third-party movements. The author points out that historically the same factors that have shaped the U.S. political system limit the success of the third-party movement, then the author goes on to list those factors. So just from reading the first third of the passage, you have a sense of the overall structure and purpose.

## 2. Read the Rest of the Passage.

Make note of the author's point-by-point examination of the effectiveness of the third-party movement, but don't try to memorize details. You can always refer back to the passage to answer questions.

## 3. Do the Questions in an Efficient Order.

Let's look again at the seven question stems attacked to this passage:

1. According to the passage, a major factor responsible for the rise of third parties in the U.S. is the
2. The author cites all of the following as contributing to the weakness of third parties EXCEPT:
3. It can be inferred that which of the following have contributed to the "nondoctrinal character of U.S. politics" (line 28)?
4. It can be inferred from the passage that the probable attitudes of many voters in the general population to the ideas initially put forth by a third party could best be described as
5. It can be inferred that the Republican Party was successful in establishing itself as a major party because
6. The author's description of the U.S. electoral system suggests that it
7. The author of this passage is concerned primarily with

*Global Questions*

Quickly scan the question stems for Global questions, specifically main idea or primary purpose. Upon inspection, if you come across the following question, question 7, you should attempt it at this point while the author's big idea is fresh in your mind:

7. The author of this passage is concerned primarily with
   (A) suggesting an appropriate role for third parties in U.S. politics
   (B) discussing the decline of third-party movements in U.S. history
   (C) explaining why third-party movements in the U.S. have failed to gain national power
   (D) describing the traditionally nonideological character of U.S. political parties
   (E) suggesting ways in which peripheral parties may increase their influence

The author's primary purpose, as introduced early in the passage, is choice (C), explaining why third-party movements in the U.S. have failed to gain national power. Choices (A) and (E) suggest the author has an advocative tone, but the correct tone is explanatory. Choice (B), by using the word "decline," distorts the primary concern, and choice (D) is too narrow in scope, because it doesn't even mention third-party movements.

Questions 1 and 2 are clearly Explicit Detail questions, so you should do those next, beginning with the one that seems the most familiar. Questions 3-6, the Inference questions, are good candidates to be saved for last. We've already discussed one of the Global questions, question 7, so let's now conclude this discussion with a brief look at the Explicit Detail questions and the Inference questions.

*Explicit Detail Questions*
Here's the complete form (with answer choices) of Question 1:

1.  According to the passage, a major factor responsible for the rise of third parties in the U.S. is the
    (A) domination of major parties by powerful economic interests
    (B) ability of third parties to transcend regional interests
    (C) ready acceptance by mainstream voters of issues with strong minority support
    (D) appeal of fringe issues to the average American voter
    (E) slowness of major parties to respond to new issues

By looking back to the passage, specifically to paragraph 4, you can see that one factor listed as responsible for the rise of third-parties is choice (E), the slowness of major parties to respond to new issues. As discussed, these issues often act as seeds of third-party movements. Choice (A) is a factor responsible for the lack of success of the third-party movement, not for its rise, and choices (B), (C), and (D) are distortions.

Question 2 is also an Explicit Detail question:

2.  The author cites all of the following as contributing to the weakness of third parties EXCEPT:
    (A) their tendency to avoid sharply defined political programs
    (B) an electoral system that denies them proportional representation
    (C) their tendency to adopt programs that fail to attract mainstream voter support
    (D) the ability of major parties to undercut their appeal
    (E) the fact that many are based on issues of only temporary relevance

The passage cites all choices as contributing to the weakening of the third-party movement EXCEPT choice (A), the correct choice.

*Inference Questions*
Finally, let's take a look at a complete Inference question, Question 4:

4. It can be inferred from the passage that the probable attitudes
   of many voters in the general population to the ideas initially
   put forth by a third party could best be described as
   (A) shocked and disbelieving
   (B) confused and indecisive
   (C) curious and open-minded
   (D) suspicious and disapproving
   (E) apathetic and cynical

You can infer from the passage that the probable attitudes of many
voters are listed in choice (D), suspicious and disapproving, because
the passage tells us in line 34 that mainstream voters usually view
third-party issues as divisive and threatening. None of the other
choices are as applicable.

Questions 3, 5, and 6 are also Inference questions:

3. It can be inferred that which of the following have contributed
   to the "nondoctrinal character of U.S. politics" (line 28)?
       I. The social and economic diversity of the country
       II. The national political structure
       III. The avoidance by major parties of sharply defined ideo-
           logical programs
   (A) I only
   (B) III only
   (C) I and II only
   (D) II and III only
   (E) I, II, and III

5. It can be inferred that the Republican Party was successful in
   establishing itself as a major party because
   (A) its political program became essentially non-doctrinal in
       character
   (B) the Whigs were unsuccessful in their attempts to steal from
       the Republican platform
   (C) it was able to abandon its traditional opposition to slavery
       without alienating its regular supporters
   (D) a more established party was simultaneously in decline
   (E) it benefited from the experience of previous third parties
       that had undergone similar transformations

6.  The author's description of the U.S. electoral system suggests that it
    (A) allows less flexibility than more centralized systems
    (B) makes the Federal government less important politically than state and local governments
    (C) often results in the dominance of third parties in distinct or isolated geographic areas
    (D) frequently polarizes the electorate around divisive social and economic issues
    (E) fails to represent voters who would be represented in some other electoral systems

For question 3 the correct inference is (E), all of the given choices contributed to the nondoctrinal character of U.S. politics. For question 5 the correct choice is (D), a more established party was simultaneously in decline; the other choices can not be inferred solely from the passage. For question 6 the answer is (E), in that the author suggests the electoral system fails to represent voters who would be represented in some other electoral system.

## REVIEW EXERCISES

Because Reading Comp primarily tests your ability to read actively, paraphrasing as you go and paying attention to purpose and structure, let's spend some time practicing those critical reading skills.

### Big Ideas and Details

It's important that you're able to pull out the main idea and supporting details quickly and easily on test day. Covering up the boxes in the side bars, read the following three mini-passages, jotting down their big idea in the margin and underlining details. Then compare your answers with ours.

> Few historians would contest the idea that Gutenberg's invention of the printing press revolutionized the production of literature. Before the press became widely available in the late 1400s, every book published had to be individually copied by a scribe working from a master manuscript. With Gutenberg's system of moveable type, however, books could be reproduced in almost limitless quantities once the laborious process of typesetting was complete . . .

**BIG IDEA**

Gutenberg revolutionized book publishing.

**DETAILS**

late 1400s, moveable type, limitless quantities, typesetting

Plate tectonics, the study of the interaction of the earth's plates, is generally accepted as the best framework for understanding how the continents formed. New research suggests, however, that the eruption of mantle plumes from beneath the plate layer may be responsible for the formation of specific phenomena in areas distant from plate boundaries. A model of mantle plumes appears to explain a wide range of observations relating to both ocean island chains and flood basalt provinces, for example . . .

| BIG IDEA |
|---|
| Mantle plume eruptions, not plate tectonics, may explain certain phenomena. |
| **DETAILS** |
| ocean island chains, flood basalt provinces |

Most of the developed countries are now agreed on the need to take international measures to reduce the emission of carbons into the atmosphere. Despite this consensus, a wide disagreement among economists as to how much emission reduction will actually cost continues to forestall policy making. Analysts who believe the energy market is efficient predict that countries that reduce carbon emission by as little as twenty percent will experience a significant depreciation in their national product. Those that hold that the market is inefficient, however, estimate much greater long-term savings in conservation and arrive at lower costs for reducing emissions . . .

| BIG IDEA |
|---|
| Economists disagree on the cost of emission reduction. |
| **DETAILS** |
| international measures, carbon emission, greater savings, conservation |

**Paraphrasing: The Key Skill in Reading Comp**

Many people have a hard time paraphrasing passages. Taking dense, academic prose and turning it into everyday English isn't easy under the pressure of time constraints. Yet this is the most important skill in Reading Comp. If you are having trouble with paraphrasing, spend some time with the following exercise.

For centuries, the Roman Empire ruled large parts of Europe, Asia, and Africa. Rome had two assets that made continued domination possible. First, its highly trained army was superior to those of its potential adversaries. Second, and more important, Rome built a sophisticated transportation network linking together all of the provinces of its far flung empire. When necessary, it could deploy powerful military forces to any part of the empire with unmatched speed.

Summarize these lines in your own words:

_____

_____

_____

Now find the best paraphrase:

(A) Rome's army defeated its opponents because it could move quickly along the empire's excellent transportation network.
(B) Rome had a big empire, a powerful army, and a good transportation system.
(C) Rome was able to maintain a big empire because it had an excellent transportation system that allowed its efficient army to move quickly from place to place.
(D) Rome ruled large parts of Europe, Asia, and Africa for centuries because its army was always better than those of its adversaries.
(E) Because it built a sophisticated transportation system, Rome was able to build a big empire in parts of Europe, Asia, and Africa.

Despite overwhelming evidence to the contrary, many people think that flying is more dangerous than driving. Different standards of media coverage account for this erroneous belief. Although extremely rare, aircraft accidents receive a lot of media attention because they are very destructive. Hundreds of people have been killed in extreme cases. Automobile accidents, on the other hand, occur with alarming frequency, but attract little media coverage because few, if any, people are killed or seriously injured in any particular mishap.

Summarize these lines in your own words:

_____

_____

_____

Now find the best paraphrase:

(A) Compared to rare but destructive aircraft accidents, car accidents are frequent but relatively minor.

(B) Because aircraft accidents get a lot of media attention, while car accidents get much less, many people wrongly believe that flying is more dangerous than driving.

(C) Driving is more dangerous than flying because different standards of media coverage have forced airlines to improve their safety standards.

(D) Many people believe that flying is more dangerous than driving, even though overwhelming evidence points to the opposite conclusion.

(E) Media coverage is responsible for the belief that flying is more dangerous than driving, even though every year more people are killed on the roads than in the air.

**Keywords**

Remember these? Kaplan keywords are words in Reading Comprehension passages that link the text together structurally and thematically. Paying attention to keywords will help you understand the passage better, and will also help you get some easy points. Here are some keywords that you should look for when reading a passage:

CONTRADICTION:
However
But
Yet
On the other hand
Rather
Instead

SUPPORT:
For example
One reason that
In addition
Also
Moreover
Consequently

EMPHASIS:
Of primary importance
Especially important
Of particular interest
Crucial
Critical
Remarkable

| PARAPHRASE ANSWERS |
| --- |
| Roman Empire: (C) |
| Flying: (E) |

109

Take a moment and circle the structural signal words in this short Reading Comprehension passage:

Gettysburg is considered by most historians to be a turning point in the American Civil War. Before Gettysburg, Confederate forces under General Robert E. Lee had defeated their Union counterparts sometimes by
(5) considerable margins—in a string of major battles. In this engagement, however, the Confederate army was defeated and driven back. Even more important than their material losses, though, was the Confederacy's loss of momentum. Union forces took the initiative, finally
(10) defeating the Confederacy less than two years later. By invading Union territory, the Confederate leadership had sought to shatter the Union's will to continue the war and to convince European nations to recognize the Confederacy as an independent nation. Instead,
(15) the Union's willingness to fight was strengthened and the Confederacy squandered its last chance for foreign support.

Words of emphasis, though rare, are the most important category of Kaplan keywords. Why? Because if you see an emphasis keyword in a sentence, you will always get a question about that sentence. Think about it—if the author thinks something is "of primary importance," it would be pretty silly for the test maker not to ask you about it.

In the Gettysburg passage, did you circle "even more important" (line 7)? You should have. You were bound to get a question about it.

By using all of the techniques discussed above, you will be able to tackle the most difficult Reading Comprehension questions. And now that you have the tools to handle the Verbal sections of the GRE, let's look at how to deal with the Quantitative sections.

# B. QUANTITATIVE

Two sections
30 minutes per section
30 questions per section

The GRE tests the same sort of mathematical concepts that the SAT does: arithmetic, algebra, and geometry. There is no trigonometry or calculus tested on the GRE. There are three formats of GRE math questions: Problem Solving, which have five answer choices each; Graph questions, which have five answer choices each and which are based on one or more graphs; and Quantitative Comparisons, which have only four answer choices each.

In addition to the math concepts that appeared on the SAT, the GRE started to test new mathematical concepts in 1994 that were tested little, if at all, in the past. You won't find sample problems in a book of released GREs, but you will, nonetheless, see them on test day. The new concepts are Median, Mode, Range, Standard Deviation, and Simple Probability.

Because the first 15 questions on each Math section are Quantitative Comparisons, let's look at these first.

## 1. QUANTITATIVE COMPARISONS

In Quantitative Comparisons, instead of solving for a particular value, you need to compare two quantities. At first, QCs may appear really difficult because of their unfamiliar format. However, once you become used to them, they can be quicker and easier than the other types of math questions.

## THE FORMAT

**The Questions**

QCs are arranged in order of increasing difficulty, with the first five questions being fairly easy and the last five being quite difficult.

In each question, you'll see two mathematical expressions. They are boxed, one in Column A, the other in Column B. Your job is to compare them.

Some questions include additional information about one or both quantities. This information is centered, unboxed, and essential to making the comparison.

### The Directions

The directions you'll see will look something like this:

<u>Directions:</u> **Each of Questions 1-15 consists of two quantities, one in column A and another in Column B. You are to compare the two quantities and answer**

(A) **if the quantity in Column A is greater;**

(B) **if the quantity in Column B is greater;**

(C) **if the two quantities are equal;**

(D) **if the relationship cannot be determined from the information given.**

<u>Common information:</u> **In a question, information concerning one or both of the quantities to be compared is centered above the two columns. A symbol that appears in both columns represents the same thing in Column A as it does in Column B.**

*Warning! Never pick choice (E) as the answer to a QC.*

## BASIC PRINCIPLES OF QUANTITATIVE COMPARISONS

Choices (A), (B), and (C) all represent definite relationships between the quantities in Column A and Column B. But choice (D) represents a relationship that cannot be determined. Here are two things to remember about choice (D) that will help you decide when to pick it:

1. **Choice (D) is never correct if both columns contain only numbers.**
   The relationship between numbers is unchanging, but choice (D) means more than one relationship is possible.

2. **Choice (D) is correct if you can demonstrate two different relationships between the columns.**
   Suppose you ran across the following QC:

| Column A | Column B |
|----------|----------|
| $2x$ | $3x$ |

If $x$ is a positive number, Column B is greater than Column A. If $x = 0$, the columns are equal. If $x$ equals any negative number, Column B is less than Column A. Because more than one relationship is possible, the answer is (D). In fact, as soon as you find a second possibility, stop work and pick choice (D).

## THE KAPLAN APPROACH TO QUANTITATIVE COMPARISONS

Here are six Kaplan strategies that will enable you to make quick comparisons. In the rest of this chapter you'll learn how they work and you'll try them on practice problems.

### 1. Compare piece by piece.
This works on QCs that compare two sums or two products.

### 2. Make one column look like the other.
This is a great approach when the columns look so different that you can't compare them directly.

### 3. Do the same thing to both columns.
Change both columns by adding, subtracting, multiplying, or dividing by the same amount on both sides in order to make the comparison more apparent.

### 4. Pick numbers.
Use this to get a handle on abstract algebra QCs.

### 5. Redraw the diagram.
Redrawing a diagram can clarify the relationships between measurements.

### 6. Avoid QC traps.
Stay alert for questions designed to fool you by leading you to the obvious, wrong answer.

Now let's look at how these strategies work.

### 1. Compare piece by piece.

| Column A | Column B |
|----------|----------|
| | |

$$w > x > 0 > y > z$$

| Column A | Column B |
|----------|----------|
| $w + y$ | $x + z$ |

In this problem, there are four variables — *w*, *x*, *y*, and *z*. Compare the value of each "piece" in each column. If every "piece" in one column is greater than a corresponding "piece" in the other column and the only operation involved is addition, the column with the greater individual values will have the greater total value. From the given information we know that $w > x$ and $y > z$. Therefore, the first term in Column A, *w*, is greater than the first term in Column B, *x*. Similarly, the second term in Column A, *y*, is greater than the second term in Column B, *z*. Because each piece in Column A is greater than the corresponding piece in Column B, Column A must be greater; the answer is (A).

**2. Make one column look like the other.**

When the quantities in Columns A and B are expressed differently, you can often make the comparison easier by changing one column to look like the other. For example, if one column is a percent, and the other a fraction, try converting the percent to a fraction.

| Column A | Column B |
|----------|----------|
| $x(x - 1)$ | $x^2 - x$ |

Here Column A has parentheses, and Column B doesn't. So make Column A look more like Column B: get rid of those parentheses. You end up with $x^2 - x$ in both columns, which means they are equal and the answer is (C).

Try another example, this time involving geometry.

| Column A | Column B |
|----------|----------|

The diameter of circle *O* is *d* and the area is *a*.

| Column A | Column B |
|----------|----------|
| $\dfrac{\pi d^2}{2}$ | $a$ |

Make Column B look more like Column A by rewriting *a*, the area of the circle, in terms of the diameter, *d*. The area of any circle equals $\pi r^2$, where *r* is the radius.

Since the radius is half the diameter, we can plug in $\frac{d}{2}$ for $r$ in the area formula to get $\pi(\frac{d}{2})^2$ in Column B. Simplifying we get $\frac{\pi d^2}{4}$.

Since both columns contain $\pi$, we can simply compare $\frac{d^2}{2}$ with $\frac{d^2}{4}$.

$\frac{d^2}{4}$ is half as much as $\frac{d^2}{2}$, and since $d^2$ must be positive, Column A is greater and choice (A) is correct.

## 3. Do the same thing to both columns.

Some QC questions become much clearer if you change not just the appearances, but the values of both columns. Treat them like two sides of an inequality, with the sign temporarily hidden.

You can add or subtract the same amount from both columns, and multiply or divide by the same positive amount without altering the relationship.

You can also square both columns if you're sure they're both positive. But watch out. Multiplying or dividing an inequality by a negative number reverses the direction of the inequality sign. Since it alters the relationship between the columns, avoid multiplying or dividing by a negative number.

In the QC below, what could you do to both columns?

| Column A | Column B |
|---|---|
| | $4a + 3 = 7b$ | |
| $20a + 10$ | $35b - 5$ |

All the terms in the two columns are multiples of 5, so divide both columns by 5 to simplify. You're left with $4a + 2$ in Column A and $7b - 1$ in Column B. This resembles the equation given in the centered information. In fact, if you add 1 to both columns, you have $4a + 3$ in Column A and $7b$ in Column B. The centered equation tells us they are equal. Thus choice (C) is correct.

In the next QC, what could you do to both columns?

Column A                    Column B

$$y > 0$$

$$1 + \frac{y}{1+y}$$                    $$1 + \frac{1}{1+y}$$

Solution: First subtract 1 from both sides. That gives you $\frac{y}{1+y}$ in Column A, and $\frac{1}{1+y}$ in Column B. Then multiply both sides by $1 + y$, which must be positive since $y$ is positive. You're left comparing $y$ with 1.

You know $y$ is greater than 0, but it could be a fraction less than 1, so it could be greater or less than 1. Since you can't say for sure which column is greater, the answer is (D).

### 4. Pick numbers.

If a QC involves variables, try picking numbers to make the relationship clearer. Here's what you do:

- Pick numbers that are easy to work with.
- Plug in the numbers and calculate the values. Note the relationship between the columns.
- Pick another number for each variable and calculate the values again.

Column A                    Column B

$$r > s > t > w > 0$$

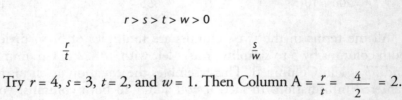

$$\frac{r}{t}$$                    $$\frac{s}{w}$$

Try $r = 4$, $s = 3$, $t = 2$, and $w = 1$. Then Column A = $\frac{r}{t} = \frac{4}{2} = 2$. And Column B = $\frac{s}{w} = \frac{3}{1} = 3$. So in this case Column B is greater than Column A.

*Always Pick More Than One Number and Calculate Again*

In the example above, we first found Column B was bigger. But that doesn't mean Column B is always bigger and that the answer is (B). It does mean the answer is not (A) or (C). But the answer could still be (D)—not enough information to decide.

If time is short, guess between (B) and (D). But whenever you can, pick another set of numbers and calculate again.

As best you can, make a special effort to find a second set of numbers that will alter the relationship. Here for example, try making $r$ a lot larger. Pick $r = 30$ and keep the other variables as they were. Now Column A = $\frac{30}{2}$ = 15. This time, Column A is greater than Column B, so answer choice (D) is correct.

### Pick different kinds of numbers.

Don't assume all variables represent positive integers. Unless you're told otherwise, variables can represent zero, negative numbers, or fractions. Since different kinds of numbers behave differently, always pick a different kind of number the second time around. In the example above, we plugged in a small positive number the first time and a larger number the second.

In the next three examples, we pick different numbers and get different results. Since we can't find constant relationships between Columns A and B, in all these cases the answer is (D).

| Column A | Column B |
|----------|----------|
| $w$ | $-w$ |

If $w = 5$, Column A = 5 and Column B = –5, so Column A is greater.

If $w = -5$, Column A = –5 and Column B = 5, so Column B is greater.

| Column A | Column B |
|----------|----------|
| $x \neq 0$ | |
| $x$ | $\frac{1}{x}$ |

If $x = 3$, Column A = 3 and Column B = $\frac{1}{3}$, so Column A is greater.

> **RULE OF THUMB**
>
> If the relationship between Columns A and B changes when you pick other numbers, (D) must be the answer.

If $x = \frac{1}{3}$, Column A = $\frac{1}{3}$ and Column B = $\frac{1}{\frac{1}{3}}$ = 3, so Column B is greater.

| Column A | Column B |
|----------|----------|
| $x$ | $x^2$ |

If $x = \frac{1}{2}$, Column A = $\frac{1}{2}$ and Column B = $\frac{1}{4}$, so Column A is greater.

If $x = 2$, Column A = 2 and Column B = 4, so Column B is greater.

**5. Redraw the diagram.**

- Redraw a diagram if the one that's given confuses you.
- Redraw scale diagrams to exaggerate crucial differences.

Some geometry diagrams may be misleading. Two angles or lengths may look equal as drawn in the diagram, but the given information tells you that there is a slight difference in their measures. The best strategy is to redraw the diagram so that their relationship can be clearly seen.

Column A                                   Column

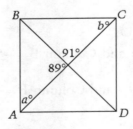

ABCD is a rectangle

a                                          b

Redraw this diagram to exaggerate the difference between the 89-degree angle and the 91-degree angle. In other words, make the larger angle much larger, and the smaller angle much smaller. The new rectangle that results is much wider than it is tall.

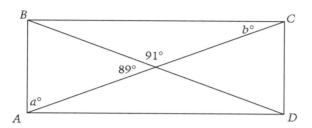

In the new diagram, where the crucial difference jumps out, *a* is clearly greater than *b*.

## 6. Avoid QC traps.

To avoid QC traps, always be alert. Don't assume anything. Be especially cautious near the end of the question set.

*Don't Be Tricked by Misleading Information*

| Column A | Column B |
|----------|----------|
| John is taller than Bob. | |
| John's weight in pounds | Bob's weight in pounds |

The test makers hope you think, "If John is taller, he must weigh more." But there's no guaranteed relationship between height and weight, so you don't have enough information. The answer is (D). Fortunately, problems like this are easy to spot if you stay alert.

*Don't Assume*

A common QC mistake is to assume that variables represent positive integers. As we saw in using the Picking Numbers strategy, fractions or negative numbers often show another relationship between the columns.

Column A       Column B

When 1 is added to the square of x the result is 37.

   x       6

> **RULE OF THUMB**
>
> Be aware of negative numbers!

It is easy to assume that $x$ must be 6, since the square of $x$ is 36. That would make choice (C) correct. However, it is possible that $x = -6$. Since $x$ could be either 6 or $-6$, the answer is (D).

*Don't Forget to Consider Other Possibilities*

Column A       Column B

$$\begin{array}{r} R \\ S \\ T \\ \hline 1W \end{array}$$

In the addition problem above, R, S, and T are different digits that are multiples of 3, and W is a digit.

   W      8

Because you're told that $R$, $S$, and $T$ are digits and different multiples of 3, most people will think of 3, 6, and 9, which add up to 18. That makes $W$ equal to 8, and Columns A and B equal. But that's too obvious for a QC at the end of the section.

There's another possibility. 0 is also a multiple of 3. So the three digits could be 0, 3, and 9, or 0, 6, and 9, which give totals of 12 and 15, respectively. That means $W$ could be 8, 2, or 5. Since the columns could be equal, or Column B could be greater, answer choice (D) must be correct.

*Don't Fall for Look-Alikes*

Column A       Column B

$\sqrt{5} + \sqrt{5}$      $\sqrt{10}$

At first glance, forgetting the rules of radicals, you might think these quantities are equal and that the answer is (C). But use some common sense to see this isn't the case. Each $\sqrt{5}$ in Column A is bigger than $\sqrt{4}$, so Column A is more than 4. The $\sqrt{10}$ in Column B is less than another familiar number, $\sqrt{16}$, so Column B is less than 4.

# TEST CONTENT

The answer is (A).

Now use Kaplan's six strategies to solve nine typical QC questions. Then check your work against our solutions.

## Practice Problems

| Column A | Column B |
|---|---|
| 1. $x^2 + 2x - 2$ | $x^2 + 2x - 1$ |

$$x = 2y$$
$$y > 0$$

| | |
|---|---|
| 2. $4^{2y}$ | $2^x$ |

$$\frac{x}{y} = \frac{z}{4}$$

$x$, $y$, and $z$ are positive.

| | |
|---|---|
| 3. $6x$ | $2yz$ |

$q$, $r$, and $s$ are positive integers.
$$qrs > 12$$

| | |
|---|---|
| 4. $\frac{qr}{5}$ | $\frac{3}{s}$ |

$$x > 1$$
$$y > 0$$

| | |
|---|---|
| 5. $y^x$ | $y^{(x+1)}$ |

$$7p + 3 = r$$
$$3p + 7 = s$$

| | |
|---|---|
| 6. $r$ | $s$ |

121

Column A                                    Column B

In triangle *XYZ*, the measure of angle *X* equals the measure of angle *Y*.

7. The degree measure        The degree measure
   of angle *Z*              of angle *X* plus the
                            degree measure of
                            angle *Y*

$$h > 1$$

8. The number of                    $\dfrac{60}{h}$
   minutes in *h*
   hours

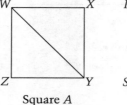

Square *A*

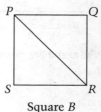

Square *B*

9. $\dfrac{\text{Perimeter of square } A}{\text{Perimeter of square } B}$        $\dfrac{\text{Length of } WY}{\text{Length of } PR}$

## ANSWER KEY

**1. (B)**

Comparing the respective pieces of the two columns, the only difference is the third piece: −2 in Column A and −1 in Column B. We don't know the value of *x*, but whatever it is, $x^2$ in Column A must have the same value as $x^2$ in Column B, and $2x$ in Column A must have the same value as $2x$ in Column B. Since any quantity minus 2 must be less than that quantity minus 1, Column B is greater than Column A.

**2. (A)**

Replacing the *x* exponent in Column B with the equivalent value given in the problem, we're comparing $4^{2y}$ to $2^{2y}$. Since *y* is greater than zero, raising 4 to the $2y$ power will result in a greater value than raising 2 to the $2y$ power.

**3. (B)**

Do the same thing to both columns until they resemble the centered information. When we divide both columns by $6y$ we get $\frac{6x}{6y}$ or $\frac{x}{y}$ in Column A, and $\frac{2yz}{6y}$, or $\frac{z}{3}$ in Column B. Since $\frac{x}{y} = \frac{z}{4}$, and $\frac{z}{3} > \frac{z}{4}$ (because $z$ is positive), $\frac{z}{3} > \frac{x}{y}$.

**4. (D)**

Do the same thing to both columns to make them look like the centered information. When we multiply both columns by $5s$ we get $qrs$ in Column A and $15$ in Column B. Since $qrs$ could be any integer greater than 12, it could be greater than, equal to, or less than 15.

**5. (D)**

Try $x = y = 2$. Then Column A = $y^x = 2^2 = 4$. Column B = $y^{x+1}$ = $2^3 = 8$, making Column B greater. But if $x = 2$ and $y = \frac{1}{2}$, Column A = $(\frac{1}{2})^2 = \frac{1}{4}$ and Column B = $(\frac{1}{2})^3 = \frac{1}{8}$. In this case, Column A is greater than Column B, so the answer is (D).

**6. (D)**

Pick a value for $p$, and see what effect this has on $r$ and $s$. If $p = 1$, $r = (7 \times 1) + 3 = 10$, and $s = (3 \times 1) + 7 = 10$, and the two columns are equal. But if $p = 0$, $r = (7 \times 0) + 3 = 3$, and $s = (3 \times 0) + 7 = 7$, and Column A is smaller than Column B. Since there are at least two different possible relationships, the answer is choice (D).

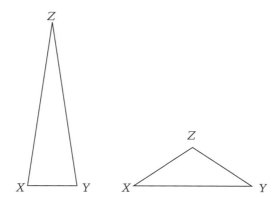

**7. (D)**

Since angle $X$ = angle $Y$, this is an isosceles triangle. We can draw two diagrams with $X$ and $Y$ as the base angles of an isosceles triangle.

In one diagram, make the triangle tall and narrow, so that angle $X$ and angle $Y$ are very large, and angle $Z$ is very small. In this case, column B is greater. In the second diagram, make the triangle short and wide, so that angle $Z$ is much larger than angle $X$ and angle $Y$. In this case, Column A is greater. Since more than one relationship between the columns is possible, the correct answer is choice (D).

**8. (A)**

The "obvious" answer here is choice (C), because there are 60 minutes in an hour, and 60 appears in Column B. But the number of minutes in $h$ hours would equal 60 times $h$, not 60 divided by $h$. Since $h$ is greater than 1, the number in Column B will be less than the actual number of minutes in $h$ hours, so Column A is greater. (A) is correct.

**9. (C)**

We don't know the exact relationship between Square $A$ and Square $B$, but it doesn't matter. The problem is actually just comparing the ratios of corresponding parts of two squares. Whatever the relationship between them is for one specific length in both squares, the same relationship will exist between them for any other corresponding length. If a side of one square is twice the length of a side of the second square, the diagonal will also be twice as long. The ratio of the perimeters of the two squares is the same as the ratio of the diagonals. Therefore, the columns are equal. (C) is correct.

# 2. PROBLEM SOLVING

In Problem Solving, you will have to solve problems that test a variety of mathematical concepts. Problem Solving questions will cover percentages, simultaneous equations, symbolism, special triangles, multiple and oddball figures, mean, median, mode, range, and probability.

## THE FORMAT

### The Questions
In each math section, questions 16 through 20 and 26 through 30 are Problem Solving questions. (Questions 21 through 25 are Graph questions, which we will discuss in a later section.) Problem Solving questions are arranged in order of increasing difficulty. Questions 16 through 18 are relatively easy; questions 19, 20, 26 and 27 are of medium difficulty, and questions 28 through 30 are hard. Keep this in mind as you practice for your test.

### The Directions
The directions that you'll see will look something like this:

> **Directions:** Each of Questions 16-20 has five answer choices. For each of these questions, select the best answer choices given.

## THE KAPLAN APPROACH TO PERCENTAGES

> Last year Julie's annual salary was $20,000. This year's raise brings her to an annual salary of $25,000. If she gets the same percent raise every year, what will her salary be next year?
> (A) $27,500
> (B) $30,000
> (C) $31,250
> (D) $32,500
> (E) $35,000

In percent problems, you're usually given two pieces of information and asked to find the third. When you see a percent problem, remember:

### KNOW YOUR PERCENTS

When you need to, you can figure out a percent equivalent on your calculator by dividing the numerator by the denominator. You'll save time by knowing some common percent equivalents.

$$\frac{1}{5} = 20\%$$

$$\frac{1}{4} = 25\%$$

$$\frac{1}{3} = 33\frac{1}{3}\%$$

$$\frac{1}{2} = 50\%$$

$$\frac{2}{3} = 66\frac{2}{3}\%$$

$$\frac{3}{4} = 75\%$$

- If you are solving for a percent:

$$\text{Percent} = \frac{\text{Part}}{\text{Whole}}$$

- If you need to solve for a part:

$$\text{Percent} \times \text{Whole} = \text{Part}$$

This problem asks for Julie's projected salary for next year—that is, her current salary plus her next raise.

You know last year's salary ($20,000) and you know this year's salary ($25,000), so you can find the difference between the two salaries:

$$\$25,000 - \$20,000 = \$5,000 = \text{her raise}$$

Now find the percent of her raise, by using the formula

$$\text{Percent} = \frac{\text{Part}}{\text{Whole}}$$

Since Julie's raise was calculated on last year's salary, divide by $20,000.

$$\text{Percent raise} = \frac{\$5,000}{\$20,000} = \frac{1}{4} = 25\%$$

You know she will get the same percent raise next year, so solve for the part. Use the formula: Percent × Whole = Part.

Her raise next year will be 25% × $25,000 = $\frac{1}{4}$ × 25,000 = $6,250.

Add that amount to this year's salary and you have her projected salary:

$$\$25,000 + \$6,250 = \$31,250 \text{ or answer choice (C).}$$

Make sure that you change the percent to either a fraction or a decimal before beginning calculations.

## Practice Problems

| Column A | Column B |
|----------|----------|
| 1. 5% of 3% of 45 | 6.75 |

---

2. If a sweater sells for $48 after a 25 percent markdown, what was its original price?
   (A) $56
   (B) $60
   (C) $64
   (D) $68
   (E) $72

## Solutions

**1. (B)**
Percent × Whole = Part. 5% of (3% of 45) = .05 × (.03 × 45) = .05 × 1.35 = .0675, which is less than 6.75 in Column B.

**2. (C)**
We want to solve for the original price, the Whole. The percent markdown is 25%, so $48 is 75% of the whole: Percent × Whole = Part.

$$75\% \times \text{Original Price} = \$48$$
$$\text{Original Price} = \frac{\$48}{0.75} = \$64.$$

# THE KAPLAN APPROACH TO SIMULTANEOUS EQUATIONS

If $p + 2q = 14$ and $3p + q = 12$, then $p =$
(A)  −2
(B)  −1
(C)   1
(D)   2
(E)   3

In order to get a numerical value for each variable, you need as many different equations as there are variables to solve for. So, if you have 2 variables, you need 2 independent equations.

You could tackle this problem by solving for one variable in terms of the other, and then plugging this expression into the other equation.

But the simultaneous equations that appear on the GRE can usually be handled in an easier way.

You can't eliminate $p$ or $q$ by adding or subtracting the equations in their present form.

But look what happens if you multiply both sides of the second equation by 2:

$$2(3p + q) = 2(12)$$
$$6p + 2q = 24$$

Now when you subtract the first equation from the second, the $q$'s will cancel out so you can solve for $p$:

$$6p + 2q = 24$$
$$-[p + 2q = 14]$$
$$\overline{\phantom{5p + 0 = 10}}$$
$$5p + 0 = 10$$
$$\text{If } 5p = 10, \; p = 2$$

## Practice Problems

1. If $x + y = 8$ and $y - x = -2$, then $y =$
   (A)   −2
   (B)   3
   (C)   5
   (D)   8
   (E)   10

2. If $m - n = 5$ and $2m + 3n = 15$, then $m + n =$
   (A)   1
   (B)   6
   (C)   7
   (D)   10
   (E)   15

**Solutions**

**1. (B)**
When you add the two equations, the $x$'s cancel out and you find that $2y = 6$, so $y = 3$.

**2. (C)**
Multiply the first equation by 2, then subtract the first equation from the second to eliminate the $m$'s and find that $5n = 5$, or $n = 1$. Plugging this value for $n$ into the first equation shows that $m = 6$, so $m + n = 7$, choice (C).

$$2m + 3n = 15 \qquad m - n = 5 \qquad m + n = 6 + 1 = 7$$
$$-2m + 2n = -10 \qquad m - 1 = 5$$
$$5n = 5 \qquad m = 6$$
$$n = 1$$

## THE KAPLAN APPROACH TO SYMBOLISM

If $a \star b = \sqrt{a + b}$ for all non-negative numbers, what is the value of $10 \star 6$ ?
(A)    0
(B)    2
(C)    4
(D)    8
(E)    16

You should be quite familiar with the arithmetic symbols $+$, $-$, $\times$, $\div$, and %. Finding the value of $10 + 2$, $18 - 4$, $4 \times 9$, or $96 \div 16$ is easy.

However, on the GRE, you may come across bizarre symbols. You may even be asked to find the value of $10 \star 2$, $5 \circledast 7$, $10 \divideontimes 6$, or $65 \heartsuit 2$.

The GRE test makers put strange symbols in questions to confuse or unnerve you. Don't let them. The question stem always tells you what the strange symbol means. Although this type of question may look difficult, it is really an exercise in plugging in.

To solve, just plug in 10 for $a$ and 6 for $b$ into the expression $\sqrt{a + b}$. That equals $\sqrt{10 + 6}$ or $\sqrt{16}$ or 4, choice (C).

## RULE OF THUMB

When a symbolism problem includes parentheses, do the operations inside the parentheses first.

How about a more involved symbolism question?

If $a$ ▲ means to multiply $a$ by 3 and $a$ ✳ means to divide $a$ by −2, what is the value of $((8✳)▲)✳$ ?

(A)　−6
(B)　0
(C)　2
(D)　3
(E)　6

First find 8✳. This means to divide 8 by −2, which is −4. Working out to the next set of parentheses, we have $(−4)▲$, which means to multiply −4 by 3, which is −12. Lastly, we find $(−12)✳$, which means to divide −12 by −2, which is 6, choice (E).

## Practice Problems

## RULE OF THUMB

When two questions include the same symbol, expect the second question to be more difficult and be extra careful.

| Column A | Column B |
|---|---|

If $x \neq 0$, let ♠ $x$ be defined by ♠ $x = x - \dfrac{1}{x}$.

1.　　−3　　　　　　　　　　♠ (−3)

2. If $r$ ❤ $s = r(r − s)$ for all integers $r$ and $s$, then $4$ ❤ $(3 ❤ 5)$ equals

(A)　−8
(B)　−2
(C)　2
(D)　20
(E)　40

Questions 3 – 4 refer to the following definition:

$c \star d = \frac{c-d}{c}$, where $c \neq 0$.

3. $12 \star 3 =$

    (A) $-3$

    (B) $\frac{1}{4}$

    (C) $\frac{2}{3}$

    (D) $\frac{3}{4}$

    (E) $3$

4. If $9 \star 4 = 15 \star k$, then $k =$

    (A) $3$

    (B) $6$

    (C) $\frac{20}{3}$

    (D) $\frac{25}{3}$

    (E) $9$

## Solutions

**1. (B)**
Plug in $-3$ for $x$: $\spadesuit\, x = -3 - \frac{1}{-3} = -3 + \frac{1}{3} = -2\frac{2}{3}$, which is greater than $-3$ in Column A.

**2. (E)**
Start in the parentheses and work out: $(3 \heartsuit 5) = 3(3–5) = 3(-2) = -6$; $4 \heartsuit (-6) = 4[4 – (-6)] = 4(10) = 40$.

**3. (D)**
Plug in 12 for $c$ and 3 for $d$: $12\star3 = \frac{12–3}{12} = \frac{9}{12} = \frac{3}{4}$.

**4. (C)**
Plug in on both sides of the equation:
$\frac{9–4}{9} = \frac{15–k}{15}$

$$\frac{5}{9} = \frac{15-k}{15}$$

Cross-multiply and solve for $k$:

$$75 = 135 - 9k$$

$$-60 = -9k$$

$$\frac{-60}{-9} = k$$

$$\frac{20}{3} = k$$

## THE KAPLAN APPROACH TO SPECIAL TRIANGLES

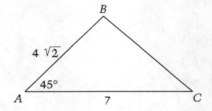

In the triangle above, what is the length of side $BC$?
(A) 4
(B) 5
(C) $4\sqrt{2}$
(D) 6
(E) $5\sqrt{2}$

| **RULE OF THUMB** |
| --- |
| Look for the special triangles in geometry problems. |

Special triangles contain a lot of information. For instance, if you know the length of one side of a 30-60-90 triangle, you can easily work out the lengths of the others. Special triangles allow you to transfer one piece of information around the whole figure.

The following are the special triangles you should look for on the GRE.

### Equilateral Triangles

All interior angles are 60° and all sides are of the same length.

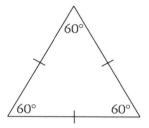

### Isosceles Triangles

Two sides are of the same length and the angles facing these sides are equal.

### Right Triangles

Contain a 90° angle. The sides are related by the Pythagorean theorem.

$a^2 + b^2 = c^2$ where $a$ and $b$ are the legs and $c$ is the hypotenuse.

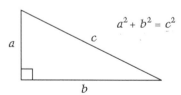

133

### The "Special" Right Triangles

Many triangle problems contain "special" right triangles, whose side lengths always come in predictable ratios. If you recognize them, you won't have to use the Pythagorean theorem to find the value of a missing side length.

### The 3-4-5 Right Triangle

(Be on the lookout for multiples of 3-4-5 as well.)

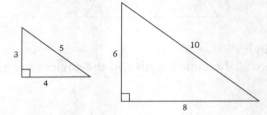

### The Isosceles Right Triangle

(Note the side ratio: 1 to 1 to $\sqrt{2}$.)

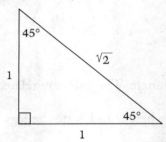

### The 30-60-90 Right Triangle

(Note the side ratio: 1 to $\sqrt{3}$ to 2, and which side is opposite which angle.)

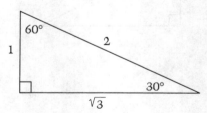

Getting back to our example, you can drop a vertical line from *B* to line *AC*. This divides the triangle into two right triangles.

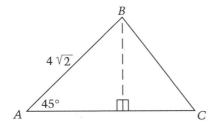

That means you know two of the angles in the triangle on the left; 90° and 45°. So this is an isosceles right triangle, with sides in the ratio of 1 to 1 to $\sqrt{2}$. The hypotenuse here is $4\sqrt{2}$, so both legs have length 4. Filling this in, you have:

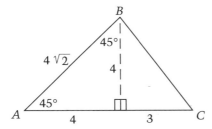

Now you can see that the legs of the smaller triangle on the right must be 4 and 3, making this a 3-4-5 right triangle, and the length of hypotenuse *BC* is 5.

### Practice Problems

| Column A | Column B |
|---|---|

1. In triangle *ABC*, if *AB* = 4, then *AC* =

    (A)   10
    (B)    9
    (C)    8
    (D)    7
    (E)    6

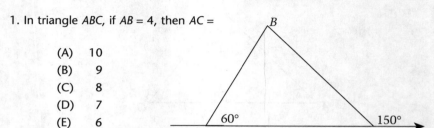

In the coordinate plane, point *R* has coordinates (0,0) and point *S* has coordinates (9,12).

2. The distance from                16
    *R* to *S*

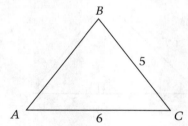

3. If the perimeter of triangle *ABC* above is 16, what is its area?

    (A)    8
    (B)    9
    (C)   10
    (D)   12
    (E)   15

### Solutions

**1. (C)**
Angle *BCA* is supplementary to the angle marked 150°, so angle *BCA* = 180° − 150° = 30°. Since the interior angles of a triangle sum to 180°, angle *A* + angle *B* + angle *BCA* = 180°, so angle *B* = 180° − 60° − 30° = 90°. So triangle *ABC* is a 30-60-90 right triangle, and its sides are in the ratio 1: $\sqrt{3}$ : 2. The side opposite the 30°, *AB*, which we know has length 4, must be half the length of the hypotenuse, *AC*. Therefore *AC* = 8, and that's answer choice (C).

**2. (B)**

Draw a diagram. Since *RS* isn't parallel to either axis, the way to compute its length is to create a right triangle with legs that are parallel to the axes, so their lengths are easy to find. We can then use the Pythagorean theorem to find the length of *RS*.

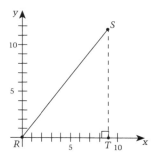

Since *S* has a *y*-coordinate of 12, it's 12 units above the *x*-axis, so the length of *ST* must be 12. And since *T* is the same number of units to the right of the *y*-axis as *S*, given by the *x*-coordinate of 9, the distance from the origin to *T* must be 9. So we have a right triangle with legs of 9 and 12. You should recognize this as a multiple of the 3-4-5 triangle. $9 = 3 \times 3$; $12 = 3 \times 4$; so the hypotenuse *RS* must be $3 \times 5$, or 15. That's the value of Column A, so Column B is greater.

**3. (D)**

To find the area you need to know the base and height. If the perimeter is 16, then $AB + BC + AC = 16$; that is, $AB = 16 - 5 - 6 = 5$. Since $AB = BC$, this is an isosceles triangle. If you drop a line from vertex *B* perpendicular to *AC*, it will divide the base in half. This divides the triangle up into two smaller right triangles:

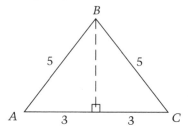

These right triangles each have one leg of 3 and a hypotenuse of 5; therefore they are 3-4-5 right triangles. So the missing leg (which is also the height of triangle *ABC* ) must have length 4. We now know that the base of *ABC* is 6 and the height is 4, so the area is $\frac{1}{2}$ × 6 × 4, or 12, answer choice (D).

## THE KAPLAN APPROACH TO MULTIPLE AND ODDBALL FIGURES

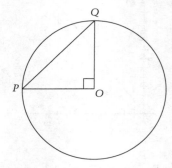

In the figure above, if the area of the circle with center *O* is 9π, what is the area of triangle *POQ*?
(A)  4.5
(B)  6
(C)  3.5π
(D)  4.5π
(E)  9

In a problem that combines figures, you have to look for the relationship between the figures.

For instance, if two figures share a side, information about that side will probably be the key.

In this case the figures don't share a side, but the triangle's legs are important features of the circle—they are radii. You can see that *OP* = *OQ* = the radius of circle *O*.

The area of the circle is 9π. The area of a circle is $\pi r^2$, where *r* is the radius. So $9\pi = \pi r^2$, $9 = r^2$, and the radius *r* is 3. The area of a triangle is $\frac{1}{2}$ base times height. Therefore, the area of $\Delta POQ$ is $\frac{1}{2}$ (leg$_1$ × leg$_2$) = $\frac{1}{2}$ (3 × 3) = $\frac{9}{2}$ = 4.5, answer choice (A).

---

**RULE OF THUMB**

Look for pieces the figures have in common.

---

But what if, instead of a number of familiar shapes, you are given something like this?

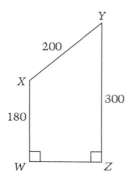

What is the perimeter of quadrilateral *WXYZ*?
(A)     680
(B)     760
(C)     840
(D)     920
(E)     1000

Try breaking the unfamiliar shape into familiar ones. Once this is done, you can use the same techniques that you would for multiple figures. Perimeter is the sum of the lengths of the sides of a figure, so you need to find the length of *WZ*. Drawing a perpendicular line from point *X* to side *YZ* will divide the figure into a right triangle and a rectangle. Call the point of intersection *A*.

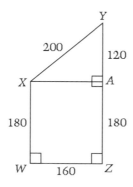

Opposite sides of a rectangle have equal length, so *WZ = XA* and *WX = ZA*. *WX* is labeled as 180, so *ZA* = 180. Since *YZ* measures 300, *AY* is 300 − 180 = 120. In right triangle *XYA*, hypotenuse *XY*

= 200 and leg $AY$ = 120; you should recognize this as a multiple of a 3-4-5 right triangle. The hypotenuse is 5 × 40, one leg is 3 × 40, so $XA$ must be 4 × 40 or 160. (If you didn't recognize this special right triangle you could have used the Pythagorean theorem to find the length of $XA$.) Since $WZ$ = $XA$ = 160, the perimeter of the figure is 180 + 200 + 300 + 160 = 840, answer choice (C).

**Practice Problems**

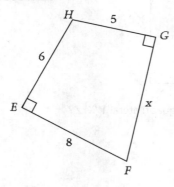

1. What is the value of *x* in the figure above?

(A)  4
(B)  $3\sqrt{3}$
(C)  $3\sqrt{5}$
(D)  $5\sqrt{3}$
(E)  9

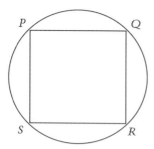

2. In the figure above, square *PQRS* is inscribed in a circle. If the area of square *PQRS* is 4, what is the radius of the circle?

   (A)  1
   (B)  $\sqrt{2}$
   (C)  2
   (D)  $2\sqrt{2}$
   (E)  $4\sqrt{2}$

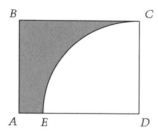

3. In the figure above, the quarter circle with center *D* has a radius of 4 and rectangle *ABCD* has a perimeter of 20. What is the perimeter of the shaded region?

   (A)   $20 - 8\pi$
   (B)   $10 + 2\pi$
   (C)   $12 + 2\pi$
   (D)   $12 + 4\pi$
   (E)    $4 + 8\pi$

**Solutions**

**1. (D)**

Draw a straight line from point $H$ to point $F$, to divide the figure into two right triangles.

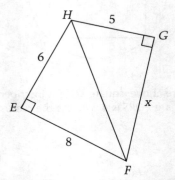

$\Delta EFH$ is a 3-4-5 right triangle with a hypotenuse of length 10. Use the Pythagorean theorem in $\Delta FGH$ to find $x$:

$$x^2 + 5^2 = 10^2$$
$$x^2 + 5^2 = 100$$
$$x^2 = 75$$
$$x = \sqrt{75}$$
$$x = \sqrt{25}\,\sqrt{3}$$
$$x = 5\,\sqrt{3}$$

**2. (B)**

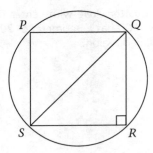

Draw in diagonal $QS$ and you will notice that it is also a diameter of the circle. Since the area of the square is 4 its sides must each be 2. The diagonal of a square is always the length of a side times $\sqrt{2}$.

Think of the diagonal as dividing the square into two isosceles right triangles. Therefore, the diagonal = $2\sqrt{2}$ = the diameter; the radius is half this amount or $\sqrt{2}$.

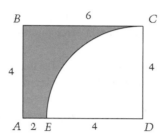

**3. (C)**

The perimeter of the shaded region is $BC + AB + AE +$ arc $EC$. The quarter circle has its center at $D$, and point $C$ lies on the circle, so side $DC$ is a radius of the circle and equals 4. Opposite sides of a rectangle are equal so $AB$ is also 4. The perimeter of the rectangle is 20, and since the two short sides account for 8, the two longer sides must account for 12, making $BC$ and $AD$ each 6. To find $AE$, subtract the length of $ED$, another radius of length 4, from the length of $AD$, which is 6; $AE = 2$. Since arc $EC$ is a quarter circle, the length of the arc $EC$ is $\frac{1}{4}$ of the circumference of a whole circle with radius 4: $\frac{1}{4} \times 2\pi r = \frac{1}{4} \times 8\pi = 2\pi$. So the perimeter of the shaded region is $6 + 4 + 2 + 2\pi = 12 + 2\pi$.

143

## THE KAPLAN APPROACH TO MEAN, MEDIAN, MODE, AND RANGE

The GRE has always tested the concept of a mean, which is also called the "arithmetic mean," for no good reason. The mean of several numbers is simply their average. Whenever you see "arithmetic mean" on the GRE, it's not a trick—they just mean "average."

The **median** of several terms is the number that evenly divides the terms into two groups; half of the terms are larger than the median and half of the terms are smaller than the median. If there is an odd number of terms, the median will be the same as the middle number (not necessarily the average or the mode). If there are an even number of terms, the median will be halfway between the two terms closest to the middle.

> For the set {4, 5, 7, 23, 5, 67, 10}, the median is 7, since this divides the set into two smaller sets of three terms each, {4, 5, 5} and {10, 23, 67}.

The **mode** is even simpler. It's just the term with the most occurrences in a set of numbers. If two or more numbers are tied for the most occurrences, then each is considered a mode.

> For the set {4, 5, 7, 23, 5, 67, 10}, the mode is 5, because it occurs the greatest number of times of any of the terms.

The **range** is the simplest of these four concepts. It's just the difference between the largest term and the smallest term in a set of numbers. Just subtract the smallest from the biggest and you will have the range.

> For the set {4, 5, 7, 23, 5, 67, 10}, the range is 63, because the greatest number, 67, minus the smallest, 4, equals 63.

## Practice Problems

| Column A | Column B |
|---|---|
| 1. The median of the integers from 1 through 31, inclusive. | 16 |
| 2. $2^6$ | The range of the series {8, 9, 9, 15, 71} |

3. The only test scores for the students in a certain class are 44, 30, 42, 30, $x$, 44, and 30. If $x$ equals one of the other scores and is a multiple of 5, what is the mode for the class?
(A)  5
(B)  6
(C) 15
(D) 30
(E) 44

4. If half the range of the increasing series {11, $A$, 23, $B$, $C$, 68, 73} is equal to its median, what is the median of the series?
(A) 23
(B) 31
(C) 33
(D) 41
(E) 62

## Solutions

**1. (C)**
"Inclusive" just means you should include the numbers on the ends —in this case, 1 and 31. The number right in the middle of this series is 16. There are 15 numbers smaller than it and 15 numbers greater than it.

**2. (A)**
$2^6$ equals 64. The range of the series in Column B equals $71 - 8$, which equals 63.

**3. (D)**
Since $x$ equals one of the other scores, it must equal either 30, 42, or 44. And since it must also be a multiple of 5, we can conclude that $x$ equals 30. That means that 4 of the students—more than earned any other score—earned a score of 30, which makes 30 the mode.

**4. (B)**
Don't get confused by all the variables; just concentrate on what you know. The range must be the difference of the smallest term and the largest term. Since this is an increasing series, the smallest term must

be 11 and the largest must be 73. The difference between them is 62, so that's the range. Half of the range, then, is 31, so 31 must equal the median of the series.

## THE KAPLAN APPROACH TO PROBABILITY

A probability is the fractional likelihood of an event occurring. It can be represented by a fraction ("the probability of it raining today is $\frac{1}{2}$"), a ratio ("the odds of it raining today are 50:50"), or a percent ("the probability of rain today is 50%"). You can translate probabilities easily into everyday language: $\frac{1}{100}$ = "One chance in a hundred" or "the odds are one in a hundred." To find probabilities, count the number of desired outcomes and divide by the number of possible outcomes. Probability = (Number of Desired Outcomes/Number of Possible Outcomes).

What is the probability of throwing a 5 on a six sided die?

There is one desired outcome—throwing a 5. There are 6 possible outcomes—one for each side of the die.
So the probability = $\frac{1}{6}$

All probabilities are between 0 and 1 inclusive. A "0" probability means there is zero chance of an event occurring (i.e. it can't happen). A "1" probability means that an event has a 100% chance of occurring (i.e. it must occur). The higher the probability, the greater chance that an event will occur. You can often eliminate answer choices by having some idea where the probability of an event occurring falls within this range.

The odds of throwing a 5 on a die are $\frac{1}{6}$, so the odds of not throwing a 5 are $\frac{5}{6}$. Therefore, you have a much greater probability of not throwing a 5 on a die than of throwing a 5.

# TEST CONTENT

## Practice Problems

Column A                          Column B

The probability of rain on Thursday is 50%. The probability that it will not rain on Friday is $\frac{1}{4}$.

1. The probability of          The probability of
   rain on Thursday            rain on Friday

   A hat contains an equal number
   of red, blue and green marbles.

2. The probability of          The probability of
   picking a red marble        picking a green
   out of the hat              marble out of the hat

3. If there are 14 women and 10 men employed in a certain office, what is the probability that one employee picked at random will be a woman?

   (A) $\frac{1}{6}$

   (B) $\frac{1}{14}$

   (C) $\frac{7}{12}$

   (D) 1

   (E) $\frac{7}{5}$

4. If Tom flips a fair coin twice, what is the probability that at least one head will be thrown?

   (A) $\frac{1}{4}$

   (B) $\frac{1}{3}$

   (C) $\frac{1}{2}$

   (D) $\frac{2}{3}$

   (E) $\frac{3}{4}$

**Solutions**

**1. (B)**
The probability of rain on Thursday is $\dfrac{1}{2}$ and the probability of rain on Friday is $\dfrac{3}{4}$.

**2. (C)**
The number of desired outcomes is the same in each case, since there are an equal number of red and green marbles. The number of possible outcomes in each case is also the same, since the marbles are all being pulled from the same hat. Therefore the probabilities are the same.

**3. (C)**
Probability = (Number of desired outcomes/Number of possible outcomes) = (Number of women/Number of people) = $\dfrac{14}{24}$ = $\dfrac{7}{12}$.

**4. (E)**
Desired outcomes = HH or HT or TH. Possible outcomes = HH or HT or TH or TT. Probability = $\dfrac{3}{4}$.

# 3. GRAPHS

In every math section, questions 21-25 will be based on one or more graphs. Exactly what ETS is trying to test with this section, we have never been able to determine, unless you need to sharpen your clerical skills before you pursue that Ph.D. in electrical engineering.

## THE BASIC PRINCIPLES OF GRAPHS

### LEVELS OF DIFFICULTY

The first two graph questions are simple; the last two graph questions are hard and can be tricky.

**1. Questions 21 and 22 will be fairly easy.**
You will have to do something like find a value from the graph(s) or compare values in the graph(s). They will be something that will only take a few steps.

**2. Questions 24 and 25 are the opposite.**
They are never so simple; they always require more than just a few steps. They may fool you into thinking that they're easy, but there will be a trick involved. Never, ever pick the obvious answer on the last two graph questions. Don't bother hoping that your test is an exception and the last graph question just happens to be pretty easy. Question 25 is never easy, even if it seems that way.

# THE KAPLAN APPROACH TO GRAPHS

We recommend a three-step approach to graph problems:

**1. Familiarize yourself with the graph(s).**
Graphs sections usually have more than one graph in them.
- Read the title(s).
- Check the scales to see how the information is measured.
- Read any accompanying notes.
- If there is more than one line on the graph, label each line according to the key so you can reference them easily when working on the questions.

**2. Answer the questions that follow.**
Graph questions require a strong understanding of fractions and percents and good attention to detail but little else.

When there are two graphs in one section, for each of questions 21 and 22 you'll probably just need to use one graph (though perhaps not the same graph). Questions 23 and 24 may use either one or both of the graphs. For 25, you will need to use both graphs, taking data from one and combining it with data from the other. If you haven't used both graphs for these hard questions, you will almost certainly get them wrong.

**3. Remember, work on all the graph questions in one piece.**
Although the first few graph questions are fairly easy, usually involving something straightforward, the average time per graph question for most students is a little greater than the average time for other problem-solving questions, so you may want to save the five graph questions within a math section for last.

**Practice Problems**

Questions 21-25 are based on the following graphs.

## MEGACORP, INC.
## REVENUE AND PROFIT DISTRIBUTION FOR FOOD AND NON-FOOD RELATED OPERATIONS, 1984–1989

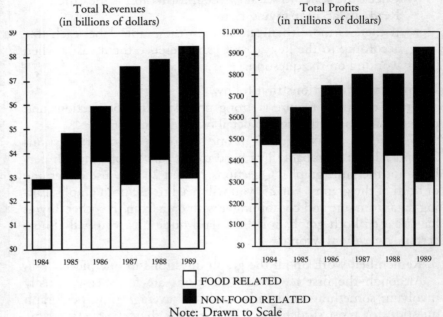

Total Revenues
(in billions of dollars)

Total Profits
(in millions of dollars)

☐ FOOD RELATED
■ NON-FOOD RELATED
Note: Drawn to Scale

## PERCENT OF REVENUES FROM FOOD-RELATED OPERATIONS IN 1989 BY CATEGORY

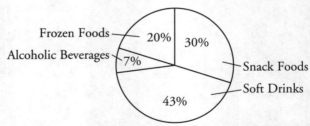

21. Approximately how much did total revenues increase from 1984 to 1987?

(A) $0.5 billion
(B) $1.5 billion
(C) $4.0 billion
(D $4.5 billion
(E) $5.0 billion

22. For the year in which profits from food-related operations increased over the previous year, total revenues were approximately
(A) $3.5 billion
(B) $4.5 billion
(C) $5.7 billion
(D) $6.0 billion
(E) $8.0 billion

23. In 1988, total profits represented approximately what percent of Megacorp's total revenues?
(A) 50%
(B) 20%
(C) 10%
(D) 5%
(E) 1%

24. For the first year in which revenues from non-food related operations surpassed $4.5 billion, total profits were approximately
(A) $250 million
(B) $450 million
(C) $550 million
(D) $650 million
(E) $800 million

25. In 1989, approximately how many millions of dollars were revenues from frozen food operations?
(A) 1,700
(B) 1,100
(C) 900
(D) 600
(E) 450

You can brush up on all of your math by referring to the Math Reference Appendix in the back of this book.

## Solutions

21. (D)
22. (E)
23. (C)
24. (E)
25. (D)

# C. ANALYTICAL

Two sections
30 minutes per section
25 questions per section
Average time per question is one minute

There are two question-types in the Analytical Section: Logic Games and Logical Reasoning. ETS has plans to introduce a third type: Analysis of Explanations. On the test, you should do the Logical Reasoning questions before the Logic Games and Analysis of Explanations.

We're going to tackle Logic Games first, because they are the most difficult Analytical question-type for many students.

## 1. LOGIC GAMES

<u>Directions:</u> **Each group of questions is based on a passage or a set of conditions. You may wish to draw a diagram to answer some of the questions. Choose the best answer for each question.**

Nothing inspires more fear in the hearts of GRE test takers than Logic Games. Why? Partly, it's because the skills tested on the section seem so unfamiliar: You need to turn a game's information to your advantage by organizing your thinking and spotting key deductions, and that's not easy to do.

Games tend to give the most trouble to students who don't have a clearly defined method of attack. And that's where Kaplan's basic principles, game-specific strategies, and Five-Step Approach to Logic Games will help most, streamlining your work so you can rack up points quickly and confidently.

## THE FOUR BASIC PRINCIPLES OF LOGIC GAMES

The rallying cry of the Logic Games-impaired is: "I can do these, if only I had more time!" Well, that's true of everybody. You can spend as much time on a game as you like when you're sitting in your own kitchen, but when your proctor says, "You have 30 minutes . . . begin," he or she is not kidding around.

Logic Games is perhaps the most speed-sensitive section of the test. The test makers know that if you could spend hours methodically trying out every choice in every question, you'd probably get the right one. But it's all about efficiency, both on the test and in your future studies.

And that brings us to the first, and somewhat paradoxical-sounding, Logic Games principle:

## 1. To go faster, you need to slow down.

To gain time in logic games, you must spend more time thinking through and analyzing the setup and the rules. This is not only the most important principle for logic games success, it's also the one that's most often ignored, probably because it just doesn't seem intuitively right; people having timing difficulties tend to speed up, not slow down. But take our word for it: By spending a little extra time up front thinking through the stimulus, the "action" of the game, and the rules, you'll be able to recognize the game's key issues and make important deductions that will actually save you time in the long run.

> ### TAKE TIME TO MAKE TIME
>
> It sounds crazy, but you really do save time in the long run by taking the time to think about a logic game's scenario before jumping into its questions.

Games are structured so that, in order to answer the questions quickly and correctly, you need to search out relevant pieces of information that combine to form valid new statements, called deductions. Now, you can either do this once, up front, and then utilize the same deductions throughout the game, OR you can choose to piece together the same basic deductions—essentially repeating the same work—for every single question.

For instance, let's say that two of the rules for a logic game go as follows:

> If Bob is chosen for the team, then Eric is also chosen.
> If Eric is chosen for the team, then Pat will not be chosen.

You can, as you read through the rules of the game, just treat those rules as two separate pieces of independent information. But there's a deduction to be made from them. Do you see it? If Bob is chosen, Eric is too. If Eric is chosen, Pat is not. That means that, if Bob is chosen, Pat is not chosen. That's an important deduction—one that will undoubtedly be required from question to question. If you don't take the time to make it up front, when you're first considering the game, you'll have to make it over and over again, every time it's necessary to answer a question. But if you do take the time to make it up front and build it into your entire conception of the game, you'll save that time later.

So, always try to take the game scenario and the rules as far as you can before moving on to the questions. Look for common elements among the rules (like Eric in the rules above); this will help you combine them and weed out major deductions. The stimulus creates a situation, and the rules place restrictions on what can and cannot happen within that situation. If you investigate the possible scenarios and look for and find major deductions up front, you'll then be able to rack up points quickly and confidently.

**2. Understand what a rule means, not just what it says.**

If you're interested in demonstrating how well you can read a statement and then spit it back verbatim, you'd be better off training to be a clerk instead of a scholar. That's why you'll never see this on the GRE:

> Rule: Arlene is not fifth in line.
> Question: Which one of the following people is not fifth in line?
> Answer: Arlene.

Some LG questions are easy, but not that easy. The GRE, after all, measures critical thinking, and virtually every sentence in Logic Games has to be filtered through some sort of analytical process before it will be of any use. You may have to use the information about Arlene to help you eliminate a choice or lead you to the right answer, but even in the simplest of cases, this will involve the application, as opposed to the mere parroting, of the rule.

So, getting back to the principle, it's not enough to just copy a rule off the page (or shorthand it, as we'll discuss momentarily); it's imperative that you think through its exact meaning, including any implications that it might have. And don't limit this behavior to the indented rules; statements in the games' introductions are very often rules in and of themselves and warrant the same meticulous consideration.

For instance, let's say a game's introduction sets up a scenario in which you have three boxes, each containing at least two of the following three types of candy—chocolates, gumdrops, and mints. Then you get the following rule:

> Box 2 does not contain any gumdrops.

What does that rule say? That there aren't any gumdrops in box 2. But what does that rule mean, when you think about it in the context of the game? That Box 2 does contain chocolates and mints. Each box contains at least two of three things, remember. So, once you eliminate one of the three things for any particular box, you know that the other two things MUST be in that box.

Part of understanding what a rule means, moreover, is grasping what the rule doesn't mean. For example, take the rule we mentioned earlier:

## NO PARROTS, PLEASE

To fully grasp a rule in Logic Games, you must know more than just what it says. You've got to know what the rule means in the context of the game and in combination with other rules.

## KAPLAN RULES

Always try to turn negative rules—Box 2 does not contain any gumdrops—into a positive statement —Box 2 must contain chocolates and mints.

## GAME WISDOM

You must know the rules of a logic game cold—what they mean, how they impact on other rules, what implications they have in the context of the game scenario.

154

RULE: If Bob is chosen for the team, then Eric is also chosen.
MEANS: Whenever Bob is chosen, Eric is too.
DOESN'T MEAN: Whenever Eric is chosen, Bob is too.

## 3. Use scratchwork and shorthand

The proper use of scratchwork can help you do your best on Logic Games. As you may recall, the directions state: "You may wish to draw a rough sketch to help answer some of the questions." Notice that they use the wording "rough sketch," not "masterpiece," "work of art," or "classic portrait for the ages." The GRE is not a drawing contest; you get no points for creating beautiful visual imagery on the page.

Although some recent games aren't even amenable to scratchwork, for most games you'll find that it is helpful to create a master sketch, one that encapsulates all of the game's information in one easy-to-reference picture. Doing so will not only give your eyes a place to gravitate toward when you need information, but it will also help to solidify in your mind the action of the game, the rules, and whatever deductions you come up with up front.

Remember to keep your scratchwork simple; the less time you spend drawing, the more time you'll have for thinking and answering questions. Pay careful attention to the scratchwork suggestions in the explanations to the four games on the Practice Test in the back of this book.

The part of your scratchwork where you jot down on your page a quick and shortened form of each rule is called "shorthand." Shorthand is a visual representation of a mental thought process and is useful only if it reminds you at a glance of the rule's meaning. Whether you shorthand a rule or commit it to memory, you should never have to look back at the game itself once you get to the questions.
The goal of the entire scratchwork process is to condense a lot of information into manageable user-friendly visual cues. It's much easier to remember rules written like so:

> B → E
> No G in 3

than ones written like this:

> If Bob is chosen for the team, then Eric is also chosen.
> Box 3 does not contain any gumdrops.

As long as you know, for instance, what the arrow from B to E means and are consistent in using it. If you can develop a personal shorthand that is instantly understandable to you, you should have a decided advantage come Test Day.

## IT'S NOT ART SCHOOL

You're applying to grad school, not art school. Don't worry about making elaborate diagrams in Logic Games. There is no "right diagram" for any game. But there is good scratchwork that will help you get points quicker and more accurately.

## WHAT IS SHORTHAND?

Shorthand is a visual representation of a mental thought process. Use shorthand to remind yourself of the meaning of a rule in a Logic Games problem.

## 4. Try to set off chains of deduction.

When hypothetical information is offered in a question stem, try to use it to set off a chain of deductions. Consider the following question: (Because this question is excerpted without the accompanying introduction and rules, ignore the specific logic of the discussion; it's just presented to make a point.)

If the speedboat is yellow, which one of the following must be true?

  (A) The car is green.
  (B) The airplane is red.
  (C) The train is black.
  (D) The car is yellow.
  (E) The train is red.

The question stem contains a "hypothetical," which is an if-clause offering information pertaining only to that particular question. The wrong approach is acknowledging that the speedboat is yellow and then proceeding to test out all of the choices. The muddled mental thought process accompanying this tragic approach might sound something like this:

"All right, the speedboat's yellow, does the car have to be green? Well, let's see, if the speedboat's yellow, AND the car is green, then the train would have to be yellow, but I can't tell what color the airplane is, and I guess this is okay, I don't know, I better try the next choice. Let's see what happens if the speedboat's yellow and the airplane is red . . ." Don't do this kind of dithering! Notice that the question doesn't ask: "What happens, if in addition to this, the car is green?" or "What happens if this is true and the airplane is red?" So why is the confused test taker above intent on answering all of these irrelevant questions? Never begin a question by trying out answer choices; that's going about it backwards. Only if you're entirely stuck or are faced with a question stem that leaves you no choice, should you resort to trial and error.

Most logic games questions are amenable to another, more efficient and systematic methodology. The correct approach is to incorporate the new piece of information into your view of the game, creating one quick sketch if you wish. How do you do this? Simple: Apply the rules and any previous deductions to the new information in order to set off a new chain of deductions. Then follow through until you've taken the new information as far as it can go. Just as you must take the game and rules as far as you can before moving on to the

### A LAST RESORT

Trial and error with the answer choices should be your last resort, not your first. It's much quicker to follow a chain of deduction until it leads you to the answer. In some cases, trial and error is necessary, but don't turn to it unless you're really stuck.

questions, you must carry the information in a question stem out as far as you can before moving on to the choices.

So make sure to stay out of answer-choice land until you have sufficiently mined the hypothetical. If the question-stem contains a hypothetical, then your job is to get as much out of that piece of information as you can before even looking at the choices. This way, YOU dictate to the test, not the other way around. You'll then be able to determine the answer and simply pick it off the page.

You'll have the chance to see these major Logic Games principles in action when you review the explanations to the games in the Practice Test in the back of this book.

## THE THREE COMMON LOGIC GAME-TYPES

Although the Logic Games section can contain a wide variety of situations and scenarios, certain game-types appear again and again. These are the most common:

### 1. Sequencing games

Logic games that require sequencing skills have long been a favorite of the test makers. No matter what the scenario in games of this type, the common denominator is that in some way, shape, or form, they all involve putting entities in order. In a typical sequence game, you may be asked to arrange the cast of characters numerically from left to right, from top to bottom, during days of the week, in a circle, and so on. The sequence may be a sequence of degree; ranking the eight smartest testtakers from 1 to 8 falls into this category. On the other hand, the sequence may be based on time, such as one that involves the finishing times of runners in a race. In some cases, there are two or even three orderings to keep track of in a single game.

*Typical Issues*

The following is a list of the key issues that underlie sequencing games. Each key issue is followed by a corresponding rule—in some cases, with several alternative ways of expressing the same rule. At the end, we'll use these rules to build a miniature logic game, so that you can see how rules work together to define and limit a game's "action." These rules all refer to a scenario in which eight events are to be sequenced from first to eighth.

> **SEQUENCING GAMES AT A GLANCE**
>
> • are historically the most common game-type
> • involve putting entities in order
> • involve orderings, which can be in time (runners finishing a race), space (people standing next to one another in line), or degree (shortest to tallest, worst to best, etc.)

- Which entities are concretely placed in the ordering?

    > X is third.

- Which entities are excluded from a specific position in the ordering?

    > Y is not fourth.

- Which entities are next to, adjacent to, or are immediately preceding or following one another?

    > X and Y are consecutive.
    > X is next to Y.
    > No event comes between X and Y.
    > X and Y are consecutive in the ordering.

- Which entities CANNOT BE next to, adjacent to, or immediately preceding or following one another?

    > X does not immediately precede or follow Z.
    > X is not immediately before or after Z.
    > At least one event comes between X and Z.
    > X and Z are not consecutive in the sequence.

- How far apart in the ordering are two particular entities?

    > Exactly two events come between X and Q.
    > At least two events come between X and Q.

- What is the relative position of two entities in the ordering?

    > Q comes before T in the sequence.
    > T comes after Q in the sequence.

### How A Sequence Game Works

Let's see how rules like those above might combine to create a simple logic game.

Eight events—Q, R, S, T, W, X, Y, and Z—are being sequenced from first to eighth.

> X is third.
> Y is not fourth.
> X and Y are consecutive in the sequence.
> Exactly two events come between X and Q.
> Q comes before T in the sequence.

How would you approach this simplified game? Remember our fourth basic principle: Use Scratchwork and Shorthand. With eight events to sequence from first to eighth, you'd probably want to draw eight dashes in the margin of your test booklet, maybe in two groups of four (so you can easily determine which dash is which). Then take the rules in order of concreteness, starting with the most concrete of all—Rule 1—which tells you that X is third. Fill that into your sketch:

Jump to the next most concrete rule—Rule 4, which tells you that exactly two events come between X and Q. Well, Q must be sixth, then:

— — X — — Q — —

Rule 5 says that Q comes before T. Because Q is sixth, T must be either seventh or eighth. To indicate this, under the sketch, write T with two arrows pointing to the seventh and eighth dashes.

Rule 3 says that X and Y are consecutive. X is third, so Y will be either second or fourth. Rule 2 clears up that matter. Y can't be fourth, says Rule 2, so it will have to be second:

— Y X — — Q — —
＾T＾

And this is how the rules work together to build a sequence game.

The questions might then present hypothetical information that would set off the "chain of deduction" we mentioned in the basic principles section.

## 2. Grouping games

A grouping game, much like every other type of game, begins with a set of entities. What sets grouping apart is the "action" of the game, or specifically, what you're asked to do with the entities. In a pure grouping game, unlike sequencing, there's no call for putting the entities in order. Instead, you'll usually be required to "select" a smaller group from the initial group or "distribute" the entities in

## GROUPING GAMES AT A GLANCE

- are a very common game type
- come in two varieties— "selection" and "distribution"
- contain number elements that are often crucial (how many chosen, how many in each group, etc.)
- action involves deciding if each entity is in or out; if in, may then need to determine where (in distribution games)

some fashion into more than one subgroup. As a distinct skill, grouping differs from sequencing in that you're not really concerned with what order the entities are in, but rather how they're grouped—who's in, who's out, and who can and cannot be with whom in various subgroups.

### Grouping Games of Selection and of Distribution

In "selection" types of grouping games, you'll be given the cast of characters and told to select from them a smaller group, based, of course, on a set of rules. For example, a game may include eight musical cassettes, from which you must choose four. Sometimes the test makers specify an exact number for the smaller group, and other times they don't. A small variation of this type occurs when the initial group of entities is itself broken up in groups to begin the game. An example would be a farmer choosing three animals from a group of three cows and five horses.

In "distribution" types of grouping games, we're more concerned with who goes where than we are with who's in and who's out. Sometimes, every entity will end up in a group—an example is placing or distributing eight marbles into two jars, four to a jar. On the other hand, it's perfectly viable for a game to mandate the placement of three marbles in each jar, leaving two marbles out in the cold.

It's important for you to be aware of the numbers that govern each particular grouping game, because although all grouping games rely on the same general skills, you have to adapt to the specific situations of each. Still, all grouping games revolve around the same basic questions: Is this entity in? Is it out? If it's not in this group, is it in that one?

Like sequencing games, grouping games have a language all their own, and it's up to you to speak that language fluently when you come across games that require this particular skill on your test.

### Typical Issues—Grouping Games of Selection

The following is a list of the key issues that underlie grouping games. Each key issue is followed by a corresponding rule—in some cases, with several alternative ways of expressing the same rule. At the end, again, we'll use these rules to build a miniature logic game.

First, grouping games of selection. These rules all refer to a scenario in which you are to select a subgroup of four from a group of eight entities—Q, R, S, T, W, X, Y, and Z:

- Which entities are definitely chosen?

    Q is selected.

- Which entities rely on a different entity's selection in order to be chosen?

> If X is selected, then Y is selected.
> X will be selected only if Y is selected.
> X will not be selected unless Y is selected.

Note: A common misconception surrounds the rule "If X is selected, then Y is selected." This works only in one direction; if X is chosen, Y must be, but if Y is chosen, X may or may not be. Remember the discussion of Basic Principle #2 above—understand not only what a rule means, but also what it doesn't mean!

- Which entities must be chosen together, or not at all?

> If Y is selected, Z is selected, and vice versa.
> Y will not be selected unless Z is selected,
> and vice versa.

- Which entities cannot both be chosen?

> If R is selected, Z is not selected.
> If Z is selected, R is not selected.
> R and Z can't both be selected.

*How Grouping Games of Selection Work*

We can combine these rules to create a rudimentary grouping game of selection:

A professor must choose a group of four books for her next seminar. She must choose from a pool of eight books—Q, R, S, T, W, X, Y, and Z.

> Q is selected.
> If X is selected then Y is selected.
> If Y is selected, Z is selected, and vice versa.
> If R is selected, Z is not selected.

A good way of dealing with this kind of game might be to write out the eight letters—four on top, four on the bottom—and then circle the ones that are definitely selected while crossing out the ones that are definitely not selected. Thus, Rule 1 would allow you to circle the Q:

The other rules can't be built into the sketch just yet, because they describe eventualities (what happens if something else happens).

Here's where you'd want to use shorthand:

> Rule 2 translates as: "If X, then Y" or "X ———> Y"
> Rule 3 might be rendered as: "Y <———> Z"
> (because the requirement is vice versa).
> Rule 4 could be shorthanded as "R ≠ Z" (because R
> and Z are mutually exclusive).

The rules would then be poised to take effect whenever a question would add new hypothetical information, setting off a chain of deduction. For instance, let's say a question reads like so:

If R is selected, which of the following must be true?

This new information would put the rules into motion. R's inclusion would set off Rule 4—"R ≠ Z"— so we'd have to circle R and cross out Z:

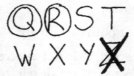

This would in turn set off Rule 3—"Y <———> Z". Because Z is out, Y is out, since they are chosen together or not at all:

Now Rule 2 comes into play. "X———> Y" means that if Y is not chosen, X can't be either (since X's inclusion would require Y's). So we can take the chain of deduction one step further:

A correct answer to this question, then, might be "X is not included." And that, in a nutshell, is how a (simplified) grouping game of selection works.

*Typical Issues—Grouping Games of Distribution*

Here are the issues involved in the other kind of grouping games—grouping games of distribution—along with the rules that govern them. These rules, by the way, refer to a scenario in which our old favorite group of eight entities—Q, R, S, T, W, X, Y, Z— have to be distributed into three different classes:

- Which entities are concretely placed in a particular subgroup?

    X is placed in class 3.

- Which entities are barred from a particular subgroup?

    Y is not placed in class 2.

- Which entities must be placed in the same subgroup?

    X is placed in the same class as Z.
    Z is placed in the same class as X.
    X and Z are placed in the same class.

- Which entities cannot be placed in the same subgroup?
    X is not placed in the same class as Y.
    Y is not placed in the same class as X.
    X and Y are not placed in the same class.

- Which entity's placement depends on the placement of a different entity?

    If Y is placed in class 1, then Q is placed in class 2.

*How Grouping Games of Distribution Work*

The above rules, neatly enough, also can combine to form a miniature grouping game of distribution:

Eight students—Q, R, S, T, W, X, Y, and Z—must be subdivided into three different classes—Classes 1, 2, and 3.
    X is placed in Class 3.
    Y is not placed in Class 2.
    X is placed in the same class as Z.
    X is not placed in the same class as Y.
    If Y is placed in Class 1, then Q is placed in Class 2.

A good scratchwork scheme for games of this type would be to draw three circles in your booklet, one for each of the three classes. Then put the eight entities in the appropriate circles as that information becomes known.

Here again, start with the most concrete rule first, which is Rule 1, which definitively places X in Class 3. Rule 2 just as definitively precludes Y from Class 2, so build that into the scratchwork, too:

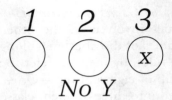

Rule 3 requires Z to join X in Class 3:

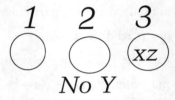

Rule 4, prohibiting Y from being in the same class as X, means that Y can't be in Class 3. But we already know that Y can't be in Class 2. We can deduce, therefore, that Y must go in Class 1. That in turn puts Rule 5 into play: If Y is in Class 1 (as it is here), Q is in Class 2:

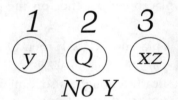

And that is the dynamic of most grouping games of distribution (though, again, in much simplified form).

## GENERAL LOGIC GAMES TIPS

Here are some other points to keep in mind on the LG section:

### IT'S LIKE MATH

Like math questions, Logic Games questions have definite right and wrong answers. Once you find the answer that works, pick it and move on. There's no need to check out the other choices.

- Some games are what you might call "hybrid games," requiring you to combine sequencing and grouping. Keep in mind that while we try to recognize games as a particular type, it's not necessary to attach a strict name to every game you encounter. For example, it really doesn't matter if you categorize a game as a sequencing game with a grouping element or as a grouping game with a sequencing element, as long as you're comfortable with both sets of skills.

- Unlike the answer choices in Logical Reasoning or Analysis of Explanations, in which the correct answer is the "best" choice, the answers in Logic Games are objectively correct or incorrect. Therefore, when you find an answer that's definitely right, have the confidence to circle it and move on, without wasting time to check the other choices. This is one way to improve your timing on the section.

- Rules that contain common elements are often the ones that lead to deductions. Consider the following three rules:

> If Sybil goes to the party, then Edna will go to the party.
> If Jacqui goes to the party, then Sherry will not go to the party.
> If Edna goes to the party, then Dale will go to the party.

Rules 1 and 2 have no entities in common, which is a sure sign that we can't deduce anything from combining them. The same goes for Rules 2 and 3. But because Rules 1 and 3 have Edna in common, a deduction is possible (although not guaranteed). In this case, combining Rules 1 and 3 would allow us to deduce another rule: If Sybil goes to the party, then Dale will go also.

- Not all rules are created equal—some are inherently more important than others. Try to focus first on the ones that have the greatest impact on the situation, specifically the ones that involve the greatest number of the entities. These are also the rules to turn to first whenever you're stuck on a question and don't know how to set off the chain of deduction.

## THE KAPLAN FIVE-STEP APPROACH TO LOGIC GAMES

Now that you've gotten some Logic Games background, it's time to see how you can marshal that knowledge into a systematic approach to games.

### 1. Get an overview.

Read carefully the game's introduction and rules, to establish the "cast of characters," the "action," and the number limits governing the game.

### 2. Visualize and map out the game.

Make a mental picture of the situation and let it guide you as you create a sketch, or some other kind of scratchwork, if need be, to help you keep track of the rules and handle new information.

---

**LOOK FOR THE COMMON ELEMENT**

Rules that deal with one or more of the same entities can often be combined to make important deductions.

---

**IS NOTHING CLICKING?**

If you find that you can't make a single important deduction by combining rules, you're probably missing something. Check the game introduction and rules again to make sure that you're not misinterpreting something.

---

**KAPLAN'S 5-STEP APPROACH TO LOGIC GAMES**

1. Get an overview.
2. Visualize and map out the game.
3. Consider the rules individually.
4. Combine the rules.
5. Work on the questions systematically.

---

### 3. Consider the rules individually.

After you've thought through the meaning and implications of each rule, you have three choices. You can:

- Build it directly into your sketch of the game situation;
- Jot down the rule in shorthand form to help you remember it;
- Underline or circle rules that don't lend themselves to the first two techniques.

### 4. Combine the rules.

Look for common elements among the rules; that's what will lead you to make deductions. Treat these deductions as additional rules, good for the whole game.

### 5. Work on the questions systematically.

Read the question stem carefully! Take special notice of such words as "must," "could," "cannot," "not," "impossible," "except." As always, use the hypothetical information offered in if-clauses to set off a chain of deductions.

## USING KAPLAN'S FIVE-STEP APPROACH

Here's how the approach can work with an actual logic game:

Five maids—Mona, Patrick, Renatta, Saffie, and Will—are scheduled to clean apartments on five days of a single week, Monday to Friday. There are three cleaning shifts available each day—a morning shift, an afternoon shift, and an evening shift. No more than one maid cleans on any given shift. Each maid works exactly two cleaning shifts during the week, but no maid works more than one cleaning shift in a single day.

Exactly two maids clean on each day of the week.
Mona and Will clean on the same days of the week.
Patrick doesn't clean on any afternoon or evening shifts during the week.
Will doesn't clean on any morning or afternoon shifts during the week.
Mona cleans on two consecutive days of the week.
Saffie's second cleaning shift of the week is on an earlier day of the week than Mona's first cleaning shift.

WHAT'S IN A NAME?

Remember, you get no points for categorizing a game; you get points for answering questions correctly. Don't worry about what to call a game. Just decide what skills it will require.

166

1. Which one of the following must be true?

   (A) Saffie cleans on Tuesday afternoon.
   (B) Patrick cleans on Monday morning.
   (C) Will cleans on Thursday evening.
   (D) Renatta cleans on Friday afternoon.
   (E) Mona cleans on Tuesday morning.

2. If Will does not clean on Friday, which one of the following could be false?

   (A) Renatta cleans on Friday.
   (B) Saffie cleans on Tuesday.
   (C) Mona cleans on Wednesday.
   (D) Saffie cleans on Monday.
   (E) Patrick cleans on Tuesday.

(Note that there are only two questions accompanying this game; a typical logic game will have three to six questions. This game is as complicated as any you're likely to see on the GRE.)

## 1. Get an overview.

We need to schedule five maids, abbreviated M, P, R, S, and W, in a particular order during a five-day calendar week, Monday to Friday. The ordering element tells us we're dealing with a sequencing game, though there is a slight grouping element involved in that a couple of rules deal with grouping issues—namely, which people can or cannot clean on the same day of the week as each other.

Be very careful about the numbers governing this game; they go a long way in defining how the game works. There are to be exactly two maids per day (never cleaning on the same shift). Each maid must clean exactly two shifts, and because maids are forbidden to take two shifts in the same day, this means that each maid will clean on exactly two days. So, in effect, 10 out of the 15 available shifts will be taken, and 5 will be left untouched.

## 2. Visualize and map out the game.

Go with whatever you feel is the most efficient way to keep track of the situation. Most people would settle on a sketch of the five days, each broken up into three shifts, like so:

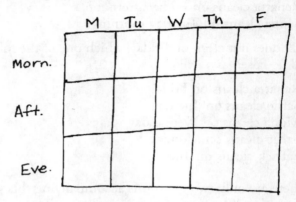

Into this sketch—one letter per box—each entity will have to go twice (each maid does two shifts, remember). So your pool of entities to place would be: MMPPRRSSWW. You might want to include five X's (or Ø's) for the five shifts that won't be taken by any of the maids.

## 3. Consider the rules individually.

We've already dealt with some of the number-related rules hidden in the game's introduction. Now let's consider this statement from the intro:

> No more than one maid cleans in any given shift.

Make sure you interpret rules like this correctly. You may have to paraphrase, in your own words, its exact meaning. In this case: Two maids per shift is no good, three is out of the question, etc. But it doesn't mean that any given shift MUST have a maid. If the test makers meant to imply that, they would have written: "Exactly one maid cleans on every given shift." Notice the difference in wording. It's subtle, but it has a huge impact on the game.

Let's consider the other rules:

1) We've already handled Rule 1. You may wish to jot down "2 a day," or something like that, to remind you of this important information.

2) Mona and Will clean on the same days, and that holds for both of the days these maids clean. Shorthand this any way that

seems fitting (one suggestion is to draw MW with a circle around it on your page).

3) and 4) We can handle these two rules together because they're so similar. You can shorthand these rules as they are, but you'd be doing yourself a great disservice. Instead, first work out their implications, which is actually a pretty simple matter: If Patrick doesn't clean afternoons or evenings, he must clean mornings. If Will doesn't clean mornings or afternoons, he must clean evenings. Always take the rules as far as you can, and then jot their implications down on your page for reference.

5) This one is pretty self-explanatory; Mona's shifts must be on consecutive days, such as Thursday and Friday. M = M might be a good way to shorthand this.

6) Here's another sequencing rule—you must place both S's for Saffie on earlier days of the week than the two M's, for Mona. That means that Saffie and Mona can't clean on the same day (although we already knew that from Rule 2), and that Mona's shifts can't come before Saffie's. Try shorthanding this as S . . . S . . . M . . . M.

## 4. Combine the rules.

This is the crucial stage for most games. Here, notice that Mona appears in three of the six indented rules; that's a good indication that combining these rules should lead somewhere useful. Combining Rule 2 and Rule 5 gives us two Mona/Will days in a row:

$$\frac{M}{W} = \frac{M}{W}$$

Will must be scheduled for evening shifts (remember, we turned Rule 4 into this positive statement). That means that Mona would take the morning or afternoon shift on these consecutive days.

Rule 6 concerns Mona as well: Two Saffies before the two Monas. How is this possible? We need two S's on different days to come before the two consecutive M's. If Saffie's cleaning shifts are as early in the week as possible, she'll clean on Monday and Tuesday. That means that the earliest day that Mona can clean (and Will as well, thanks to Rule 2) is Wednesday. There's our first really key deduction:

**Mona and Will cannot clean on Monday and Tuesday; they must clean Wednesday, Thursday, or Friday.**

Do we stop there? No, of course not. The difference between the Logic Games expert and the Logic Games novice is that the expert knows how to press on when further deductive possibilities exist. If you relate this deduction back to Rule 5, it becomes clear that Mona and Will must clean on Wednesday and Thursday OR on Thursday and Friday. This brings us to another big deduction:

> **Either way, Mona and Will must clean on Thursday. Thanks to Rule 4, we can slot Will in for Thursday evening. Mona will then take Thursday morning OR afternoon. The other Mona/Will day must be either Wednesday or Friday, to remain consecutive.**

Here's what your completed sketch may look like, with as many of the rules built into it as possible.

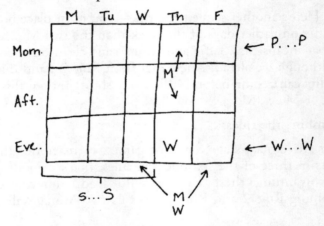

Now that we've combined the rules, and have even uncovered a few big deductions, it's time to move on to the questions.

### 5. Work on the questions systematically.

Now you'll see how all the work we did up front pays off. Question 1 offers no hypothetical information; it simply asks what must be true. And because we've already deduced a few things that must be true, we can scan the choices for one that matches any one of our newly-discovered pieces of information. It doesn't take long to spot choice (C)—it's our big deduction staring us right in the face. You shouldn't even waste time checking the other choices. Instead, have the confidence that you've done the right work the right way, and circle (C) and move on. [Just for the record, for those of you who are curious, (A), (B), and (D) could be true, but need not be, whereas (E), as we discovered earlier, is an impossibility.]

Question 2 contains a hypothetical: No Will on Friday. One glance at our sketch tells us that the second Mona/Will cluster must therefore be placed on Wednesday, next to the Thursday Mona/Will group. Saffie must then clean on Monday and Tuesday, in order to satisfy Rule 6 (although we don't yet know the exact shifts she takes during those days).

That brings us to the two questions that test takers ask all too infrequently: WHO'S LEFT?, and more importantly, WHERE CAN THEY GO? Two P's and two R's are left to place, with one spot on Monday, one spot on Tuesday, and two spots on Friday open to place them. How can this be done? Friday can't get both P's or both R's (from the last sentence in the introduction), so it will have to get one of each, with P in the morning and R in either the afternoon or evening. The other P and the other R will join S on Monday or Tuesday, in either order. Of course, whichever day P is on, he must be in the morning, whereas the exact shifts for R and S are ambiguous.

Look at how far the chain of deductions takes us, beginning with the simple statement in the question stem:

**If Will doesn't clean on Friday, then . . .**

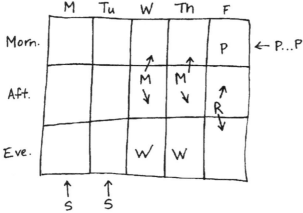

With all of this information at our disposal, there's not a question in the world that we can't answer correctly. This one asks for a statement that could be false—which means that the four wrong choices will all be things that must be true. And in fact, choices (A) through (D) match the situation in this question perfectly, while (E) only could be true: Patrick's first cleaning shift of the week could be on Tuesday, but it just as easily could be on Monday as well. (His second shift must be on Friday, of course.) (E) is therefore the only choice that could be false.

# 2. LOGICAL REASONING

**Directions:** Each group of questions is based on a passage or a set of conditions. You may wish to draw a diagram to answer some of the questions. Choose the best answer for each question.

Most people find GRE Logical Reasoning to be much easier than Logic Games. In fact, many people don't do any preparation for this question type at all. It's ironic, then, that this is also one of the most stubborn item types on the test—that is, it's one of the toughest to improve at. That's because there aren't really any quick fixes in Logical Reasoning. You can only get better by understanding arguments better.

It's not totally clear how many Logical Reasoning questions will show up on your GRE. It used to be that there were always 6 logical reasoning questions per section, but there have been a number of experimental sections recently with 9 logical reasoning questions (and only 16 games questions). So don't be surprised if you see a section like that.

## THE FIVE BASIC PRINCIPLES OF LOGICAL REASONING

### 1. Know the structure of the argument

Success on this section hinges on your ability to identify the evidence and conclusion parts of the argument. There is no general rule about where conclusion and evidence appear in the argument: The conclusion could be the first sentence, followed by the evidence, or else it could be the last sentence, with the evidence preceding it. Consider the following short stimulus:

> The Brookdale Public Library will require extensive physical rehabilitation to meet the new building codes just passed by the town council. For one thing, the electrical system is inadequate, causing the lights to flicker sporadically. Furthermore, there are too few emergency exits, and even those are poorly marked and sometimes locked.

Let's suppose that the author of the argument above were only allowed one sentence to convey her meaning. Do you think that she would waste her lone opportunity on the statement "the electrical system at the Brookdale Public Library is inadequate, causing the lights to flicker sporadically"? Would she walk away satisfied that she got her main point across? Probably not. Given a single opportunity, she would have to state the first sentence: "The Brookdale Public Library will require extensive physical rehabilitation etc." This is her conclusion. If you pressed her for her reasons for making this statement, she would then cite the electrical and structural problems with the building. This is the evidence for her conclusion.

> **STRUCTURAL SIGNALS**
>
> Certain key words can help you isolate the conclusion and the evidence in a stimulus. Clues that signal evidence include: *because, since, for, as a result of,* and *due to*. Clues that signal the conclusion include: *consequently, hence, therefore, thus, clearly, so,* and *accordingly*.

## 2. Preview the question stem

Looking over the question stem before you read the stimulus will alert you in advance of what to focus on in your initial reading of the stimulus. In effect, it gives you a jump on the questions. For example, let's say the question attached to the original library argument above asked the following:

> The author supports her point about the need for rehabilitation at the Brookdale Library by citing which of the following?

If you were to preview this question stem before reading the stimulus, you would know what to look for in advance—namely, evidence, the "support" provided for the conclusion. Similarly, if the question asked you to find an assumption that the author is relying on, this would tell you in advance that there was a crucial piece of the argument missing, and you can begin to think about it right off the bat.

> **KNOW WHAT YOU'RE LOOKING FOR**
>
> Previewing the question stem before reading the stimulus makes you a better, more directed reader. You'll know what you're looking for in advance.

## 3. Paraphrase the author's point

After you read the stimulus, you'll want to paraphrase the author's main argument, i.e., restate the author's ideas in your own words. Frequently, the authors in LR say pretty simple things in complex ways. But if you mentally translate the verbiage into a simpler form, you'll find the whole thing more manageable.

In the library argument, for instance, you probably don't want to deal with the full complexity of the author's stated conclusion:

> The Brookdale Public Library will require extensive physical rehabilitation to meet the new building codes just passed by the town council.

Instead, you probably want to carry a much simpler form of the point in your mind, something like:

> **IN YOUR OWN WORDS**
>
> It's much easier to understand and remember an argument if you restate it simply, in your own words.

The library will need fixing up to meet new codes.

Often, by the time you begin reading through answer choices, you run the risk of losing sight of the gist of the stimulus. After all, you can only concentrate on a certain amount of information at one time. Restating the argument in your own words will not only help you get the author's point in the first place, but it'll also help you hold on to it until you've found the correct answer.

### 4. Try to pre-phrase an answer

You must try to approach the answer choices with at least a faint idea of what the answer should look like. This is not to say that you should ponder the question for minutes until you're able to write out your own answer; it's still a multiple-choice test, so the right answer is on the page. Just try to get in the habit of instinctively thinking through the question and framing an answer in your own mind.

For instance, let's say a question for the library argument went like this:

> The author's argument depends on which of the following assumptions about the new building codes?

Having thought about the stimulus argument, an answer to this question may have sprung immediately to mind: namely, the assumption that the new codes are tougher than the old codes. After all, the library will have to be rehabilitated to meet the new codes, according to the author. Clearly, the assumption is that the new codes are more stringent than the old. And that's the kind of statement you would look for among the choices.

### 5. Keep in mind the scope of the argument

One of the most important Logical Reasoning skills, particularly when you're at the point of actually selecting one of the five choices, is the ability to focus in on the scope of the argument. The majority of wrong choices on this section are wrong because they are "outside the scope." In everyday language, that simply means that these choices contain elements that don't match the author's ideas or that simply go beyond the context of the stimulus. Some common examples of scope problems are choices that are too narrow, or too broad, or literally have nothing to do with the author's points. Also, watch for and eliminate choices that are too extreme to match the argument's scope; they're usually signaled by words like "all," "always," "never," "none," and so on. Choices that are more qualified are often correct for arguments that are moderate in tone and contain such words as "usually," "sometimes," "probably," etc. To illustrate the scope principle, let's look again at the question mentioned above:

## SCOPE IT OUT

A remarkable number of wrong answers in Logical Reasoning have scope problems. Always be on the lookout for choices that are too extreme, that contain value judgments that are not relevant to the argument, or that don't match the stimulus in tone or subject matter.

The author's argument depends on which of the following assumptions about the new building codes?

Let's say one of the choices read as follows:

(A) The new building codes are far too stringent.

Knowing the scope of the argument would help you to eliminate this choice very quickly. You know that this argument is just a claim about what the new codes will require—that the library be rehabilitated. It's not an argument about whether the requirements of the new codes are good, or justifiable, or ridiculously strict. That kind of value judgment is outside the scope of this argument. Recognizing scope problems is a great way of eliminating dozens of wrong answers quickly.

## THE FIVE COMMON LOGICAL REASONING QUESTION-TYPES

Now that you're familiar with the basic principles of Logical Reasoning, let's look at the most common types of questions that you'll be asked. As we said earlier, certain question-types crop up again and again on the GRE, and it pays to be familiar with them. Of the types discussed below, the first three predominate, but try to become familiar with the others as well.

### 1. Assumption Questions

An assumption bridges the gap between an argument's evidence and conclusion. It's a piece of support that isn't explicitly stated but that is required for the conclusion to remain valid. When a question asks you to find an author's assumption, it's asking you to find the statement without which the argument falls apart.

In order to test whether a statement is necessarily assumed by an author, therefore, we can employ the **Denial Test**. Here's how it works: Simply deny or negate the statement and see if the argument falls apart. If it does, that choice is the correct assumption. If, on the other hand, the argument is unaffected, the choice is wrong. Consider, as an example, this simple stimulus:

> Allyson plays volleyball for Central High School.
> Therefore, Allyson must be over six feet tall.

You should recognize the second sentence as the conclusion, and the first sentence as the support, or evidence, for it. But is the argument complete? Obviously not. The piece that's missing—the unstated

---

### THE MISSING LINK

Some arguments lack an important bridge between their evidence and their conclusion. That bridge is the necessary assumption—a key part of many arguments that remains unspoken.

175

link between the evidence and conclusion—is the assumption, and you could probably pre-phrase this one pretty easily:

> All volleyball players for Central High School are over six feet tall.

To test whether this really is a necessary assumption to the argument, let's apply the Denial Test to it, by negating it. What if it's not true that all volleyball players for Central High School are over six feet tall? Can we still logically conclude that Allyson must be taller than six feet? No, we can't. Sure, it's possible that she is, but just as possible that she's not. By denying the statement, then, the argument falls to pieces; it's simply no longer valid. And that's our conclusive proof that the statement above is a necessary assumption that the author of this stimulus is relying on.

As we've just seen, you can often pre-phrase the answer to an assumption question. By previewing the question stem, you'll know what to look for. And stimuli for assumption questions just "feel" like they're missing something. Often, the answer will jump right out at you, as in this case. In more difficult assumption questions, the answers may not be as obvious. But in either case, you can use the Denial Test to quickly check whichever choice seems correct.

Here are some of the ways in which assumption questions are worded:

• Which one of the following is assumed by the author?
• The argument depends on the assumption that . . .
• The validity of the argument above depends on which one of the following?

## 2. Strengthen/Weaken the Argument

Determining an argument's necessary assumption, as we've just seen, is required to answer Assumption questions. But it also is required for another common question-type, Strengthen-and-Weaken-the-Argument questions.

One way to weaken an argument is to break down a central piece of evidence. Another way is to attack the validity of any assumptions that the author may be making. The answer to many Weaken-the-Argument questions is the one that reveals an author's assumption to be unreasonable; conversely, the answer to many Strengthen-the-Argument questions provides additional support by affirming the truth of an assumption or by presenting more persuasive evidence.

Weakening questions tend to be more common on the GRE than strengthening questions. But here are a few concepts that apply to both question types:

- Weakening an argument is not the same thing as disproving it, whereas strengthening is not the same as proving the conclusion to be true. A strengthener tips the scale toward believing in the validity of the conclusion, whereas a weakener tips the scale in the other direction, toward doubting the conclusion.
- Don't be careless. Wrong answer choices in these question-types often have exactly the opposite of the desired effect. That is, if you're asked to strengthen a stimulus argument, it's quite likely that one or more of the wrong choices will contain information that actually weakens the argument. By the same token, weaken questions may contain a choice that strengthens the argument. So once again, pay close attention to what the question stem asks.

The stems associated with these two question types are usually self-explanatory. Here's a list of what you can expect to see on Test Day: Weaken:

- Which one of the following, if true, would most weaken the argument above?
- Which one of the following, if true, would most seriously undermine the argument above?

Strengthen:

- Which one of the following, if true, would most strengthen the argument?
- Which one of the following, if true, would provide the most support for the conclusion in the argument above?
- The argument above would be more persuasive if which one of the following were found to be true?

## 3. Inference Questions

Another of the most common question types you'll encounter on the Logical Reasoning section is the Inference question. The process of inferring is a matter of considering one or more statements as evidence and then drawing a conclusion from them.

Sometimes the inference is very close to the author's overall main point. Other times, it deals with a less central point. In Logical Reasoning, the difference between an inference and an assumption is that the conclusion's validity doesn't logically depend on an inference, as it does on a necessary assumption. A valid inference is merely something that must be true if the statements in the passage are true—an extension of the argument rather than a necessary part of it.

Be careful. Unlike an assumption, an inference need not have anything to do with the author's conclusion; it may simply be a

> **INFERENCE QUESTIONS AT A GLANCE**
>
> - one of the most popular LR question types
> - answer must be true if statements in the stimulus are true
> - often stick close to the author's main point
> - question stems vary considerably in appearance
> - can be checked by applying the Denial Test

piece of information derived from one or more pieces of evidence. However, the Denial Test works for inferences as well as for assumptions: A valid inference always makes more sense than its opposite. If you deny or negate an answer choice, and it has little or no effect on the argument, then chances are that the choice is not inferable from the passage.

Here are some tips for making proper inferences (useful for Reading Comprehension, as well!). A good inference:

- stays in line with the gist of the passage
- stays in line with the author's tone
- stays in line with the author's point of view
- stays within the scope of the argument or the main idea
- is neither denied by, nor irrelevant to, the argument or discussion
- always makes more sense than its opposite

Here's a quick rundown of the various forms that inference questions are likely to take on your test:

- Which one of the following is implied by the argument above?
- The author suggests that . . .
- If all the statements above are true, which one of the following must also be true?
- The author of the passage would most likely agree with which one of the following?

### 4. Parallel Reasoning Questions

Parallel Reasoning questions require you to identify the answer choice that contains the argument most similar, or parallel, to that in the stimulus in terms of the reasoning employed. Your task is to abstract the stimulus argument's form, with as little content as possible, and then locate the answer choice that has the form most similar to that of the stimulus. Do not let yourself be drawn to a choice based on its subject matter. A stimulus about music may have an answer choice that also involves music, but that doesn't mean that the reasoning in the two arguments are similar.

### 5. Paradox Questions

A paradox exists when an argument contains two or more seemingly inconsistent statements. You'll know you're dealing with a paradoxical situation if the argument ends with what seems to be a bizarre contradiction. Another sure sign of a paradox is when the argument builds to a certain point, and then the exact opposite of what you would expect to happen happens.

---

## PARALLEL REASONING AT A GLANCE

- must mimic structure or form, not content of stimulus
- sometimes amenable to algebraic symbolization
- key is to summarize argument's overall form and match it to that of the correct choice

---

## PARADOX QUESTIONS AT A GLANCE

- correct choice will resolve apparent discrepancy or contradiction
- correct choice should have an intuitive click
- correct choice will often involve realizing that two groups presented as identical are actually not

# No mailboxes nearby?
# We understand.

# Call 1-800-KAP-TEST

# KAPLAN
## The answer to the test question

# THE KAPLAN FOUR-STEP APPROACH TO LOGICAL REASONING

Now that you've learned the basic Logical Reasoning principles and have been exposed to the full range of question-types, it's time to learn how to use all of that knowledge to formulate a systematic approach to Logical Reasoning. We've developed a four-step approach that you can use to attack each and every question on the section.

### 1. Preview the question stem.

As we mentioned in the discussion of basic principles, previewing the stem is a great way to focus your reading of the stimulus, so that you know exactly what you're looking for.

### 2. Read the stimulus.

With the question stem in mind, read the stimulus, paraphrasing as you go. Remember to read actively and critically, pinpointing evidence and conclusion. Also get a sense for how strong or weak the argument is.

### 3. Try to pre-phrase an answer.

Sometimes, if you've read the stimulus critically enough, you'll know the answer without even looking at the choices. It will be much easier to find it if you have a sense of what you're looking for among the choices.

### 4. Choose an answer

If you were able to pre-phrase an answer, skim the choices looking for something that sounds like what you have in mind. If you couldn't think of anything, read and evaluate each choice, throwing out the ones that are outside the scope of the argument. After settling on an answer, you may wish to briefly double-check the question stem to make sure that you're indeed answering the question that was asked.

> ## THE KAPLAN 4-STEP APPROACH TO LOGICAL REASONING
>
> 1. Preview the question stem.
> 2. Read the stimulus.
> 3. Try to pre-phrase an answer.
> 4. Choose an answer.

## USING KAPLAN'S FOUR-STEP APPROACH

Now let's try this approach on a genuine Logical Reasoning item:

> A study of twenty overweight men revealed that each man experienced significant weight loss after adding SlimDown, an artificial food supplement, to his daily diet. For three months, each man consumed one SlimDown portion every morning after exercising, and then followed his normal diet for the rest of the day. Clearly, anyone who consumes one portion of SlimDown every day for at least three months will lose weight and will look and feel their best.

> Which one of the following is an assumption on which the argument depends?

> (A) The men in the study will gain back the weight if they discontinue the SlimDown program.
> (B) No other dietary supplement will have the same effect on overweight men.
> (C) The daily exercise regimen was not responsible for the effects noted in the study.
> (D) Women won't experience similar weight reductions if they adhere to the SlimDown program for three months.
> (E) Overweight men will achieve only partial weight loss if they don't remain on the SlimDown program for a full three months.

### 1. Preview the question stem.

We see, quite clearly, that we're dealing with an assumption question. Good. We can immediately adopt an "assumption mindset," which basically means that, before even reading the first word of the stimulus, we know that the conclusion will be lacking an important piece of supporting evidence. We now turn to the stimulus, already on the lookout for this missing link.

### 2. Read the stimulus.

Sentence 1 introduces a study of twenty men using a food supplement product, resulting in weight loss for all twenty. Sentence 2 describes how they used it: once a day, for three months, after morning exercise. So far so good; it feels as if we're building up to something. The structural signal usually indicates that some sort of conclusion follows, and in fact it does: The author concludes in sentence 3 that anyone who has one portion of the product daily for three months will lose weight too.

You must read critically! Notice that the conclusion doesn't say that anyone who follows the same routine as the twenty men will have the same results; it says that anyone who simply consumes the product in the same way will have the same results. You should have begun to sense the inevitable lack of crucial information at this point. The evidence in sentence 2 describes a routine that includes taking the supplement after daily exercise, whereas the conclusion focuses primarily on the supplement and entirely ignores the part about the exercise. The conclusion, therefore, doesn't stem logically from the evidence in the first two sentences. This blends seamlessly into Step 3.

### 3. Pre-phrase an answer.

As expected, the argument is beginning to look as if it has a serious shortcoming. Of course, we expected this because we previewed the question stem before reading the stimulus.

In really simplistic terms, the argument proceeds like so: "A bunch of guys did A and B for 3 months and had X result. If anyone does A for 3 months, that person will experience X result too." Sound a little fishy? You bet. The author must be assuming that A (the product), not B (exercise), must be the crucial thing that leads to the result. If not (the Denial Test), the conclusion makes no sense.

So, you might pre-phrase the answer like this: "Something about the exercise thing needs to be cleared up." That's it. Did you think your pre-phrasing had to be something fancy and glamorous? Well, it doesn't. All you need is an inkling of what the question is looking for, and in this case, it just seems that if we don't shore up the exercise issue, the argument will remain invalid and incomplete. So, with our vague idea of a possible assumption, we can turn to step 4, which is . . .

### 4. Choose an answer.

Because we were able to pre-phrase something, it's best to skim the choices looking for it. And, lo and behold, there's our idea, stated in choice (C). (C) clears up the exercise issue. Yes, this author must assume (C) to make the conclusion that eating SlimDown alone will cause the men to lose weight.

At this point, if you're stuck for time, you simply choose (C) and move on. If you have more time, you may as well quickly check the remaining choices, to find (we hope) that none of them fits the bill.

Of course, once you grasp the structure of the argument and have located the author's central assumption, you should be able to answer any question they throw at you. This one takes the form of an Assumption question. But it could have just as easily been phrased as a Weaken the Argument question.

> ## THE ART OF PRE-PHRASING
>
> Your pre-phrasing of an answer need not be elaborate or terribly specific. Your goal is just to get an idea of what you're looking for, so the correct answer will jump out at you.

# 3. ANALYSIS OF EXPLANATIONS

The newest type of Analytical Reasoning question-type is Analysis of Explanations, which ETS has been trying out for the last couple of years. Because this question-type is so new and still undergoing revision, it's not totally clear how many of them you can expect. It can also be a pretty weird and intimidating question-type at first glance, so it pays to take some time to understand it. However, it is far from certain that you will see it on a scored section of the test, and so studying it should be your lowest priority.

### Format and Directions

A typical Analysis of Explanations set will consist of the following:

- The Situation
- The Result
- A group of two to four Adequate Explanation questions
- A group of two to four Relevance questions

**The Situation** is more or less just what it sounds like: a description of a real-life situation with characters and action. For instance, a Situation might involve, say, an archeologist trying to decide which of two locations to dig next—Site A, which has all of the tell-tale signs that usually indicate a potentially rich archeological dig, and Site B, where the conditions are not nearly as promising.

**The Result** follows the Situation, and it is usually somewhat mysterious. For instance, the Result of our hypothetical Situation above might be that the archeologist picks Site B instead of Site A as the next site to dig.

Your job at this point is to isolate the key issue brought up by the Result. It will usually take the form of a question—in this case, why did the archeologist choose Site B instead of Site A? The Situation will usually be full of details that suggest one explanation or another. You've got to be sensitive to those details, so that, after reading the Situation and the Result, several different possible explanations for the Result should occur to you.

Two groups of questions will then follow: Adequate Explanation questions and Relevance questions (the order in which the groups appear will vary). **The Adequate Explanation group** will give you a series of statements and ask you whether or not each could serve as an adequate explanation for the Result. For instance, the first item might be the statement: "As a result of a legal dispute with the owner of Site A, the archeologist and her team were forbidden access to the site." Well, yes, that would adequately explain why the archeologist chose Site B over Site A. The answer for that statement, then, would be yes, and you would choose (A) for that question. If the answer had been no, you'd have selected choice (B).

Either just before or just after the Adequate Explanation questions will come the **Relevance group**. This group provides statements as well, but here the question is whether or not the statements would be relevant to a possible adequate explanation. Here again, the answer is yes (choice A) or no (choice B). A statement for our hypothetical Situation might read: "Much of the fighting in the recent civil war has taken place in the vicinity of Site A." Here, you'd want to choose (A), yes, because this certainly would be relevant to a possible explanation for the result—namely, that the archeologist chose Site B to avoid having her people blown up in the civil war fighting.

That, in a nutshell, is the basic layout of this very odd question-type. For the record, the official directions (which probably wouldn't make a lot of sense to you if you came across them before knowing what the question-type was all about) will look something like this:

> <u>Directions:</u> **Each group of numbered statements below is preceded by a question for which the answer can be either "Yes" or "No." Decide the answer to the question for each individual statement in the group and mark your answer key accordingly, marking answer choice A if the answer is "Yes" and marking answer choice B if the answer is "No." Make sure you do not mark answer choices C, D, or E. Do not make assumptions about how many "Yes" answers and how many "No" answers there should be for each group.**

What this all means, of course, is that statements that are adequate explanations (in the Adequate Explanations group) and statements that are relevant (in the Relevance group) will get A's. Statements that are NOT adequate explanations (in the one group) and statements that are irrelevant (in the other) will get B's. You never select (C), (D), or (E) in this section. Never.

## THE THREE BASIC PRINCIPLES OF ANALYSIS OF EXPLANATIONS

In order to better explain the basic principles of this question-type, why don't we look at a typical Situation and Result:

Situation:
Louise Dorango was an extremely talented junior executive with Ipsilon, Inc., a small computer software company. Her abilities were no secret in the industry, and she was constantly being courted by recruiters from other software companies, who would invite her to long lunches at expensive restaurants. In fact, she spent so much time seeing these recruiters that she often was absent from important meetings, and soon fell behind on many of her projects. One afternoon, her lunch with one such recruiter lasted so long that she missed a meeting with her supervisor, Warren Wise. When Louise finally came back, Warren asked that she step into his office.

Result:
That afternoon, Louise packed up her desk and left the offices of Ipsilon, Inc., never to return.

Here are the basic principles to keep in mind when approaching something like the above:

### 1. Determine the key question raised by the Result.

Since, as mentioned above, the Result will almost always be somewhat mysterious, the key question will typically be: Why did this result come about? Or, in this case: Why did Louise Dorango leave Ipsilon? Was she fired? Did she quit? Did she get a better offer somewhere else and tell Warren Wise to go jump in a lake? To a certain extent, the test makers are asking you to think like a private investigator. Something happened; now your job is to find out why it happened.

### 2. Look for suggestive elements in the Situation.

Like any private investigator, the way to proceed is to look for clues. The clues in A-of-E are what we call suggestive elements—details that would suggest one possible explanation or another for the Result. And the place to look for them is in the Situation.

---

### DETECTIVE WORK

Your job is to find out why the result happened.

---

In the example above, are there any details there that would suggest an explanation for Louise's abrupt departure? Yes. What about all of these recruiters that Louise has been courted by? Doesn't their interest in her suggest that she's receiving job offers from them all the time? And doesn't the fact that she just had a really long lunch with one of these recruiters strengthen that possibility? Maybe Louise accepted an offer over lunch, and the reason she was so late back to the office was that they were going over the details of her new employment. All of these details—the courtship by recruiters, the extended lunch—are suggestive elements, leading us toward a possible explanation for the result: namely, that Louise was offered and accepted another job, quit, and therefore left Ipsilon that very day, never to return.

But before you pat yourself on the back for solving the mystery, take note that there are other kinds of suggestive elements in the Situation—ones that lead toward a very different explanation of the result. Notice that Louise's long lunches have caused her to miss important meetings and to fall behind on many of her projects. Notice too that, on the day in question, Louise's lingering at lunch caused her to miss a meeting with Warren Wise, her supervisor. Don't those elements suggest that Louise might have annoyed her supervisor once too often, and that, when Warren asked that she step into his office, it was to give her the boot? Here again, the answer is yes.

In fact, you'll find that the key question in most A-of-E sets will be open-ended in this way. Some elements will suggest one possible explanation, while other elements will suggest another. (As we'll see in the discussion of the Four-Step Approach to A-of-E, we recommend that you actually circle these suggestive elements in the Situation as you read, in order to focus your investigative thinking.) And that's where the third basic principle comes in:

### 3. Keep an open mind.

As you know, your job in A-of-E is NOT to find the one true explanation for the Result. It's to determine whether certain statements are relevant to, or could serve as, a possible explanation for the Result. So it's important that you not decide in your own mind why poor old Louise left Ipsilon. If you reject one of the explanations being subtly suggested in the Situation—if you decide that one explanation is right and the others are wrong—you'll be in bad shape when the questions come around.

> ## ATTENTION TO DETAIL
>
> When you're reading the Situation, keep an eye out for details that would suggest possible explanations.

To succeed on A-of-E, in other words, you've got to have an open mind. You've got to be willing to entertain several possible explanations in your mind at the same time. Otherwise, if you close your mind to other possibilities, you won't be able to recognize relevant statements when the time comes to answer the questions.

## THE TWO ANALYSIS-OF-EXPLANATIONS QUESTION-TYPES

Now let's look at the actual Analysis of Explanations questions. The questions, after all, are where you get the actual points. As in Reading Comp, you don't get any points for just getting through the passage; you've got to get questions right to score.

With each set-up situation, as we saw, you'll get two sets of 2 to 4 questions: Adequate Explanation Questions and Relevance Questions.

### 1. Adequate Explanation Questions

Explanation Questions will ask you if a given statement is an adequate explanation of the result. They look like this:

> Question: Assuming that the following statement is true, could it serve as the basis of an adequate explanation of the result? To be considered an adequate explanation, a statement need not be complete in all its details.

This will be followed by a series of statements. You must answer the question—yes or no—for each of these statements. For instance, a statement for the Louise Dorango set might read like this:

> 1. Because of her increasing tendency to fall behind on projects, Louise was fired when she returned to the office.

Is this what you'd call "the basis of an adequate explanation of the result"? Certainly. It's consistent with the facts of the Situation, and it explains Louise's behavior in the Result. So, for question 1, you'd choose (A), for yes.

But what about a statement like this:

> 2. Warren Wise was a co-founder of Ipsilon Inc., and he had himself conducted Louise's job interview.

Is that an adequate explanation? Hardly. How would Wise's history as a co-founder of Ipsilon (and as the person who originally conducted Louise's interview) explain Louise's abrupt departure? It can't, and that's why the answer to question 2 would be (B), for no.

Do you see the difference between (A)s and (B)s here? (A)s, adequate explanations, don't have to explain every detail of the Result explicitly (notice that the statement in question 1 doesn't go on to say, ". . . so Louise packed up and left that very day."), but they do have to offer a solid explanatory basis for the Result. (B)s, on the other hand, will just seem off somehow. They just won't do the job of explaining the Result.

## 2. Relevance Questions

The other kind of A-of-E question is somewhat more subtle. Relevance Questions ask you if a given statement is simply relevant to any reasonable explanation of the result. They look like this:

> Question: Assuming that the following statement is true, is it relevant to a possible adequate explanation of the result? To be relevant to an explanation, a statement must either support or weaken that explanation.

These questions are a little harder than Explanation questions because you don't just have to distinguish between statements that do explain the Result and statements that don't. Instead, you've got to judge whether a given statement would be *relevant* to such an explanation. Would it weaken a possible explanation? Would it strengthen one? Here, the judgments to be made are finer and subtler. For instance, let's say you got the following statement:

3. Warren only called Louise into his office to explain the new voice-mail system to her.

Is this relevant? Well, it would certainly weaken the possibility that Warren called her into the office to fire her, wouldn't it? So yes, this is a relevant statement, because it weakens one possible explanation. Notice that it doesn't have to devastate a possible explanation. It's still possible, of course, that Warren fired her after showing her the voicemail system (maybe they got into an argument about the telephones, who knows?). But the statement for Question 3 certainly has relevance, so you would answer (A).

What does an irrelevant statement look like? Have a look at this next one:

4. The recruiter with whom Louise had lunch had eaten at that particular restaurant once before.

What explanation of the Result could this statement be relevant to? The recruiter's lunching habits are way off the topic here. Without stretching and coming up with a really far-fetched explanation of events, there's no way you can make a statement like Question 4 relevant. That's why the correct answer for 4 would be (B).

In fact, that's a good rule of thumb for Relevance Questions. If you find yourself stretching to find an explanation to fit the statement, then you're probably dealing with a (B), with an irrelevant statement.

## THE KAPLAN FOUR-STEP APPROACH TO ANALYSIS OF EXPLANATIONS

Now that you've got a good handle on the basics of Analysis of Explanations, it's time to put it all together into a step-by-step approach to the question-type. Here are the four steps of the Kaplan Four-Step Approach to Analysis of Explanations:

### 1. Analyze the Situation
Read the situation carefully. Try to grasp the most important points in the situation. Some of the situations will be lengthy and complex. Don't try to memorize them! Get a clear sense of who's who and what the central issues are. Keep an eye out for suggestive elements and circle key phrases as you go.

### 2. Analyze the Result
Decide precisely what needs to be explained. What's the key question to be answered? Keep the scope of the Result in mind. If the Result concerns Louise's departure from the office, don't worry about the employment background of other characters in the Situation, like Warren Wise and the recruiter.

### 3. Think about Possible Explanations
Decide what kind of explanations would bridge the gap between the Situation and the Result. The Suggestive Elements should guide your thinking.

Remember to keep an open mind. Always be prepared to run into an explanation you haven't considered.

### 4. Attack the Questions
After you've developed a good sense of the situation and an exact understanding of the result, and after you've got an idea of what sorts of explanations could account for the result, you're ready for the questions.

We find that doing the Adequate Explanation Questions first is a good idea. Doing so may alert you to one or two possible explana-

> **THE KAPLAN 4-STEP APPROACH TO ANALYSIS OF EXPLANATIONS**
>
> 1. Analyze the Situation.
> 2. Analyze the Result.
> 3. Think about possible explanations.
> 4. Attack the questions.

tions for the Result that you may not have thought of in Step 3, making the Relevance Questions easier.

## USING THE KAPLAN FOUR-STEP APPROACH

Now let's see how this approach works on another actual A-of-E set:

Situation: The Ho River Valley had been cultivated by small farmers for centuries, though with limited success. While the valley was blessed with good soil and plentiful rain, the red weevil, an indigenous insect notoriously resistant to pesticides, had always done extensive damage to anything grown there. Because of the valley's limited agricultural productivity, the Government Power Agency in 1990 began to promote a plan to build a hydroelectric plant on the Ho, damming the river and flooding the valley. Hoping to forestall this plan, which would have driven them from land that they and their forebears had cultivated for generations, the local farmers agreed to try to improve the valley's agricultural output by using Morphomil, a powerful and still-experimental pesticide, on their crop to destroy the weevils. Despite warnings from environmentalists about the potential harms of the pesticide, the farmers began systematically spraying their fields with Morphomil in the spring of 1991. As a result, the red weevil population plummeted, and the Ho River Valley's harvest that autumn was three times as large as any in the past.

Result: By the end of 1993, two-and-a-half years after first using the new pesticide, all residents of the Ho River Valley had left their ancestral homes and moved to other parts of the country.

Question: Assuming that the following statement is true, is it relevant to a possible adequate explanation of the result? To be relevant to an explanation, a statement must either support or weaken that explanation.

1. A 1992 study found trace quantities of Morphomil in the fruits and vegetables grown in the Ho River Valley.

2. Morphomil had been proven effective in killing a wide variety of crop-destroying pests, including the red weevil.

3. Most of the people who left the Ho River Valley in 1993 relocated to other agricultural areas.

4. In 1992, the government banned all sales of Morphomil pesticide.

5. A 1991 study indicated that the country's demand for electrical power would grow at a faster pace than previously believed.

Question: Assuming that the following statements are true, could it serve as the basis of an adequate explanation of the result? To be considered an adequate explanation, a statement need not be complete in all its details.

6. Despite higher crop yields in the Ho River Valley, the Government Power Agency was given the go-ahead in 1992 to build the hydroelectric plant.

7. The widespread use of the highly toxic Morphomil pesticide rendered the Ho River Valley unfit for human habitation.

8. The Government Power Agency revised its plan in 1992, proposing the construction of a series of smaller hydroelectric plants on several rivers besides the Ho.

9. In early 1993, the Government Power Agency succeeded in having the entire Ho River Valley officially condemned.

## 1. Analyze the Situation

Get a fix on the basic outline of the Situation: It involves a conflict between the Government Power Authority (GPA) and the farmers of the Ho Valley. The GPA wants to flood the valley to build a hydroelectric plant. The farmers want to stop the plan. They figure that if they can convince the GPA that the valley can be productive agriculturally, the GPA will change its mind. So the farmers decide to use a questionable pesticide on their crops, hoping to kill the red weevils and boost agricultural production. They use the pesticide, and—lo and behold—the weevils die and production skyrockets.

What are the suggestive elements here? Well, the warnings from environmentalists about the pesticide seem ominous, so that may play a role in the result. Also the dramatic increase in agricultural yield. These are the things to keep in mind when you start to think about explanations for the Result.

## 2. Analyze the Result.

What happens? Well, by the end of 1993, all of the farmers have moved out of the valley. Does that mean that they lost their bid, that the valley was flooded after all? Not necessarily. Always make sure you know precisely what needs to be explained in the result. The key question here is NOT why did the valley get flooded after all. We don't know whether the valley is flooded or not. Rather, the key question is simply: Why did the farmers leave? THAT is what we're looking to explain.

## 3. Think about Possible Explanations.

Well, as we saw, there's one obvious possible explanation for the result. The GPA went ahead and flooded the valley anyway, even though agricultural output was way up. That would certainly explain why the farmers left: They didn't want to drown!

But there are elements in the Situation that suggest another possible explanation. Remember that "powerful and still-experimental" pesticide that the farmers used on their fields. Environmentalists warned that use of the pesticide had "potential harms." This suggests that maybe the pesticide, while killing off all of the weevils, may have made the valley unfit for humans as well as insects. There are definite hints in the Situation that the use of the pesticide may have been responsible for the exodus of farmers from the valley.

> ### AVOID TUNNEL VISION
>
> Don't fixate on one explanation of the Result. Keep an open mind to other possible explanations.

So remember your third basic principle: Keep an open mind. Don't just assume that the valley was flooded and that that's why the farmers left. There are other possible explanations for their flight.

## 4. Attack the Adequate Explanation Questions first, then the Relevance Questions.

Remember, in some sets the Adequate Explanations Questions come first; in other sets, the Relevance Questions come first. Either way, you should do the Adequate Explanation Questions first. So here, where the Relevance Questions come first, you want to hop to questions 6 through 9 first. Only after you've finished those, would you come back to questions 1 through 5.

Here are the answers to the questions, with commentary, in that order:

5. (A) This is certainly the basis of an adequate explanation. If the GPA got the go-ahead to flood the valley and build the plant, the first step would be to get all of the farmers to move out of the valley.

6. (A) Yes, this was the second possible explanation that we mentioned above. It too would explain why all of the farmers high-tailed it out of the valley.

7. (B) How would this explain the exodus from the Ho Valley? If the big Ho plant wasn't built, there would be no need for the Ho farmers to leave.

8. (A) Here again, this would adequately explain the exodus of farmers. If the Ho Valley was officially condemned, everyone would have to leave it.

1. (A) This is relevant. If the pesticide was getting into the agricultural products, then the increased output of the valley would be commercially useless. This would be a perfect excuse for the GPA to go ahead and flood the valley, forcing the farmers to leave.

2. (B) This doesn't really tell us much that the Situation hasn't already told us. We already know that the pesticide works. This doesn't really strengthen or weaken any possible explanation that comes easily to mind.

3. (B) So what?

4. (A) This would strengthen the "environmental apocalypse" theory: The pesticide was so bad that it poisoned the whole valley. Interestingly, it also would strengthen the other theory. If the pesticide was banned, the Ho farmers couldn't use it anymore. Agricultural output would go back to its old low level, and the GPA would be much more likely to go ahead with the plan to flood the valley.

5. (A) This would strengthen the explanation that the GPA plan went into effect and that the valley was slated for flooding. If demand for electricity went up, the Ho Valley's value as the site of a hydroelectric plant would more likely be seen as more important than its value as a source of agricultural products.

---

## Analysis of Explanations Tips

Here's are some useful tips for the A-of-E section:
• Do Explanation questions first.
• Always remember which question-type you're solving for.
• Remember: A weakener is relevant to the possible explanation.
• Keep your facts straight.
• Note the chronology of the result.
• Think narrowly; consider the scope.
• Don't memorize details.
• Watch out for "B"s.
• Keep an open mind.
• Use common sense.
• Consider each statement by itself only. Don't apply one statement to another.
• When in doubt—guess!

## ANALYSIS OF EXPLANATIONS PRACTICE

Now's your chance to try a full set on your own. Good luck!

Situation: In the spring of 1990, the town of Falberg was considering new legislation that would legalize high-stakes gambling. The town already allowed gambling for small stakes, but the new law would increase bet limits from $5 to $250 and triple the number of slot machines allowed. Critics of the proposal said that the resulting gambling explosion would destroy their way of life by driving their traditional businesses out, flooding the town with thousands of visitors every year, bringing in organized crime, and driving up street crime. They pointed out that even limited gambling had driven most stores that sell wares off Main Street, and replaced them with gas stations, convenience stores, and cheap motels. Proponents of the legislation argued that it would create jobs and bring about an economic rebirth in an area where many traditional industries, such as mining and agriculture, were failing. When the governor of the state endorsed the proposal, it was widely believed that the legislation would be passed.

Result: Within two years after the legislation was voted on, many of Falberg's oldest residents, and many of those residents whose families had lived in Falberg the longest, moved out.

Question: Assuming that the following statement is true, is it relevant to a possible adequate explanation of the result? To be relevant to an explanation, a statement must either support or weaken that explanation.

10. The proposal to legalize high-stakes gambling in Falberg was defeated by a sizable majority.

11. When five-dollar-a-bet gambling was legalized in Poltava, a nearby community, the town did not experience a decrease in total population.

12. Following the vote on the proposal to legalize high-stakes gambling in Falberg, the traditional area industries of mining and agriculture did not experience the continued depression that some had feared.

13. When a similar measure to legalize high-stakes gambling in Falberg came to a vote in 1975, it met with defeat.

**ANSWERS**

10. A
11. B
12. A
13. B
14. A
15. B
16. A

<u>Question:</u> Assuming that the following statement is true, could it serve as the basis of an adequate explanation of the result? To be considered an adequate explanation, a statement need not be complete in all its details.

14. The proposal to legalize high-stakes gambling was passed, and the resulting boom caused property values and property taxes to climb so high that only residents involved in high-profit businesses could afford to pay them.

15. A year after the vote in Falberg, a nearby county in the same state passed legislation almost identical to the Falberg proposal to legalize high-stakes gambling.

16. The summer after the vote on the gambling proposal was the third consecutive year in which severe flooding did extensive damage to area farms.

## WHAT'S NEXT?

Now that we've covered Level 1 in depth for all three section-types, it's time to move on to Level 2 in the Kaplan Three-Level Master Plan for the GRE: Test Mechanics.

# CHAPTER 3

# TEST MECHANICS

The first year of graduate school is a frenzied experience for many students. It's no surprise, then, that the GRE, the test specifically designed to predict success in the first year of graduate school, is a highly-speeded, time-intensive test that demands excellent time-management skills.

So when you're comfortable with the content of the test, namely, the type of material discussed in the previous chapters, your next challenge will be to take it to the next level—test mechanics—which will enable you to manage an entire section at a time.

On most of the tests you take in school, you wouldn't dream of not making at least a try at every single one of the questions. If a question seems particularly difficult, you spend significantly more time on it, because you'll probably be given more points for answering a hard question correct. Not so on the GRE. Remember, every GRE question is worth a single point, no matter how hard. And because there are so many questions to do in so little time, you'd be nuts to spend three minutes getting a point for a hard question and then not have time to get a couple of quick points from two easy questions later in the section.

Given this combination—limited time and all questions equal in weight—you've got to develop a way of handling the test sections to make sure you get as many points as you can as quickly and easily as you can. The following principles will help you do just that.

## GET TO ALL THE EASY QUESTIONS

One of the most critical strategies is to make sure you do all the easy questions. Remember that in the math and short verbal sections, the questions go from easy to hard. For instance, the hardest Sentence Completion question, #7, will be harder than the easiest Analogy question that follows it. Likewise, you're more likely to get the first

---

**IT'S NOT JUST ABOUT CORRECT ANSWERS**

For complete GRE success, you've got to get as many correct answers as possible in the time you're given. Knowing the strategies is not enough. You've got to perfect your time management skills so that you get a chance to use those strategies on as many questions as possible.

---

**FACTORS FOR SUCCESS**

• In order to meet the stringent time requirements of the GRE, you've got to cultivate the following:
• a sense of timing
• an ability to skip around without getting mixed up
• an ability to assess the difficulty level of a question, passage, or game
• a cool head

few Antonyms correct than the last few Analogies, even though the Antonyms are at the end of the section. So if you persistently have trouble finishing sections, make sure to skip around; just keep good track of your answers when you mark them in your answer grid.

By all means, also come back and do as many of the difficult questions as you have time for. But if you run out of time, you're much better off running out of time on questions that you may have had difficulty with, rather than on potentially doable material. Of course, because there's no guessing penalty, always fill in an answer to every question on the test, whether you get to it or not.

## LEARN TO RECOGNIZE AND SEEK OUT QUESTIONS YOU CAN DO

All of the Reading Comprehension and Analytical Questions will be presented without a clear order of difficulty. That means you should peek ahead in the section you're working on to see if what follows is easier than what you're doing now. If you find that the second Reading Comp passage in a verbal section is about Picasso and you happen to be an art history major, go ahead and do that passage first. Or if you find sequencing games particularly easy, seek out the sequencing games when you are in the Analytical sections and do them first.

## DON'T WASTE TIME ON QUESTIONS YOU CAN'T DO

We know that foregoing a possibly tough question is easier said than done; we all have the natural instinct to plow through test sections in their given order. But it just doesn't pay off on the GRE. If you dig in your heels on a tough question, refusing to move on until you've cracked it, well, you're letting your test macho get in the way of your test score. A test section, not to mention life itself, is too short to waste on lost causes.

## REMAIN CALM

It's imperative that you remain calm and composed while working through a section. You can't allow yourself to be rattled by one hard logic game or reading comp passage to the degree that it throws off your performance on the rest of the section. Expect to find at least one difficult passage or game; but remember, you won't be the only one to have trouble with it. The test is curved in such a way as to take the tough material into account. Having trouble with a difficult logic game isn't going to ruin your score, but getting upset about it and letting it throw you off-track will. When you understand that part of the test maker's goal is to reward those who keep their composure, you'll recognize the importance of not panicking when you run into challenging material.

## KEEP TRACK OF TIME

Of course, the last thing you want to happen is to have time called on a particular section before you've gotten to half the questions. It's essential, therefore, that you pace yourself, keeping in mind the general guidelines for how long to spend on any individual question, passage, or game. No one is saying that you should spend, for instance, exactly 60 seconds on every Logical Reasoning question. But you should have a sense of how long you have to do each question, so you know when you're exceeding the limit and should start to move faster.

Keeping track of time is also important for guessing. Remember, there's no penalty for a wrong answer on the GRE! So it pays to leave a little time at the end to guess on the questions that you haven't answered. For instance, let's say you never get a chance to do the last logic game. If you just leave the grids for those questions blank, you're going to get no points for that entire game. If, on the other hand, you give yourself a little time at the end to fill in a guess for each of those questions, you'll have a very good chance of getting lucky on at least one or two questions. That would up your raw score by one or two points, which could make a significant difference in your scaled score.

So, when working on a section, always remember to keep track of time. Don't spend a wildly disproportionate amount of time on any one question or group of questions. Also, give yourself thirty seconds or so at the end of each section to fill in answers for any questions you haven't gotten to. After all, a correct guess is worth just as much as any other correct answer.

## MANAGING THE ANSWER GRID

Another key to the GRE is knowing how to handle the answer grid. You not only have to get right answers, remember; you've also got to get those right answers onto the answer grid in an efficient and

> ### THE GUESSING GAME
>
> We've said it before and we'll say it again: If you can't do a question or can't get to it, guess! Fill in an answer—any answer—on the answer grid. There's no penalty if you're wrong, but you get a big, fat, juicy point if you're right.

## GRID TECHNIQUE IS IMPORTANT

Yes, it's purely bookkeeping, but you won't get the points if you put your answers in the wrong place or if you waste time searching for the right place to put your answers. Take the time now to develop some good answer grid habits.

accurate way. It sounds simple, but it's extremely important: Don't make mistakes filling out your answer grid! When time is short, it's easy to get confused going back and forth between your test book and your grid. If you know the answer, but misgrid, you won't get the points. Here are a few methods of avoiding mistakes on the answer grid:

### Always Circle The Questions You Skip

Put a big circle in your test book around the number of any question you skip. When you go back, such questions will be easy to locate. Also, if you accidentally skip a box on the grid, you can more easily check your grid against your book to see where you went wrong.

### Always Circle the Answers You Choose

Circle the correct answers in your test booklet but don't transfer the answers to the grid right away. That wastes too much time, especially if you're doing a lot of skipping around. Circling your answers in the test book will also make it easier to check your grid against your book.

### Grid Five or More Answers At Once

As we said, don't transfer your answers to the grid after every question. Transfer your answers after every five questions or at the end of each reading comp passage or logic game (find the method that works best for you). That way, you won't keep breaking your concentration to mark the grid. You'll save time and improve accuracy. Just make sure you're not left at the end of the section with ungridded answers!

## WHAT'S NEXT?

Now that you've been through the first two levels of GRE preparation, Test Content and Test Mechanics, it's time to move up to the third and final level of GRE preparation—Test Mentality.

# CHAPTER 4

# TEST MENTALITY

In this test-prep section, we first looked at the content that makes up each specific section of the GRE, focusing on the strategies and techniques that you'll need to tackle individual questions, games, and passages. Then we discussed the mechanics involved in moving from individual items to working through full-length sections. Now we're ready to turn our attention to the often overlooked attitudinal aspects of the test. We'll then combine these factors with what we learned in the Test Content and Test Mechanics chapters to put the finishing touches on your comprehensive GRE approach.

We've already armed you with the weapons that you need to do well on the GRE. But you must wield those weapons with the right frame of mind and in the right spirit. This involves taking a certain stance toward the entire test. Here's what's involved:

> **THE BASIC PRINCIPLES OF GOOD TEST MENTALITY**
>
> - test awareness
> - stamina
> - confidence
> - the right attitude

## TEST AWARENESS

To do your best on the GRE, you must always keep in mind that the test is like no other test you've taken before, both in terms of its content and in terms of its scoring system. If you took a test in high school or college and got a quarter of the questions wrong, you'd probably receive a pretty lousy grade. But on the GRE, you can get a quarter of the questions wrong (about 42) and still earn an average score of about 650! The test is geared so that only the very best test takers are able to finish every section. But even these people rarely get every question right.

What does this mean for you? Well, just as you shouldn't let one tough Reading Comp passage ruin an entire section, you shouldn't let what you consider to be a sub-par performance on one section ruin your performance on the entire test. A lousy performance on one single section will not by itself spoil your score—unless you literally miss almost every question. If you allow that sub-par section to rattle you, however, it can have a cumulative negative effect that

> **NOBODY'S PERFECT**
>
> Remember that the GRE isn't like most tests you've taken. You can get a lot of questions wrong and still get a great score. So don't get rattled if you miss a few questions.

## BE COOL

Losing a few extra points here and there won't do serious damage to your score but losing your head will. Keeping your composure is an important test-taking skill.

sets in motion a downward spiral. It's that kind of thing that could potentially do serious damage to your score. Losing a few extra points won't do you in, but losing your head will.

Remember, if you feel that you've done poorly on a section, don't sweat it. It could be the experimental one. And even if it's not, chances are it's just a difficult section, which will be figured into the scoring curve anyway. The point is that you must remain calm and collected. Simply do your best on each section, and once a section is over, forget about it and move on.

## STAMINA

You must work on your test-taking stamina. Overall, the GRE is a fairly grueling experience, and some test takers simply run out of gas on the final few sections. To avoid this, you must prepare by taking as many full-length practice tests as possible in the week or two before the test, so that on test day, five sections plus a writing sample will seem like a breeze (well, maybe not a breeze, but at least not a hurricane).

One option is to buy *Practicing to Take the GRE General Test, Vol. #9*, which is a book of released tests from ETS. There are seven real GREs in this book, and they can be great practice for all the strategies that you're learning in this book. Unfortunately, only one of these seven tests comes with explanations—the rest just have answer keys—so it's difficult to get much better just by using *Practicing to Take the GRE*. Also, the tests are out of date. Since that book was published, ETS has revised the Analytical and Quantitative sections, adding the new "Analysis of Explanations" question type in Analytical and questions on probability, median, mode, and range in Quantitative.

## GET IN SHAPE

You wouldn't run a marathon without working on your stamina well in advance of the race, would you? The same goes for taking the GRE.

Another option, if you have some time and need a really great score, would be to take the full Kaplan course. We'll give you access to every released test plus loads of additional material, so you can really build up your GRE stamina. As a bonus, you'll also have the benefit of our expert live instruction: all-in-one tutoring in every aspect of the GRE. If you decide to go this route, call 1-800-KAP-TEST for a Kaplan center location near you.

## CONFIDENCE

Confidence feeds on itself, and unfortunately, so does the opposite of confidence—self-doubt. Confidence in your ability leads to quick, sure answers and an ease of concentration that translates into more points. If you lack concentration, you end up reading sentences and answer choices two, three, or four times. This leads to timing difficulties, which only continue the downward spiral, causing anxiety and a tendency to rush in order to finish sections.

If you subscribe to the GRE Mindset that we've described, however, you'll gear all of your practice toward the major goal of taking control of the test. Learn our techniques and then practice them on real test material, such as that found in *Practicing to Take the GRE* (even if it is somewhat out of date). That's the way to score your best on test day.

## ATTITUDE

Those who approach the GRE as an obstacle and who rail against the necessity of taking it usually don't fare as well as those who see the GRE as an opportunity to show off the reading and reasoning skills that graduate schools are looking for. Those who look forward to doing battle with the GRE—or, at least, who enjoy the opportunity to distinguish themselves from the rest of the applicant pack—tend to score better than do those who resent or dread it.

It may sound a little dubious, but take our word for it: Attitude adjustment is proven to raise points. Here are a few steps you can take to make sure you develop the right GRE attitude:

- Look at the GRE as a challenge, but try not to obsess over it; you certainly don't want to psyche yourself out of the game.
- Remember that, yes, the GRE is obviously important, but, contrary to what some people think, this one test will not single-handedly determine the outcome of your life. In many cases, it's not even the most important piece of your graduate application.
- Try to have fun with the test. Learning how to match your wits against the test makers can be a very satisfying experience, and the reading and thinking skills you'll acquire will benefit you in graduate school as well as in your future career.
- Remember that you're more prepared than most people. You've trained with Kaplan. You have the tools you need, plus the know-how to use those tools.

> **ATTITUDE ADJUSTMENT**
>
> Your attitude toward the test does affect your performance. You don't have to "think nice thoughts" about the GRE, but you should have a good mental stance toward the test.

## WHAT'S NEXT?

Now that we've covered the three levels of GRE test preparation, we are going to provide you with information on two issues that may be important to you: whether you should take the GRE on computer and whether you should take a GRE Subject Test.

# CHAPTER 5

# TESTS, TESTS, AND MORE TESTS

There are two topics that we promised to cover but haven't discussed yet: the Computer-Adaptive GRE and the GRE Subject Tests. So let's talk about them now.

## THE COMPUTER-ADAPTIVE GRE

You can take the GRE on a computer. It's pretty weird, so here's how it works. You only see one question at a time. Instead of having a pre-determined mixture of easy, medium, and hard questions, the Computer-Adaptive Test (CAT) will select questions for you based on how well you are doing. The first question will be of medium difficulty. If you get it right, the second question will be a little harder; if you get it wrong, the second will be a little easier.

If you keep getting questions right, the test will get harder and harder; if you slip and make some mistakes, the test will adjust and start giving you easier problems, but if you answer them all correctly, it will go back to the hard ones. It gives you enough questions to ensure that scores are not based on luck—if you get one hard question wrong you might just have been unlucky, but if you get ten hard questions wrong, then luck has little to do with it. So the test is self-adjusting and self-correcting.

Because of this format, the CAT is very different *structurally* from the traditional test. Every problem that you see is based on how you answered the prior problem. That means you cannot return to a question once you've answered it, because that would throw off the sequence. Once you answer a question it's part of your score, for better or worse. That means you cannot skip around within a section and do questions in the order that you like.

> ### WHEN THE GOING GETS TOUGH . . .
>
> When you get a question right on the CAT, the next question is harder. When you get a question wrong, the next question is easier.

Another major consequence is that hard problems count more than easy ones. It has to be this way, because everyone gets a different mix of easy and hard problems, and the very purpose of this adaptive format is to see how far you get into the hard problems. Imagine two students: one who gets mostly easy questions, and one who gets very difficult questions. The test maker wants to reward the student who makes it to the hard questions, so these questions count more and that student gets a better score. No matter how much more comfortable you might be sticking to the easy questions, you definitely want to get to the hard questions if you can, because that's where the points are.

### The Five Sections
Everyone who finishes each section gets the same number of questions. The test consists of up to five CAT sections, total, but only three of them will count toward your score. They will not necessarily be presented in this order:

- 30-minute Verbal Section. The section has a maximum number of 30 questions. You must answer at least 24 of them to receive a score.

- 45-minute Math Section. The section has a maximum of 28 questions. You must answer at least 23 of them to receive a score.

- 60-minute Analytical Section. The section has a maximum of 35 questions. You must answer at least 28 of them to receive a score.

In addition to these three scored sections, you will most likely have one "experimental" CAT section which will look just like one of the three sections above and will not count toward your score. So if you get two Analytical sections, for instance, you will know that one of them was unscored, but you won't know which one. The very last section on the test is called the "Research Section." This section, like the experimental section, will not count toward your score; but, unlike the experimental section, you will know which section is Research. The Research Section is last and is optional. There is no reason whatsoever for you to complete the research section, unless you feel like doing the Educational Testing Service a favor.

## THIS CAT HAS FIVE LIVES

There are five sections on the CAT, but you don't have to do the final one—the research section.

## YOU'VE GOT BETTER THINGS TO DO

There's no reason for you to answer the questions in the Research Section because it has no effect on your score.

## Timing

There is no time limit per question. You can take as much time on each question as you like, as long as you answer the minimum number of questions in each section in the allotted time. Most students are finding that the CAT sections are easier to finish than the sections on the paper-and-pencil exam (but that doesn't necessarily mean you get a higher score). You must answer at least 24 of the Verbal questions, 23 of the Math questions, and 28 of the Analytical questions. If you don't, the computer won't have enough information to figure out your performance on that section. What are the rest of the questions used for? Fine tuning.

## Cancelling

When you finish the CAT you will be given a prompt asking you whether or not you want to cancel your scores. If you do not cancel your scores at that time, you will never be able to do so because your scores will immediately be recorded and given to you.

## CAT: The Upside

There are many good things about CAT, such as:

- There is a little timer at the top of the computer screen to help you pace yourself (you can hide it if it distracts you).
- There will be just a few other test takers in the room with you—it won't be like taking it in one of those massive lecture halls with distractions everywhere.
- You get a pause of one minute between each section. The pause is optional, but you should always use it to relax and stretch.
- You can sign up for the CAT the day before and registration is very easy.
- The CAT is much more convenient for your schedule than the pencil-and-paper exam. It's offered at more than 175 centers three to five days a week (depending on the center) all year long.
- Perhaps the CAT's best feature is that it gives you your scores immediately and will send them to schools just 10 to 15 days later.

> ### INSTANT FEEDBACK
>
> The CAT will give you your scores immediately and send them to your school of choice in about two weeks.

## CAT: The Downside

There are many not-so-good things about the CAT:

- The CAT is more expensive, $40 more than the regular test—the CAT is $96 instead of $56.
- You cannot skip around on this test; you must answer the questions one at a time in the order the computer gives them to you.
- Because the answer choices are presented without letters (A, B,

C, D, or E) next to them, it's easier to mismark a choice.

- You can't cross an answer choice off and never look at it again on the CAT, so you have to be more disciplined about not reconsidering choices you've already eliminated.
- You have to scroll through Reading Comprehension passages, as the entire passage won't necessarily fit on the screen.
- You can't write on your computer screen the way you can on the paper test (though people have tried), so you have to use scratch paper (*official* ETS scratch paper, not your own) and transfer your answers to the computer, which takes time.
- Lastly, many people find that computer screens tire them and cause eyestrain—especially after three hours!

The greatest distinction of the CAT is simply that it's *very different*. It's a new test format, and it's given in a new way—by computer. The computer has a mouse; in fact, the test is mouse-only. You won't use the keyboard. Also, the test makes use of computer functions, such as HELP and QUIT, which take some getting used to. For these reasons, make sure you go through ETS's official CAT Tutorial diskette, which Kaplan makes available to all its course students. The tutorial is your only opportunity to acquaint yourself with this format before you start playing for keeps.

### Computer Basics

Let's preview the primary computer functions that you will use on the CAT. ETS calls them "Testing Tools," but they're basically just boxes that you can click with your mouse. (They are also explained in the CAT Diskette described above.)

TIME
Clicking on this box turns the time display at the top of the screen on and off. When you have five minutes left in a section, the clock flashes and the display changes from Hours/Minutes to Hours/Minutes/Seconds.

HELP
Directions and other stuff from the tutorial—you should know all this already and the test clock won't pause just because you click on "Help."

QUIT
Ends the test.

NEXT
Confirms your response to the question and moves you to the next screen. Your response won't count until you hit this button.

SCROLL BAR
Similar to that on a Macintosh computer, this is a thin, vertical column with up/down arrows at either end. Clicking on the arrows moves you up or down the page you're reading.

**CAT Scores vs. Paper 'n' Pencil Scores**

There is little reason to believe that your score would be either much higher or lower on the CAT than it would be on the paper-and-pencil test. ETS has rigorously pre-tested and "normed" the CAT to make sure that people score pretty much the same as they would on the traditional exam. Norming is a scientifically valid process, and it's fairly easy to do.

If you feel that you would be much more comfortable taking the test on computer in a small room with just a few other people, then you might do a little better on the CAT. If you despise computers and everything they stand for, you should probably stick to the paper-and-pencil format. Other than that, your scores probably wouldn't be very different from one to the other.

One thing to consider: The norming process was not specifically applied to Kaplan students, and it may be that Kaplan students do better on the paper-and-pencil exam than they would on the CAT, even though that's not true of the population at large. Why? Because some Kaplan strategies don't work on the CAT. That fact won't hurt the population at large, because they don't know about the strategies anyway, but it could mean that a Kaplan student's score on the CAT would be a little bit different than it would have been on the paper-and-pencil test. How much different? Probably no more than 10 to 20 points per 200 to 800 score, and even then only if you really use these particular strategies a great deal in a paper-and-pencil test and with a lot of success. But let's take a look at the particular Kaplan strategies that don't work on the CAT, and you can decide for yourself whether they are techniques that really work well for you. Reasons that Kaplan students (in particular) might not want to take the CAT:

- There's no skipping around within a section. If you get a lot of mileage out of this strategy—that is, if you skip questions all the time and come back to them, or you always do the Reading Comp passages in the order that you want, then you probably don't want to take the CAT. But if you always do the questions in whatever order they're presented in, then this difference between the CAT and the paper-and-pencil test won't affect you.
- It's harder to eliminate choices based on the difficulty level of the question. Remember, difficult questions never have "obvi-

> **KAPLAN RULES OF THUMB**
>
> Any Kaplan strategy about any particular kind of question—like Q.C.s or Logic Games or Analogies—will work fine on the CAT. But any strategy that has to do with the structure of the test as a whole—such as skipping around or order of difficulty—will NOT work. Bear this in mind as you study for the exam.

ous" answers. On the paper-and-pencil GRE, you know how difficult a question is by where it shows up in a section.

- It's harder to use systematic process of elimination on the CAT. Answer choices are not presented with letters A, B, C, D, or E next to them. They are simply listed. Some students are very good at putting marks through answer choices they've eliminated—this helps them be less distracted and not be tempted to read the choice again if they're stuck.

## So Why Do People Take the CAT?

One good reason to take the CAT is time. Your schools get the scores just two to three weeks after you take it. That gives you more time to prepare.

Another reason some people take it is that they can see their scores before they decide which schools they want to send them to. On the paper-and-pencil test, you have to decide which schools to send score reports to before you take the exam, or you pay extra. This isn't a very strong reason, though, in and of itself.

Finally, many students take the CAT because they have to take a GRE Subject Test such as Biology or Psychology. If you plan on taking a Subject Test but don't want to take it on the same day as the General Test, you might consider taking the General Test on another date on computer. The Subject Tests are not offered on computer.

If any or all of these reasons apply to you, and you feel that they outweigh the reasons stated above for not taking the CAT, then go ahead and take it.

## Grin and Bear It

If you must take the CAT, here are some handy strategies to keep in mind:

1. If you get lots of mileage from the strategy of eliminating answer choices based on difficulty level, you can apply it on the CAT, though in a different and limited way. It won't be spelled out for you like on the paper-and-pencil test, but as you progress through the questions, you should have a good idea of how you're doing. If you've practiced a lot on real questions, it's fairly easy to maintain a pretty clear sense of the difficulty level of your questions and to eliminate answer choices accordingly. For instance, if you're confident that you've been answering most of the questions correctly, then you should be seeing harder and harder questions—if that seems to be the case, you can safely eliminate answer choices that look too obvious or easy for a difficult question.

2. If crossing off answer choices on paper tests really helps to clarify your thinking and to use a process of elimination, you may want to consider making a grid on your scratch paper before you begin the CAT. Use it to mark off answer choices that you have eliminated, as shown below. That way you can tell at a glance which answer choices are still running. If process of elimination works well for you, it will be worth the 10 seconds it takes to scratch out a simple grid, like this one:

| A | × | × |   | × |   | × |   |   | × | × |   | × |   |
|---|---|---|---|---|---|---|---|---|---|---|---|---|---|
| B |   | × | × | × |   |   | × | × | × | × |   | × |   |
| C |   |   |   |   | × |   |   |   | × |   |   |   | × |
| D | × |   | × |   | × |   |   | × |   | × |   | × |   |
| E | × | × |   | × |   |   | × |   |   | × |   |   |   |

3. The timer in the corner can work to your advantage, but if you find yourself looking at it so frequently that it becomes a distraction, you should turn it off for 10 or 15 minutes and try to re-focus your attention on the test, even if you lose track of time somewhat. The CAT rewards focus and accuracy much more than it does speed.

## SUBJECT TESTS

Subject Tests are designed to test the fundamental knowledge most important for successful graduate study in a particular subject area. In order to do well on a Subject Test, you basically need to have an extensive background in the particular subject area. In this section, we'll answer the most common questions about Subject Tests.

### Do I Have To Take A Subject Test?
Not every graduate school or program requires Subject Tests, so check admissions requirements at the schools that you're interested in early.

### What's The Purpose Of Subject Tests?
Unlike the GRE General Test, which assesses skills that have been developed over a long period of time and are not related to a particular subject area, Subject Tests assess knowledge of a particular field of study. They enable admissions officers to compare students from different colleges with different standards and curricula.

> **SUBJECT TEST BASICS**
>
> Subject Tests are designed to test your knowledge in a particular field of study. Find out whether the programs that you're thinking about applying to require any Subject Tests.

## What Are Subject Tests Like?

Except for the Revised Music test, Subject Tests consist exclusively of multiple choice questions that are designed to assess knowledge of the areas of the subject that are included in the typical under-graduate curriculum.

On Subject Tests, you'll earn 1 point for each multiple choice question that you answer correctly but lose 1/4 point for each incorrectly answered question. Unanswered questions aren't counted in the scoring. Your raw score is the number of correctly answered questions minus 1/4 of the incorrectly answered questions. This raw score is then converted into a scaled score, which can range from 200 to 900. The range varies from test to test.

Some Subject Tests also contain subtests, which provide more specific information about your strengths and weaknesses. The same questions that contribute to your subtest scores also contribute to your overall score. Subtest scores, which range from 20 to 99, are reported along with the overall score. For further information on scoring, you should consult the relevant Subject Test Descriptive Booklet, available from ETS.

## Are There Any Different Test-Taking Strategies for the Subject Tests?

Because the multiple choice questions on Subject tests have a wrong-answer penalty of 1/4 point, you should adopt a different test-taking strategy for your Subject Test than the one you're going to use for the GRE General Test. There's no penalty for guessing incorrectly on the GRE General Test, so you should guess whenever you can't answer a question. On the Subject Tests, however, you shouldn't attempt to fill in an answer for every question on the test because there's no penalty for not answering a question. You should guess only if you can eliminate one or more of the answer choices.

## When Should I Take the Subject Test?

Subject tests are offered on the same days as the paper-and-pencil versions of the GRE General Test, but they are not offered in June. On these days, the General Test is given in the morning, and the Subject tests are given in the afternoon. Although you can take the General and Subject tests on the same day, we don't recommend it. Your testing day will be six hours or more, and by the afternoon you'll may find your concentration waning, which will probably result in a lower score on the Subject Test.

An alternative is to take the Computer-Adaptive Test (CAT) early in the same week that you are taking the Subject Test. Some Subject Tests may also be available through the computer-based testing program. For more information, call 1 (800) 808-0900.

### A DIFFERENT CUP OF TEA

Unlike the GRE General Test, GRE Subjects Tests penalize wrong answers. You should guess on a question only if you can eliminate one or more of the answer choices.

**How Many Subject Tests Are There and What Fields Do They Cover?**

There are 16 Subject Tests. Here's a list of them, along with a brief description:

BIOCHEMISTRY, CELL, AND MOLECULAR BIOLOGY. This test consists of 180 questions and is divided among three subscore areas: biochemistry, cell biology, and molecular biology and genetics.

BIOLOGY. This test consists of 205 questions divided among three subscore areas: cellular and molecular biology, organismal biology, and ecology and evolution ecology.

CHEMISTRY. This test consists of 150 questions. There are no subscores, and the questions cover the following topics: analytical chemistry, inorganic chemistry, organic chemistry, and physical chemistry.

COMPUTER SCIENCE. This test consists of 80 questions. There are no subscores, and the questions cover the following topics: software systems and methodology, computer organization and architecture, theory, mathematical background, and other, more advanced topics, such as modeling, simulation, and artificial intelligence.

ECONOMICS. This test consists of 130 questions. A majority of the questions cover micro- and macroeconomics, but about seven percent of the questions cover basic statistics. The rest of the test covers other areas of economics.

REVISED EDUCATION. This test consists of 200 questions drawn from three broad categories: learning and development, curriculum and instruction, and contexts of education. There are no sub-scores.

ENGINEERING. This test consists of 140 questions divided among two subscore areas: engineering and mathematics. The engineering subscore is taken from the 105 questions based on material learned by most engineers during their first two years of college, including basic physics and chemistry. The mathematics subscores is taken from the 35 questions based on the mathematical facts needed to work efficiently in engineering and on the application of calculus.

GEOLOGY. This test consists of 195 questions divided among three sub-score areas. The first area includes questions dealing with stratigraphy, sedimentology, paleontology, geomorphology, hydrology, and oceanography. The second area includes questions dealing with structural field relations, mechanics, and processes; tectonics, isostasy, gravity, and magnetism; earthquakes and seismology; heat and electrical properties; and planetology. The third area includes questions dealing with mineralogy, petrology, geochemistry, isotope geology, and economic mineral deposits and resources.

HISTORY. This test consists of 195 questions divided among two subscore areas: European history and U.S. history. There are also a small number of questions that deal with African, Asian, or Latin American history. These questions contribute to the overall score but not to the subscores.

LITERATURE IN ENGLISH. This test consists of 230 questions on literature in the English language. There are two basic types of questions: Factual questions that test the student's knowledge of writers typically covered in the undergraduate curriculum, and interpretive questions test the student's ability to read various types of literature critically.

MATHEMATICS. This test consists of 66 questions on the content of various undergraduate courses in mathematics. Most of the test assesses the student's knowledge of calculus, abstract algebra, linear algebra, and real analysis. About a quarter of the test, however, requires knowledge in other areas of math.

REVISED MUSIC. This test consists of 101 multiple-choice questions and 23 free-response questions. The test has two sections. In Section I, the multiple choice questions test knowledge of the history and theory of music from the middle ages to the modern era. The free response questions in this section cover the fundamentals of music theory. In Section II, the multiple choice questions require the student to analyze taped excerpts of music. The free-response questions consist of dictation, part-writing exercises, and counterpoint exercises. This test has three subscores—history and theory, listening and literature, and aural skills. This test is only offered in October and December.

PHYSICS. This test consists of 100 questions covering mostly material covered in the first three years of undergraduate physics. Topics include classical mechanics, electromagnetism, atomic physics, optics and wave phenomena, quantum mechanics, thermodynamics and statistical mechanics, special relativity, and laboratory methods. About nine percent of the test covers advanced topics, such as nuclear and particle physics, condensed matter physics, and astrophysics.

POLITICAL SCIENCE. This test consists of 170 questions that are drawn from the following areas: U. S. government, comparative political systems, political theory, international relations, and methodology.

PSYCHOLOGY: This test consists of 220 questions drawn from courses most commonly included in the undergraduate curriculum. Questions fall into three categories. The experimental or natural science oriented category includes questions in learning, cognitive psychology, sensation and perception, ethology and comparative psychology, and physiological psychology. The social or social science oriented category includes questions in abnormal psychology, developmental psychology, social psychology, and personality. Finally, the general category includes questions in the history of psychology, tests and measurements, research design and statistics, and applied psychology. The psychology test contains two subscores—an experimental psychology subscore consisting of questions from category one and a social psychology subscore consisting of questions from category two.

SOCIOLOGY: This test consists of 190 questions drawn from the major subfields in the undergraduate sociology curriculum: general theory, methodology and statistics, criminology and deviance, demography, family and gender roles, organizations, race and ethnic relations, social change, social institutions, social psychology, social stratification, and urban, rural, and community sociology.

For more information, you should consult the relevant Subject Test Descriptive Booklet, available from ETS.

## WHAT'S NEXT?

Before setting you off on the Practice Test, let's conclude with a recap of some of the most important principles and strategies for success on the GRE:

- In many sections of the test, the test questions are presented in order of difficulty. Because you get the same amount of points for getting an easy or a hard question correct, try to answer the questions that are easiest for you first.

- There is no penalty for wrong answers on the GRE. Always guess if you can't answer a question or don't get to it. Never, ever, leave a question blank.

- Never spend an excessive amount of time on any one question. If you're stumped, skip it and return to it when you've finished the other questions in the section.

Take these points—and all of the others that you've learned in this section—as you proceed now to the Practice Test. Good luck!

# THE PRACTICE TEST

Start with number 1 for each new section. If a section has fewer questions than answer spaces, leave the extra spaces blank.

**SECTION 1**

| | | | |
|---|---|---|---|
| 1 Ⓐ Ⓑ Ⓒ Ⓓ Ⓔ | 11 Ⓐ Ⓑ Ⓒ Ⓓ Ⓔ | 21 Ⓐ Ⓑ Ⓒ Ⓓ Ⓔ | 31 Ⓐ Ⓑ Ⓒ Ⓓ Ⓔ |
| 2 Ⓐ Ⓑ Ⓒ Ⓓ Ⓔ | 12 Ⓐ Ⓑ Ⓒ Ⓓ Ⓔ | 22 Ⓐ Ⓑ Ⓒ Ⓓ Ⓔ | 32 Ⓐ Ⓑ Ⓒ Ⓓ Ⓔ |
| 3 Ⓐ Ⓑ Ⓒ Ⓓ Ⓔ | 13 Ⓐ Ⓑ Ⓒ Ⓓ Ⓔ | 23 Ⓐ Ⓑ Ⓒ Ⓓ Ⓔ | 33 Ⓐ Ⓑ Ⓒ Ⓓ Ⓔ |
| 4 Ⓐ Ⓑ Ⓒ Ⓓ Ⓔ | 14 Ⓐ Ⓑ Ⓒ Ⓓ Ⓔ | 24 Ⓐ Ⓑ Ⓒ Ⓓ Ⓔ | 34 Ⓐ Ⓑ Ⓒ Ⓓ Ⓔ |
| 5 Ⓐ Ⓑ Ⓒ Ⓓ Ⓔ | 15 Ⓐ Ⓑ Ⓒ Ⓓ Ⓔ | 25 Ⓐ Ⓑ Ⓒ Ⓓ Ⓔ | 35 Ⓐ Ⓑ Ⓒ Ⓓ Ⓔ |
| 6 Ⓐ Ⓑ Ⓒ Ⓓ Ⓔ | 16 Ⓐ Ⓑ Ⓒ Ⓓ Ⓔ | 26 Ⓐ Ⓑ Ⓒ Ⓓ Ⓔ | 36 Ⓐ Ⓑ Ⓒ Ⓓ Ⓔ |
| 7 Ⓐ Ⓑ Ⓒ Ⓓ Ⓔ | 17 Ⓐ Ⓑ Ⓒ Ⓓ Ⓔ | 27 Ⓐ Ⓑ Ⓒ Ⓓ Ⓔ | 37 Ⓐ Ⓑ Ⓒ Ⓓ Ⓔ |
| 8 Ⓐ Ⓑ Ⓒ Ⓓ Ⓔ | 18 Ⓐ Ⓑ Ⓒ Ⓓ Ⓔ | 28 Ⓐ Ⓑ Ⓒ Ⓓ Ⓔ | 38 Ⓐ Ⓑ Ⓒ Ⓓ Ⓔ |
| 9 Ⓐ Ⓑ Ⓒ Ⓓ Ⓔ | 19 Ⓐ Ⓑ Ⓒ Ⓓ Ⓔ | 29 Ⓐ Ⓑ Ⓒ Ⓓ Ⓔ | 39 Ⓐ Ⓑ Ⓒ Ⓓ Ⓔ |
| 10 Ⓐ Ⓑ Ⓒ Ⓓ Ⓔ | 20 Ⓐ Ⓑ Ⓒ Ⓓ Ⓔ | 30 Ⓐ Ⓑ Ⓒ Ⓓ Ⓔ | 40 Ⓐ Ⓑ Ⓒ Ⓓ Ⓔ |

**SECTION 2**

| | | | |
|---|---|---|---|
| 1 Ⓐ Ⓑ Ⓒ Ⓓ Ⓔ | 11 Ⓐ Ⓑ Ⓒ Ⓓ Ⓔ | 21 Ⓐ Ⓑ Ⓒ Ⓓ Ⓔ | 31 Ⓐ Ⓑ Ⓒ Ⓓ Ⓔ |
| 2 Ⓐ Ⓑ Ⓒ Ⓓ Ⓔ | 12 Ⓐ Ⓑ Ⓒ Ⓓ Ⓔ | 22 Ⓐ Ⓑ Ⓒ Ⓓ Ⓔ | 32 Ⓐ Ⓑ Ⓒ Ⓓ Ⓔ |
| 3 Ⓐ Ⓑ Ⓒ Ⓓ Ⓔ | 13 Ⓐ Ⓑ Ⓒ Ⓓ Ⓔ | 23 Ⓐ Ⓑ Ⓒ Ⓓ Ⓔ | 33 Ⓐ Ⓑ Ⓒ Ⓓ Ⓔ |
| 4 Ⓐ Ⓑ Ⓒ Ⓓ Ⓔ | 14 Ⓐ Ⓑ Ⓒ Ⓓ Ⓔ | 24 Ⓐ Ⓑ Ⓒ Ⓓ Ⓔ | 34 Ⓐ Ⓑ Ⓒ Ⓓ Ⓔ |
| 5 Ⓐ Ⓑ Ⓒ Ⓓ Ⓔ | 15 Ⓐ Ⓑ Ⓒ Ⓓ Ⓔ | 25 Ⓐ Ⓑ Ⓒ Ⓓ Ⓔ | 35 Ⓐ Ⓑ Ⓒ Ⓓ Ⓔ |
| 6 Ⓐ Ⓑ Ⓒ Ⓓ Ⓔ | 16 Ⓐ Ⓑ Ⓒ Ⓓ Ⓔ | 26 Ⓐ Ⓑ Ⓒ Ⓓ Ⓔ | 36 Ⓐ Ⓑ Ⓒ Ⓓ Ⓔ |
| 7 Ⓐ Ⓑ Ⓒ Ⓓ Ⓔ | 17 Ⓐ Ⓑ Ⓒ Ⓓ Ⓔ | 27 Ⓐ Ⓑ Ⓒ Ⓓ Ⓔ | 37 Ⓐ Ⓑ Ⓒ Ⓓ Ⓔ |
| 8 Ⓐ Ⓑ Ⓒ Ⓓ Ⓔ | 18 Ⓐ Ⓑ Ⓒ Ⓓ Ⓔ | 28 Ⓐ Ⓑ Ⓒ Ⓓ Ⓔ | 38 Ⓐ Ⓑ Ⓒ Ⓓ Ⓔ |
| 9 Ⓐ Ⓑ Ⓒ Ⓓ Ⓔ | 19 Ⓐ Ⓑ Ⓒ Ⓓ Ⓔ | 29 Ⓐ Ⓑ Ⓒ Ⓓ Ⓔ | 39 Ⓐ Ⓑ Ⓒ Ⓓ Ⓔ |
| 10 Ⓐ Ⓑ Ⓒ Ⓓ Ⓔ | 20 Ⓐ Ⓑ Ⓒ Ⓓ Ⓔ | 30 Ⓐ Ⓑ Ⓒ Ⓓ Ⓔ | 40 Ⓐ Ⓑ Ⓒ Ⓓ Ⓔ |

**SECTION 3**

| | | | |
|---|---|---|---|
| 1 Ⓐ Ⓑ Ⓒ Ⓓ Ⓔ | 11 Ⓐ Ⓑ Ⓒ Ⓓ Ⓔ | 21 Ⓐ Ⓑ Ⓒ Ⓓ Ⓔ | 31 Ⓐ Ⓑ Ⓒ Ⓓ Ⓔ |
| 2 Ⓐ Ⓑ Ⓒ Ⓓ Ⓔ | 12 Ⓐ Ⓑ Ⓒ Ⓓ Ⓔ | 22 Ⓐ Ⓑ Ⓒ Ⓓ Ⓔ | 32 Ⓐ Ⓑ Ⓒ Ⓓ Ⓔ |
| 3 Ⓐ Ⓑ Ⓒ Ⓓ Ⓔ | 13 Ⓐ Ⓑ Ⓒ Ⓓ Ⓔ | 23 Ⓐ Ⓑ Ⓒ Ⓓ Ⓔ | 33 Ⓐ Ⓑ Ⓒ Ⓓ Ⓔ |
| 4 Ⓐ Ⓑ Ⓒ Ⓓ Ⓔ | 14 Ⓐ Ⓑ Ⓒ Ⓓ Ⓔ | 24 Ⓐ Ⓑ Ⓒ Ⓓ Ⓔ | 34 Ⓐ Ⓑ Ⓒ Ⓓ Ⓔ |
| 5 Ⓐ Ⓑ Ⓒ Ⓓ Ⓔ | 15 Ⓐ Ⓑ Ⓒ Ⓓ Ⓔ | 25 Ⓐ Ⓑ Ⓒ Ⓓ Ⓔ | 35 Ⓐ Ⓑ Ⓒ Ⓓ Ⓔ |
| 6 Ⓐ Ⓑ Ⓒ Ⓓ Ⓔ | 16 Ⓐ Ⓑ Ⓒ Ⓓ Ⓔ | 26 Ⓐ Ⓑ Ⓒ Ⓓ Ⓔ | 36 Ⓐ Ⓑ Ⓒ Ⓓ Ⓔ |
| 7 Ⓐ Ⓑ Ⓒ Ⓓ Ⓔ | 17 Ⓐ Ⓑ Ⓒ Ⓓ Ⓔ | 27 Ⓐ Ⓑ Ⓒ Ⓓ Ⓔ | 37 Ⓐ Ⓑ Ⓒ Ⓓ Ⓔ |
| 8 Ⓐ Ⓑ Ⓒ Ⓓ Ⓔ | 18 Ⓐ Ⓑ Ⓒ Ⓓ Ⓔ | 28 Ⓐ Ⓑ Ⓒ Ⓓ Ⓔ | 38 Ⓐ Ⓑ Ⓒ Ⓓ Ⓔ |
| 9 Ⓐ Ⓑ Ⓒ Ⓓ Ⓔ | 19 Ⓐ Ⓑ Ⓒ Ⓓ Ⓔ | 29 Ⓐ Ⓑ Ⓒ Ⓓ Ⓔ | 39 Ⓐ Ⓑ Ⓒ Ⓓ Ⓔ |
| 10 Ⓐ Ⓑ Ⓒ Ⓓ Ⓔ | 20 Ⓐ Ⓑ Ⓒ Ⓓ Ⓔ | 30 Ⓐ Ⓑ Ⓒ Ⓓ Ⓔ | 40 Ⓐ Ⓑ Ⓒ Ⓓ Ⓔ |

**SECTION 4**

| | | | |
|---|---|---|---|
| 1 Ⓐ Ⓑ Ⓒ Ⓓ Ⓔ | 11 Ⓐ Ⓑ Ⓒ Ⓓ Ⓔ | 21 Ⓐ Ⓑ Ⓒ Ⓓ Ⓔ | 31 Ⓐ Ⓑ Ⓒ Ⓓ Ⓔ |
| 2 Ⓐ Ⓑ Ⓒ Ⓓ Ⓔ | 12 Ⓐ Ⓑ Ⓒ Ⓓ Ⓔ | 22 Ⓐ Ⓑ Ⓒ Ⓓ Ⓔ | 32 Ⓐ Ⓑ Ⓒ Ⓓ Ⓔ |
| 3 Ⓐ Ⓑ Ⓒ Ⓓ Ⓔ | 13 Ⓐ Ⓑ Ⓒ Ⓓ Ⓔ | 23 Ⓐ Ⓑ Ⓒ Ⓓ Ⓔ | 33 Ⓐ Ⓑ Ⓒ Ⓓ Ⓔ |
| 4 Ⓐ Ⓑ Ⓒ Ⓓ Ⓔ | 14 Ⓐ Ⓑ Ⓒ Ⓓ Ⓔ | 24 Ⓐ Ⓑ Ⓒ Ⓓ Ⓔ | 34 Ⓐ Ⓑ Ⓒ Ⓓ Ⓔ |
| 5 Ⓐ Ⓑ Ⓒ Ⓓ Ⓔ | 15 Ⓐ Ⓑ Ⓒ Ⓓ Ⓔ | 25 Ⓐ Ⓑ Ⓒ Ⓓ Ⓔ | 35 Ⓐ Ⓑ Ⓒ Ⓓ Ⓔ |
| 6 Ⓐ Ⓑ Ⓒ Ⓓ Ⓔ | 16 Ⓐ Ⓑ Ⓒ Ⓓ Ⓔ | 26 Ⓐ Ⓑ Ⓒ Ⓓ Ⓔ | 36 Ⓐ Ⓑ Ⓒ Ⓓ Ⓔ |
| 7 Ⓐ Ⓑ Ⓒ Ⓓ Ⓔ | 17 Ⓐ Ⓑ Ⓒ Ⓓ Ⓔ | 27 Ⓐ Ⓑ Ⓒ Ⓓ Ⓔ | 37 Ⓐ Ⓑ Ⓒ Ⓓ Ⓔ |
| 8 Ⓐ Ⓑ Ⓒ Ⓓ Ⓔ | 18 Ⓐ Ⓑ Ⓒ Ⓓ Ⓔ | 28 Ⓐ Ⓑ Ⓒ Ⓓ Ⓔ | 38 Ⓐ Ⓑ Ⓒ Ⓓ Ⓔ |
| 9 Ⓐ Ⓑ Ⓒ Ⓓ Ⓔ | 19 Ⓐ Ⓑ Ⓒ Ⓓ Ⓔ | 29 Ⓐ Ⓑ Ⓒ Ⓓ Ⓔ | 39 Ⓐ Ⓑ Ⓒ Ⓓ Ⓔ |
| 10 Ⓐ Ⓑ Ⓒ Ⓓ Ⓔ | 20 Ⓐ Ⓑ Ⓒ Ⓓ Ⓔ | 30 Ⓐ Ⓑ Ⓒ Ⓓ Ⓔ | 40 Ⓐ Ⓑ Ⓒ Ⓓ Ⓔ |

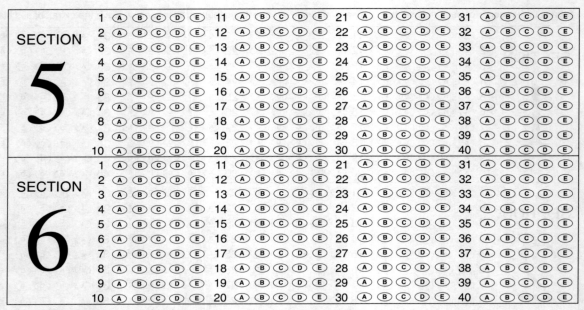

*Remove this scoresheet and use it to complete the practice test.*

# INSTRUCTIONS
# FOR TAKING
# THE PRACTICE TEST

Before taking this practice test, find a quiet place where you can work uninterrupted for 2-½ hours or so. Make sure you have a comfortable desk and several #2 pencils.

This practice test includes six scored multiple-choice sections. Keep in mind that on the actual GRE, there will be an additional section—the experimental section—which will not contribute to your score.

Use the answer grid on the previous page to record your answers.

Once you start the practice test, don't stop until you've gone through all six sections. Remember, you can review any questions within a section, but you may not go back or forward a section.

You'll find the answer key and score converter following the test.

Good luck.

Directions: Each group of questions is based on a passage or a set of conditions. You may wish to draw a diagram to answer some of the questions. Choose the best answer for each question.

Questions 1–3

A spice farmer must harvest exactly five spices grown on her farm. The spices must be harvested consecutively, the harvest of one being completed before the harvest of the next begins. The five spices to be harvested are allspice, cloves, nutmeg, sage, and thyme.

Nutmeg must be harvested before thyme.
Cloves must be harvested immediately after allspice.
Sage must not be harvested first.

1. Which of the following is an acceptable order for the harvesting of the five spices?

   (A) nutmeg, sage, allspice, cloves, thyme
   (B) sage, nutmeg, thyme, allspice, cloves
   (C) allspice, sage, thyme, cloves, nutmeg
   (D) cloves, nutmeg, allspice, sage, thyme
   (E) allspice, cloves, thyme, sage, nutmeg

2. If nutmeg is the fourth spice harvested, which of the following must be false?

   (A) Allspice is the first spice harvested.
   (B) Sage is harvested immediately after cloves.
   (C) Exactly one crop is harvested between sage and thyme.
   (D) Nutmeg is harvested immediately after cloves.
   (E) Thyme is the last spice harvested.

3. If sage is the second spice harvested, allspice must be which of the following?

   (A) the first or the third spice harvested
   (B) the first or the fourth spice harvested
   (C) the third or the fourth spice harvested
   (D) the third or the fifth spice harvested
   (E) the fourth or the fifth spice harvested

4. If a judge is appointed for life, she will make courtroom decisions that reflect the accumulated wisdom inherent in this country's judicial history, relying upon the law and reason rather than upon trends in political thinking. If, on the other hand, the judge is appointed or elected for short terms in office, her decisions will be heavily influenced by the prevailing political climate. In sum, the outcome of many court cases will be determined by the method by which the presiding judge has been installed in her post.
Which one of the following, if true, does NOT support the argument in the passage above?

   (A) Surveys indicate that judges enjoy their work and want to remain in office as long as possible.
   (B) Judges appointed for life are just as informed about political matters as are judges who are elected or appointed for short terms.
   (C) The rulings of judges who must run for re-election are generally approved of by the voters who live in their elective districts.
   (D) Most judges appointed for life hand down identical rulings on similar cases throughout their long careers.
   (E) Only judges who are elected or appointed for short terms of office employ pollsters to read the mood of the electorate.

GO ON TO THE NEXT PAGE.

5. There are those who claim that reductions in the spending on and deployment of weapons systems would result in a so-called "climate of peace," thereby diminishing the likelihood of armed conflict. The facts show otherwise. These self-proclaimed pacifists are either the victims or the propagators of a false argument.

Which of the following is an assumption underlying the conclusion of the passage above?

(A) Military actions involving our forces can be instigated by any number of different factors.
(B) Our build-up of weapons systems and combat personnel has prevented our adversaries from increasing their own spending on defense.
(C) The increased defense spending of the past ten years has lessened the need for significant military expenditure in future decades.
(D) At the present time, state-of-the-art weapons systems and the augmentation of combat personnel are equally important to a nation's defense.
(E) An established correlation between greater spending on weapons systems and a decreased incidence of conflict will persist.

6. Should present trends continue, within five years it will be cheaper for audio enthusiasts to build their stereo systems around sets of separate, high quality tuners and amplifiers, rather than around integrated tuners and amplifiers, known as receivers. While receivers have been considered the necessary compromise for those with budget restrictions, recent trends in retail pricing seem destined to change that perception. The average retail price of a high quality tuner has declined at a rate of 20 percent each of the last two years, and the average retail price of a high quality amplifier has declined at the rate of 35 percent for each of those years. At the same time, the average retail price of integrated receivers has declined only 12 percent.

In evaluating the claim made in the passage above, information about which of the following would be most useful?

(A) The average life expectancy of stereo tuners as compared to the average life expectancy of stereo amplifiers
(B) The number of integrated receivers sold each year and the number of sets of separate tuners and amplifiers sold each year
(C) The present average retail price of an integrated receiver and the present average retail price of a tuner and amplifier set
(D) The number of separate tuner and amplifier sets expected to be purchased over the next five years and the number of integrated receivers expected to be purchased over the next five years
(E) The percentage of audio enthusiasts who prefer separate tuner and amplifier sets to integrated receivers

GO ON TO THE NEXT PAGE.

T-7

## Questions 7–10

An editor must choose five articles to be published in the upcoming issue of an arts review. The only articles available for publication are theater articles F, G, H, and J, and dance articles K, L, M, and O.

At least three of the five published articles must be dance articles.

If J is chosen, then M cannot be.

If F is chosen, then J must also be chosen.

7. If M is not chosen for the issue, which of the following must be chosen?
   (A) F
   (B) G
   (C) H
   (D) J
   (E) K

8. How many acceptable groupings of articles include J?
   (A) one
   (B) two
   (C) three
   (D) four
   (E) five

9. The choice of which article makes only one group of articles acceptable?
   (A) F
   (B) G
   (C) J
   (D) L
   (E) M

10. If G is chosen for the issue, which of the following must be true?

    (A) J is not chosen.
    (B) Exactly three dance articles are chosen.
    (C) H is not chosen.
    (D) All four of the dance articles are chosen.
    (E) F is not chosen.

GO ON TO THE NEXT PAGE.

Questions 11-14

An obedience school is experimenting with a new training system. To test the system, three trainers (Luis, Molly, and Oprah) and three dogs (Lassie, Mugs, and Onyx) are assigned to three different rooms, one trainer and one dog per room. The initial assignment is as follows:

> Room 1: Luis and Lassie
> Room 2: Molly and Mugs
> Room 3: Oprah and Onyx

The participants have learned five different commands, each of which they will execute as soon as the command is given.

> Command W requires the trainer in Room 1 to move to Room 2, the trainer in Room 2 to move to Room 3, and the trainer in Room 3 to move to Room 1.
> Command X requires the dogs in Rooms 1 and 2 to change places.
> Command Y requires the dogs in Rooms 2 and 3 to change places.
> Command Z requires the dogs in Rooms 3 and 1 to change places.
> Command A requires each of the dogs to go to the room containing the trainer it was matched with in the initial assignment.

11. If the participants in the initial assignment are given exactly one command, Command W, which of the following will be true in the resulting arrangement?

    (A) Oprah and Mugs will be in the same room.
    (B) Molly will be in Room 3.
    (C) Molly and Lassie will be in the same room.
    (D) Luis will be in Room 3.
    (E) Luis and Onyx will be in the same room.

12. Which of the following commands or series of commands will yield a final arrangement in which Onyx is in Room 2?

    (A) One call of W
    (B) Two calls of X
    (C) Two calls of W followed by one call of A
    (D) Two calls of W followed by one call of Z
    (E) Two calls of X followed by one call of Z

13. Which of the following sequences of commands will yield a final arrangement in which Oprah and Lassie are in Room 2?

    (A) X, Y, W
    (B) X, W, W
    (C) Z, W, A
    (D) X, Y, A, W
    (E) Z, W, W, X

14. Which of the following sequences of commands could result in a final arrangement in which Molly and Onyx are in Room 1, Oprah and Mugs are in Room 2, and Luis and Lassie are in Room 3?

    (A) Z, W, X
    (B) W, Y, Z
    (C) W, A, Y, W
    (D) W, Z, W, X
    (E) X, Z, W, W

GO ON TO THE NEXT PAGE.

Questions 15-18

There are eight apartments in a two-story building, four on each floor. The top floor is called Level A, the bottom floor is Level B. The rooms on each level are numbered 1 through 4 in order from one end of the building to the other, such that the apartments on Level A are directly above the apartments with the same numbers on Level B. Exactly seven people–P, Q, R, S, T, V, and W–live in the building, one to an apartment. One of the apartments is empty.

W's apartment is directly above S's apartment.

S and Q live on different levels.

P's apartment is adjacent to T's apartment on the same level.

T's apartment is directly between two other apartments on the same level.

W's apartment is adjacent to the empty apartment on the same level.

15. Which of the following must be on Level B?

(A)   P's apartment
(B)   Q's apartment
(C)   R's apartment
(D)   V's apartment
(E)   the empty apartment

16. If W lives in Apartment 2 on Level A, which of the following must be true?

(A)   V lives in Apartment 1 on Level B.
(B)   The empty apartment is Apartment 3 on Level A.
(C)   R's apartment is on Level A.
(D)   P lives in Apartment 4 on Level A.
(E)   T lives in Apartment 3 on Level B.

17. If R lives in Apartment 3 on Level A, directly above P's apartment, in which apartment must V live?

(A)   Apartment 1 on Level A
(B)   Apartment 4 on Level A
(C)   Apartment 1 on Level B
(D)   Apartment 2 on Level B
(E)   Apartment 4 on Level B

18. If Q lives in Apartment 2 on Level A, directly above T's apartment, which of the following could possibly be Apartment 1 on Level A?

(A)   P's apartment
(B)   S's apartment
(C)   V's apartment
(D)   W's apartment
(E)   the empty apartment

GO ON TO THE NEXT PAGE.

Questions 19-22

Exactly seven people are present in the game room of a club. Three of those present–F, G, and H–are senior club members, two–K and M–are junior club members, and two–P and R–are club applicants. They decide that two of those present will play backgammon, two will play chess, and three will play dominoes.

Each person present can play only one of the three games.
There must be a senior club member playing each game.
G cannot play the same game that R plays.
H and P must play the same game.
M cannot play dominoes.

19. Which of the following is an acceptable grouping of people playing backgammon, chess, and dominoes, respectively?

    (A)  G, K; H, P; F, M, R
    (B)  G, M; K, R; F, H, P
    (C)  F, R; G, P; H, K, M
    (D)  H, P; G, M; F, K, R
    (E)  F, M; H, P; G, K, R

20. If K and R play the same game, which of the following must be true?

    (A)  H plays dominoes.
    (B)  P plays chess.
    (C)  G plays backgammon.
    (D)  F plays dominoes.
    (E)  M plays backgammon.

21. If R plays backgammon, how many different groupings of people and games are possible?

    (A)  one
    (B)  two
    (C)  three
    (D)  four
    (E)  six

22. Which of the following pairs CANNOT play the same game?

    (A)  H and R
    (B)  K and M
    (C)  F and M
    (D)  G and M
    (E)  P and R

23. European nations are starting to decrease the percentage of their foreign aid that is "tied"–that is, given only on the condition that it be spent to obtain goods and materials produced by the country from which the aid originates. By doing so, European nations hope to avoid the ethical criticism that has been recently leveled at some foreign aid donors, notably Japan.

Which of the following can most reasonably be inferred from the passage?

    (A)  Many non-European nations give foreign aid solely for the purpose of benefiting their domestic economies.
    (B)  Only ethical considerations, and not those of self-interest, should be considered when foreign aid decisions are made.
    (C)  Many of the problems faced by underdeveloped countries could be eliminated if a smaller percentage of the foreign aid they obtain were "tied" to specific purchases and uses.
    (D)  Much of Japan's foreign aid returns to Japan in the form of purchase orders for Japanese products and equipment.
    (E)  Non-European nations are unwilling to offer foreign aid that is not "tied" to the purchase of their own manufactures.

GO ON TO THE NEXT PAGE.

24. Our environment can stand only so much more "progress." We must take a few steps backward and accept some inconvenience if we want to secure the health and well-being of our planet. This is not merely a matter of using manual mowers instead of power mowers, or foregoing a few outdoor barbecues. Something must be done about the 51.1 percent of total ozone that is contributed by vehicles and fuel. The percentage must be cut regardless of the cost or inconvenience. Such concerns are irrelevant here; what needs to be done must be done.

The author of the passage above makes which of the following arguments?

(A) People will have to go back to living as they did a century ago if they want to save the environment.
(B) If people would be willing to drive their cars less, pollution would be drastically reduced.
(C) People can continue to use power lawn mowers and have barbecues as long as industry cuts down on its use of fuel.
(D) People must accept drastic and costly measures as they are necessary to save the environment.
(E) Lack of concern for the environment leads people to continue their overuse of the automobile.

25. If you stop in the movie studio's commissary during lunch time, you may be able to meet the actors. Although the actors always eat elsewhere on workdays when the commissary does not serve fish, they always eat there on workdays when the commissary does serve fish. If all the statements above are true, and it is true that the actors are eating in the commissary, which of the following must also be true?

(A) It is not a workday, or the commissary is serving fish, or both.
(B) It is a workday, or the commissary is serving fish, or both.
(C) It is not a workday and the commissary is not serving fish.
(D) It is not a workday and the commissary is serving fish.
(E) It is a workday and the commissary is serving fish.

# STOP

IF YOU FINISH BEFORE TIME IS CALLED, YOU MAY CHECK YOUR WORK ON THIS SECTION ONLY.
DO NOT TURN TO ANY OTHER SECTION IN THE TEST.

NO TEST MATERIAL ON THIS PAGE.

Time–30 minutes
38 Questions

Directions: Each sentence below has one or two blanks, each blank indicating that something has been omitted. Beneath the sentence are five lettered words or sets of words. Choose the word or set of words for each blank that best fits the meaning of the sentence as a whole.

1. The fundamental_____between dogs and cats is for the most part a myth; members of these species often coexist_____.

   (A) antipathy .. amiably
   (B) disharmony .. uneasily
   (C) compatibility .. together
   (D) relationship .. peacefully
   (E) difference .. placidly

2. His desire to state his case completely was certainly reasonable; however, his lengthy technical explanations were monotonous and tended to_____rather than _____the jury.

   (A) enlighten .. inform
   (B) interest .. persuade
   (C) provoke .. influence
   (D) allay .. pacify
   (E) bore .. convince

3. In some countries, government restrictions are so _____that businesses operate with nearly complete impunity.

   (A) traditional
   (B) judicious
   (C) ambiguous
   (D) exacting
   (E) lax

4. The recent Oxford edition of the works of Shakespeare is_____because it not only departs frequently from the readings of most other modern editions, but also challenges many of the basic_____of textual criticism.

   (A) controversial .. conventions
   (B) typical .. innovations
   (C) inadequate .. norms
   (D) curious .. projects
   (E) pretentious .. explanations

5. The early form of writing known as Linear B was _____in 1952, but no one has yet succeeded in the_____of the still more ancient Linear A.

   (A) superseded .. explanation
   (B) encoded .. transcription
   (C) obliterated .. analysis
   (D) deciphered .. interpretation
   (E) discovered .. obfuscation

6. Considering everything she had been through, her reaction was quite normal and even_____: I was therefore surprised at the number of_____comments and raised eyebrows that her response elicited.

   (A) commendable .. complimentary
   (B) odious .. insulting
   (C) apologetic .. conciliatory
   (D) commonplace .. typical
   (E) laudable .. derogatory

7. The purpose of the proposed insurance policy is to_____the burden of medical costs, thereby removing what is for many people a major_____medical care.

   (A) augment .. problem with
   (B) eliminate .. perquisite of
   (C) ameliorate .. study of
   (D) assuage .. impediment to
   (E) clarify .. explanation for

GO ON TO THE NEXT PAGE.

Directions: In each of the following questions, a related pair of words or phrases is followed by five lettered pairs of words or phrases. Select the lettered pair that best expresses a relationship similar to that expressed in the original pair.

8. NOVEL : BOOK ::

   (A) epic : poem
   (B) house : library
   (C) tale : fable
   (D) number : page
   (E) play : theater

9. HUNGRY : RAVENOUS ::

   (A) thirsty : desirous
   (B) large : titanic
   (C) famous : eminent
   (D) dizzy : disoriented
   (E) obese : gluttonous

10. BOUQUET : FLOWER ::

   (A) humidor : tobacco
   (B) mosaic : tile
   (C) tapestry : color
   (D) pile : block
   (E) sacristy : vestment

11. REALIST : QUIXOTIC ::

   (A) scholar : pedantic
   (B) fool : idiotic
   (C) idler : lethargic
   (D) tormentor : sympathetic
   (E) diner : dyspeptic

12. SHARD : GLASS ::

   (A) grain : sand
   (B) morsel : meal
   (C) strand : rope
   (D) scrap : quilt
   (E) splinter : wood

13. FILTER : IMPURITY ::

   (A) expurgate : obscenity
   (B) whitewash : infraction
   (C) testify : perjury
   (D) perform : penance
   (E) vacuum : carpet

14. PARAPHRASE : VERBATIM ::

   (A) approximation : precise
   (B) description : vivid
   (C) quotation : apt
   (D) interpretation : valid
   (E) significance : uncertain

15. ONCOLOGY : TUMOR ::

   (A) chronology : time
   (B) theology : tenet
   (C) oral : sound
   (D) philology : religion
   (E) taxonomy : classification

16. INTRANSIGENT : FLEXIBILITY ::

   (A) transient : mobility
   (B) disinterested : partisanship
   (C) dissimilar : variation
   (D) progressive : transition
   (E) ineluctable : modality

GO ON TO THE NEXT PAGE.

Directions: Each passage in this group is followed by several questions. After reading the passage, choose the best response to each question. Your replies are to be based on what is stated or implied in the passage.

There can be nothing simpler than an elementary particle: it is an indivisible shard of matter, without internal structure and without detectable shape or size. One might expect commensurate simplicity in the
(5) theories that describe such particles and the forces through which they interact; at the least, one might expect the structure of the world to be explained with a minimum number of particles and forces. Judged by this criterion of parsimony, a description of nature that
(10) has evolved in the past several years can be accounted a reasonable success. Matter is built out of just two classes of elementary particles: the leptons, such as the electron, and the quarks, which are constituents of the proton, the neutron and many related particles. Four
(15) basic forces act between the elementary particles. Gravitation and electromagnetism have long been familiar in the macroscopic world; the weak force and the strong force are observed only in subnuclear events. In principle this complement of particles and forces could
(20) account for the entire observed hierarchy of material structure, from the nuclei of atoms to stars and galaxies.

An understanding of nature at this level of detail is a remarkable achievement; nevertheless, it is possible to imagine what a still simpler theory might be like. The
(25) existence of two disparate classes of elementary particles is not fully satisfying; ideally, one class would suffice. Similarly, the existence of four forces seems a needless complication; one force might explain all the interactions of elementary particles. An ambitious new
(30) theory now promises at least a partial unification along these lines. The theory does not embrace gravitation, which is by far the feeblest of the forces and may be fundamentally different from the others. If gravitation is excluded, however, the theory unifies all elementary
(35) particles and forces.

The first step in the construction of the unified theory was the demonstration that the weak, the strong, and the electromagnetic forces could all be described by theories of the same general kind. The
(40) three forces remained distinct, but they could be seen to operate through the same mechanism. In the course of this development a deep connection was discovered between the weak force and electromagnetism, a connection that hinted at a still grander synthesis. The
(45) new theory is the leading candidate for accomplishing the synthesis. It incorporates the leptons and the quarks into a single family and provides a means of transforming one kind of particle into the other. At the same time the weak, the strong, and the electro-magneticforces are
(50) understood as aspects of a single underlying force. With only one class of particles and one force (plus gravitation), the unified theory is a model of frugality.

17. All of the following are differences between the two theories described by the author EXCEPT

(A) the second theory is simpler than the first
(B) the first theory encompasses gravitation while the second does not
(C) the second theory includes only one class of elementary particles
(D) the first theory accounts for only part of the hierarchy of material structure
(E) the second theory unifies forces that the first theory regards as distinct

18. The primary purpose of the passage is to

(A) correct a misconception in a currently accepted theory of the nature of matter
(B) describe efforts to arrive at a simplified theory of elementary particles and forces
(C) predict the success of a new effort to unify gravitation with other basic forces
(D) explain why scientists prefer simpler explanations over more complex ones
(E) summarize what is known about the basic components of matter

19. According to the passage, which of the following are true of quarks?

I. They are the elementary building blocks for neutrons.
II. Scientists have described them as having no internal structure.
III. Some scientists group them with leptons in a single class of particles.

(A) I only
(B) III only
(C) I and II only
(D) II and III only
(E) I, II, and III

GO ON TO THE NEXT PAGE.

20. The author considers which of the following in judging the usefulness of a theory of elementary particles and forces?

    I.   The simplicity of the theory
   II.   The ability of the theory to account for the largest possible number of known phenomena
  III.   The possibility of proving or disproving the theory by experiment

  (A)  I only
  (B)  II only
  (C)  I and II only
  (D)  I and III only
  (E)  II and III only

21. It can be inferred that the author considers the failure to unify gravitation with other forces in the theory he describes to be

  (A)  a disqualifying defect
  (B)  an unjustified deviation
  (C)  a needless oversimplification
  (D)  an unfortunate oversight
  (E)  an unavoidable limitation

22. The author organizes the passage by

  (A)  enumerating distinctions among several different kinds of elementary particles
  (B)  stating a criterion for judging theories of nature, and using it to evaluate two theories
  (C)  explaining three methods of grouping particles and forces
  (D)  criticizing an inaccurate view of elemental nature and proposing an alternative approach
  (E)  outlining an assumption about scientific verification, then criticizing the assumption

23. It can be inferred that the author would be likely to consider a new theory of nature superior to present theories if it were to

  (A)  account for a larger number of macroscopic structures than present theories
  (B)  reduce the four basic forces to two more fundamental, incompatible forces
  (C)  propose a smaller number of fundamental particles and forces than current theories
  (D)  successfully account for the observable behavior of bodies due to gravity
  (E)  hypothesize that protons but not neutrons are formed by combinations of more fundamental particles

GO ON TO THE NEXT PAGE.

The majority of white abolitionists and the majority of suffragists worked hard to convince their compatriots that the changes they advocated were not revolutionary, that far from undermining the accepted
(5) distribution of power they would eliminate deviations from the democratic principle it was supposedly based on. Non-Garrisonian abolitionists repeatedly disavowed miscegenationist or revolutionary intentions. And as for the suffragists, despite the presence in the movement of
(10) socialists, and in the final years of a few blacks, immigrants and workers, the racism and nativism in the movement's thinking were not an aberration and did not conflict with the movement's objective of suffrage. Far from saying, as presentist historians do, that the white abolitionists and
(15) suffragists compromised the abiding principles of equality and the equal right of all to life, liberty and the pursuit of happiness, I suggest just the opposite: the non-Garrisonian majority of white abolitionists and the majority of suffragists showed what those principles
(20) meant in their respective generations, because they traced the farthest acceptable boundaries around them.

24. The author's main point is that

(A)   the actions of the abolitionist and suffragist movements compromised their stated principles
(B)   the underlying beliefs of abolitionists and suffragists were closer than is usually believed
(C)   abolitionists' and suffragists' thinking about equality was limited by the assumptions of their time
(D)   presentist historians have willfully misrepresented the ideology of abolitionists and suffragists
(E)   historians should impose their own value systems when evaluating events of the past

25. Which of the following does the author imply about the principle of equality?

I.    It does not have a fixed meaning.
II.   Suffragists applied it more consistently than abolitionists.
III.  Abolitionists and suffragists compromised it to gain their political objectives.

(A)   I only
(B)   II only
(C)   III only
(D)   I and II only
(E)   II and III only

26. The author takes exception to the views of presentist historians by

(A)   charging that they ignore pertinent evidence
(B)   presenting new information that had not been available before
(C)   applying a different interpretation to the same set of facts
(D)   refuting the accuracy of their historical data
(E)   exposing a logical contradiction in their arguments

27. Which of the following is suggested about the abolitionist movement?

(A)   Its members disguised their objectives from the public.
(B)   It contained different groupings characterized by varied philosophies.
(C)   It undermined its principles by accommodating public concerns.
(D)   A majority of its members misunderstood its objectives.
(E)   Its progress was hindered by the actions of radical factions within it.

GO ON TO THE NEXT PAGE.

Directions: Each question below consists of a word printed in capital letters, followed by five lettered words or phrases. Choose the lettered word or phrase that is most nearly opposite in meaning to the word in capital letters.

Since some of the questions require you to distinguish fine shades of meaning, be sure to consider all the choices before deciding which one is best.

28. UNDERMINE:

    (A) appreciate    (B) donate
    (C) bolster    (D) decay
    (E) simplify

29. OBSEQUIOUS:

    (A) original    (B) haughty
    (C) casual    (D) virtuous
    (E) informative

30. BLANCH:

    (A) stand    (B) repay
    (C) flush    (D) relax
    (E) cope

31. DISSIPATED:

    (A) temperate    (B) pleased
    (C) inundated    (D) encouraged
    (E) planned

32. FECUNDITY:

    (A) levity    (B) sanity
    (C) cowardice    (D) sterility
    (E) ventilation

33. ENCUMBER:

    (A) animate    (B) inaugurate
    (C) bleach    (D) disburden
    (E) obliterate

34. DISSEMINATE:

    (A) fertilize    (B) ordain
    (C) suppress    (D) explain thoroughly
    (E) make an impression

35. RESTIVE:

    (A) morose    (B) intangible
    (C) fatigued    (D) patient
    (E) curious

36. SYNCOPATED:

    (A) carefully executed    (B) normally accented
    (C) brightly illuminated    (D) easily understood
    (E) justly represented

37. VITUPERATIVE:

    (A) lethal    (B) incapacitated
    (C) laudatory    (D) insulated
    (E) prominent

38. SATURNINE:

    (A) magnanimous    (B) ebullient
    (C) finicky    (D) unnatural
    (E) impoverished

# STOP

IF YOU FINISH BEFORE TIME IS CALLED, YOU MAY CHECK YOUR WORK ON THIS SECTION ONLY.
DO NOT TURN TO ANY OTHER SECTION IN THE TEST.

| Time-30 minutes |
| :---: |
| 30 questions |

Figures:    You may assume that the position of points, lines, angles, etc. are in the order shown and that all lengths and angle measures may be assumed to be positive.

You may assume that lines that look straight are straight.

Figures are in a plane unless otherwise stated.

Figures are not drawn to scale unless otherwise stated.

Directions:    Questions 1-15 provide two quantities, one in Column A and another in Column B. Compare the two quantities and answer

A    if the quantity in Column A is greater;
B    if the quantity in Column B is greater;
C    if the two quantities are equal;
D    if the relationship cannot be determined from the information given.

Common Information:    In each question, information relating to one or both of the quantities in Column A and Column B is centered above the two columns. A symbol that appears in both columns represents the same thing in Column A as it does in Column B.

| Column A | Column B | Sample Answers |
| :---: | :---: | :---: |

Example 1:     $3 \times 4$     $3 + 4$     ● Ⓑ Ⓒ Ⓓ Ⓔ

Examples 2-4 refer to the figure below.

Example 2:    $x$     $y$     Ⓐ Ⓑ Ⓒ ● Ⓔ
(Because we cannot assume the angles are equal, even though they appear that way.)

Example 3:    $x + y$     90     Ⓐ Ⓑ ● Ⓓ Ⓔ
(Because the sum of the angles is 180°.)

Example 4:    $x$     90     Ⓐ ● Ⓒ Ⓓ Ⓔ
(Since $\triangle ABC$ is a right triangle, $x$ is less than 90°.)

A   if the quantity in Column A is greater;
B   if the quantity in Column B is greater;
C   if the two quantities are equal;
D   if the relationship cannot be determined from the information given.

| | Column A | Column B | | | Column A | Column B |
|---|---|---|---|---|---|---|
| 1. | 0.0260 | 0.0256 | | 6. | $\dfrac{12 \times 1}{12 + 1}$ | $\dfrac{12 + 1}{12 \times 1}$ |

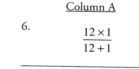

7.    $(a + 1)(b + 1)$        $ab + 1$

In the two-digit number $jk$, the value of the digit $j$ is twice the value of the digit $k$.

8.          $k$            6

$\triangle ABD$ and $\triangle CDB$ are right triangles.

2.     $w^2 + x^2$        $y^2 + z^2$

$$x + 4y = 6$$
$$x = 2y$$

3.         $x$           $y$

4.     $\sqrt{4^2 + 5^2}$     $\sqrt{3^2 + 6^2}$

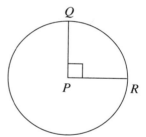

$P$ is the center of the circle and the area of sector $PQR$ is 4.

9.    The area of circle $P$       $4\pi$

In a certain accounting firm, there are exactly 3 types of employees: managerial, technical, and clerical. The firm has 120 employees and 25 percent of the employees are managerial.

5.    The number of managerial employees      Two-thirds of the number of clerical employees

GO ON TO THE NEXT PAGE.

A  if the quantity in Column A is greater;
B  if the quantity in Column B is greater;
C  if the two quantities are equal;
D  if the relationship cannot be determined from the information given.

| Column A | Column B |
|----------|----------|

Henry purchased $x$ apples and Jack purchased 10 apples less than $\frac{1}{3}$ of the number of apples Henry purchased.

10. The number of apples Jack purchased      $\dfrac{x-30}{3}$

---

11. The volume of a rectangular solid with a length of 5 feet, a width of 4 feet, and a height of $x$ feet     The volume of a rectangular solid with a length of 10 feet, a width of 8 feet, and a height of $y$ feet

---

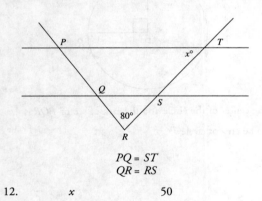

$PQ = ST$
$QR = RS$

12.      $x$           50

| Column A | Column B |
|----------|----------|

$$2 \times 16 \times 64 = 2 \times 4^n \times 256$$

13.      $n$           2

---

$$y \neq 0$$
$$-\frac{2}{y} + \frac{1}{3} = -\frac{1}{2y}$$

14.      $y$           4

---

The perimeter of isosceles $\triangle ABC$ is 40 and the length of side $BC$ is 12.

15.      The length of side $AB$        14

GO ON TO THE NEXT PAGE.

**Directions:** Each of Questions 16-30 has five answer choices. For each of these questions, select the best of the answer choices given.

16. If $\dfrac{p-q}{p} = \dfrac{2}{7}$, then $\dfrac{q}{p} =$

(A) $\dfrac{2}{5}$   (B) $\dfrac{5}{7}$   (C) 1

(D) $\dfrac{7}{5}$   (E) $\dfrac{7}{2}$

17. Which of the following numbers is both a multiple of 8 and a factor of 72?

(A)   4
(B)   9
(C)   16
(D)   24
(E)   36

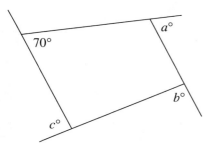

18. In the figure above, what is the value of $a + b + c$?

(A)   110
(B)   250
(C)   290
(D)   330
(E)   430

19. John has 4 ties, 12 shirts, and 3 belts. If each day he wears exactly one tie, one shirt, and one belt, what is the maximum number of days he can go without repeating a particular combination?

(A)   12
(B)   21
(C)   84
(D)   108
(E)   144

20. Which of the following is the greatest?

(A)   $\dfrac{0.00003}{0.0007}$

(B)   $\dfrac{0.0008}{0.0005}$

(C)   $\dfrac{0.007}{0.0008}$

(D)   $\dfrac{0.006}{0.0005}$

(E)   $\dfrac{0.01}{0.008}$

GO ON TO THE NEXT PAGE

## U.S PHYSICIANS IN SELECTED SPECIALTIES BY SEX, 1986

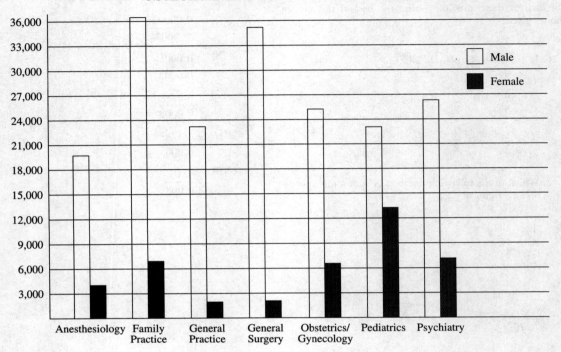

## GENERAL SURGERY PHYSICIANS BY AGE, 1986

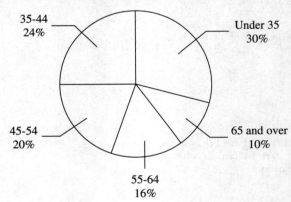

GO ON TO THE NEXT PAGE.

21. Approximately what percent of all general practice physicians in 1986 were male?

    (A)   23%
    (B)   50%
    (C)   75%
    (D)   82%
    (E)   90%

22. Which of the following physician specialties had the lowest ratio of males to females in 1986?

    (A)   Family practice
    (B)   General surgery
    (C)   Obstetrics/gynecology
    (D)   Pediatrics
    (E)   Psychiatry

23. In 1986, approximately how many general surgery physicians were between the ages of 45 and 54, inclusive?

    (A)   5,440
    (B)   6,300
    (C)   7,350
    (D)   7,800
    (E)   8,900

24. If in 1986 all the family practice physicians represented 7.5 percent of all the physicians in the United States, approximately how many physicians were there total?

    (A)   300,000
    (B)   360,000
    (C)   430,000
    (D)   485,000
    (E)   570,000

25. If the number of female general surgeon physicians in the under-35 category represented 3.5 percent of all the general surgeon physicians, approximately how many male general surgeon physicians were under 35 years?

    (A)   9,200
    (B)   9,800
    (C)   10,750
    (D)   11,260
    (E)   11,980

GO ON TO THE NEXT PAGE.

26. $|3| + |-4| + |3 - 4| =$

    (A)  14
    (B)  8
    (C)  7
    (D)  2
    (E)  0

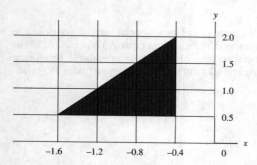

27. What is the area of the shaded region in the figure above?

    (A)  0.5
    (B)  0.7
    (C)  0.9
    (D)  2.7
    (E)  4.5

28. A computer can perform 30 identical tasks in 6 hours. At that rate, what is the minimum number of computers that should be assigned to complete 80 of the tasks within 3 hours?

    (A)  6
    (B)  7
    (C)  8
    (D)  12
    (E)  16

29. The volume of the cube in the figure above is 8. If point A is the midpoint of an edge of this cube, what is the perimeter of $\triangle ABC$?

    (A)  5

    (B)  $2 + 2\sqrt{3}$

    (C)  $2 + 2\sqrt{5}$

    (D)  7

    (E)  $6 + \sqrt{5}$

30. Which of the following is 850 percent greater than $8 \times 10^3$ ?

    (A)  $8.5 \times 10^3$
    (B)  $6.4 \times 10^4$
    (C)  $6.8 \times 10^4$
    (D)  $7.6 \times 10^4$
    (E)  $1.6 \times 10^5$

# STOP

IF YOU FINISH BEFORE TIME IS CALLED, YOU MAY CHECK YOUR WORK ON THIS SECTION ONLY.
DO NOT TURN TO ANY OTHER SECTION IN THE TEST.

Directions: Each sentence below has one or two blanks, each blank indicating that something has been omitted. Beneath the sentence are five lettered words or sets of words. Choose the word or set of words for each blank that best fits the meaning of the sentence as a whole.

1. Her concern for the earthquake victims _____her reputation as a callous person.

   (A) restored
   (B) rescinded
   (C) created
   (D) proved
   (E) belied

2. Due to unforeseen circumstances, the original plans were no longer _____ and were therefore _____.

   (A) relevant .. adaptable
   (B) applicable .. rejected
   (C) expedient .. adopted
   (D) acceptable .. appraised
   (E) capable .. allayed

3. The microscopic cross-section of a sandstone generally shows a_____surface, each tiny layer representing an _____of deposition that may have taken centuries or even millennia to accumulate.

   (A) ridged .. enlargement
   (B) multi-faceted .. angle
   (C) distinctive .. area
   (D) stratified .. interval
   (E) coarse .. episode

4. The convict has always insisted upon his own_____and now at last there is new evidence to_____him.

   (A) defensiveness .. incarcerate
   (B) culpability .. exonerate
   (C) blamelessness .. anathematize
   (D) innocence .. vindicate
   (E) contrition .. condemn

5. The theory of plate tectonics was the subject of much _____ when it was first proposed by Alfred Wegener, but now most geophysicists _____its validity.

   (A) opposition .. grant
   (B) consideration .. see
   (C) acclamation .. boost
   (D) prognostication .. learn
   (E) contention .. bar

6. Despite her professed_____, the glint in her eyes demonstrated her_____ with the topic.

   (A) intelligence .. obsession
   (B) interest .. concern
   (C) obliviousness .. confusion
   (D) indifference .. fascination
   (E) expertise .. unfamiliarity

7. Lacking sacred scriptures or _____, Shinto is more properly regarded as a legacy of traditional religious practices and basic values than as a formal system of belief.

   (A) followers
   (B) customs
   (C) dogma
   (D) relics
   (E) faith

GO ON TO THE NEXT PAGE.

Directions: In each of the following questions, a related pair of words or phrases is followed by five lettered pairs of words or phrases. Select the lettered pair that best expresses a relationship similar to that expressed in the original pair.

8.  IMPECCABLE : FLAW ::

    (A)  impeachable : crime
    (B)  obstreperous : permission
    (C)  impetuous : warning
    (D)  moribund : living
    (E)  absurd : sense

9.  SEISMOGRAPH : EARTHQUAKE ::

    (A)  stethoscope : health
    (B)  speedometer : truck
    (C)  telescope : astronomy
    (D)  thermometer : temperature
    (E)  abacus : arithmetic

10. GUZZLE : DRINK ::

    (A)  elucidate : clarify
    (B)  ingest : eat
    (C)  boast : describe
    (D)  stride : walk
    (E)  admonish : condemn

11. ORATOR : ARTICULATE ::

    (A)  soldier : merciless
    (B)  celebrity : talented
    (C)  judge : unbiased
    (D)  novice : unfamiliar
    (E)  dignitary : respectful

12. BADGE : POLICEMAN ::

    (A)  placard : demonstrator
    (B)  tattoo : sailor
    (C)  number : convict
    (D)  pedigree : dog
    (E)  fingerprint : defendant

13. SCRUTINIZE : OBSERVE ::

    (A)  excite : pique
    (B)  beseech : request
    (C)  search : discover
    (D)  smile : grin
    (E)  dive : jump

14. INDULGE : EPICUREAN ::

    (A)  frighten: ugly
    (B)  retract : revocable
    (C)  hesitate : unproductive
    (D)  revenge : vindictive
    (E)  understand : comprehensible

15. FLOOD : DILUVIAL ::

    (A)  punishment : criminal
    (B)  bacteria : biological
    (C)  verdict : judicial
    (D)  light : candescent
    (E)  heart : cardiac

16. SPHINX : PERPLEX ::

    (A)  oracle : interpret
    (B)  prophet : prepare
    (C)  siren : lure
    (D)  jester : astound
    (E)  minotaur : anger

GO ON TO THE NEXT PAGE.

Directions: Each passage in this group is followed by several questions. After reading the passage, choose the best response to each question. Your replies are to be based on what is stated or implied in the passage.

Although the schooling of fish is a familiar form of animal social behavior, how the school is formed and maintained is only beginning to be understood in detail. It had been thought that each fish maintains its
(5) position chiefly by means of vision. Our work has shown that, as each fish maintains its position, the lateral line, an organ sensitive to transitory changes in water displacement, is as important as vision. In each species a fish has a "preferred" distance and angle from
(10) its nearest neighbor. The ideal separation and bearing, however, are not maintained rigidly. The result is a probabilistic arrangement that appears like a random aggregation. The tendency of the fish to remain at the preferred distance and angle, however, serves to
(15) maintain the structure. Each fish, having established its position, uses its eyes and its lateral lines simultaneously to measure the speed of all the other fish in the school. It then adjusts its own speed to match a weighted average that emphasizes the contribution of nearby fish.

17. According to the passage, the structure of a fish school is dependent upon which of the following?

I.   Rigidly formed random aggregations
II.  The tendency of each fish to remain at a preferred distance from neighboring fish
III. Measurements of a weighted average by individual fish

(A) II only
(B) III only
(C) I and II only
(D) I and III only
(E) II and III only

18. Which of the following best describes the author's attitude toward the theory that the structure of fish schools is maintained primarily through vision?

(A) Heated opposition
(B) Careful neutrality
(C) Considered dissatisfaction
(D) Cautious approval
(E) Unqualified enthusiasm

19. The passage suggests that, after establishing its position in the school formation, an individual fish will subsequently

(A) maintain its preferred position primarily by visual and auditory means
(B) rigorously avoid changes that would interfere with the overall structure of the school
(C) make continuous sensory readjustments to its position within the school
(D) make unexpected shifts in position only if threatened by external danger
(E) surrender its ability to make quick, instinctive judgments

GO ON TO THE NEXT PAGE.

Whether as a result of some mysterious tendency in the national psyche or as a spontaneous reaction to their turbulent historical experience after the break-up of the Mycenaean world, the Greeks felt that to live with

(5) changing, undefined, unmeasured, seemingly random impressions–to live, in short, with what was expressed by the Greek word "chaos"–was to live in a state of constant anxiety.

If the apparent mutability of the physical world

(10) and of the human condition was a source of pain and bewilderment to the Greeks, the discovery of a permanent pattern or an unchanging substratum by which apparently chaotic experience could be measured and explained was a source of satisfaction, even joy, which

(15) had something of a religious nature. For the recognition of order and measure in phenomena did more than simply satisfy their intellectual curiosity or gratify a desire for tidiness; it also served as the basis of a spiritual ideal. "Measure and commensurability are everywhere

(20) identified with beauty and excellence" was Plato's way of putting it in a dialogue in which measure is identified as a primary characteristic of the ultimate good. Rational definability and spirituality were never mutually exclusive categories in Greek thought. If the quest for order

(25) and clarity was in essence the search for a kind of spiritual ideal, it was not an ideal to be perceived in rapturous emotional mysticism but rather one to be arrived at by patient analysis.

We see this process at work especially in Greek

(30) philosophy, which in various ways was aimed at alleviating the anxiety which is inherent in the more spontaneous expression of lyric poetry. The Milesian philosophers of the sixth century were interested above all in discovering a primary substance from which all other phenomena

(35) could be explained. Neat, clear, and sublimely undisturbed by the social world of humanity, which took shape and dissolved within the natural order of things, it was an austere ideal, an astringent antidote to the apparent senselessness of life. The person who contemplated it

(40) deeply could feel a part of a great system which was impersonal but predictable, and, like Lucretius, who revived the Milesian attitude in a later age, he or she could derive a peculiar peace from it. As time passed and Greek philosophy developed, the urge to find order in

(45) experience was shifted from physics to the realm of mathematical abstraction by the Pythagoreans, and to the world of human behavior by various thinkers of the later fifth century; and, finally, Plato and Aristotle attempted to weave all these foci of interest into comprehensive

(50) pictures of the relationship between human life and the world as a whole. But in all these epochs the basic quest–the search for a "kosmos"–remained the same.

20. The author's primary purpose is to

(A) evaluate conflicting viewpoints
(B) challenge an accepted opinion
(C) question philosophical principles
(D) enumerate historical facts
(E) describe a cultural phenomenon

21. The author indicates that the discovery of "an unchanging substratum" (line 12) served primarily to

(A) alter the Greeks' perception of the mutability of existence
(B) help eradicate severe social problems
(C) alleviate painful memories of national suffering
(D) calm a restless intellectual curiosity
(E) foster a more mystical understanding of the physical world

22. It can be inferred from the passage that rational thought and spiritual ideals were categories of experience that were

(A) unimportant and unfamiliar to most ordinary Greeks
(B) advocated by the Milesians and rejected by the Pythagoreans
(C) neglected by most philosophers before Plato and Aristotle
(D) seen by the Greeks as essentially compatible
(E) embraced mainly by Greek poets

23. All of the following can be inferred about the Greeks' anxiety over the possibility of "chaos" EXCEPT that it

(A) had sources in their national consciousness
(B) was reflected in specific aspects of their religion
(C) was related to their sense of change in the physical world
(D) led to a striving for order in their philosophy
(E) was expressed in their lyric poetry

GO ON TO THE NEXT PAGE.

24. The author implies that the Milesian philosophers of the sixth century sought relief from worldly anxiety by

    (A) focusing narrowly on inherently human questions
    (B) establishing sharp distinctions between spiritual and rational understanding
    (C) focusing primarily on an impersonal natural order
    (D) attempting to integrate rational and mystical worldviews
    (E) withdrawing from the physical world into the realm of mathematical abstraction

25. Which of the following best describes the organization of lines 15–24 of the passage ("For . . . thought")?

    (A) The author summarizes two viewpoints, cites historical evidence, and then declines to support either of the viewpoints.
    (B) The author makes an observation, admits to evidence that weakens the viewpoint, and then revises his observation.
    (C) The author specifies two distinct arguments, examines both in detail, then advances a third argument which reconciles the other two.
    (D) The author clarifies a previous statement, offers an example, and then draws a further conclusion based on these ideas.
    (E) The author states a thesis, mentions an opposed thesis and cites evidence supporting it, and then restates his original thesis.

26. According to the passage, the Pythagoreans differed from the Milesians primarily in that the Pythagoreans

    (A) focused on mathematical abstractions rather than physical phenomena
    (B) placed a renewed emphasis on understanding human behavior
    (C) focused primarily on a rational means to understanding truth
    (D) attempted to identify a fundamental physical unit of matter
    (E) stressed concrete reality over formal theory

27. In the context of the author's overall argument, which of the following best characterizes the Greeks' "search for a 'kosmos'" (lines 51–52)?

    (A) A mystical quest for a strong national identity
    (B) Efforts to replace a sterile philosophical rationalism with revitalized religious values
    (C) Attempts to end conflict among key philosophical schools
    (D) A search for order and measure in an unpredictable world
    (E) A search for an alternative to a narrow preoccupation with beauty and excellence

GO ON TO THE NEXT PAGE.

# 4 4 4 4 4 4 4 4 4

28. ENMITY:

    (A) friendship
    (B) reverence
    (C) boredom
    (D) stylishness
    (E) awkwardness

29. DILATE:

    (A) enclose
    (B) shrink
    (C) hurry
    (D) inflate
    (E) erase

30. CHARLATAN:

    (A) genuine expert
    (B) powerful leader
    (C) false idol
    (D) unknown enemy
    (E) hardened villain

31. PERIPHERAL:

    (A) civilized
    (B) partial
    (C) central
    (D) unharmed
    (E) stable

32. MERITORIOUS:

    (A) effulgent
    (B) stationary
    (C) uneven
    (D) narrow-minded
    (E) unpraiseworthy

33. DISCHARGE:

    (A) heal
    (B) advance
    (C) enlist
    (D) penalize
    (E) delay

34. MALEDICTION:

    (A) blessing
    (B) preparation
    (C) good omen
    (D) liberation
    (E) pursuit

35. MAWKISH:

    (A) unsentimental
    (B) sophisticated
    (C) graceful
    (D) tense
    (E) descriptive

36. TEMERITY:

    (A) blandness
    (B) caution
    (C) severity
    (D) strength
    (E) charm

37. JEJUNE:

    (A) morose
    (B) natural
    (C) mature
    (D) contrived
    (E) accurate

38. VITIATE:

    (A) deaden
    (B) trust
    (C) rectify
    (D) drain
    (E) amuse

# STOP

IF YOU FINISH BEFORE TIME IS CALLED, YOU MAY CHECK YOUR WORK ON THIS SECTION ONLY.
DO NOT TURN TO ANY OTHER SECTION IN THE TEST.

NO TEST MATERIAL ON THIS PAGE

Time–30 minutes
25 Questions

Directions: Each group of questions is based on a passage or a set of conditions. You may wish to draw a diagram to answer some of the questions. Choose the best answer for each question.

Questions 1-4

A new kind of lock is opened by pushing symbols in sequence on a keyboard. The sequence is called a combination. All acceptable combinations must consist of exactly five symbols–four letters and one single-digit number. Acceptable combinations must also conform to the following rules:

The number must be either the second or third symbol in the combination.

The fourth and fifth symbols in the combination must not be the same.

If the third symbol is a number, then the fifth must be either B or D.

If the third symbol is a letter, then there must be no F's or G's in the combination.

The first symbol must be a letter closer to the beginning of the alphabet than any other symbol in the combination.

1. Which of the following sequences of symbols is an acceptable combination?

(A)  E, R, 2, K, B
(B)  F, 6, T, T, Y
(C)  B, W, 4, G, G
(D)  C, 7, M, Q, D
(E)  A, X, L, 3, P

2. Which of the following could possibly be the first symbol in an acceptable sequence?

(A)  F
(B)  7
(C)  Y
(D)  3
(E)  E

3. A combination whose first symbol is B and whose fourth symbol is G could have which of the following as its second, third, and fifth symbols, respectively?

(A)  J, 6, D
(B)  A, 9, T
(C)  9, Z, X
(D)  3, H, G
(E)  M, 4, S

4. The combination C, Q, 8, P, F can be made acceptable by doing which of the following?

(A)  Replacing the F with a B
(B)  Reversing the C and the P
(C)  Reversing the Q and the 8
(D)  Replacing the F with a D
(E)  Replacing the C with an A

GO ON TO THE NEXT PAGE.

5. Some scientists argue that if fish are as common in unfished areas of the oceans as they are in the areas we now fish, current estimates of the amount of protein that our planet supports are far too low. Thus, even if the Earth's population continues to grow at its present rate, we can ensure the availability of protein for even the poorest of countries over the next two decades.

Which of the following, if true, would most weaken the argument above?

(A) Some scientists believe that the unfished areas of the ocean support substantially fewer fish per cubic kilometer than do the areas currently fished.

(B) The technology needed to fish new areas of the oceans is more expensive than that now used in ocean fishing.

(C) Increasing the supply of other sources of protein, such as beef and poultry, would be less expensive than fishing new parts of the oceans.

(D) The rate of increase of the Earth's population will slowly decline over the next two decades.

(E) It will take at least thirty years to develop the technology necessary for fishing the unfished areas of the ocean.

6. Travelers may enter and remain in the Republic for up to 59 days. If a traveler is to stay for more than 7 days, however, a special visa is required.
If the statements above are true, which of the following must also be true?

(A) A traveler who is staying in the Republic for 14 days must have a special visa.

(B) Many travelers who stay in the Republic do not need visas.

(C) Some travelers who stay in the Republic for more than 7 days do not have the appropriate visas.

(D) Travelers who stay less than 7 days in the Republic do not need visas.

(E) Travelers who merely pass through the Republic while en route to other destinations do not need visas.

7. Despite a steady stream of pessimistic forecasts, our economy continues to grow and prosper. Over the last fifteen years the service sector of our economy has greatly expanded. Last year alone, 500,000 Americans found employment in the service sector. In the face of evidence such as this, one cannot argue that our economy is wilting.

Which of the following, if true, would most seriously undermine the conclusion drawn above?

(A) Many Americans who took jobs in the service sector last year were also offered jobs in other sectors of the economy.

(B) Most of the job growth in the service sector can be attributed to people forced out of the declining manufacturing sector.

(C) American society has developed many programs that greatly offset the consequences of a sluggish economy.

(D) Forty years ago the American economy experienced a period of prosperity far greater than that of today.

(E) The importance of the service sector in determining the well-being of the overall American economy has decreased somewhat in the past ten years.

GO ON TO THE NEXT PAGE.

<u>Questions 8-12</u>

There are three bells in a clock tower. One of the bells produces a low-pitched ring, one produces a medium-pitched ring, and one produces a high-pitched ring. The bell-ringer must decide on a sequence of eight rings to play on special occasions. He decides that, for the sequence, the low bell must be rung exactly three times, the medium bell must be rung exactly three times, and the high bell must be rung exactly twice. The bell-ringer's choice of sequence is further limited by the following rules:

    The sixth ring must be that of the medium bell.
    The low bell must not be rung twice in succession.
    The high bell must be rung twice in succession.

8. Which of the following is an acceptable eight-ring sequence?

  (A)  medium, low, high, low, high, medium, low, medium
  (B)  low, high, high, low, medium, medium, low, medium
  (C)  medium, low, high, high, medium, low, medium, low
  (D)  medium, high, high, low, low, medium, low, medium
  (E)  low, medium, low, low, medium, medium, high, high

9. If the high bell is rung fifth in the sequence, all of the following must be true EXCEPT:

  (A)  The low bell is rung first.
  (B)  The medium bell is rung second.
  (C)  The low bell is rung third.
  (D)  The high bell is rung fourth.
  (E)  The low bell is rung seventh.

10. If the medium bell is rung fourth, the high bell CANNOT be rung

  (A)  first
  (B)  second
  (C)  third
  (D)  fifth
  (E)  eighth

11. Which of the following CANNOT be the order of bells rung third, fourth, and fifth, respectively?

  (A)  high, medium, low
  (B)  low, medium, low
  (C)  high, high, low
  (D)  high, medium, medium
  (E)  high, low, medium

12. Which of the following is IMPOSSIBLE?

  (A)  The high bell is rung first.
  (B)  The low bell is rung second.
  (C)  The medium bell is rung third.
  (D)  The high bell is rung fourth.
  (E)  The low bell is rung fifth.

GO ON TO THE NEXT PAGE.

Questions 13-17

A large corporation has branches in the following six cities–Atlanta, Beijing, Caracas, Dakar, Edinburgh, and Fresno. Memos of two types, Priority 1 and Priority 2, are sent from the head office to the branches.

Priority 1 memos are sent directly from the head office to either Atlanta or Dakar.

Priority 2 memos are sent directly from the head office to either Atlanta or Beijing.

Any branch that receives a memo directly from the head office must pass it on to at least one other branch. That other branch can pass it on to yet another branch, though it is not required to do so. The passing of memos from branch to branch must conform to the following rules:

> Atlanta can send memos of either type to Caracas only.
>
> Beijing can send Priority 1 memos to Edinburgh only and Priority 2 memos to Fresno only.
>
> Caracas can send memos of either type to either Beijing or Dakar.
>
> Dakar can send Priority 1 memos to Caracas only and Priority 2 memos to Edinburgh only.
>
> Edinburgh can send memos of either type to either Fresno or Atlanta.
>
> Fresno cannot send memos to any other branches.

13. A memo that is sent from the home office to Atlanta must be sent on to which of the following?

   (A)  Beijing
   (B)  Caracas
   (C)  Dakar
   (D)  Edinburgh
   (E)  Fresno

14. A memo that is sent from Edinburgh to Fresno could NOT be which of the following?

   (A)  A Priority 1 memo that was initially sent to Atlanta
   (B)  A Priority 1 memo that was sent to Edinburgh from Beijing
   (C)  A Priority 1 memo that was initially sent to Dakar
   (D)  A Priority 2 memo that was sent to Edinburgh from Dakar
   (E)  A Priority 2 memo that was initially sent to Beijing

15. A Priority 2 memo that was not originally sent to Atlanta could have been seen by a maximum of how many branches?

   (A)  two
   (B)  three
   (C)  four
   (D)  five
   (E)  six

16. A memo that reaches Edinburgh without having passed through Atlanta must have been seen in a minimum of how many branches besides Edinburgh?

   (A)  one
   (B)  two
   (C)  three
   (D)  four
   (E)  five

17. Which of the following cannot be the complete progress of a memo from the head office?

   (A)  Atlanta to Caracas to Beijing
   (B)  Atlanta to Caracas to Beijing to Edinburgh
   (C)  Atlanta to Caracas to Dakar to Edinburgh
   (D)  Beijing to Edinburgh to Fresno
   (E)  Dakar to Caracas to Beijing

GO ON TO THE NEXT PAGE.

T-37

Questions 18-22

An athlete has six trophies to place on an empty three-shelf display case. The six trophies are bowling trophies F, G, and H and tennis trophies J, K, and L. The three shelves of the display case are labeled 1 to 3 from top to bottom. Any of the shelves can remain empty. The athlete's placement of trophies must conform to the following conditions:

    J and L cannot be on the same shelf.
    F must be on the shelf immediately above the shelf that
       L is on.
    No single shelf can hold all three bowling trophies.
    K cannot be on Shelf 2.

18. If G and H are on Shelf 2, which of the following must be true?

    (A)    K is on Shelf 1.
    (B)    L is on Shelf 2.
    (C)    J is on Shelf 3.
    (D)    G and J are on the same shelf.
    (E)    F and K are on the same shelf.

19. If no tennis trophies are on Shelf 3, which pair of trophies must be on the same shelf?

    (A)    F and G
    (B)    L and H
    (C)    L and G
    (D)    K and J
    (E)    G and H

20. If J is on Shelf 2, which of the following must also be on Shelf 2?

    (A)    K
    (B)    G
    (C)    F
    (D)    L
    (E)    H

21. If Shelf 1 remains empty, which of the following must be FALSE?

    (A)    H and F are on the same shelf.
    (B)    There are exactly three trophies on Shelf 2.
    (C)    G and H are on the same shelf.
    (D)    There are exactly two trophies on Shelf 3.
    (E)    G and K are on the same shelf.

22. If L and G are on the same shelf, and if one of the shelves remains empty, which of the following must be true?

    (A)    If H is on Shelf 3, then J is on Shelf 2.
    (B)    K and L are on the same shelf.
    (C)    If H is on Shelf 2, then J is on Shelf 3.
    (D)    F and K are on the same shelf.
    (E)    If J is on Shelf 2, then H is on Shelf 1.

GO ON TO THE NEXT PAGE.

23. Painting wood furniture requires less time than does finishing the furniture with a stain and polyurethane. On the other hand, a finish of stain and polyurethane lasts much longer than does paint. Yet one further fact in favor of paint is that it costs significantly less than does stain and polyurethane. Therefore, if reducing work time and saving money are more important to people, they will paint their wood furniture rather than finish it with stain and polyurethane.
The argument in the passage above makes which of the following assumptions?

(A) It is better to paint wood furniture than it is to stain and polyurethane it.
(B) Most people consider reducing work time and saving money to be more important than the longevity of a finish.
(C) Most people prefer to paint or to stain and polyurethane wood furniture, rather than to leave the wood unfinished.
(D) Work time, cost, and longevity are equally important factors in deciding whether to paint wood furniture or stain and polyurethane it.
(E) Work time, cost, and longevity are the only important differences between painting wood furniture and finishing it with stain and polyurethane.

24. Young Cowonga lion cubs in the wild often engage in aggressive play with their siblings. This activity is instigated by the cubs' mother. Cowonga lion cubs born in captivity, however, never engage in this aggressive play. Some zoologists have concluded that this particular form of play teaches the young lions the skills needed for successful hunting in the wild, and that such play is not instigated in captivity because the development of hunting skills is unnecessary in such an environment.
The zoologists' conclusion would be most strengthened if it could be demonstrated that

(A) all Cowonga lion cubs raised in the wild are capable of hunting successfully
(B) other predatory animals also engage in aggressive play at a young age
(C) no Cowonga lion cub that has been raised in captivity is able to hunt successfully in the wild
(D) the skills used in aggressive play are similar to the skills necessary for successful hunting
(E) female lions that were raised in captivity will not instigate aggressive play among their offspring

25. According to a recent school survey, the number of students who regularly attend religious services on campus has increased fifty percent from the figure ten years ago. It must be an increased religiosity at our college that has massively reduced incidences of cheating on exams during this period. Which of the following, if true, most significantly weakens the inference above?

(A) Most of the students who now attend campus services do so only for social reasons.
(B) Campus chaplains have time and again spoken about the importance of academic honesty.
(C) Fifteen years ago, the college switched from an honor system to faculty-proctored exams.
(D) Not all students responded to the survey.
(E) Cheating was never a major problem at this school.

## STOP

IF YOU FINISH BEFORE TIME IS CALLED, YOU MAY CHECK YOUR WORK ON THIS SECTION ONLY.
DO NOT TURN TO ANY OTHER SECTION IN THE TEST.

| Time–30 minutes |
| :---: |
| 30 Questions |

<u>Numbers:</u>   The numbers in this section are real numbers.

<u>Figures:</u>   You may assume that the position of points, lines, angles, etc. are in the order shown and that all lengths and angle measures may be assumed to be positive.

You may assume that lines that look straight are straight.

Figures are in a plane unless otherwise stated.

Figures are not drawn to scale unless otherwise stated.

<u>Directions:</u>   Questions 1-15 provide two quantities, one in Column A and another in Column B. Compare the two quantities and answer

A   if the quantity in Column A is greater;
B   if the quantity in Column B is greater;
C   if the two quantities are equal;
D   if the relationship cannot be determined from the information given.

<u>Common</u>
<u>Information:</u>   In each question, information relating to one or both of the quantities in Column A and Column B is centered above the two columns. A symbol that appears in both columns represents the same thing in Column A as it does in Column B.

| | Column A | Column B | <u>Sample Answers</u> |
| :--- | :--- | :--- | :--- |
| <u>Example 1:</u> | $3 \times 4$ | $3 + 4$ | ● Ⓑ Ⓒ Ⓓ Ⓔ |

Examples 2-4 refer to the figure below.

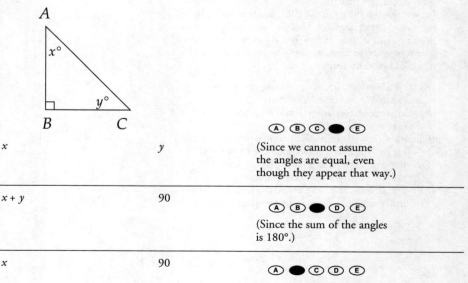

| | | | |
| :--- | :--- | :--- | :--- |
| <u>Example 2:</u> | $x$ | $y$ | Ⓐ Ⓑ Ⓒ ● Ⓔ |
| | | | (Since we cannot assume the angles are equal, even though they appear that way.) |
| <u>Example 3:</u> | $x + y$ | 90 | Ⓐ Ⓑ ● Ⓓ Ⓔ |
| | | | (Since the sum of the angles is 180°.) |
| <u>Example 4:</u> | $x$ | 90 | Ⓐ ● Ⓒ Ⓓ Ⓔ |
| | | | (Since $\triangle ABC$ is a right triangle, $x$ is less than 90°.) |

A   if the quantity in Column A is greater;
B   if the quantity in Column B is greater;
C   if the two quantities are equal;
D   if the relationship cannot be determined from the information given.

Column A　　　　　　Column B

$y = (x + 3)^2$

1.　The value of $y$　　　　9
　　when $x = 1$

2.　The number of miles　　The number of
　　traveled by a car that　miles traveled by a
　　traveled for 4 hours at　train that traveled
　　an average speed of　　for $2^{1}/_{2}$ hours at
　　40 miles per hour　　　an average speed
　　　　　　　　　　　　of 70 miles per hour

3.　The number of cookies　The number of
　　in a bag that weighs　grapes in a bag
　　3 kilograms　　　　that weighs
　　　　　　　　　　　2 kilograms

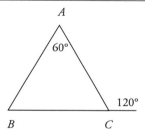

4.　$AB$　　　　　　　$BC$

$8a + 8b = 24$

5.　The length of　　　　2
　　segment $PQ$

Column A　　　　　　Column B

$x < y$

6.　$y - x$　　　　　　$x - y$

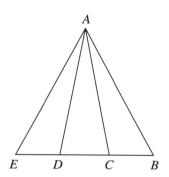

The area of triangular region $ABE$ is 75.

7.　The area of　　　　The area of
　　$\triangle ABC$　　　　$\triangle ADE$

| | $x$ | |
|---|---|---|
| $\frac{1}{3}$ | $\frac{2}{9}$ | $y$ |
| | $\frac{4}{5}$ | |

The sum of the numbers in the horizontal
row of boxes equals the sum of the numbers in the
vertical row of boxes.

8.　$x$　　　　　　　　$y$

GO ON TO THE NEXT PAGE.

A   if the quantity in Column A is greater;
B   if the quantity in Column B is greater;
C   if the two quantities are equal;
D   if the relationship cannot be determined from the information given.

| Column A | Column B |
|---|---|

9.

$$\dfrac{\dfrac{1}{3}\times\dfrac{1}{4}}{\dfrac{2}{3}\times\dfrac{1}{2}}$$

$$\dfrac{\dfrac{2}{3}\times\dfrac{1}{2}}{\dfrac{1}{3}\times\dfrac{1}{4}}$$

Eileen drives due north from town $A$ to town $B$ for a distance of 60 miles, then drives due east from town $B$ to town $C$ for a distance of 80 miles.

10.   The distance from town            120
      $A$ to town $C$ in miles

11.   $(\sqrt{7}-2)(\sqrt{7}+2)$        $(2-\sqrt{7})(-\sqrt{7}-2)$

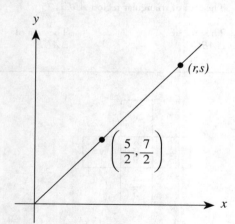

12.   $r$                               $s$

| Column A | Column B |
|---|---|

$x$ is an integer greater than 0.

13.   $1-\left(\dfrac{1}{4}\right)^{x}$        0.95

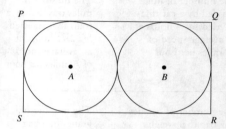

The two circles with centers $A$ and $B$ have the same radius.

14.   The sum of the           The perimeter of
      circumferences         rectangles $PQRS$
      of the two circles

15.   $3^{17}+3^{18}+3^{19}$        $3^{20}$

GO ON TO THE NEXT PAGE.

Directions: Each of Questions 16-30 has five answer choices. For each of these questions, select the best of the answer choices given.

16. If $4 + y = 14 - 4y$, then $y =$

(A)  $-4$

(B)  $0$

(C)  $\dfrac{5}{8}$

(D)  $\dfrac{4}{5}$

(E)  $2$

17. $\dfrac{4}{5} + \dfrac{5}{4} =$

(A)  $1$

(B)  $\dfrac{9}{8}$

(C)  $\dfrac{6}{5}$

(D)  $\dfrac{41}{20}$

(E)  $\dfrac{23}{10}$

18. If $3^m = 81$, then $m^3 =$

(A)  9
(B)  16
(C)  27
(D)  54
(E)  64

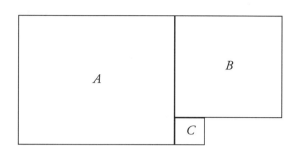

19. In the figure above, there are 3 square gardening areas. The area of square $A$ is 81 square meters and the area of square $B$ is 49 square meters. What is the area, in square meters, of square $C$?

(A)  2
(B)  4
(C)  9
(D)  27
(E)  32

20. In a certain history class, all except 23 students scored under 85 on a test. If 18 students scored over 85 on this test, how many students are there in this history class?

(A)  33
(B)  37
(C)  39
(D)  41
(E)  It cannot be determined from the information given.

GO ON TO THE NEXT PAGE.

### ENERGY USE BY YEAR, COUNTRY Y, 1950-1980
(in millions of kilowatt-hours)

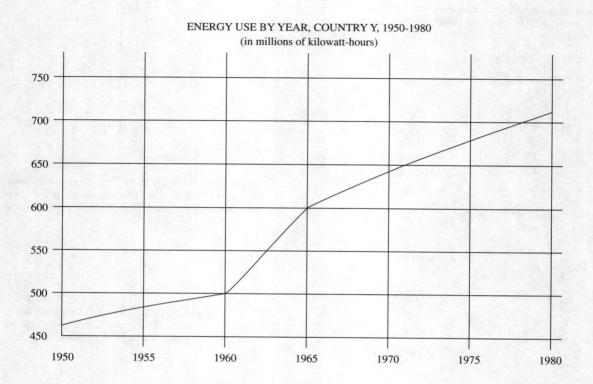

### ENERGY USE BY TYPE, COUNTRY Y

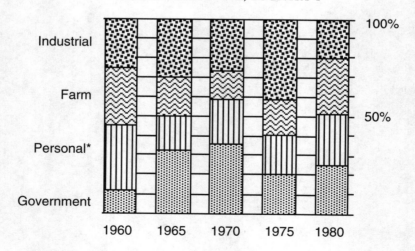

*Total personal use = population x per-capita personal use

21. In which of the following years was the energy use in country *Y* closest to 650 million kilowatt-hours?

    (A)  1960
    (B)  1965
    (C)  1970
    (D)  1975
    (E)  1980

22. In 1965, how many of the categories shown had energy use greater than 150 million kilowatt-hours?

    (A)  None
    (B)  One
    (C)  Two
    (D)  Three
    (E)  Four

23. In which of the following years was industrial use of energy greatest in country *Y*?

    (A)  1960
    (B)  1965
    (C)  1970
    (D)  1975
    (E)  1980

24. If the population of country *Y* increased by 20 percent from 1960 to 1965, approximately what was the percent decrease in the per-capita personal use of energy between those two years?

    (A)  0%
    (B)  17%
    (C)  25%
    (D)  47%
    (E)  It cannot be determined from the information given.

25. Which of the following can be inferred from the graphs?

    I.    Farm use of energy increased between 1960 and 1980.
    II.   In 1980, industrial use of energy was greater than industrial use of energy in 1965.
    III.  More people were employed by the government of country *Y* in 1980 than in 1960.

    (A)  I only
    (B)  II only
    (C)  I and II only
    (D)  II and III only
    (E)  I, II, and III

GO ON TO THE NEXT PAGE.

26. If the average of two numbers is $3y$ and one of the numbers is $y - z$, what is the other number, in terms of $y$ and $z$?

(A) $y + z$
(B) $3y + z$
(C) $4y - z$
(D) $5y - z$
(E) $5y + z$

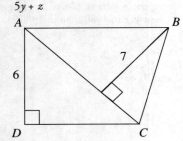

27. In the figure above, the area of $\triangle ABC$ is 35. What is the length of $DC$?

(A) 6
(B) 8
(C) $6\sqrt{2}$
(D) 10
(E) $6\sqrt{3}$

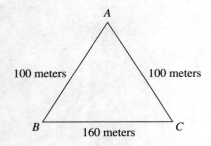

28. In the figure above is a triangular field. What is the minimum distance, in meters, that a person would have to walk to go from point $A$ to a point on side $BC$?

(A) 60
(B) 80
(C) 100
(D) 140
(E) 180

29. If the ratio of $2a$ to $b$ is 8 times the ratio of $b$ to $a$, then $\dfrac{b}{a}$ could be

(A) 4
(B) 2
(C) 1
(D) $\dfrac{1}{2}$
(E) $\dfrac{1}{4}$

30. A certain dentist earns $n$ dollars for each filling she puts in, plus $x$ dollars for every 15 minutes she works. If in a certain week she works 14 hours and puts in 21 fillings, how much does she earn for the week, in dollars?

(A) $\dfrac{7}{2}x + 21n$
(B) $7x + 14n$
(C) $14x + 21n$
(D) $56x + 21n$
(E) $56x + \dfrac{21}{4}n$

## S T O P

IF YOU FINISH BEFORE TIME IS CALLED, YOU MAY CHECK YOUR WORK ON THIS SECTION ONLY.
DO NOT TURN TO ANY OTHER SECTION IN THE TEST.

# PRACTICE TEST
## ANSWER KEY

| I. Analytical | II. Verbal | III. Math | IV. Verbal | V. Analytical | VI. Math |
|---|---|---|---|---|---|
| 1.....A | 1.....A | 1.....A | 1.....E | 1.....D | 1.....A |
| 2.....D | 2.....E | 2.....C | 2.....B | 2.....E | 2.....B |
| 3.....C | 3.....E | 3.....A | 3.....D | 3.....A | 3.....D |
| 4.....B | 4.....A | 4.....B | 4.....D | 4.....D | 4.....C |
| 5.....E | 5.....D | 5.....D | 5.....A | 5.....E | 5.....A |
| 6.....C | 6.....E | 6.....B | 6.....D | 6.....A | 6.....A |
| 7.....E | 7.....D | 7.....D | 7.....C | 7.....B | 7.....D |
| 8.....C | 8.....A | 8.....B | 8.....E | 8.....B | 8.....B |
| 9.....A | 9.....B | 9.....A | 9.....D | 9.....E | 9.....B |
| 10....E | 10....B | 10....C | 10....D | 10....D | 10....B |
| 11....B | 11....D | 11....D | 11....C | 11....D | 11....C |
| 12....C | 12....E | 12....C | 12....C | 12....C | 12....B |
| 13....B | 13....A | 13....B | 13....B | 13....B | 13....D |
| 14....C | 14....A | 14....A | 14....D | 14....E | 14....A |
| 15....A | 15....E | 15....D | 15....E | 15....A | 15....B |
| 16....E | 16....B | 16....B | 16....C | 16....C | 16....E |
| 17....E | 17....D | 17....D | 17....E | 17....D | 17....D |
| 18....C | 18....B | 18....B | 18....C | 18....B | 18....E |
| 19....D | 19....E | 19....E | 19....C | 19....D | 19....B |
| 20....D | 20....C | 20....D | 20....E | 20....C | 20....E |
| 21....A | 21....E | 21....E | 21....A | 21....D | 21....C |
| 22....B | 22....B | 22....D | 22....D | 22....A | 22....C |
| 23....D | 23....C | 23....C | 23....B | 23....E | 23....D |
| 24....D | 24....C | 24....E | 24....C | 24....C | 24....D |
| 25....A | 25....A | 25....B | 25....D | 25....A | 25....A |
| | 26....C | 26....B | 26....A | | 26....E |
| | 27....B | 27....C | 27....D | | 27....B |
| | 28....C | 28....A | 28....A | | 28....A |
| | 29....B | 29....C | 29....B | | 29....D |
| | 30....C | 30....D | 30....A | | 30....D |
| | 31....A | | 31....C | | |
| | 32....D | | 32....E | | |
| | 33....D | | 33....C | | |
| | 34....C | | 34....A | | |
| | 35....D | | 35....A | | |
| | 36....B | | 36....B | | |
| | 37....C | | 37....C | | |
| | 38....B | | 38....C | | |

# CALCULATE YOUR SCORE

## STEP 1

Add together your total number correct for the Analytical, Verbal, and Quantitative sections.
This is your raw score for each measure.

## ANALYTICAL

**SECTION 1** _____ (# correct)

**SECTION 5** _____ (# correct)

_____

**TOTAL CORRECT** _____ (raw score)

## VERBAL

**SECTION 2** _____ (# correct)

**SECTION 4** _____ (# correct)

_____

**TOTAL CORRECT** _____ (raw score)

## QUANTITATIVE

**SECTION 3** _____ (# correct)

**SECTION 6** _____ (# correct)

_____

**TOTAL CORRECT** _____ (raw score)

# STEP 2

Find your raw score on the table below and read across to find your scaled score and your percentile.

## QUANTITATIVE

| RAW SCORE | SCALED SCORE | PERCENTILE RANK |
|-----------|--------------|-----------------|
| 0 | 200 | 1 |
| 1 | 200 | 1 |
| 2 | 200 | 1 |
| 3 | 200 | 1 |
| 4 | 200 | 1 |
| 5 | 200 | 1 |
| 6 | 200 | 1 |
| 7 | 200 | 1 |
| 8 | 200 | 1 |
| 9 | 200 | 1 |
| 10 | 210 | 1 |
| 11 | 220 | 1 |
| 12 | 240 | 1 |
| 13 | 260 | 1 |
| 14 | 270 | 1 |
| 15 | 280 | 2 |
| 16 | 290 | 2 |
| 17 | 300 | 3 |
| 18 | 310 | 4 |
| 19 | 310 | 5 |
| 20 | 320 | 5 |
| 21 | 330 | 6 |
| 22 | 340 | 7 |
| 23 | 360 | 9 |
| 24 | 370 | 10 |
| 25 | 380 | 13 |
| 26 | 390 | 14 |
| 27 | 400 | 16 |
| 28 | 410 | 18 |
| 29 | 420 | 20 |
| 30 | 420 | 22 |
| 31 | 430 | 24 |
| 32 | 440 | 26 |
| 33 | 460 | 28 |
| 34 | 470 | 32 |
| 35 | 480 | 35 |
| 36 | 490 | 37 |
| 37 | 500 | 40 |
| 38 | 510 | 42 |
| 39 | 520 | 45 |
| 40 | 530 | 48 |
| 41 | 540 | 49 |
| 42 | 540 | 51 |
| 43 | 560 | 57 |
| 44 | 570 | 59 |
| 45 | 580 | 61 |
| 46 | 600 | 66 |
| 47 | 610 | 68 |
| 48 | 630 | 72 |
| 49 | 640 | 74 |
| 50 | 660 | 78 |
| 51 | 670 | 80 |
| 52 | 690 | 84 |
| 53 | 690 | 86 |
| 54 | 700 | 89 |
| 55 | 720 | 92 |
| 56 | 730 | 94 |
| 57 | 750 | 97 |
| 58 | 770 | 97 |
| 59 | 780 | 97 |
| 60 | 800 | 97 |

## VERBAL

| RAW SCORE | SCALED SCORE | PERCENTILE RANK |
|-----------|--------------|-----------------|
| 0 | 200 | 1 |
| 1 | 200 | 1 |
| 2 | 200 | 1 |
| 3 | 200 | 1 |
| 4 | 200 | 1 |
| 5 | 200 | 1 |
| 6 | 200 | 1 |
| 7 | 200 | 1 |
| 8 | 200 | 1 |
| 9 | 200 | 1 |
| 10 | 200 | 1 |
| 11 | 200 | 1 |
| 12 | 200 | 1 |
| 13 | 220 | 1 |
| 14 | 230 | 1 |
| 15 | 240 | 1 |
| 16 | 250 | 1 |
| 17 | 260 | 1 |
| 18 | 270 | 2 |
| 19 | 270 | 3 |
| 20 | 280 | 4 |
| 21 | 290 | 5 |
| 22 | 300 | 6 |
| 23 | 310 | 7 |
| 24 | 320 | 9 |
| 25 | 320 | 10 |
| 26 | 330 | 12 |
| 27 | 330 | 14 |
| 28 | 340 | 16 |
| 29 | 350 | 16 |
| 30 | 360 | 20 |
| 31 | 360 | 22 |
| 32 | 360 | 24 |
| 33 | 370 | 24 |
| 34 | 380 | 26 |
| 35 | 390 | 30 |
| 36 | 400 | 33 |
| 37 | 410 | 36 |
| 38 | 420 | 38 |
| 39 | 420 | 41 |

| | | |
|---|---|---|
| 40 | 420 | 41 |
| 41 | 430 | 44 |
| 42 | 440 | 48 |
| 43 | 450 | 51 |
| 44 | 460 | 54 |
| 45 | 470 | 56 |
| 46 | 470 | 59 |
| 47 | 480 | 61 |
| 48 | 490 | 67 |
| 49 | 510 | 69 |
| 50 | 520 | 72 |
| 51 | 530 | 74 |
| 52 | 530 | 76 |
| 53 | 540 | 78 |
| 54 | 550 | 80 |
| 55 | 560 | 82 |
| 56 | 570 | 84 |
| 57 | 580 | 85 |
| 58 | 590 | 87 |
| 59 | 590 | 89 |
| 60 | 600 | 90 |
| 61 | 610 | 92 |
| 62 | 620 | 93 |
| 63 | 630 | 94 |
| 64 | 640 | 95 |
| 65 | 650 | 95 |
| 66 | 660 | 96 |
| 67 | 670 | 97 |
| 68 | 680 | 98 |
| 69 | 690 | 98 |
| 70 | 700 | 99 |
| 71 | 710 | 99 |
| 72 | 720 | 99 |
| 73 | 740 | 99 |
| 74 | 760 | 99 |
| 75 | 780 | 99 |
| 76 | 800 | 99 |

## ANALYTICAL

| RAW SCORE | SCALED SCORE | PERCENTILE RANK |
|---|---|---|
| 0 | 200 | 1 |
| 1 | 210 | 1 |
| 2 | 230 | 1 |
| 3 | 230 | 1 |
| 4 | 250 | 1 |
| 5 | 260 | 1 |
| 6 | 280 | 1 |
| 7 | 300 | 1 |
| 8 | 310 | 1 |
| 9 | 330 | 1 |
| 10 | 330 | 1 |
| 11 | 340 | 1 |
| 12 | 360 | 2 |
| 13 | 370 | 3 |
| 14 | 390 | 4 |
| 15 | 400 | 6 |
| 16 | 420 | 7 |
| 17 | 420 | 10 |
| 18 | 430 | 12 |
| 19 | 450 | 15 |
| 20 | 460 | 17 |
| 21 | 470 | 20 |
| 22 | 490 | 23 |
| 23 | 500 | 27 |
| 24 | 500 | 31 |
| 25 | 520 | 35 |
| 26 | 530 | 38 |
| 27 | 550 | 40 |
| 28 | 560 | 46 |
| 29 | 580 | 49 |
| 30 | 580 | 55 |
| 31 | 590 | 58 |
| 32 | 600 | 64 |
| 33 | 620 | 67 |
| 34 | 640 | 72 |
| 35 | 650 | 74 |
| 36 | 660 | 76 |
| 37 | 670 | 81 |
| 38 | 680 | 85 |
| 39 | 690 | 87 |
| 40 | 700 | 88 |
| 41 | 710 | 91 |
| 42 | 720 | 92 |
| 43 | 730 | 95 |
| 44 | 740 | 96 |
| 45 | 750 | 97 |
| 46 | 760 | 98 |
| 47 | 770 | 99 |
| 48 | 780 | 99 |
| 49 | 790 | 99 |
| 50 | 800 | 99 |

# PRACTICE TEST
# EXPLANATIONS

## GAME I: QUESTIONS 1-3

**The Action:** 5 spices to arrange: *A, C, N, S* and *T*.

**The Rules:**

1) *N* must be harvested before *T*.

2) Cloves must be harvested **immediately** after allspice—no other spice can come between them.

3) *S* can't be first.

There are no overlaps here—no spices are mentioned by more than one rule. We know from Rule 1 that *T* isn't first, from Rule 2 we know *C* isn't first and from Rule 3 we know that *S* isn't first, so the first spice is either *N* or *A*.

**1** **A-** Let's take Rule 3 first and try to throw out answer choices. (B) has sage in the number one spot, so it's out. Rule 2 gives us our *AC* unit—*A* has to be immediately before *C*—choice (C) has *A* first and *C* fourth, and (D) has *C* before *A*, so they're both out. Rule 1 gives us our answer—*N* is before *T*, and choice (E) has *N* coming after *T*. (E)'s out, so it's (A) for Question 1.

**2** **D-** If we put *N* fourth, what are the consequences? Rule 1 springs to mind—nutmeg is before thyme. If *N* is fourth, *T* must be fifth. Now we have our *AC* unit, and we have *S*. We know *S* can't be first, and it can't be second either, since we can't separate *A* and *C*. *S* is third, so we've completed our sequence—*A, C, S, N, T*. Choice (D) must be false, since cloves can't be immediately followed by nutmeg. We need cloves, sage, and nutmeg second, third and fourth. We don't have to go through the others as long as you know that only sequence *A, C, S, N* and *T* will work, and, again, it's (D) for Question 2.

**3** **C-** First, put *S* in the second slot and look for a spot for *A*—it's joined with *C*, which limits our options. *A* can't be first since *C* would then be second and the second slot is taken, so eliminate choices (A) and (B). *A* can't be last since *C* comes after *A*, so scratch (D) and (E), leaving (C). So (C), third and fourth, is correct, and that's it for that game, which was short and quite easy.

**4** **B-** We need a statement that weakens or has no effect on the logic. The conclusion here is that the way a judge came into his job often determines the result of a case. Judges decide differently depending on their term length—short termers think in light of political influences, while lifelong judges rely on a tradition of judicial wisdom. The author provides no supporting evidence, so the wrong choices will likely be evidence that strengthens the argument. (A) gives support, asserting that if judges want to keep their jobs, they're likely to be swayed by voters, to improve their election chances. (C) shows that short termers rule in ways that the voters approve of. In (E), we find that only short term judges use pollsters—people who track public opinion. So (A), (C) and (E) lend credence to the allegations about the political sensitivity of short term judges. (D) supports the viewpoint on lifelong judges, saying that appointed judges show consistency, implying that those judges turn a blind eye to politics. We're left with (B). If long termers act on their political knowledge, they're as fickle as the short termers. If they don't act on their political knowledge, it's simply irrelevant. (B) doesn't support the argument, and it's correct for Question 4.

**5** **E-** The author believes that a climate of peace has been created by spending on weapons systems and supports this claim by indicating that a decrease in conflicts can be attributed to the robust deployment of weapons systems. The author sees a causal connection between defense readiness maintained by greater spending and the lower number of attacks. (E) is the assumption underlying this connection. The author must assume that had defense spending not gone up, the number of attacks would have increased.

(A), in its reference to the causes of military action, is outside the scope. In (B), the author doesn't tell us that more defense spending has prevented military actions, and it is certainly not a necessary assumption. There's no claim about the future of peace for (C). Finally, (D)'s equation of weapons and personnel is silly–if the author has an opinion on this issue, he's keeping it to himself, so we can't ascribe this view to him. (E)'s the answer for Question 5.

**6** C- Within five years it will be cheaper to buy tuners and amplifiers separately instead of buying an integrated receiver. Previously, a receiver combining both tuner and amp was cheaper than the two purchased separately. What has changed? In other words, what's the basis of the author's claim? It's a recent trend showing that the average retail prices of tuners and amps have declined 20% and 35% respectively, while the average retail price of an integrated receiver has declined only 12%. But percentages often can't be compared unless you know the actual numbers. Try plugging in numbers. If tuners and amps each used to cost $1,000 apiece, while receivers used to cost only $100 apiece, then the 20% decline in the tuner and the 35% decline in the amp over the past two years wouldn't have brought them near the cost of a receiver. Tuners would cost $800 and amps $650 while a 12% decline in the price of a receiver would bring its price to under $90. In five years a receiver will probably still be the

better bargain. While the author implies that the price gap has been closing in the past two years, we don't know how much it has closed or the rate at which it will close in the next five years, so (C) is correct.

(A), (B), (D) and (E) don't help you decide the significance of the percent decline in the average prices. The life expectancy of stereo equipment, (A), is outside the scope. As for (B), this doesn't tell you anything about which component costs less—outside the scope. So is (D)— sales projections tell you nothing about the actual cost of the equipment. (E) is even farther out in left field in talking about the consumers rather than the equipment, so it's (C) for Question 6.

## GAME II : QUESTIONS 7-10

**The Action:** 8 articles—5 must be selected. Let's put theater articles in capitals and dance articles in lower case: F, G, H, J, k, l, m, o.

**The Rules:**

1) We need at least three lower case letters, so we either have three lower case and two capitals, or four lower case and one capital. If you're told that one lower case isn't chosen, you can circle the other three. This kind of unpacking of rules can help you make realizations at the top of the game.

2) If J is chosen, m can't be. Put this together with Rule 1, and you see that if you cross out m, you know you can circle k, l and o, and if you choose m, you have to cross out J.

3) If you choose F, you must choose J. Note: This doesn't mean that if you have J you have F.

**Rule Overview:**

Both Rule 2 and Rule 3 mention J, and you can combine them. If you have J, you can't have m and in order to have F, you must have

*J*, so this tells us that you can't have *F* and *m* in the same group.

**7** **E-** Question 7 tells us that *m* isn't chosen, and since *m* is a lower case letter you have to choose the three remaining ones. So cross out *m*, circle *k*, *l* and *o* and you need go no further. We're asked which must be chosen—(E) suggests *k*, and it's our answer. (A) through (D) are all capital letters, so they're out and it's (E) for Question 7.

**8** **C-** Let's make out a roster, circle *J*, and see what happens. Rule 2 tells us that if *J* is chosen, *m* is not, and if we cross out *m* we circle *k*, *l* and *o*. We have *J*, *k*, *l* and *o* circled. Any of the remaining letters can be fifth—*F*, *G* or *H*. There are three possible groupings— *J*, *k*, *l*, *o*, *F*; *J*, *k*, *l*, *o*, *G* and *J*, *k*, *l*, *o*, *H*, so (C), three, is correct for Question 8.

**9** **A-** We just know that the choice of one article will make only one group of published articles acceptable, so let's start with the entities that we know the most about. As we saw in Question 8, choosing *J* yields three possible groups, not just one, so we can eliminate (C). *m*, (E), was mentioned in Rule 2 and in our deduced rule about *F* and *m* being incompatible. If you circle *m*, you have to cross out *J* and *F*, but the rest is wide open, so we can eliminate (E). What about *F*? If you circle *F*, Rule 3 says you have to circle *J*, and when you circle *J*, Rule 2 says you have to cross out *m*, and once you cross out *m*, you have to circle *k*, *l* and *o*, and those are your five articles, *F*, *J*, *k*, *l*, *o*, so (A) is correct for Question 9.

**10** **E-** If you circle *G*, what follows? Nothing obvious, so our best bet is to try out the choices by attempting to disprove them. (A)—must it follow if *G* is chosen that *J* is not chosen? Well, what happens if *J* is chosen? If *G* and *J* are circled, we need three lower case letters to satisfy Rule 1, and *k*, *l* and *o* will fit the bill quite nicely, since we know we can't have *m* according to Rule 2, so as a group, *G*, *J*, *k*, *l*, *o* is perfectly acceptable. We can have *G* and *J*, so we can eliminate (A). (B) looks a little wordy—let's jump to (C), which says *H* is not chosen. If you circle *G* and *H*, you could fill out an acceptable group—you could have *G*, *H*, *k*, *l*, *m* or *G*, *H*, *l*, *m*, *o* or *G*, *H*, *k*, *l*, *o*, etc. Let's jump to (E) which says *F* isn't chosen. Well, if we circle *F* along with *G*, we know that we have to circle *J*, since Rule 3 says if *F* is chosen, *J* is chosen. But we have to choose five, and we've got three capitals circled here— there'd be no way to get three lower case letters. If *G* is chosen, *F* can't be chosen—since we can disprove the statement in (E), choice (E) is correct.

For the record let's look at choices (B) and (D). The grouping *G*, *J*, *k*, *l*, *o* shows that (D) needn't be true and the grouping *G*, *k*, *l*, *m*, *o* shows that (B) needn't be true. Again, it's (E) for Question 10.

## GAME III: QUESTIONS 11-14

**The Action:** This oddball game involves matching up dogs and trainers, then moving them around according to different commands. We have three trainers, *L*, *M* and *O* for short and three dogs with the same initials—*l*, *m*, and *o*. We have three rooms, rooms 1, 2 and 3. We start with an initial room assignment for each trainer and each dog: *Ll* in Room 1; *Mm* in Room 2 and *Oo* in Room 3.

**The Rules:**

1) Command W involves trainers only—the trainer in Room 1 moves to Room 2, the trainer in Room 2 moves to Room 3, and the trainer in Room 3 moves to Room 1.

2) With command X, the dogs in Rooms 1 and 2 switch places, and the dog in Room 3 stays put.

3) When command Y is called, the dogs in Rooms 2 and 3 switch places.

4) When command Z is called, the dogs in Rooms 1 and 3 switch places.

5) Command A is trickier—the dogs return to their original trainers. So *l* returns to *L*, *m* to *M* and *o* to *O*.

**11** B- Question 11 is basic—*Ll* in Room 1, *Mm* in Room 2, and *Oo* in Room 3. Command W is called, and Luis in Room 1 moves to Room 2, Molly in Room 2 moves to Room 3 and Oprah in Room 3 moves to Room 1. So we have in Room 1, *Ol*—the lower case letters, the dogs, have stayed put—in Room 2 *Lm* and in Room 3 *Mo*. Which choice is true of that arrangement? (B), Molly is in Room 3. Yes, she's there with Onyx.

Looking at the wrong choices, (A) is out because Oprah is with Lassie, not with Mugs. (C) is out because Molly is with Onyx. (D) is out since Luis is in Room 2, and (E) is out because Luis is with Mugs, not with Onyx. Again, it's (B) for Question 11.

**12** C- We need to get Onyx to Room 2 from Room 3. One *Y* would do it—the dogs in Rooms 2 and 3 would switch, but that's not a choice. The only single command here is the one call of *W* in choice (A), but that moves trainers, not dogs, so it's out. The two calls of *X* suggested by (B) would leave Onyx where she started in Room 3. What about (C), two *W*s, then one *A*? Well, the *W* command

moves only trainers so we'd have Oprah in Room 1, Luis in Room 2, and Molly in Room 3. A second call of *W* would move Molly to Room 1, Oprah to Room 2 and Luis to Room 3. Then if we got a call of *A*, all of the dogs would seek out their original trainers—Mugs with Molly in Room 1, Onyx with Oprah in Room 2 and Lassie with Luis in Room 3— Onyx would end up in Room 2—that's what we're looking for.

Let's see why choices (D) and (E) are wrong. (D) suggests two *W*s and one *Z*—the two *W*s give us *Ml* in Room 1; *Om* in Room 2 and *Lo* in Room 3 and the *Z* would switch the dogs in Rooms 1 and 3, putting Onyx in Room 1, not in Room 2. The same for (E)—it puts Onyx in Room 1 because the two *X* calls cancel each other out and the *Z* would switch Lassie and Onyx—we're trying to get Onyx into Room 2, not Room 1. So (C) is correct for Question 12.

**13** B- There's a long way and a short way to do Question 13—the long way is to try out each sequence and see which one yields *O* and *l* in Room 2. The short, and smart way, is to think it through—see where *O* and *l* are in the original arrangement and see what commands would move them to Room 2. Thus, to get Oprah from her original position in Room 3 to the desired position in Room 2 you'd have to use *W*, the only one that moves trainers, twice. The first *W* moves Oprah to Room 1, and the second *W* moves her to Room 2. We also want to get Lassie from Room 1 to Room 2, and to do that we need one *X*. Do any of the choices have two *W*s and one *X*? (B) does, and it's correct for Question 13.

Let's look through the wrong choices. (A)'s sequence of *X*, *Y* and *W* puts Oprah in Room 1 and Lassie in Room 3. (C)'s suggestion of *Z*, *W* and *A* puts Oprah again in Room 1, but Lassie in Room 2. (D) puts *O* and *l* together but in Room 1 rather than Room 2. (E) puts

Oprah in Room 2, but Lassie's in Room 3. Again, it's (B) for Question 13.

**14** C- We can answer this question the same way we answered Question 13. We want to get Molly and Onyx in Room 1, Oprah and Mugs in Room 2 and Luis and Lassie in Room 3. Let's deal with the trainers first. In order to get from *L, M, O* to *M, O, L*, you call *W* twice. Call *W* once, you'll get *O, L, M* in rooms 1, 2 and 3 respectively—call it again and you'll get *M, O, L* which is what we want. Now for the dogs—how to go from *l, m, o* to *o, m, l*? One call of *Z* will do it. Command *Z* will make the dogs in Rooms 1 and 3 change places, giving us *o, m, l* as desired. But two *W*s and one *Z* isn't a choice, so there must be some other way to get this arrangement. What if we tried calling *A* between the two calls of *W*? The first *W* would give us Oprah in 1, Luis in 2, and Molly in 3 with the dogs in their original positions. But if you called *A*, the dogs would seek out their original trainers, so you'd have Oprah and Onyx in Room 1, Luis and Lassie in Room 2 and Molly and Mugs in Room 3. Keeping in mind that we'll have a second W for the trainers, what will line up the dogs? *Y* will, putting Mugs in Room 2 and Lassie in Room 3 and we'd have our dogs all set. Our second *W* will get the trainers in the proper place, so we've got our answer, *W, A, Y, W,* (C).

## GAME IV: QUESTIONS 15-18

**The Action:**

7 people to distribute in 8 apartments—1 will remain empty. You can think of it as seven people and one non-person to be distributed in the eight apartments which are arranged in two levels of four adjacent apartments. The action of the game is taking your people, *P, Q, R, S, T, V, W* and *E* for the empty apartment, and filling them in the eight apartments. We'll make A level the top and B level the bottom.

**The Rules:**

1) *W* lives directly above *S*, which tells us that there has to be another apartment. *W* is on the A level and *S* is on the B level .

2) *S* and *Q* are on different levels, so *Q* must be on *A* level.

3) *P* and *T* are adjacent on the same level. Adjacent means it could be either *TP* or *PT*.

4) This jibes nicely with Rule 3—it tells us that *T* is not in one of the end apartments—*T* is not in apartment 1 or in apartment 4. We know from Rule 3 that *P* is in an apartment on one side of *T*, and Rule 4 tells us someone else is on the other side of *T*. So *T* is in either apartment 2 or apartment 3.

5) *W* is next to the empty apartment on the same level. We know that *W* is on level A, so the empty apartment is on level A.

**Recap:** So far we have *W*, the empty apartment and *Q* on level A, *S* on level B—who's still up in the air? *P, T, V* and *R*. But we know that *P* and *T* have to be adjacent on the same level, and they can't be on level A, since there are 3 apartments filled there, so by deduction we know that *P* and *T* are on level B. *V* and *R* are left—one will be on A, the other on B.

**15** A- Who must be on level B? Well, the only definite person on level B among the choices is (A), *P*, the correct answer. As for the others, choice (B), *Q* and (E), the empty apartment, are both on A. As for (C) and (D), *R* and *V*, we know that one's on A, the other on B but we don't know which is which. Again it's (A) for Question 15.

**16** E- Here we learn about *W*—*W* lives in apartment A-2, level A, apartment 2. With *W* there, we put *S* directly underneath in apartment B-2. We also know that the empty apartment is either A-1 or A-3 so that it's adjacent to *W* on the same level. *T* has to be in either B-2 or B-3, because it can't be on the end, so since B-2 is occupied by *S*, *T* has to go in B-3 and we can put *P* in B-4, so (E) is correct.

As for (D), *P* is in apartment 4 on B level, not on A level. And with choices (A) and (C), we have no more light on the *R* and *V* issue here. We know one's on A, the other's on B, but that's all we know. As for (B), we know the empty apartment could be either 1 or 3 on level A. Again, (E) is correct.

**17** E- We're told that *R* is in A-3 and that *R* is directly above *P*. So *P* is in B-3, and we need a place for *V*. Once we have *P* in apartment B-3, we know that since *T* can't be on the end so it can't be in B-1 or B-4, it has to be next to *P* in apartment B-2. Now turn to your other large unit, the *W*, *S*, empty unit. Either *W* and *S* could be in the two apartment 1's or in the two apartment 4's. But they can't be in the two apartment 4's since the empty apartment has to be next to *W* on the same level. The apartment next to A-4 is A-3 and that's occupied by *R*. So *W* and *S* have to be in A-1 and B-1 respectively, and the empty apartment goes next to *W* in A-2. *Q* would go into A-4 and we've got the place for *V*—only B-4 is left. That's (E), which is correct for Question 17.

**18** C- Put *Q* in A-2, directly above *T*, which is in B-2. The question asks about apartment A-1, so we'll keep an eye on it as we make our deductions.

Now we turn to our *W*, *S*, empty apartment unit. Since *W* and the empty apartment have to be adjacent on level A, there's only one place for them—in A-3 and 4, in either order. So only two people could go in apartment A-1. *Q*, *W* and the empty apartment are out of the running, and *T*, *P* and *S* are out because they're

on level B. It's between *V* and *R*—but since we're only looking for possibility here, either one will do. *R* is not an answer choice but *V* is—it's (C), which is correct for Question 18.

## GAME V: QUESTIONS 19-22

**The Action:** 7 people to distribute into 3 groups. Let's put senior members in capitals, *F*, *G*, *H*, and the junior members and applicants in lower case letters, *k*, *m* and *p*, *r* —the only distinction that's significant is senior members from the rest since there has to be one senior member in each game. There are three different groups—backgammon with two people, chess with two and dominoes with three.

**The Rules:**

1) Seven people—seven slots.

2) We have three senior members, so we have one capital letter in each group.

3) *G* and *r* don't play the same game.

4) *H* and *p* must play the same game. They could play backgammon or chess or they could be two-thirds of the domino group, so if *H* and someone other than *p* are playing the same game, (or *p* and someone else), they must play dominoes.

5) *m* doesn't play dominoes.

**19** D- Try Rule 5—both (A) and (C) violate it by having *m* play dominoes. Rule 4 looks helpful—*H* and *p* play the same game, but all the remaining choices, (B), (D) and (E) comply. Rule 3 tells us that *G* and *r* can't play the same game—(E) has them together. Rule 2 says we need a senior in each game. (B) has *F* and *H*, two seniors both playing dominoes and no senior playing chess, so (B) is out and it's (D) for Question 19.

**20** D- Neither *k* nor *r* is a senior and we need a senior for each game—and only dominoes has three people playing it. Who can be the senior? It can't be *H*, since *H* is with *p*. It can't be *G* either since G and *r* can't play the same game, so it's *F*. *F*, *k* and *r* are playing dominoes, making (D) correct.

**21** A- Since *r* is lower case we know that the other backgammon player must be a senior. *G* and *r* can't play together, so *G*'s out. Since *H* and *p* are together, it can't be *H*. It must be *F*, so *F* and *r* are playing backgammon.

Now go to your largest unit—the *Hp* unit. Either *H* and *p* are the entire chess group or two-thirds of the domino group. If they play chess, *G*, *m* and *k* play dominoes but *m* can't play dominoes, so this won't work and *H* and *p* must play dominoes. With *F* in backgammon and *H* in dominoes the other senior, *G*, must play chess with *m*; and *k* must play dominoes with *H* and *p*. When *r* plays backgammon, there's only one grouping possible, so (A), one, is the correct answer for Question 21.

**22** B- Which group can't play the same game? What about *H* and *r*? Remember when *H* is with someone else, *p* comes along so we'd have *H*, *p* and *r* together, and they'd have to play dominoes. That would leave, say, *F* and *m* playing backgammon and *G* and *k* playing chess—no problem, so (A) can't be our answer. Nix (E), *p* and *r*, since we know that *H*, *p* and *r* playing dominoes is okay. What about (B)? Well, *k* and *m* are both lower case, and we need a capital for each, so *k*, *m* plus a capital would play dominoes (since there are three of them.) But *m* can't play dominoes, so *k* and *m* can't play together, making (B) correct for Question 22.

For the record, *F* and *m*, (C), would be fine. We could have *F* and *m* playing backgammon, *G* and *k* playing chess and *H*, *p* and *r* playing dominoes. We've seen (D)'s suggestion of *G* and *m* before. *G* and *m* could play backgammon, *F* and *k* chess, and *H*, *p* and *r* dominoes.

The impossible pair is (B), the correct answer for Question 22.

**23** D- According to the passage, when foreign aid money is tied, nation A gives money to nation B with the understanding that B will use the money only to buy A's products. That way, nation A makes most of its money back. The author says that European nations are phasing out this practice in order to avoid criticism leveled at other donors, "notably Japan." The inference to be drawn here is that Japan has been criticized for tying its foreign aid, so (D) is the inference we're looking for.

(A) isn't inferable because the passage discusses only **one** non-European nation, Japan, and its foreign aid policy. (E) says the same thing, that non-European nations are out for their own profit—one comment about Japan doesn't let you make sweeping inferences about non-European nations.

Choices (B) and (C) make statements of opinion—(B) about the role of ethical considerations and (C) about how to help underdeveloped countries—the author doesn't make any policy recommendations so (B) and (C) are wrong. Once again it's (D) for Question 23.

**24** D- The author argues that we must accept inconvenience if we want to secure the well-being of our world. Most pollution is caused by vehicle fuel and, according to the author, it "must be cut regardless of the costs." That's best summarized by (D). We must do what's necessary, no matter how drastic and costly, to save the environment.

The closest choice is probably (B), but the "if then" statement in (B) argues that a lower rate of car use would be sufficient to drastically reduce pollution. The author doesn't say that driving less is **sufficient** to cut pollution, but rather that it is **necessary** to cut pollution. (C) brings in the use of fuel by industry, which is outside the scope here. (A)'s saying that we've got to go back to the 19th century is too extreme to describe this argument. Finally, (E) states a causal relationship not implied in the stimulus—that people overuse their cars because they don't care about the environment. Again, (D)'s correct for Question 24.

**25** A- When the commissary serves fish on workdays, all the actors eat there. When the commissary doesn't serve fish on workdays, none of the actors eat there. What happens on a non-workday? We don't know. So you're asked what it means when all the actors are eating in the commissary. One possibility is that it's a workday and they're serving fish, but there's still the question of non-workdays. If all we know is that the actors are eating in the commissary, it's a workday and fish is served or it's not a workday and fish may or may not be served on non-workdays. No choice says exactly this, but (A) comes the closest. (A) gives you three possibilities—that it's not a workday, that the commissary is serving fish, which would have to be true on a workday, or both, that it's a non-workday and fish is being served, so it's (A) for Question 25.

(E) was tricky—it lists only one of the possible types of days when the actors could be found in the commissary, the workday with fish. (B) also doesn't say anything about non-workdays. (C) and (D) have the opposite problem, claiming that any day the actors are in the commissary is a non-workday, but we know that's not true because the actors always eat in the commissary on workdays when they're serving fish. (A) is correct for Question 25.

**1** **A-** We're told that the fundamental (blank) between cats and dogs is a myth, that the species actually coexist quite (blankly). We need a contrast, and we find it in (A)—"antipathy" means aversion or dislike, and "amiably" means agreeably.

In (B), if the members of the species coexisted "uneasily," their "disharmony" wouldn't be a myth. In (C), both "compatibility" and "together" imply that dogs and cats are good friends. In (D), it doesn't make sense to say that the "relationship" between dogs and cats is a myth. In (E), no one could claim that there's no "difference" between dogs and cats.

**2** **E-** The clue is the signal "rather than"— we need a contrast between what the speaker intended and what he achieved. The word "monotonous" clues you into boredom, and "bore" in (E), followed by "convince" makes the contrast we need.

In (A), "enlighten" and "inform" are similar. "Interest" and "persuade," (B), don't show contrast. In (C), "provoke" and "influence" don't express a contrast. "Allay" in (D) means to relieve, which is similar to "pacify," which means to calm or to make peace. No contrast here, and again, it's (E) for Question 2.

**3** **E-** The blank is part of a cause and effect structure as the keyword "that" indicates. Because government restrictions are so something, businesses can operate with nearly complete impunity. There's an absence of restrictions, so we need a word that cancels out restrictions. Would a "traditional" restriction, (A), be canceled out? No. (B), "judicious," means wise or having sound judgment, but a wise restriction would probably be effective. In (C), "ambiguous" means unclear, but though ambiguity might interfere with the effectiveness of restrictions, it doesn't cancel them out. (D), "exacting" means very strict, which is the

opposite of what we want. (E), lax, means loose, careless or sloppy. This describes restrictions that aren't very strict, and it's correct for Question 3.

**4** **A-** The first blank describes a book— the recent Oxford edition of the works of Shakespeare is (blank). The word "because" tells us that what follows is an explanation of why this book is whatever it is. The "not only but also" structure tells us that there are **two** reasons why: it departs from the readings of other editions, and it challenges basic (blanks) of textual criticism. In (A), we could say that challenging "conventions" could make a book "controversial." Conventions are accepted practices, so challenging conventions would make a book controversial. What else have we got? (B) gives us the book is "typical" because it challenges "innovations." Typical doesn't fit in with the "departs from other editions" part. How about (C)? Challenging "norms," which are rules or patterns, wouldn't make something "inadequate." (D)—a book that is different might be called "curious," but could you call a book curious for challenging "projects"? Finally, (E) says the book is "pretentious" because it challenges "explanations"—no good. So the best answer for Question 4 is (A).

**5** **D-** In Question 5 we learn that an early form of writing, Linear B, was (blank) in 1952. The keyword "but" tells us that Linear A, an older form, met with a contrasting fate, so we'll look for a pair of contrasting words. The words "no one has yet succeeded in" precede the second blank, so instead of a word that is contrasted with the first blank, we need a word that means about the same thing. That leads us to pick (D)—the words "deciphered" and "interpretation" are similar since both imply understanding.

The word "superseded" in (A) means replaced

by something more up to date—not giving an "explanation" of something. (B)—in the context of ancient languages, a "transcription" would probably be a decoded version of something. That would be the opposite of "encoding" something. (C)'s "obliterated" and "analysis" imply a contrast—wiping something out is different from figuring it out. In (E) "discovered" and "obfuscation" are more at odds than they are alike. Obfuscation means confusion, while a discovery usually sheds light on a situation.

**6** E- The clue here is the structure "quite normal and even (blank)"—the missing word has a more positive meaning than the word "normal." Then we get "I was therefore surprised," which tips us off to look for contrast. "Commendable" and "complimentary" in (A) are both positive. In (B), "odious" means hateful, so odious and "insulting" are both negative. "Conciliatory" in (C) means placating or reconciling, which fits in with "apologetic." "Commonplace" and "typical" in (D) mean the same thing. Only correct choice (E) is left—"laudable" means praiseworthy while "derogatory" means belittling or detracting.

**7** D- Whatever we're doing to the burden of medical costs is causing the removal of the second blank, signalled by "thereby." In (A), it doesn't make sense to say that to "augment" or add to the burden would remove a "problem"—it could make the problem worse. In (B), a "perquisite" is a reward over and above one's salary. But would "eliminating" a burden remove a perquisite? In (C), to "ameliorate" means to improve, but you can't talk about removing a major "study of" medical care. (D) is perfect. To "assuage" means to make less severe and an "impediment" is an obstacle. Assuaging the burden would remove an impediment to medical care, so (D)'s correct. As for (E), to "clarify" means to "explain"

or make clear, and explaining the burden of medical costs wouldn't remove an explanation.

**8** A- A "novel" is a type of "book." That's an easy bridge. In (A), is an "epic" a type of "poem"? Yes, an epic is a long narrative poem, so (A) is right. In (B), a "house" isn't a type of "library." (C) is tempting—"tales" and "fables" are related, but a fable is a kind of tale, not vice versa, so it's not parallel. In (D), a "number" is not a type of "page" and in (E) a "play" isn't a type of "theater."

**9** B- "Ravenous" means extremely "hungry"—the second word is an extreme version of the first word. In (A), "desirous" means desiring or wanting something—it's not an extreme form of "thirsty." (B) is perfect—"titanic" is an amplification of "large." Titanic means gigantic, so (B) is the answer.

"Eminent" and "famous" in (C) mean the same thing. (D)'s "disoriented" and "dizzy" are close in meaning. To be disoriented means to have lost your bearings, and when you're dizzy, you feel as if you're going to fall down. (E)'s "obese" and "gluttonous" could be related, but don't have to be. Gluttonous comes from gluttony—it means excessive eating or drinking. Gluttony doesn't have to result in obesity and it's not an extreme form of it.

**10** B- A bouquet is an arrangement of flowers, so the first word will be an arrangement of the second word. The first word in (A) is archaic—a "humidor" is a container for "tobacco"—a container for tobacco is not the same as a formal arrangement of it. The next choice, (B), is more like it. A "mosaic" is made of "tiles," just as a bouquet is made up of flowers. That's a good match. In (C), a "tapestry" is not made of "color," it's made of threads woven to make a design. You can't argue that a tapestry is an arrangement of colors. (D) also has problems. A "pile" of "blocks" could be an arrangement. But a bouquet isn't just an arrangement of flowers—it's an orderly arrangement. In the same way, a mosaic is an orderly arrangement of tiles. A pile isn't a formal arrangement. What about "sacristy" and "vestment" in (E)? A sacristy is a room in a church where priests' clothes or vestments are kept, so vestments are stored in a sacristy. The correct answer is (B).

**11** D- "Quixotic" means impractical, after the hero of *Don Quixote*. A "realist" is a person who is especially realistic. Realistic is the opposite of quixotic, so a realist is never quixotic. In (A), "pedantic" people show off their learning. Many "scholars" are pedantic, so this won't work. In (B), a "fool" is foolish— a synonym for "idiotic." The same relationship holds true for (C)—an "idler" is a "lethargic" person. (D) looks good—a "tormentor" is vicious or cruel. The opposite sort of person would be kinder and more "sympathetic"—a tormentor is never sympathetic. (E) "dyspeptic" means suffering from indigestion. A "diner" is someone who eats—some diners get dyspeptic, some don't, so (D)'s correct.

**12** E- A "shard" is a broken fragment of "glass" or crockery. Glass, when it shatters, creates shards, so a shard is a piece of broken glass. (E) shows the same analogy—a "splinter" is a piece of broken "wood." As for the wrong choices, in (A), a "grain" is the basic unit that "sand" comes in, but you can't talk about breaking sand. (B)'s "morsel" means a bit of food, but a "meal" doesn't shatter into morsels. In (C), a "rope" is composed of "strands" and (D) a "quilt" is made from "scraps." The correct answer is (E).

**13** A- The word "filter" is used as a verb. When you use a filter, an "impurity" is removed, so you filter to remove an impurity. The word "expurgate" in (A) means to censor to remove "obscenities"—you expurgate to remove an obscenity. To "whitewash," (B), is to misrepresent a bad thing to make it look better. An infraction isn't removed by whitewashing it, it's only covered up, so (B) isn't parallel. In (C), "perjury" is the crime of lying under oath. To "testify" doesn't mean to remove a false statement. In (D) "penance" is something you do to atone for a sin, but you don't "perform" to remove penance. And in (E) you don't "vacuum" to remove a "carpet." So (A) is correct.

**14** A- "Paraphrase" means restatement of a text using different words. "Verbatim" means "word for word" or exact. "A paraphrase is not verbatim"—the words are near opposites. The only choices opposite in meaning are "approximation" and "precise," in (A). An "approximation" is an estimate, while something that's "precise" is exact, so an approximation is not precise. A "description" might or might not be "vivid" in (B). In (C), "apt" means appropriate, so a "quotation" could be apt. There's no relationship in (D), "interpretation" and "valid" or in (E), "significance" and "uncertain." (A) is correct.

**15** E- Even if you didn't know what "oncology" means, you might have guessed the study of something because of the "ology" ending, and judging from the other word it's probably the study of "tumors." The choices look like sciences too. (A)'s pairing of "chronology" and "time" looks okay, but not dead on. There's a science called chronology, the science of arranging time into periods. Chronology is not exactly the study of time— it's a science involved with mapping events in time. Likewise, (B) is almost there. The "theo" in "theology" comes from the Greek word for god, and theology means the study of gods or religious beliefs. "Tenet," on the other hand, means a particular belief or principle. It's too narrow to say theology is the study of tenets. We can eliminate (C) because "aural" is not the study of "sound"—that would be closer to acoustics. In (D), "philology" is a field that includes the study of literary history, language history and systems of writing, not the study of "religion." "Taxonomy," (E) is the study of "classification," the correct answer. Taxonomy is also used to refer specifically to the classification of organisms.

**16** B- "Intransigent" means unyielding— the opposite of flexible. Our bridge is "a person who is intransigent is lacking in flexibility." The only pair that looks good is (B), "disinterested" and "partisanship." One who's disinterested is unbiased—he doesn't have an interest in either side of a dispute. "Partisan" means partial to a particular party or cause. That's the opposite of disinterested. So partisanship, the quality of being biased, is lacking in a person who could be described as disinterested.

In (A), "transient" means transitory, so you wouldn't say that someone transient lacks "mobility." In (C), "dissimilar" means not similar, along the same lines as "variation." You can't say that something "progressive" lacks "transition," so (D) is no good. The word "ineluctable" in (E) means inescapable, while "modality" is a longer way of saying mode.

The longer of the two reading comp passages appears first. The author's main concern, the aim of science to derive a theory which describes particles and their forces as simply as possible, becomes apparent early in the first paragraph. Simplicity is so important that the author sets it up as a criterion for judging the specific theory of nature. Then the author outlines a recently developed theory which he considers to be a remarkable achievement for its frugality and level of detail. He then asserts that an even simpler theory is conceivable and goes on to mention one which promises at least a partial unification of elementary particles and forces. The last half of the second paragraph and the final paragraph describe this theory in greater detail.

**17** D- We need either a choice that describes the similarity between the theories, or one that falsifies information about them. (D) should raise your suspicions. The author acknowledged at the end of the first paragraph that the first theory could account for the entire observed hierarchy of material structure. (D) is right, but let's look at the others.

(A) is a valid difference between the two theories—the second is presented as a simpler alternative to the first. (B) is also a real difference. The first theory encompass gravitation and the second unifies three of the four forces, which makes it a better theory, but it doesn't account for gravitation. The first theory includes leptons and quarks, while the second combines these two classes into just one, so (C) is valid. In a similar way, the second theory unifies three of the four forces outlined in the first theory, so (E) is valid. Again, it's (D) for Question 17.

**18** B- Question 18 asks for the primary purpose, and we know that the author is concerned with theories that describe, simply and precisely, particles and their forces. The author's primary purpose is to describe attempts to develop a simplified theory of nature. Skimming through the choices, (B) looks good. (E) doesn't fit at all. You might say the author summarizes the theories describing matter, but he doesn't summarize all that is known about matter itself. As for (A), the author doesn't cite a misconception in either of the theories he describes. At most, he mentions ways in which the first could be simplified but this doesn't imply that there's a misconception. The author does refer to the second theory as a leading candidate for achieving unification, but predicting its success, (C), is far from his primary purpose. As for (D), although it's implied that scientists in general do prefer simpler theories, their reasons for this preference are never discussed. Again, it's (B) for Question 18.

**19** E- Question 19 is a scattered detail question concerning quarks. In the first paragraph we're told that quarks are constituents of the proton and the neutron. It's reasonable, then, to say that quarks are the elementary building blocks of protons and neutrons, option I. Since option I is correct, we can eliminate choices which exclude it, (B) and (D). The remaining choices are either I only, I and II only, or I, II and III. You could skip II and go to III. If you're sure III is right, you can assume that II is also and pick (E). It turns out that III can be easily checked at the end of paragraph three where the author states that a new theory incorporates the leptons and quarks into a single family or class, so option III is correct. For a complete list, let's look at option II. In the very first sentence the author tells us that elementary particles don't have an internal structure and since quarks are elementary particles, option II is indeed correct and (E) is our answer.

**20** C- It should be clear that the author has some very definite criteria for judging the usefulness or worth of various theories of nature. As for option I, "simplicity" should leap off the page at you—it's what this passage is all about. We can eliminate (B) and (E). The author also takes the theory's completeness into consideration. He commends the first theory he describes because it accounts for the entire observed hierarchy of material structure and therefore option II is correct. We know that (C) must be correct because there is no I, II and III choice. But let's look at III anyway. Does the author ever mention proving either of those two theories he describes? Proof is of no concern to him—there's no mention in the passage of any experiments, or of wanting to find experimental proof. So III is out and (C) it is.

**21** E- We've mentioned that the second theory doesn't include gravitation in its attempt to unify the four basic forces. We need the author's opinion about this omission. The author introduces the theory in the second paragraph, describing it as an ambitious theory which promises at least a partial unification of elementary particles and forces. The failure to include gravitation and achieve complete unification doesn't dampen the author's enthusiasm and he seems to suggest that gravitation's omission can't be helped, at least at this stage. So, although the omission is a limitation—it prevents total unification—it is also unavoidable. It looks like (E) does the trick. You could see the limitation as a defect, (A), but the author never gives the impression that the omission of gravitation disqualifies the theory. As for (B), "deviation" is a funny word—deviation from what? More important, we've already seen that the author doesn't consider the omission to be unjustified. For the same reason, (C) can be eliminated. If the omission of gravitation can't be avoided, then it certainly isn't a needless oversimplification. Finally (D) is out because there's no way that gravitation's omission could be an oversight. A scientist just forgot about one of the four basic forces when developing a theory of nature? No, the idea is that, for now at least, gravitation just can't be fit in, and (E) is correct.

**22** **B-** The passage begins with the author's discussion of the simplicity of elementary particles and the theories which describe them. In the third sentence, the author sets forth simplicity as a standard for judging theories of nature. In the rest of the passage, the author measures two specific theories against this standard. (B) summarizes this setup nicely and it's our answer. (A) is way off base. Although the author might be said to enumerate distinctions between how the two theories treat elementary particles, he doesn't enumerate distinctions among the particles. (C) is easy to eliminate—the author describes only two methods of grouping particles and forces—not three. As for (D), the author doesn't criticize the first theory he describes or call it inaccurate—he commends it. Finally, (E) goes overboard. As we mentioned in our discussion of option III in Question 20, the author is not interested in scientific verification. Nothing is ever mentioned about proving or verifying either of the theories he describes. Again, (B) is correct.

**23** **C-** Question 23, our last one for this passage, shouldn't be difficult. It asks us to put ourselves in the author's shoes and figure out what sort of theory he would find superior to present theories. We already know—a simpler theory. The author's criteria for judging a theory are its simplicity and its ability to account for the largest possible number of known phenomena. Which choice represents a theory with one or both of these characteristics? (A) misrepresents the two theories described in the passage. The author says that the first theory could account for the entire observed hierarchy of material structure. The second does also, even though gravitation must be thrown in as a separate force. A theory that could account for a larger number of structures isn't what's needed. As for (B), why would the author approve of a theory that

reduces the four basic forces to two which are incompatible? (C) is on the right track. The author would prefer a theory that accounts for all matter with the fewest particles and forces and this is offered by (C), the correct answer. (D) is out because it wouldn't represent an improvement on currently existing theories. They account for gravitation, although they haven't yet unified it with the other three forces. Finally, (E) represents a step backwards. The current theories hypothesize that both protons and neutrons are formed by combinations of elementary particles. Again, it's (C).

The second passage is short but dense, and the author doesn't arrive at her main point until the last sentence. We see that the author sets herself in opposition to presentist historians, people who believe that white abolitionists and suffragists comprise the abiding principles of equality and the equal right of all to life, liberty and the pursuit of happiness. Their evidence is presented in the first three sentences. First, a majority of both groups tried to assure people that the changes they advocated weren't revolutionary and served to support rather than to undermine the status quo. A certain group of abolitionists disclaimed miscegenationist intentions—they were careful to assert that their interest in obtaining freedom for blacks didn't mean they were advocating mixing of races. And finally, suffragists saw no conflict between racism or nativism and their movement's objectives. Presentist historians apparently think that, by denying any revolutionary intentions and miscegenationist intentions, and by justifying nativism and racism, both groups were undermining their own principles and because their objectives, the abolition of slavery and voting rights for all, go hand in hand with our present conception of equality, presentist historians think that both groups undermine the principle of equality at the same time. The author uses the same evidence to argue that the actions of both groups served not to show how far these groups deviated from a fixed principle of equality, but to show what the principle meant in their own generations. The author thinks that the principle of equality is not unchanging, but means different things for different generations and that presentist historians err when they judge these movements by our conception of equality.

**24** C- We need the author's main point, which we just formulated—the actions of abolitionists and suffragists demonstrate the meaning that equality had in their time. (C) expresses this, and it's the correct answer. (A) is wrong because it's the presentist historians who believe that the actions of the abolitionists and suffragists compromised their principles. (B) has nothing to do with the author's discussion. A comparison of beliefs never occurs. As for (D), the author charges presentist historians with misinterpreting abolitionist and suffragist ideology, not with willfully misrepresenting it. Finally, (E) constitutes a criticism the author makes about presentist historians—that they impose their own value systems on the past, rather than interpreting actions in the appropriate historical context. Again, it's (C) for Question 24.

**25** A- We can infer something about the author's concept of the principle of equality—it's clear that the author thinks the principle of equality is not abiding. Rather, she thinks, it encompasses different things for people at different times. We can give the nod to option I, which eliminates (B), (C) and (E). Since the only choices left include option I only or options I and II only, option III can be eliminated. Option II—does the author suggest that the suffragists applied the principle of equality more consistently than

abolitionists? No, if anything, she implies that they applied it equally consistently. We're left with (A) as our answer. We know option III can't be true—presentist historians say that abolitionists and suffragists compromised the principle of equality, not the author, who thinks their actions conform to their generation's conception of equality.

**26** C- Question 26 deals with the logical structure of the author's argument, how she argues her case against the presentist historians. She uses the same evidence to support her views that they do, cites the actions of the suffragists and abolitionists, states that the presentist historians knew of these actions, then presents her own interpretation of these same actions. She's applying a different interpretation to the same set of facts, and (C) is our answer. The author doesn't cite any new evidence, so both (A) and (B) can be ruled out. As for (D), the author refutes not the accuracy of the historians' data, but the accuracy of their interpretation. Finally, the author doesn't claim that the historians' argument is flawed by a logical contradiction, (E). She claims instead that they erred by assuming that equality is an abiding value and by measuring the actions of past groups against this concept of equality. Again, it's (C) for Question 26.

**27** B- We need to know what the author suggests about the abolitionist movement. Well, in her references to this movement, the author mentions the non-Garrisonian abolitionists. If there were non-Garrisonian abolitionists, it seems reasonable to assume that Garrisonian abolitionists existed. Also, the author refers to a majority of white abolitionists who made certain denials. This implies that there was a minority of abolitionists who didn't make such denials and also that there were black abolitionists. In other words, the abolitionist movement was sub-divided into different groups and these groups didn't always share identical ideologies. This corresponds closely to (B), the correct answer. As for (A), the passage does state that some abolitionists denied that they had revolutionary or miscegenationist intentions, but these denials don't seem to be an attempt to disguise their real intentions. (C) is wrong because the author thinks the abolitionists did live by their principles. As for (D), presentist historians might claim that abolitionists undermined their objectives by making certain disclaimers to the public. But even they wouldn't say that these disclaimers were the result of abolitionists misunderstanding their objectives. Finally, the passage makes no mention of radical factions within the abolitionist movement and the effects of abolitionists' actions on their movement's progress is never discussed so (E) is out. Again, it's (B) for Question 27.

**28** C- Our first word is "undermine," which means to weaken or cause to collapse, especially by secret means. The opposite would be something like build up or make stronger. The best choice here is (C), "bolster," meaning to support. The only other tempting choice was (A), "appreciate," but a better opposite for appreciate would be "resent."

**29** B- "Obsequious" in Question 29 means servile or submissive. The opposite of obsequious would be something like snooty or arrogant. "Haughty," (B), fits perfectly. A haughty person is overly arrogant while an obsequious person is overly eager to please. None of the other choices comes close.

**30** C- The word "blanch" may be familiar to you if you cook. Foods like broccoli are blanched by plunging them in boiling water so they lose color. In the same way, a per-

son might blanch from fear, shock or dismay. Since blanch means to whiten or turn pale, the opposite would be to redden or blush. (C), "flush" is what we need. None of the other answer choices are particularly colorful.

**31** A- The word "dissipated" is a pejorative reference to someone devoted to the pursuit of pleasure—the opposite of dissipation is restraint or moderation. (A) is correct because "temperate" means moderate or self-restrained. None of the other answer choices have to do with moderation. "Inundated" means overwhelmed or deluged.

**32** D- "Fecundity" means fertility, the capacity for producing life, whether it be children or vegetation. Clearly the opposite would be (D), "sterility" which refers to an inability to reproduce. None of the other choices comes close, and the only unusual word is (A)'s "levity," which means silliness or frivolity.

**33** D- In Question 33, "encumber" means to block or weigh down. A good synonym would be oppress. The best opposite is (D), "disburden," which means to free from oppression. "Animate" (A), means to make alive—its opposite would be something like deaden. To "inaugurate," (B), means to begin or commence. To "bleach" means to pale or whiten and to "obliterate" means to erase or remove.

**34** C- The word "disseminate" isn't so easy to figure out if you don't know it—it means to spread widely. Ideas, theories, and beliefs can all be disseminated. The opposite of spreading an idea is "suppressing" it, (C). None of the other choices works.

**35** D- "Restive" looks like the word rested, but the two don't mean the same thing at all. Restive can mean stubborn or restless. A mule that won't move is restive, as is a fidgety child. We need something like obedient, quiet or settled, and it's "patient," (D). "Morose" in (A) means gloomy. "Intangible" means untouchable or elusive. "Fatigued" means tired and the opposite of "curious" would be indifferent.

**36** B- If you didn't know what "syncopated" means, you might have guessed it had something to do with rhythm from the expression "out of sync." That would lead you to (B), "normally accented." Syncopation refers to a pattern or rhythm in which stress is shifted onto normally unaccented beats.

The opposite of (A)'s "carefully executed" would be haphazard, and (C)'s "brightly illuminated" is the opposite of dim. Obscure would be an antonym for (D)'s "easily understood." "Justly represented," in (E) isn't easy to match, but even if you couldn't eliminate all the choices, you could have at least narrowed the field. So it's (B) for Question 36.

**37** C- "Vituperative" means verbally abusive. The opposite of defaming someone with vituperative remarks would be praising them—(C)'s "laudatory" means expressing praise. As for the other choices, "lethal" means deadly and "incapacitated" means incapable or unfit. In (D), "insulated" means protected, as in insulation, and "prominent," (E), means famous.

**38** B- "Saturnine" is probably the hardest word in the section. It means heavy, gloomy, sluggish, so its opposite is cheerful or lively. The answer is (B), "ebullient" which means bubbling with enthusiasm or high-spirited. (A)'s "magnanimous" means generous or high-minded. "Finicky," (C), means fussy or picky. The opposite of (D), "unnatural" is natural and (E), "impoverished" means poor.

**1** **A-** To compare these two quantities, work column by column starting with the decimal point and working to the right. Both have a zero in the tenths column, so no difference there. In the hundredths column, both have a 2, so we go to thousandths. <u>Column A</u> has a 6 and <u>Column B</u> has a 5—there are more thousandths in A than in B, so <u>Column A</u> is larger and (A) is the correct answer.

**2** **C-** Right triangles $ABD$ and $CDB$ share a hypotenuse, segment $DB$. The squared quantities should clue you to use the Pythagorean theorem. See that $w$ and $x$ are lengths of the legs of right triangle $ABD$. Side $AD$ has length $w$, side $AB$ has length $x$. Also, $y$ and $z$ are lengths of the legs of right triangle $CDB$. Side $CD$ has length $z$, side $CB$ has length $y$. Where $a$ and $b$ are lengths of the legs of a right triangle, and $C$ is the length of the hypotenuse, $a^2 + b^2 = c^2$, so $w^2 + x^2 =$ length $BD^2$. $y^2 + z^2$ also equals length $DB^2$, the quantities are equal and the answer is (C).

**3** **A-** We have $x + 4y = 6$ and $x = 2y$, and we want to compare $x$ and $y$, so substitute $2y$ for $x$ in the first equation. Using that information, solve for the other variable. Substitute $2y$ for $x$ into $x + 4y = 6$ and get $2y + 4y = 6$ or $6y = 6$. Divide both sides by 6 and we get $y = 1$. If $y = 1$ and $x = 2y$ as the second equation tells us, $x$ must equal 2. 2 is greater than 1 so the quantity in <u>Column A</u> is greater.

**4** **B-** Question 4 looks hard—but you don't have to simplify to find the relationship. With positive numbers, you can square both without changing the relationship. That leaves you with $4^2 + 5^2$ in <u>Column A</u> and $3^2 + 6^2$ in <u>Column B</u>. $4^2$ is 16, $5^2$ is 25, 16 + 25 is 41. In <u>Column B</u> we have $3^2$, that's 9 + $6^2$, that's 36, 9 + 36 is 45. 45 is greater than 41, <u>Column B</u> is greater than <u>Column A</u>, and

the answer is (B).

**5** **D-** <u>Column A</u> asks for the number of managerial employees—that's easy. There are 120 employees in the firm, and 25 percent of them are managerial. One-fourth of 120 is 30, the value of <u>Column A.</u>

<u>Column B</u> asks for two-thirds of the clerical employees. But we can't figure out how many workers are clerical workers, so we can't find two-thirds of that number. We can't determine a relationship, and the answer is choice (D).

**6** **B-** We have $12 \times 1$ over $12 + 1$ in <u>Column A</u>—$12 \times 1$ is 12 and $12 + 1$ is 13. So we have $\frac{12}{13}$ in <u>Column A</u>. In <u>Column B</u> we have $12 + 1 = 13$ in the numerator, and $12 \times 1 = 12$ in the denominator. So $\frac{12}{13}$ in <u>Column A</u> versus $\frac{13}{12}$ in <u>Column B</u>—of course, $\frac{12}{13}$ is less than 1 while $\frac{13}{12}$ is greater than 1, and the answer is (B).

**7** **D-** You might suspect (D) because there are no variable restrictions. To make the columns look as much alike as you can, multiply out <u>Column A</u>. You'll get $a \times b$ or $ab$, plus $1 \times b$, plus $1 \times a$, plus $1 \times 1$ or 1. So you get $ab + a + b + 1$. <u>Column B</u> has $ab + 1$. We can subtract $ab$ from both sides, and it won't change the relationship and we have $1 + a + b$ in <u>Column A</u>, and 1 in <u>Column B</u>. Subtract 1 from both sides and we have $a + b$ in <u>Column A</u> and 0 in <u>Column B</u>. But consider that $a$ and $b$ could be negative numbers. Since $a + b$ could be positive, negative or zero, the answer is (D).

**8** **B-** In the two-digit number $jk$ the value of digit $j$ is twice the value of digit $k$. We have to compare the value of $k$ in Column A with 6 in Column B. If you plug in 6 for $k$, then go back, you see that the value of digit $j$ is twice digit $k$. We know that $j$ isn't just a number—it's a digit, which means it's 0, 1, 2, 3, 4, 5, 6, 7, 8 or 9. So 12, twice the value of 6, can't be $j$. In other words, $k$ has to be something less than 6, so the answer must be (B), the value in Column B is greater.

**9** **A-** We have a circle with right angle $QPR$ as a central angle. The area of sector $PQR$ is 4 and we're asked to compare the area of the circle with $4\pi$. There's a shortcut—the right angle defines the sector, and you have the area of that sector. A 90 degree angle cuts off one-fourth of the circle. If you multiply by four, you have the area of the circle. So in Column A you have $4 \times 4$, and in Column B, you have $4\pi$. $\pi$ is about 3.14, and 4 is bigger than that, so Column A, $4 \times 4$, must be bigger than $4\pi$, and the answer is (A).

**10** **C-** Henry purchased $x$ apples and Jack purchased 10 apples less than one-third the number of apples Henry purchased. "One-third of" means the same as "one-third times" and the number of apples Henry purchased is $x$. So this boils down to $j$ equals $\frac{1}{3} x - 10$. You can plug this in for Column A. We have $\frac{1}{3} x -10$ in Column A and in Column B we have $x - \frac{30}{3}$. Now you can clear the fraction in Column B. Let's split Column B to two frac-

tions. $\frac{x}{3} - \frac{30}{3}$. We leave the $\frac{x}{3}$ alone and cancel the factor of 3 from the numerator and denominator of $\frac{30}{3}$ and we're left with $\frac{x}{3} -10$. What's $\frac{x}{3}$? It's one-third of $x$, so these two quantities are equal. Column A equals $\frac{1}{3} x -10$, while Column B also equals $\frac{1}{3} x -10$, so the answer is (C).

**11** **D-** You can suspect (D) because there are unrestricted variables. In Column A we have the volume of a rectangular solid with length 5 feet, width 4 feet and height $x$ feet. The formula is length times width times height, so we have 5 times 4 times $x$, or $20x$. In Column B we need the volume of rectangular solid with length 10 feet, width 8 feet and height $y$ feet. 10 times 8 times $y$ gives you a volume of 80y. Now you may think, I've got $20x$, and 80y, so $80y$ must be bigger because there's more $y$s than $x$s. That would be true if $x$ and $y$ were close together, but the variables are unrestricted, and the answer is (D).

**12** **C-** We want to compare 50 with $x$, one of the angles formed by the intersection of $ST$ and $PT$. Now angle $QRS$ is labeled 80. We also know $PQ$ and $ST$ have the same length and $QR$ and $RS$ have the same length. If you add $PQ$ and $QR$, you get $PR$. If you add $ST$ and $RS$, you get $RT$. If you add equals to equals, you get equals, so $PQ + QR$ must be the same as $ST + RS$, which means that $PR$ and $RT$ are the same. You have isoceles triangle $PRT$ and we're given one angle that has measure 80 and the second angle that has measure $x$. The angle measuring $x$ is opposite equal side $PR$. That means the other angle must have the same measure, because it's opposite the other equal side. The sum of the interior angles in a triangle always equals 180 degrees. $x + x + 80$ must equal 180, $2x$ must equal 100, $x = 50$. So $x$ and 50 are equal, and the answer is (C).

**13** **B-** First we can cancel factors of 2 from $2 \times 16 \times 64$ on the left, and $2 \times 4^n \times 256$ on the right. If we cancel a factor of 2 we have $16 \times 64$ on the left, $4^n \times 256$ on the right. 64 goes into 256 four times, so let's cancel a factor of 64. That leaves us 16 on the left and $4^n \times 4$ on the right. We can cancel a factor of 4 and we're left with 4 on the left and $4^n$ on the right. If $4 = 4^n$, $n$ must equal 1, so we have $n = 1$ for <u>Column A</u>. <u>Column B</u> is 2, so the answer is (B).

**14** **A-** Try to solve the centered equation for $y$. First get all the $y$'s on one side by adding $\frac{2}{y}$ to both sides. This gives $\frac{1}{3} = \frac{2}{y} - \frac{1}{2y}$. Multiplying both sides by $y$ gives $\frac{y}{3} = 2 - \frac{1}{2} = 1\frac{1}{2}$. Multiplying both sides by 3 gives $y = 3 \times 1\frac{1}{2} = 4\frac{1}{2}$. So Column A is greater than Column B.

**15** **D-** The perimeter of $ABC$ is 40 and the length of $BC$ is 12, and we want to compare the length of $AB$ with 14. In an isosceles triangle there are two sides with equal length, but we don't know whether side $BC$ is one of those sides or not. If side $BC$ is the unequal side, we have two unknown sides plus 12 and they have a sum of 40, the perimeter. The two remaining sides have a sum of 28, so each is 14. That would mean that $AB$ and $AC$ would have length 14. Then the answer would be

(C). If $BC$ is one of the equal sides, we have two sides length 12 and a third unknown side, and the sum is 40. $12 + 12$ is 24, so that the third side has length 16. $AB$ could be one of the sides length 12, or the side length 12. There are three possible lengths for side $AB$, 16, 14 and 12 so the answer is (D).

**16** **B-** Isolate $\frac{q}{p}$. Multiplying both sides of the equation by $p$ gives $p - q = \frac{2p}{7}$. Subtracting $p$ from both sides gives $-q = \frac{2p}{7} - p = \frac{2p}{7} - \frac{7p}{7} = -\frac{5p}{7}$. So $-q = -\frac{5p}{7}$, or $q = \frac{5p}{7}$. Dividing both sides by $p$ gives $\frac{q}{p} = \frac{5}{7}$.

**17** D- We need the number that's a multiple of 8 and a factor of 72. 4 and 9 aren't multiples of 8, so you can eliminate (A) and (B). 16 is, 24 is, but 36, (E), isn't. We're down to just 16 and 24; count by 16s and see if 16 is a factor of 72: 16, 32, 48, 64, 80. Well, that's not a factor of 72, so 24, (D) is correct.

**18** B- We need the value of $a + b + c$. We know that $a$, $b$ and $c$ are exterior angles of our quadrilateral in the diagram and there's a fourth exterior angle which isn't labeled. But the measure of the interior angle next to it is given to us—it's 70 degrees. The sum of the exterior angles of any figure is always 360 degrees. So we can figure out the measure of the missing angle, then subtract it from 360 and get the sum of the other three. The unlabeled angle must be 110 degrees. Now we know $110 + a + b + c = 360$, we subtract to get the sum of $a$, $b$ and $c$ and we get 250, (B) as the correct answer.

**19** E- John has 4 ties, 12 shirts and 3 belts, and we need the number of days he can go without repeating. So we multiply the number of ties times the number of shirts times the number of belts. 4 ties, 12 shirts— 48 combinations. Multiply by 3 choices of belt, and you get $3 \times 48$ or 144 combinations, (E).

**20** D- Move the decimal points to the right until they disappear—but keep track of how many places you move the decimal. In (A) we have .00003 in the numerator. Move 5 places to the right to change it to 3. Then we change from .0007 to 70 in the denominator and we

end up with $\frac{3}{70}$. In (B) we have .0008 on top, .0005 on the bottom—we get $\frac{8}{5}$. We have $\frac{70}{8}$ for (C). In (D), we end up with $\frac{60}{5}$ and $\frac{10}{8}$ in (E). Clearly (D), 12, is the largest value.

**Graphs:** Questions 21-25

**21** E- The bar graph doesn't give us the total number of general practice physicians, but if we add the number of males to the number of females, we get the total number of g. p. physicians. To find the percent who are male, we take the number of males and put it over the total number and that will give us our percent. We have around 2,000 women and around 23,000 men, making the total about 25,000. Well if there are around 25,000 g.p. physicians all together and between 2 and 3,000 of them are female, that's what percent of 25,000? It's around 10 percent. About 22,500 are male, which gives us 90 percent, (E).

**22** D- We're looking for the lowest ratio of males to females so we have to get the smallest number of males and the largest number of females. Skimming the bar graphs, we can see that in pediatrics the female graph and the male graph are closer than any of the others. Pediatrics is (D), the correct answer.

**23** C- To refer to ages of physicians, we need to find the slice of the pie that goes from 45 to 54—it's 20 percent but 20 percent of what? We're not looking for a percent, we're looking for a number of doctors. For general surgery the male bar goes up to about 35,000 and the female bar goes up to about 2,000—about 37,000 total. So 20 percent of 37,000 is the number of general surgery physicians between ages 45 and 54, inclusive. What's 20 percent of 37,000, or $\frac{1}{5}$ of 37,000? Well, let's see, $\frac{1}{5}$ of 35,000 is 7,000, $\frac{1}{5}$ of 2,000 is 400, making 7,400. (C) is 7,350, the correct answer.

**24** E- We'll have to find the total number of family practice physicians, which represents 7.5 percent of all the physicians in the United States, then we can find 100 percent of that number. The male bar of family practice physicians goes just over 36,000, so we'll say it's 36,000 plus. The number of females goes just over 6,000 so we'll call that 6,000 plus, so we have about 43,000 all together. This is 7.5 percent of all the physicians. 7.5 percent is awkward—it's three-quarters of 10 percent, which is $\frac{3}{4} \times \frac{1}{10}$, or $\frac{3}{40}$. So 43,000 is $\frac{3}{40}$ of the total number of doctors. To change 43,000 into the number of total physicians, we multiply it by $\frac{40}{3}$. Think of it this way, we have an equation now, $\frac{3}{40}$ of the number we're looking for, we'll call it $N$, the number of physicians, equals 43,000. We want to get $N$ by

itself, so we have to get rid of that $\frac{3}{40}$. So we multiply by the reciprocal, $\frac{40}{3}$ and that leaves us $N$ by itself on the left. But the hard part is multiplying $\frac{40}{3} \times 43,000$. What's $\frac{40}{3}$? It's $13\frac{1}{3}$ and that's easier to multiply, $13 \times 43$ is 559, so $13 \times 43,000$ is 559,000—you can look at your choices and estimate. Only one is close to 559,000—(E), 570,000 and we're going to add on to that, so (E), 570,000, is the correct answer.

**25** B- How many male general surgeon physicians were under 35 years old? The pie chart breaks down general surgery physicians by age, so we'll be working with it and since we're looking for a number of general surgery physicians, we know that we're going to have to find the total number of general surgery physicians, then break it down according to the percentages on the pie chart.

We're told the number of female general surgery physicians in the under 35 category represented 3.5 percent of all the general surgery physicians. What this does is break that slice of the pie for under 35 into two smaller slices, one for men under 35 and one for women under 35. Now we know that the whole slice for under 35 year olds is 30 percent of the total and we've just been told that the number of females under 35 is 3.5 percent of the total. So the difference between 30 percent and 3.5 percent must be the men in the under 35 category, which leaves 26.5 percent, which we have to multiply by the total number of general surgery physicians.

We figured out in Question 23 that there were 37,000 total general surgery physicians, and 26.5 percent of those are men under 35. What's 26.5 percent of 37,000? One quarter of 37,000 is 9,250 and that's very close to (A), but remember we've still got another 1.5 percent to go. One percent of 37,000 is 370 and half of that, or .5 percent will be 185, so if you add 370 and 185 to 9,250 you end up with a total of 9,805 which is very close to (B), the correct answer.

**26** B- We want to find the sum of the absolute value of three, the absolute value of −4 and the absolute value of 3 − 4. Well, the absolute value of 3 is 3, the absolute value of −4 is 4. What's the absolute value of 3 − 4? Do the subtraction inside the absolute value sign first, and we get −1. What's the absolute value of −1? It's 1, so we have 3 + 4 + 1 or 8 as our sum for Question 26, (B).

**27** C- This looks like a right triangle on a coordinate grid, but it's not a normal coordinate grid—the lines on the grid don't represent integer units, they represent units of less than an integer. Going up on the $y$ axis, we have .5, 1.0, 1.5 and 2.0, so the lines each represent half an integer and, going to the left, the lines are labeled −0.4, −0.8, −1.2, so these each represent .4, and yet the diagram's not drawn to scale. Going left to right, the vertical lines are actually farther apart than the horizontal lines, which represent more value on the number line. Now, to find the area of the shaded region, a triangle, we need a base and a height. This is a right triangle because its base lies on the horizontal line on our grid and its height, the side to the right, lies right on a vertical line on the grid. What's the length of the bottom side? The far right end point is at −0.4 and the far left end point is at −1.6, and the difference is 1.2 units, so the base is 1.2. The lower right vertex has value .5 and the upper right vertex has value 2.0—the difference is 1.5, so that's the height. The base is 1.2 and the height is 1.5, and the formula for the area of a right triangle is one half base times height. We have 1.2 as our base, we can call that $\frac{6}{5}$, 1.5 is $\frac{3}{2}$ so the area is $\frac{1}{2} \times \frac{6}{5} \times \frac{3}{2}$, that's $\frac{9}{10}$ or .9, choice (C).

**28** A- You could find the number of tasks per hour from one computer, but that would add extra steps, because you want to find out how many computers you need to do a certain number of tasks in three hours. Well, if it can do 30 tasks in six hours, it can do 15 tasks in three hours. So if you have two computers that's 30 tasks, three is 45, four is 60, five is 75, six is 90. You can't get by with five because you have to get 80 tasks done, so you'll need six computers, (A).

**29** C- One side of triangle $ABC$ is an edge of our cube, segment $BC$. But segments $AB$ and $AC$ aren't lengths of the edge of the cube or fractions of a length of an edge of the cube. Well, let's find the length of an edge of the cube. If the cube has volume 8, that's the length of an edge to the third power. 2 cubed is 8, so the length of an edge of this cube is 2. We need $AB$ and $AC$, and so we have to concentrate on smaller right triangles on the same face of the cube that includes triangle $ABC$.

On the upper left, directly above point $A$ is an unlabeled vertex—let's call that point $Y$—and down below point $A$ is an unlabeled vertex— we'll call that point $X$. Look at triangle $AXC$. It's a right triangle because angle $AXC$ is one of the angles formed by two edges of a cube— and $AC$ is its hypotenuse. $AX$ is half an edge of the cube because point A's the midpoint of edge $XY$. That means that $AX$ has length 1 and $XC$ is an edge of the cube, so it has length 2. The legs of this right triangle are 1 and 2, so we can use the Pythagorean theorem to find the length of $AC$. $AX^2$ is $1^2$, $XC^2$ is $2^2$, $1^2$ is 1, $2^2$ is 4, the sum of 1 and 4 is 5, $AC^2$ is 5 and $AC$ has length $\sqrt{5}$. $AB$ is identical to $AC$ because triangle $AYB$ is identical to triangle $AXC$, so $AB$ also has length $\sqrt{5}$ and the perimeter of $ABC$ is $2 + 2\sqrt{5}$, choice (C).

**30** D- The catch here is that it's not which of the following is 850 percent **of** $8 \times 10^3$, it's which of the following is 850 percent **greater than** $8 \times 10^3$. Well, what's bigger, 850 percent of 1 or a number that's 850 percent greater than 1? 850 percent of 1 is $8.5 \times 1$ or $8\frac{1}{2}$. But a number that's 850 percent greater than 1 is 1 + 850 percent of 1, it's 1 + 8.5 or 9.5. So the number we want is $9.5 \times 8 \times 10^3$. $9.5 \times 8 = 76$, so the answer is $76 \times 10^3$, or $7.6 \times 10^4$, in scientific notation.

# SECTION 4

**1** **E-** "Callous" means unfeeling, uncaring, but if this person has concern for the earthquake victims, her reputation must be an unfounded one, so the correct choice will mean "contradicted" or "proved false." This is one of the meanings of "belied," correct choice (E). (B), "rescinded," is the second best answer. It means revoked or withdrawn, but you don't say that a reputation is rescinded. (A), (C), and (D) are the opposite of what we're looking for—they don't make sense in this context.

**2** **B-** "No longer" and "therefore" show strong contrast—something is done with the original plans because they are no longer something else. (B) expresses this contrast, "applicable..rejected," and if we plug in these words—the plans could no longer be applied so they were tossed aside. In (A), there's no contrast between something being "relevant," or pertinent, and its being "adaptable," capable of being changed to fit a new situation. In (C), "expedient" means convenient—it makes no sense for something not expedient to be "adopted" or taken up. In (D), "appraised" means judged or rated, which doesn't follow from no longer being "acceptable." In (E) it doesn't make sense to say that the plans were no longer "capable" or that the plans were "allayed," or minimized—again, (B) is best for Question 2.

**3** **D-** The second half of the sentence is about each tiny layer of the surface of the cross-section of the sandstone. This must explain what the first part alludes to, so the first blank must mean layered—otherwise, what tiny layers is the author talking about? On this basis, (D) is the best answer since "stratified" means layered. In (A), a "ridge" isn't really a layer. In (B), a "facet" is a face or flat surface, so "multi-faceted" can't be right.

"Distinctive," in (C) means distinguishing or individual. And "coarse" in (E) means rough. Looking at the second blank, "enlargement," in (A), has nothing to do with the formation of the stone. In (B), if the phrase "angle of deposition" means anything at all, it's an obscure geological term and can't be what we want here. The remaining choices could refer to the time or place in which material is deposited. Since (D) has the best answer for the first blank and a possible answer for the second blank, it's correct for Question 3.

**4** **D-** The phrase "and now" suggests that the second part of the sentence will say something consistent with the first part. Whatever the convict has always insisted upon, the new evidence must support his claim. (D) gets this connection right—"innocence..vindicate." To "vindicate" means to clear from an accusation, to prove innocent. The convict has always insisted upon his own innocence and now at last there is new evidence to vindicate him—this makes perfect sense and it's the answer. In (A), "defensiveness" is a tendency to defend oneself and "incarcerate" means to put in prison. In (B), "culpability" is guilt, as in the word culprit, and "exonerate" means to clear from guilt. In (C), to "anathematize" someone means to curse him or pronounce a strong sentence against him but that doesn't go with "blamelessness." In (E) "contrition" is a sense of remorse, while to "condemn" someone means to pass judgment against him. This is probably second best, but it doesn't follow as logically as (D), so (D) is correct.

**5** **A-** The word "but" signals a contrast between the opinion of plate tectonics when the theory was first proposed, and the opinion of it now—either people disbelieved the theory at first and believe it now or vice

290

versa. (A), "opposition..grant" provides the contrast. If most geophysicists now grant its validity, they believe in it. That's the opposite of opposing it, so (A) is the answer. In (B), "consideration" is a neutral term—people are thinking about the theory, but it doesn't provide the necessary contrasts with "see," which implies that physicists now recognize the validity of the theory. In (C), "acclamation" means loud praise and "boost" means to support enthusiastically—no contrast there. In (D), a "prognostication" is a prediction of the future, which doesn't make sense in this context and "learn its validity" doesn't make sense either, so (D) isn't a good choice. In (E), "contention" is argument and to "bar" means to exclude or forbid—there is no contrast with this pair. Again, (A) is the correct answer to Question 5.

**6** D- "Despite" clues you in to a contrast between something "professed," claimed or pretended, and reality, indicated by the glint in her eyes. A glint in someone's eye is a sign of strong interest, so "obsession" and "fascination," in (A) and (D) are tempting. We want a contrast with strong interest, so the first word is something like disinterest. We find "indifference" in (D) and "obliviousness" in (C). Since both words in (D) fit, it must be correct. None of the others offers the kind of contrasts we need. There's no contrast between "intelligence" and "obsession," in (A), between "interest" and "concern" in (B), or between "obliviousness" and "confusion" in (C). We get a contrast in (E) between "expertise" and "unfamiliarity," but the words don't make sense—a glint in someone's eye isn't a sign of unfamiliarity.

**7** C- We're looking for something that goes with sacred scriptures and implies a formal system of belief, but something whose absence doesn't rule out "a legacy of tradition-al religious practices and basic values." We can eliminate choices (A), (B), and (E) because if Shinto lacked "followers," "customs," or "faith" it wouldn't be a legacy of traditional religious practices and basic values. "Relics," (D), are sacred objects but relics don't make something a formal system of beliefs. The best choice is (C)—a "dogma" is a formal religious belief.

**8** E- Something "impeccable" is perfect, it doesn't have a "flaw." In (A) "impeachable" means subject to accusation, so something impeachable is not necessarily without "crime." "Obstreperous," in (B) means loud or unruly, not without "permission." "Impetuous," in (C) means rash or without care rather than without "warning." In (D), "moribund" means in the process of dying, so it's inappropriate to use "living." In (E), "absurd" means without "sense," so this is the correct answer.

**9** D- A "seismograph" is an instrument used to measure an "earthquake," so we need another instrument used to measure something. In (A), a "stethoscope" is an instrument used to listen to a patient's chest. Only indirectly can this be used to measure a patient's "health." In (B), a "speedometer" doesn't measure a "truck"—it measures the speed of any kind of vehicle. In (C), a "telescope" doesn't measure "astronomy." A telescope is an instrument used to observe far away objects. In (D), a "thermometer" measures "temperature," so this looks like a promising answer. In (E), an "abacus" is used in arithmetic as a calculator but it doesn't measure "arithmetic." So (D) is the best answer.

**10** D- To "guzzle" is to "drink" very quickly, taking big gulps, so the relationship is one of speed or degree. In (A), "elucidate" and "clarify" mean to make clearer. One doesn't imply greater speed or volume than the other. Similarly, with (B) to "ingest" is to "eat" or drink—it doesn't mean to eat in big bites. In (C), to "boast" and to "describe" are two unrelated ways of talking. In (D), to "stride" is to "walk" quickly, taking big steps, so this may be the answer. In (E), "condemn" is stronger than the first word "admonish," meaning to rebuke—the opposite of how the stem pair is presented. So (D) is the best answer.

**11** C- An "orator" is a public speaker and "articulate" means able to express oneself well. You can form the bridge "a successful orator is one who is articulate." With that in mind, (A) may seem tempting but the profession of "soldier" isn't defined as aspiring towards being "merciless." In (B) a "celebrity" is a famous person, not by definition a "talented" one. (C) is good—a good "judge" has to be "unbiased." It's safe to say that a biased judge is a bad judge in the same way that an inarticulate orator is a bad orator. In (D), a "novice" is a beginner—it wouldn't be unusual for a novice to be "unfamiliar" but that's not what makes a good novice. In (E), a "dignitary" is a person of high rank, and such a person doesn't need to be "respectful." (C) is correct.

**12** C- A "badge" is the identification worn by a "policeman." In (A), a "placard" is a sign carried by a "demonstrator." There's a link here but a placard isn't an official ID and a demonstrator doesn't necessarily carry a placard. (B) is wrong because although there is a tradition for a "sailor" to have a "tattoo," a tattoo isn't an official identification of a sailor. In (C) a "convict" wears a "number" on his uniform to identify him, so this is plausible. In (D) the "pedigree" of a "dog" is the dog's lineage or genealogy, not something worn by the dog as identification. In (E), even though a "fingerprint" may be used to identify a "defendant," everybody has fingerprints. So the best answer is (C).

**13** B- To "scrutinize" means to "observe" intently, so the relationship is one of degree. In (A), to "pique" interest is to "excite" interest. The words mean the same thing. In (B) to "beseech" means to "request" with great fervor—this is more like it. In (C) to "search" is the process you go through to "discover" something. That's different from the stem pair. In (D) to "grin" is to "smile" broadly—this reverses the original pair. And in (E) to "dive" means to "jump" in a certain way or under certain conditions, not to jump intently. The best answer is (B).

**14** D- If you didn't know what "epicurean" means, you might have had trouble here, but you can still eliminate some choices. There must be some relationship between "epicurean" and "indulge." Could (A) have the same relationship? No, because there really is no relationship between "frightened" and "ugly." Something ugly doesn't necessarily frighten people. Same with (C)—there's no relationship between "hesitate" and "unproductive." There are good relationships for the other choices but let's see if we can eliminate them. In (E) the relationship is that something "comprehensible" can be "understood." Do you think that something "epicurean" can be "indulged"? That sounds odd—just about everyone or everything can be indulged. In (B) "revocable" means can be taken back, so the relationship is something revocable can be "retracted." That's the same relationship that we just saw in (E), another clue that they must be wrong. If (B) and (E) share the same relationship, they can't both be right, so they must both be wrong. That leaves us with (D) and there our relationship is something like someone "vindictive" is likely to "revenge" himself and that sounds better. In fact, an epicurean person is one who is likely to indulge himself, so (D) is correct here.

**15** E- "Diluvial" means having to do with a "flood." You may have heard the word anti-diluvian, meaning "before the flood," Noah's flood—in other words, a long time ago. So our bridge is "having to do with." In (A), "criminal" can mean having to do with crime but it doesn't mean having to do with "punishment." In (B), "biological" means having to do with living things. "Bacteria" are living things but to define biological as having to do with bacteria would be too narrow. In (C), "judicial" means having to do with the administration of justice. A "verdict" is the decision about the guilt or innocence of a defendant, a small part of the "judicial" process. (D)'s "candescent" means giving off "light" rather than having to do with light. This leaves (E) and "cardiac" means having to do with the "heart," so (E) is correct.

**16** C- It is in the nature of a "sphinx" to "perplex." This comes from Greek mythology—the sphinx was a monster that asked a riddle that no one could answer. "Sphinx" can be used to mean anything that is difficult to understand, so our bridge is that a sphinx is known for perplexing. In (A), an "oracle" is a soothsayer, someone who predicts the future—an oracle doesn't "interpret." In (B), a "prophet" is someone who foretells the future. This may help someone to "prepare" but you don't say that a prophet is known for preparing. In (C), a "siren" can mean a beautiful or a seductive woman who "lures" men. So (C) looks good—a siren lures in the same way that a sphinx perplexes. In (D), the role of a "jester" is to amuse, not necessarily to "astound." In (E), a "minotaur" is a mythological monster—it didn't, by definition, "anger" someone. So (C) is correct.

The first reading comp passage is short and it's followed by three questions—the remaining passage will be long with eight questions. The style of this natural science passage is factual, descriptive and straightforward, although the discussion does get fairly detailed. The topic is clear from the first sentence: our knowledge of how fish schools are formed and how their structure is maintained. The next two sentences get more specific and express the author's main point, that, contrary to the previous theory, the structure of fish schools is primarily dependent on vision. The tone is objective and positive, but it's worth noting that since the author is contrasting the new knowledge about lateral lines with older, outdated knowledge, he must be skeptical of the notion that vision is the primary means of forming and maintaining fish schools. The rest of the passage is a more technical report of how the schools are structured, how individual fish actually behave in forming schools—this is detail and the best way to deal with it is to read it attentively, but more quickly than the earlier lines.

**17** E- This Roman numeral format question focuses on detail. The stem is asking what the structure of fish schools depends on, and the options focus on the more technical elements in the last half of the passage. The author states that ideal positions of individual fish aren't maintained rigidly and this contradicts option I right away. The idea of random aggregation appears: the school formation results from a probabilistic arrangement that appears like a random aggregation, so the idea is that fish are positioned probabilistically, but not rigidly. Option II is true, repeating the idea in the next sentence that fish school structure is maintained by the preference of fish to have a certain distance from their neighbors. Option III is true too. It's a paraphrase of the last two sentences, that each fish uses its vision and lateral line first to measure the speed of the

other fish, then to adjust its own speed to conform, based primarily on the position and
movements of other fish. So options II and III
are true and (E) is the right choice.

**18** C- You know the primary purpose here
is to present new ideas that challenge the
emphasis of the old theory. So you're probably
safe in assuming that the author's attitude
toward the old idea will be at least somewhat
negative. You can therefore cross off choices
that sound neutral or positive, (B), (D), and
(E). The negative choices are (A) and (C). (A)
is out because it is much too extreme—the
author is not offended or indignant, nor does
he or she argue that vision is insignificant—
quite the contrary. This leaves (C), the best
choice. The author disagrees with the old theory since it overlooks the role of the lateral
line, but the disagreement is tempered by an
acknowledgment that the old theory did recognize the role of vision. So it's a qualified or
measured disagreement—the adjective "considered" works well here. Again, it's (C) for
Question 18.

**19** C- Question 19 involves inference as the
word "suggests" in the stem suggests. It
refers to the latter, more detailed half of the
passage, and that's where correct answer (C) is.
It's logically suggested by the last couple of
sentences where you're told that once it estab-
lishes its position, each fish uses its eyes and
lateral line to measure the movements of nearby fish in order to maintain appropriate speed
and position. Since the school is moving, each
fish's adjustments must be ongoing and continuous, as (C) states. (A) is wrong because
auditory organs aren't mentioned. Lateral lines
correspond to a sense of touch, not hearing.
(B) and (D) both have words that should strike
you as improbable. Nothing suggests that each
fish rigorously avoids any disruptive move-

ments, (B), or that the fish would make sud-
den unexpected movements only in the presence of danger, (D). The idea in (E) also isn't
mentioned. It's never suggested that a fish,
once part of a school, completely loses its ability to act on its own. Again, (C) is our answer
for Question 19.

The second passage is divided into three para-
graphs. If you figure out what each paragraph
covers, you've understood the passage's hand-
ful of ideas, plus you've sketched out a rough
mental map. In this passage, the first ten or fifteen lines take you through the first paragraph
and into the second and if you were careful
you picked up the author's broad topic area,
(ancient Greek social anxiety), the style of the
writing (dense and scholarly) and the tone or
attitude (expository and neutral).

The second paragraph gives you the central
point—what the Greeks apparently succeeded
in doing was discovering a way of measuring
and explaining chaotic experience so that
chaos was no longer so threatening and anxiety producing. This recognition of order in the
midst of chaos served as the basis of a spiritual
ideal for the Greeks. So by the end of the second paragraph you have the author's central
idea plus all the information about style, tone,
and topics in the beginning. The first sentence
of the last paragraph tells you the search for
order and clarity in the midst of chaos is
reflected especially in Greek philosophy. The
rest of the paragraph is a description of how
various philosophers and schools of philosophy offered solutions to the problem of finding order and measure in a disorderly world.

**20** **E-** This kind of primary purpose question is common, and here the right answer is (E). In this case, both the noun and the verb are right on the money. The verb is exactly right for this author's expository neutral tone, and a cultural phenomenon, the Greeks' perception of chaos and their solution to the problem, is what the author is "describing." The verbs in (B) and (C), "challenge" and "question" eliminate them right away—no opinion is given but the author's own, and philosophy in (C) is discussed only in the last paragraph. The noun phrase in (A), "conflicting viewpoints" is wrong. (D) is the most tempting—the author is looking at history and mentioning certain facts, but this misses the author's purpose, which is not to simply list facts but rather to describe and define something in the form of a thesis. Again, it's (E) for Question 20.

**21** **A-** This is from the first sentence of the second paragraph and it's the central idea that's being focused on, that the discovery of this substratum helped bring a satisfying new sense of order into experience, thus reforming the Greeks' perception of worldly chaos. The choice that paraphrases this point is (A), the perception of constant change was altered by the idea of a permanent principle of order lying underneath it—this is the main point of the passage. (B) is out because severe social problems are never mentioned, at least not in any concrete way. As for (C), it misses the point made in the sentence the question refers to. The passage does refer to pain and bewilderment and to an earlier period of political turbulence, but this choice goes overboard with its notions of painful memories and national humiliation and so on. As for (D), a few lines into the second paragraph the author says directly that the discovery did much more than satisfy intellectual curiosity. And (E) also

contradicts the author, distorting a detail at the end of the paragraph. It's not mysticism, but rationality and careful analysis that lead to order and clarity, so it's (A) for Question 21.

**22** **D-** The author is arguing in the second, third and fourth sentences that the Greeks identified rational thought and spiritual ideals as inseparable. Rationality, order, measure, and so forth became equivalent to spiritual ideals for the Greeks. Toward the end of the second paragraph the author states that rationality and spirituality are not mutually exclusive. The choice that's most clearly consistent with this is (D). As for (A), the passage never suggests that ordinary Greeks were unfamiliar with or uninterested in the concepts of rational thought and spiritual ideals. The passage suggests quite the contrary. (B) and (C) are both inconsistent with the passage as well. All the philosophers mentioned accepted the notion that rationality was the key, amounting to an ideal to understanding the world. (E) picks up on the mention of poetry at the beginning of the last paragraph, but the point there is that Greek poetry manifested the sense of cultural anxiety that philosophy tried to alleviate. Again it's (D) for Question 22.

**23** **B-** This question is looking for the choice that isn't mentioned as reflecting the Greeks' anxieties about chaos. The one that's never mentioned is (B), that it was reflected in aspects of their religion. We don't actually learn anything about Greek religion in the passage—we just don't know and we certainly can't infer anything about specific aspects. Each of the other choices is mentioned specifically. (A) is implied in the long opening sentence of the first paragraph—the national psyche and historical experience both relate to national consciousness. (C), the sense of change in the physical world is mentioned at the start of paragraph two. (D), the striving for order and philosophy is discussed throughout the third paragraph. And finally (E), lyric poetry, is mentioned at the start of the paragraph as one place where the sense of anxiety was expressed directly. Again it's (B).

**24** C- Your mental map should have taken you straight to the last paragraph—the Milesians are discussed in the first several sentences. (C) encapsulates what the passage says, that Milesians were interested primarily in understanding a fundamental order in nature, outside the disturbing world of human society. (A) gets it backwards—the Milesians apparently ignored questions that were inherently human. (B) and (D) contradict the passage. None of the philosophies mentioned did what these choices suggest, either to sharply distinguish between rationality and spirituality, (B), or to integrate rationality and mysticism, (D). (E), finally, describes the approach of the Pythagoreans who were absorbed by the logic and order of mathematics, rather than by attempts to explain physical phenomena. It's (C) for Question 24.

**25** D- This question is similar to the primary purpose question we just saw, Question 20, which asked you for an abstract description of the author's primary purpose. In both, you're being asked not the actual content, but the logical progression of the contents. Is he or she making a series of disconnected assertions? Making a point and backing it up with factual evidence, or what? What's the author up to logically in the lines referred to? In the preceding sentence the author is talking about the Greeks' discovery of order and measure, and that it helped them get a secure handle on chaotic experience. The discovery was a relief—its impact was almost religious in nature. In the next sentence, the author says that this recognition, discovery, of order and measure was much more than merely intellectually satisfying—it served as a basic part of their spiritual values. The author quotes Plato to support his point, to give an idea of the significance of measure. In the last of the three sentences the author finishes up with a statement that pulls the strands of the thesis together and puts the basic point into clear cultural perspective. Rational definability or measure was never regarded by the Greeks as inconsistent with spirituality—(D) is the choice that describes things best. The problem with (A) is that the author isn't summarizing two viewpoints but discussing one thesis. As for (B), the author neither mentions evidence that weakens his thesis nor revises it. (C) is out because the author is not discussing two separate arguments that need to be reconciled by a third. It's just one argument that's the topic here. (E), finally, is wrong for the same reason—the author discusses one thesis only and never suggests any other.

**26** A- We know from our rough map of the structure that except for one reference to Plato in the middle of the second paragraph, philosophy is discussed only in the last paragraph, so that's where you'll find out about the Pythagoreans. The main thing about them was that they concentrated on mathematical abstraction. They shifted the focus in philosophy from the physical realm to the mathematical. The Milesians focused on physical phenomena, and that's the idea you see immediately in (A), the correct choice. (B) lists an idea that mentions the Pythagoreans—thinkers who came **after** the Pythagoreans focused on human behavior. (C) won't work because both of these schools and all other philosophies mentioned used rationality as the means to truth. (D) picks up what characterized the Milesians—we want the Pythagorean side of the contrast. (E) gets things backward—the Pythagoreans stressed mathematical theory over physical matter. Again, it's (A) for Question 26.

**27** D- The last sentence is saying that in all these various periods of Greek history and philosophy, the basic preoccupation of the Greeks was with the search for a kosmos. The term kosmos hasn't been used before, but because this sentence is at the end of the passage and because it's phrased as a summary, you should realize that the basic quest here must be the same one the author has been talking about all along. So this refers to the central problem for Greek society—how to find order and measure in a seemingly confusing and disorderly world. This search for a kosmos then is the passage's main idea, and correct choice (D) restates it. (A) is out because the word "mystical" is incorrect, since the author states at the end of paragraph two that the Greeks stressed rationalism over mysticism. (B) and (E) are inconsistent with some major points. In (B), the idea that the Greeks would have regarded rationalism as sterile is completely wrong. And in (E), the ideals of beauty and excellence, as mentioned in paragraph two, are preeminent and fundamental within the Greeks' world view. Finally, (C) talks about ending conflict among important schools of philosophy. This last sentence about the search for kosmos is talking about a quest you find in Greek thought as a whole, a much bigger topic than mere conflicts among philosophers.

**28** A- "Enmity" is the state of being an enemy—the opposite is "friendship," (A). "Reverence," (B), means great respect, the opposite of contempt. The opposite of "boredom," (C), is interest. The opposite of (D), "stylishness," is a lack of style, and the opposite of (E), "awkwardness" is skillfulness.

**29** B- "Dilate" means expand and widen. The opposite is contract, so (B), "shrink" is what we're looking for. (A), "enclose" means confine. The opposite of "hurry," (C), is delay. "Inflate," (D), means expand or fill with air. The opposite of (E), "erase," might be preserve or set down.

**30** A- A "charlatan" is a fraud or a quack. (A), "genuine expert," is a possible answer. The opposite of a "powerful leader," (B), is a follower or maybe a weak leader. The opposite of a "false idol," (C), is a true god or a hero. The opposite of an "unknown enemy," (D), is a known enemy, an unknown friend or a known friend. The opposite of (E), "hardened villain," might be innocent person or first offender. So it's (A).

**31** C- "Peripheral" means having to do with the periphery, the outer edge of something. The opposite of peripheral is "central," (C). The opposite of (A), "civilized," is crude or savage. (B), "partial," means favoring or biased, or incomplete—it has lots of opposites but peripheral isn't one of them. Harmed is the opposite of "unharmed," and the opposite of (E), "stable," is weak or inconstant. (C) is correct.

**32** E- "Meritorious" means full of merit, deserving reward. Its opposite is "unpraiseworthy," (E), the best choice. "Effulgent," (A), means shiny—its opposite is dull. (B), "stationary" means not moving. Neither (C), "uneven" nor (D), "narrow-minded" works , so (E) is correct.

**33** C- "Discharge" means unburden, eject or exude. However, it has a more specific meaning in military context, to release or remove someone from service. The opposite is to "enlist," (C). The opposite of (A), "heal," is make sick. The opposite of (B), "advance," is retreat. (D) "penalize" means punish. The opposite of "delay," (E), is hasten.

**34** A- A "malediction" is a curse. We want something like benediction, and we find "blessing" in correct (A). The opposite of "preparation," (B), is lack of preparation. (C), "good omen," has bad omen as its opposite. The opposite of (D), "liberation," is captivity. The opposite of "pursuit," (E), is tough, but it sure isn't malediction, so (A) is correct.

**35** A- "Mawkish" means sickeningly sentimental. "Unsentimental," (A), is the answer here. The opposite of (B), "sophisticated" is naive or simple. The opposite of "graceful," (C), is clumsy. The opposite of "tense," (D), is relaxed. There are various antonyms to "descriptive," (E), but mawkish isn't one.

**36** B- "Temerity" means recklessness or foolish daring. Its opposite is hesitancy or carefulness. "Blandness," (A), is a lack of character, not a lack of courage. (B), "caution," fits—one with temerity lacks caution. The opposite of (C), "severity," is leniency. The opposite of (D), "strength," is weakness. "Charm," (E), is personal appeal. The best answer is (B), caution.

**37** C- "Jejune" can mean immature or sophomoric. The opposite would be adult or correct choice (C), "mature." "Morose," (A), means sad or moody. The opposite of "natural," (B), is artificial. (D), "contrived," means deliberately planned. Its opposite is natural. "Accurate," (E), means precise or exact.

**38** C- "Vitiate" means corrupt, put wrong, spoil or make worse, and the opposite is improve or correct. The closest choice is "rectify," (C). (A), "deaden," is way off. The opposite of "trust," (B), is distrust or suspect. The opposite of "drain," (D), is fill up. And the opposite of "amuse," (E), is bore or upset.

## GAME I: QUESTIONS 1-4

**The Action:** A lock has to be opened by pressing a combination of symbols. Each combination has 5 symbols: 4 letters and 1 number.

**The Rules:**

1) This rule sets limits on the game—you'll be working with two basic options. Option 1 is the first situation described, where the number is second in the sequence. Option 2 is the second situation, where the number is the third symbol in the sequence.

2) I put a mark underneath the 4th and 5th space in each of my options.

3) We're dealing with Option 2, the one with the number in the third position. In Option 2, the 5th symbol must be either *B* or *D*, so we can write that under the 5th space in Option 2, *B* or *D* only.

4) The third symbol is a letter so you're dealing with Option 1. In that combination there can't be any *F*'s or *G*'s.

5) There are different ways to take note of this—some of you may have chosen to circle the rule, others of you might have put something into your scratch work. Just don't forget it!

**Recap:** In Option 1, the number appears in the second place, there can't be an *F* or a *G*, and the 4th and 5th letters can't be the same. In Option 2, the number is in the third place, the fifth must be *B* or *D*, and the 4th place and the 5th place can't be the same. And the overall rule for the game is that the first letter has to be the letter that's closest to the beginning of the alphabet.

**1** **D-** The quickest way to get through this is to take the rules and check the choices against them. Rule 1 eliminates (E) since it has the number in the 4th position. (C) can be thrown out because it has G in the 4th and the 5th positions—a Rule 2 no-no. Move on to Rule 3—the only one left with a number in the third position is (A) and (A) obeys Rule 3. Rule 4 applies to (B) and (D) because it talks about having a number in the second position—you can't have any *F*'s or *G*'s and (B) violates that rule with an *F* in the first position. Rule 5 eliminates (A). The letter *B* at the end of (A) violates Rule 5. (A) begins with the letter *E*, meaning that all the rest of the letters must appear later in the alphabet than *E*, and *B* doesn't. That leaves correct choice (D).

**2** **E-** You can eliminate (B) and D) right off—numbers only appear in the second or the third position. Then (C) goes, since you can't start a sequence with *Y*—think about the alphabet—*X, Y, Z*. Only one letter comes after *Y*, so you'd be left with only one letter to fill the rest of the sequence, and Rule 2 says that you can't have the 4th and 5th symbols the same. That leaves with (A), *F*, and (E), *E*. Seeing the F should make you suspicious—in Option 1 you can't use *F* at all, and in Option 2, where you've got the number in third place. In Option 2 you must end the sequence with *B* or *D*. If you start with *F*, you begin with a letter later in the alphabet than *B* or *D* violating Rule 5. So *F* can't begin the sequence in Option 2 and *E*, (E), is the correct answer.

**3** **A-** You're told about a combination with *B* first and *G* fourth. When you see *G*, you know you'll be dealing with Option 2 only because Option 1 can't contain *G*'s. In Option 2, *B* is first, and you don't know what's second. The number is third, *G* is fourth and fifth is either *B* or *D*, since in Option 2 fifth is either *B* or *D*. You've used *B* first, so you're left with only *D* for the fifth position. Your sequence has *B* first, you don't know what's second, a number third, *G* fourth, and *D* fifth. *D* has to be fifth and only (A) gives you that option, so it's correct.

**4** **D-** The first thing is to figure out why the combination isn't acceptable. You have a number third so it's Option 2. You end with *B* or *D* and this one ends with *F*, so we need to switch that *F* for a *B* or a *D* and make the sequence correct. (A) offers to replace *F* with *B* but remember Rule 5—the first symbol must be closest to the beginning of the alphabet. If you replace *F* with *B* you break that rule because the sequence begins with *C*. The only way to put *B* at the end of this and still have an acceptable sequence would be to change the *C* to an *A* but you can't do that, so (A) won't work. Skim down to (D), replace the *F* with a *D*, which works with the rules for Option 2, the sequence ends with a *D*, and *D* comes later in the alphabet than *C* so you're obeying Rule 5. So (D) is correct. As for the others, if you do (B) and reverse the *C* and *P* you have Option 2 ending with an *F*—not acceptable. With (C) you reverse the *Q* and the 8 and you have Option 1 with the number second—but you can't have an *F* in Option 1, so (C) won't work. Finally, (E) says replace the *C* with an *A*. Well, we talked about that when we were talking about (A). If you did (A) and (E) together you'd have an acceptable sequence but replacing the *C* with an *A* does not solve the problem of having the *F* at the end which isn't acceptable when the number is third. So (D) is correct.

**5** **E-** The first sentence is evidence: some scientists argue that our planet may support more sources of protein than we think if presently unfished areas have as many fish in them as do the areas presently fished. The author then concludes that we can provide protein to the whole world even if population grows at its present rate. But his conclusion isn't expressed conditionally, and his evidence is. He's just *assuming* that there are as many fish in the unfished part of the ocean as there are in the fished part. Furthermore, he's assuming that the scientists are right, that those fish would mean the world supports more protein than we believe. To conclude that we can feed the hungry masses, the author must assume that we can get the fish in the unfished areas—maybe those areas are unfished because we can't fish them. Since we need to weaken the argument we need an answer choice that contradicts one of these assumptions, and correct choice (E) denies the last one. (E) says it will take 30 years before we can fish those areas, so we can't ensure the availability of protein to everyone over the next two decades. As for the others, (A) supplies the view of some scientists that fish are less common in the unfished areas. This isn't as damaging as (E). (B) is close, but the cost of the technology isn't as damning an obstacle as its availability. (C) focuses on cost. The author doesn't argue that the world can be fed *cheaply*. And (D), by cutting the population growth certainly doesn't weaken the argument. So (E) is correct.

**6** **A-** It's possible for travelers to enter and remain in the Republic for anywhere from 1 to 59 days, but there's at least one condition for stays of longer than 7 days. Although it's possible to stay for more than 7 days, if you do so, you need a special visa. Correct choice (A) is simply a statement in which the antecedent, or "if" clause, of the original is affirmed and the consequent, or "then" clause, flows from it, just as it's supposed to. If a traveler wants to stay 14 days, then a special visa is required. This jibes perfectly with the if-then statement in the stimulus, so (A) it is.

(B) and (D) are wrong because each implies that some travelers don't need visas. We don't know that travelers staying less than 7 days don't need anything. Maybe all travelers to the Republic need visas of some kind, so neither

(B) nor (D) must be true. (C) fails by bringing up the topic of whether or not people have the visas they require. All the stimulus tells us is when a special visa is required. (E) comes out of thin air. Nothing precludes the possibility that every person in the Republic needs a visa, even those just passing through, so (E) isn't inferable from the stimulus, and (A) is correct.

**7** **B-** The conclusion here is that the U.S. economy continues to grow and prosper. As evidence, the author cites the expansion over the last 15 years of the service sector, where last year alone 500,000 Americans found employment. He assumes that this growth correlates to growth in the economy. But what if declines in other sectors offset the growth in service? If, as correct choice (B) says, growth in the service sector can be at least partly attributed to a decline in the manufacturing and heavy industry sectors, then growth in the service sector can't be a reliable indicator of growth in the overall economy. (A) tends to support the conclusion—job offers imply health, contributing to a sense that the economy isn't in bad shape. (C) doesn't do much to affect the author's conclusion. Just because the American economy isn't sluggish doesn't mean it's growing and prospering. (D) can be eliminated because the author is claiming that the American economy is prospering—he isn't claiming that it's prospering more than ever. Finally, (E) weakens the argument a bit, suggesting that some of the evidence for the claim of economic growth and health isn't as central as the author believes. But using the service sector as a barometer of economic growth may be valid, regardless of the doubt (E) casts on how much of that growth is caused by the service sector. Since (E)'s ability to weaken the argument is dubious while (B)'s is certain, it's (B) for Question 7.

## GAME II: QUESTIONS 8-12

**The Action:** 3 bells, a high, a medium, and a low, and 8 rings. You ring the low bell 3 times, the medium bell 3 times, and the high bell 2 times.

**The Rules:**

1) The sixth ring is the medium bell—put it in.

2) You'll have to split the low rings up—they will always be separated by medium and high rings.

3) The two high bells will stick together throughout the game.

**8** **B-** Starting with Rule 1, (C) has a low bell sixth which can't be true. Rule 2 won't let us ring the low bell twice in succession, so dump (D) and (E). And Rule 3 eliminates (A) by splitting up the high bells, leaving us with (B), the correct answer.

**9** **E-** We have to ring the high bell fifth, so we've got to ring the other high bell fourth—the two high bells have to stay together and we've got the medium bell ringing sixth. Now we have to split up the low bells. We'll have to put two before this high, high, medium set, and one after. So we'll put one low first, one low third, then fill the space between with a medium. The beginning looks like this—low, medium, low, high, high, medium. You've got one low and one medium left. Does it matter which goes in 7 and which in 8? No, either way would be acceptable. (A), the low bell is first, yes. (B) the medium bell is second, yes. (C) the low bell is third, yes. (D), the high bell is fourth, yes. (E), the low bell is rung seventh—it could be true, but it could be eighth, so (E) could be true but doesn't have to be true so it's correct.

**10** D- We're told that we have a medium bell fourth and we know that there's a medium bell sixth. Sketching it out, we have eight spots for bells to be rung, and mediums fourth and sixth. Where can't the high bell be rung? Remember when we're talking about the high bell, we're talking about both high bells because they stay together. So you can't ring a high bell in five because there's no room for the other high bell next to it. So (D) is correct for Question 10.

(A) puts the high bell first, and you'd ring the other high bell second and split up the low bells third, fifth, and seventh. (B) puts the high bell second and you can use the same sequence and ring a high bell second. (C) puts a high bell third, the other high bell second, and splits up the low bells by placing one first, one fifth, and one seventh. And (E) puts the high bell eighth. You can ring the other high bell seventh and still split up the lows by placing one first, one third, and one fifth. So (D) is the correct answer.

**11** D- If you sketch out a sequence, one of the things you can see is that the third, fourth, and fifth group buts up against the medium bell in sixth. So all high and medium bells would be unacceptable in three, four, and five because you'd have a solid group of high and medium in the center and no way to split up those low bells on the ends. (D) has a high in third, a medium in fourth, and a medium in fifth, and it's the correct answer. As for the wrong choices, (A) has high, medium, low in three, four, and five. That works if we put a low first, the other high second, next to the high bell in three, and a medium and a low in seven and eight, if the high bells are together and the lows are split up. (B) has low, medium, and low, in three, four, and five. That makes it easy to split up the lows—we can put the third one in first and we still have two spaces at the end to keep the two highs together. (C) has the two highs in three and four and a low in five. We put a low first and a medium in space two next to the high in space three. That leaves seven and eight to put the other low and the other medium. Finally, (E) has high, low, and medium in three, four, and five. You put the high bell in second so it's next to first and third, and you put one low first and the other in seven or eight, with the other medium to keep them split up. (D) is correct.

**12** C- (A) mentions ringing the high bell first. This may have "rung a bell" because, having done questions 9 and 10, we've discussed whether or not it's possible to ring the high bell first—yes, it's acceptable. If you remembered that, you don't need to work out a sequence again. Let's skip to (D)—it says the high bell is fourth—you know that this is all right from Question 9. How about (E), ringing the low bell fifth? When we worked on Question 10 in trying out the possibilities we put the low bell fifth, so you know that this is acceptable. (B) says the low bell is rung second—what I did was put the low bell second and the medium first, put the two highs third and fourth, a low fifth, medium sixth, low seven, medium eight. That's acceptable, so (C) is correct—you can't ring the medium bell third. If you have a medium bell ringing third and another sixth, you have three groups of two spaces, first and second, fourth and fifth, seventh and eighth. One of those pairs has to contain the high bells but then you have three low bells to split up, and no way to do that. So the correct answer is (C).

## GAME III: QUESTIONS 13-17

**The Action:**

Try a simple tack—break it into two flow charts, one following the priority 1 mail and one following the priority 2 mail—it's actually much simpler.

**Information overload? Here's a breakdown.**

6 cities, 2 types of memos, and the basic idea that they're sent from the head office to the branches. The second introductory paragraph: any branch that receives a memo from the head office has to pass it on to at least one other branch. The other branch can pass it on but it doesn't have to.

The real key to your work on this game is the second set of rules about which branches can send memos to which other branches. Look at the last rule—it says that Fresno can't send memos to any other branches. What that means in terms of the game is something very simple: Fresno is a dead end. Let's look at the questions.

**13** **B-** One thing to notice is that you have to consider both priority 1 and priority 2, because both are sent from home to Atlanta. Check out both flow charts, and you notice that when memos go to Atlanta, in both cases, the next place they go is to Caracas. So the memos must leave Atlanta and go to Caracas, and that makes (B) correct. All of the wrong choices are only "could be trues"—you could send the memo on to Beijing, you could send it on to Dakar, to Edinburgh, to Fresno but you don't have to.

**14** **E-** Four of the choices describe routes of travel that the memo *could* have followed and one describes a route that the memo *could not* have followed and that's (E), a priority 2 memo initially sent to Beijing. Take a look at the priority 2 flow chart—start at the home

office, send the memo to Beijing, and then send it where? The only place that you can send it is Fresno and Fresno is a dead end. So it can't be a memo sent from Edinburgh to Fresno, so (E)'s correct. All the others work. (A), you can send a priority 1 memo from Atlanta, to Caracas, to Beijing, to Edinburgh, to Fresno. (B), you can send a priority 1 memo to Dakar, to Caracas, to Beijing, to Edinburgh, and then to Fresno. (C) is fine, a priority 1 memo can be sent to Dakar, and then to Caracas, Beijing, Edinburgh and Fresno. (D) is also fine, a priority 2 memo can be sent to Atlanta, to Caracas, to Dakar, to Edinburgh, and then to Fresno.

**15** **A-** If it wasn't originally sent to Atlanta, where was it sent? Priority 2, the only places something can go from home are Atlanta and Beijing. If it didn't go to Atlanta, it went to Beijing. This will ring a bell because we're following the same path that we followed in the last question. The only place a priority 2 memo can go after Beijing is Fresno, a dead end. Only two branches, Beijing and Fresno, could have seen the memo, and (A) is correct.

**16** **C-** If the memo didn't go through Atlanta, where did it go? A priority 1 memo would go to Dakar and a priority 2 memo would go to Beijing. We want it to end up in Edinburgh—does that ring a bell? In priority 2 we're dealing with the same path—a priority 2 memo starting at home going to Beijing goes to Fresno, a dead end, so it can't do what this question asks. So all you have to do is concentrate on your priority 1 system and see how a memo would go from Dakar to Edinburgh. After it goes to Dakar, the only place it can go is to Caracas, and from Caracas you could send it back to Dakar but you want it to move toward Edinburgh. Send it to Beijing and the only place it can go is

Edinburgh. So you take a priority 1 memo and send it from home to Dakar, to Caracas, to Beijing, then to Edinburgh. The question asks you how many branches saw this memo besides Edinburgh. Dakar, Caracas, and Beijing, that's three, and the answer is (C).

**17** D- Here you'll have to try out both priority 1 and priority 2 memos. (A) asks if you can go from Atlanta to Caracas to Beijing. Yes, in both priority 1 and priority 2. (B) talks about going from Atlanta to Caracas to Beijing to Edinburgh. In (A) you saw in both priority 1 and priority 2 you can go from Atlanta to Caracas to Beijing. Can you keep going to Edinburgh? Yes, in priority 1—that's where you go from Beijing with priority 1 memos, so (B) won't do it. (C), in priority 2 you can go from Atlanta, to Caracas, to Dakar, to Edinburgh. (D) suggests sending a memo from Beijing, to Edinburgh, to Fresno. A priority 1 memo can't go to Beijing from the head office. The only way to get a priority 1 memo to Beijing is through Atlanta or Dakar, to Caracas, and then on to Beijing. So (D) can't be the complete path of a priority 1 memo from the home office because it can't start in Beijing. As far as priority 2, when something leaves the priority 2 head office and goes to Beijing, the only other place it can go is Fresno, the dead end. (D) describes a path that's impossible for both priority 1 and priority 2 and it's correct. (E) suggests sending from Dakar to Caracas to Beijing. That works in priority 1, you can start in the home office, go to Dakar, go to Caracas, go to Beijing. So, again, the answer is (D).

## GAME IV: QUESTIONS 18-22

**The Action:**
You have to sequence trophies on shelves one, two, and three, from top to bottom.

**The Rules:**
2) Rule 2 seems to be the most helpful so let's look at it first. *F* must be on the shelf immediately above the shelf that *L* is on. You have two basic options. In Option 1 you place *F* on shelf one and L on shelf two. With Option 2 you put *F* on shelf 2 and *L* on shelf three.

1) In Option 1, we can write next to shelf two no *J*, and in Option 2, we can write next to shelf three no *J*.

3) No shelf can hold all three bowling trophies.

4) *K* can't be on shelf two—that's for either option.

**18** B- *G* and *H* are on shelf two, so if you remember that three bowling trophies can't be on the same shelf, this tells us that we must work with Option 1. If you put *G* and *H* on shelf two in Option 2, you'd be breaking Rule 3—you'd have all three bowling trophies on the same shelf. So you'll have F on shelf one, and *L*, *G*, and *H* on shelf two. What must be true? Take a look at (B), *L* is on shelf two. Yes, we just went through the deduction whereby you realize you must use Option 1 in which *F* is on shelf one and *L* is on shelf two. So (B) is the correct answer.

**19** D- Right away we realize that you can't use Option 2 here because Option 2 already has a tennis trophy on shelf three, *L*, so you will work with Option 1, *F* on the first shelf and *L* on the second shelf. You know that neither *J* nor *K* can appear on shelf two in Option 1. *J* and *K* are tennis trophies, so if the question specifies that you can't have a tennis trophy on shelf three and you can't have these two trophies on shelf two, then the only place for them is on shelf one. In other words, *K* and *J* must be on the same shelf, so (D) is correct for Question 19.

**20** C- This question is directing you to Option 2, because you already know that *J* isn't allowed on shelf two in Option 1. With Option 2 you know that *F* must appear on shelf two, so (C) is correct.

**21** D- In only one option can shelf one remain empty, Option 2. The rest of the question says "Which of the following must be false?" which means "Which of the following arrangements won't work?" First, let's look at the basic situation. We have Option 2 and we have *F* on two and L on three, and shelf one remains empty. That tells us that we can do something with *J* and *K*. We know in Option 2 that *J* can't go on shelf three and shelf one is empty, so the only other place for it is shelf two. We know that *K* can't be on shelf two and shelf one is empty, so the only home for K is shelf three. So we have shelf one empty, shelf two with *F* and *J*, and shelf three with *L* and *K*. What to do with *G* and *H*? The only thing we can't do is put them on shelf two because that would violate Rule 3. So if we keep them together we have to put them on shelf three. If we split them up, we can put *G* on two and *H* on three or vice versa. (A), can we put *H* and *F* on the same shelf? Sure, we've already said we can put one of *G* and *H* on shelf two and one on shelf three. (B), can we put exactly three trophies on shelf two? Sure, we just did with (A). We put *F*, *J*, and *H* together on shelf two and that left us with *L*, *K*, and *G* together on shelf three. (C)—can we put *G* and *H* on the same shelf? Yes, as long as they're on shelf three and not on shelf two. (D), can we put exactly two trophies on shelf three? We have on shelf three, *L* and *K*. To have exactly two trophies on shelf three, we would put both *G* and *H* somewhere else and we can't put *G* and *H* together on shelf two because that would violate Rule 3. So (D) is our answer here—it's the thing we can't do. (E), "can I put *G* and *K* on the same shelf?" Yes,

whether *G* is alone or together with *H*, it's possible to do this and (D)'s correct.

**22** A- This is hard because the "if" clause doesn't narrow it down to one of the two options. *L* and *G* can be on the same shelf in both options, which makes your work more complicated. In both options there's just one empty shelf—in Option 1 it's shelf three, and in Option 2 it's shelf one. Let's see if we can make any more deductions about both options. In Option 1, if we have to leave shelf three empty, we can figure out what to do with *K* and *J* because they can't be on shelf two and shelf three is empty, so shelf one has *F*, *K*, and *J* and shelf two has *L* and *G* and the only thing left is *H*, on either shelf one or shelf two. In Option 2 we know that *K* can't be on shelf two, and shelf one has to be empty, so the only place for *K* is shelf three. *J* can't be on shelf three in Option 2, shelf one is empty, so *J* is on shelf two. So we end up with *F* and *J* on shelf two, *L*, *K*, and *G* on shelf three and shelf one empty, and *H* is a floater.

For the answer to be correct, it must be true in both options—you hit pay dirt right away, because (A) is correct. It says if *H* is on shelf three, then *J* is on shelf two. The only way to put *H* on shelf three is Option 2, where shelf three is open. You can put *H* on shelf three, and in Option 2, *J* is on shelf two, so (A)'s correct. (B) describes *K* and *L* as being on the same shelf, but that's true only in Option 2. (C) says if *H* is on shelf two, *J* is on shelf three, but *J* is never on shelf three. (D) has *F* and *K* on the same shelf, that's true in Option 1 only and not in Option 2. And (E) has *J* on shelf two. That's Option 2, but it goes on to say that *H* is on shelf one and in Option 2 shelf one is empty. Again, (A) is correct.

**23** E- What if someone prefers the look of finished furniture over the look of painted furniture? Would that factor outweigh the person's desire to reduce work time and costs? We don't know—the author assumes that only the three factors he discusses, work time, cost, and longevity determine a person's decision to paint rather than to finish. (E) says more or less the same thing and is our answer. As for (A), the author concludes that some people might prefer painting because it costs less and it saves work time, not because it is necessarily better than finishing. (B) is a distortion of the author's conclusions. The author needn't assume that most people will consider saving time and cost more important than longevity. (C) is wrong because it falls outside the scope. The discussion is limited only to people who will paint or finish—it doesn't include people who will do neither. As for (D), the author doesn't assume that work time, cost, and longevity are equally important factors in deciding whether to paint or to finish. It's (E) for Question 23.

**24** C- We need to find evidence that will strengthen the zoologists' conclusion, so we want to establish some connection between cubs living in captivity and an inability to hunt successfully in the wild. (C) does the trick—if cubs raised in captivity could hunt successfully in the wild, it would suggest that aggressive play is not a factor in learning to hunt. But (C) demonstrates that Cowonga lion cubs raised in captivity can't hunt success-fully in the wild. Unless there are other differ-ences, the aggressive play could very well be the cause of this. (A) doesn't strengthen a con-nection between hunting and aggressive play—maybe the wild cubs would be equally successful at hunting if they didn't play aggres-sively. (B)—that other predatory animals also engage in aggressive play when young doesn't mean that this play is necessary for successful hunting in later life. (D) is irrelevant—just because the skills used in play are similar to the skills necessary for hunting doesn't mean that cubs learn the hunting skills through play. And (E) doesn't strengthen the zoologists' conclu-sion—it simply repeats the part of the evidence they cite in support of their argument. So (C) is correct .

**25** A- Two assumptions hold this argument together. First, the author decides that the survey means that the student body has become more religious. Then she decides that this is what has reduced cheating. So we'll look for a choice that suggests that either increased attendance at religious services or reduced cheating could be attributed to factors other than these. We get the former in (A). If most students attend services for social reasons, then this majority isn't attending because of increased religiosity, and this would destroy the author's primary assumption. (B) would *strengthen* the author's argument since it sums up her second assumption. If the students had really become religious, the author would be justified in asserting that the religiosity was a factor in the decrease of cheating. (C) lists the change in exam procedures made 15 years ago, but the survey compares attendance today with attendance ten years ago, and the author's implicitly speaking of the last decade. (D) tries to attack the author's evidence, positing that not all students responded to the survey. But a survey just needs a sufficiently representative sample. (E) takes us way out of the ballpark—who said cheating was a major problem? All we know is that it's been massively reduced. The answer is (A).

**1** **A-** We have to plug 1 in for $x$ and solve the equation for $y$. Well, $x + 3$ is $1 + 3$—that's what's inside the parentheses and we do that first. We have $1 + 3 = 4$ inside the parentheses. $y = 4^2$, $4^2$ is 16, and 16 is greater than 9, so the answer is (A).

**2** **B-** In both columns we'll use the basic formula: rate × time = distance. In Column A, 40 mph × 4 hours traveled gives you 160 miles. In Column B, 70 mph × $2\frac{1}{2}$ hours, $2 \times 70 = 140$, half of 70 is 35, and $140 + 35 = 175$ miles in Column B. 175 is greater than 160, so the answer is (B).

**3** **D-** This is intended to conjure up a picture of heavy cookies in one bag and light grapes in the other, but you can't assume that because cookies are usually bigger than grapes, these cookies weigh more than these grapes. Since you don't know how much each cookie and each grape weighs, you can't find the number of cookies or grapes, so it's (D).

**4** **C-** Here we have triangle $ABC$—base $BC$ has been extended on one side so we have an exterior angle drawn in and labeled 120 degrees. We want to compare side lengths $AB$ and $BC$—in any triangle, the largest side will be opposite the largest angle, so we want to see which of these sides is opposite a larger angle. Since angle $A$ is labeled 60 degrees, is angle $C$ less than, equal to or greater than 60? Notice that the adjacent angle is 120 degrees–the two together form a straight line, so their sum is 180 degrees. $180 - 120 = 60$, so angle $C$ is a 60 degree angle. Since the angles are equal, the sides are equal, and the answer is (C).

**5** **A-** Notice the way the diagram is set up—$a + b$ is the same as $PQ$. Our equa-

tion is $8a + 8b = 24$. Divide by 8. We end up with $a + b = 3$. $PQ$ is 3 and since 3 is greater than 2, the answer is (A).

**6** **A-** All we know is that $x$ is less than $y$ but though we don't know their values, we may know enough to determine a relationship. In Column A we have $y - x$, the larger number minus the smaller number, so you must get a positive difference, even if both numbers are negative. In Column B you have the smaller number minus the larger number—the difference is the same except this time it is negative. So you can determine a relationship—you know the answer is (A), the quantity in Column A is always greater than the quantity in Column B.

**7** **D-** Remember, area equals $\frac{1}{2}$ × base × height. Both triangles have the same height, because they have the same apex point $A$ and each of them has its base a part of segment $EB$. So the one with the larger base has the larger area. Which is bigger, $CB$ or $DE$? We have no way to figure it out. We are not given any relationships or lengths for any of those segments, so the answer is (D).

**8** **B-** There's one box that's in both rows–the one in the middle with value $\frac{2}{9}$. In fact, we have $\frac{1}{3} + \frac{2}{9} + y$ in the horizontal row, $x + \frac{2}{9} + \frac{4}{5}$ in the vertical row and we are comparing $x$ and $y$. Since $\frac{2}{9}$ is part of both rows, we can throw it out. So we have $\frac{1}{3} + y = \frac{4}{5} + x$. We have $\frac{1}{3} + y$ and that is the same as $\frac{4}{5} + x$. Since $\frac{4}{5}$ is greater than $\frac{1}{3}$, the number we add to $\frac{4}{5}$ has to be less than the number we add to $\frac{1}{3}$ for the sums to be the same. Since $\frac{4}{5}$ is greater than $\frac{1}{3}$, $x$ must be less than $y$. The answer is (B).

**9** **B-** Looking at the fraction in <u>Column A</u> we have $\frac{1}{3} \times \frac{1}{4}$ in the numerator, $\frac{2}{3} \times \frac{1}{2}$ in the denominator. We can cancel the factor of $\frac{1}{3}$ from the numerator and denominator, right? Cancel a $\frac{1}{3}$ from each and you end up with $1 \times \frac{1}{4}$ in the numerator, $2 \times \frac{1}{2}$ in the denominator. Using the same approach, we can cancel a factor of $\frac{1}{4}$, so we're left with $1 \times 1$ in the numerator and $2 \times 2$ in the denominator, the value of <u>Column A</u> is $\frac{1}{4}$. Now take a look at <u>Column B</u>. It's the reciprocal of the value in Column A. You have $\frac{2}{3} \times \frac{1}{2}$ in the numerator and $\frac{1}{3} \times \frac{1}{4}$ in the denominator. So you have $\frac{4}{1}$ as your value for <u>Column B</u>.

You have 4 in Column B, $\frac{1}{4}$ in Column A, and the answer is (B).

**10** **B-** Make a map—if you have trouble with geometry, this will make it much easier. Eileen drives due north from town $A$ to town $B$ for 60 miles. Start at a point and draw a line straight up. Label the point you started at $A$ and the point above it, $B$. Label the length of the distance from $A$ to $B$ 60. Next she drives due east from town $B$ to town $C$ for a distance of 80 miles. Start at point $B$, draw a line straight over to the right, call the right endpoint $C$ and label distance $BC$ 80. You have a right angle, angle $ABC$. Well, the distance from town $A$ to town $C$ is the hypotenuse of a right triangle if you draw line $AC$. The two legs are 60 and 80 and this is one of our Pythagorean ratios. It is a 6 to 8 to 10 triangle except this time it is 60, 80, 100. So the distance from $A$ to $C$ is 100 miles, the same as our value for <u>Column A</u>, so the answer is (B).

**11** **C-** Let's see if we can do something to make these look more alike by getting both sets of binomials so the $\sqrt{7}$ s are in the front. We have $\sqrt{7} - 2$. Is that a positive or negative quantity? $2^2$ is 4, $3^2$ is 9 so $\sqrt{7}$ is between 2 and 3. We have $\sqrt{7} - 2$, that is positive, times $\sqrt{7} + 2$, that is positive again. Two positives in <u>Column A</u> and the product of two positives is always positive. What do we have in <u>Column B</u>? $2 - \sqrt{7}$, that is a negative number times negative $\sqrt{7} - 2$. $-\sqrt{7}$ is a negative, $-2$ is negative, that quantity is negative. You have the product of two negatives in <u>Column</u>

B, but a product of two negatives is positive also, so you can't tell which is greater. Let's see if we can make these quantities look more alike. With the last one on the right, $-\sqrt{7}-2$, if we divide the whole thing by $-1$, we're left with a positive $\sqrt{7}$ and a positive 2, $\sqrt{7}+2$. On the right in Column B we have $(2-\sqrt{7})\times(-1)\times(\sqrt{7}+2)$, and $(\sqrt{7}+2)$ is also in Column A so we can cancel. Those two factors are the same, right? We have $-1\times(2-\sqrt{7})$. Let's distribute again. What is $-1\times 2$? It's $-2$. What is $-1\times-\sqrt{7}$? It's $+\sqrt{7}$ so we end up with $+\sqrt{7}+-2$ or $\sqrt{7}-2$. It's exactly the same as the factor in Column A. So the quantities are equal and the answer is (C).

**12** B- We can see from our diagram that $r$ and $s$ are the coordinates of a point on our line. We have a line on the graph with one point with coordinates $(\frac{5}{2},\frac{7}{2})$. The line also goes through the origin $(0,0)$, so what can we figure out about this line? Well, draw in the line $x=y$, a line which makes a 45 degree angle with the $x$-axis that goes from the lower left to the upper right—you notice that it goes through the point $(\frac{5}{2},\frac{5}{2})$, because any point on line $x=y$ has the same $x$ coordinate and $y$ coordinate. Point $(\frac{5}{2},\frac{7}{2})$ falls above point $(\frac{5}{2},$

$\frac{5}{2})$, because the $y$ coordinate is greater, it's above the $x=y$ line. Similarly, point $(r,s)$ lies above the $x=y$ line so the $y$ coordinate is greater than the $x$ coordinate and the $y$ coordinate of that point is $s$. Where we have coordinates $(r,s)$, $r$ is the $x$ coordinate, $s$ is the $y$ coordinate, $s$ is greater than $r$ in this case. The answer is (B), the quantity in Column B is greater.

**13** D- We have $1-(\frac{1}{4})$ to the $x$ power in Column A and we have 0.95 in Column B. That's a bizarre comparison, isn't it? Converting Column B, .95 into fraction form, $.95=\frac{95}{100}=\frac{19}{20}$. What do we have in Column A if $x=1$? We have $1-\frac{1}{4}$ or $\frac{3}{4}$. $\frac{19}{20}$ is greater than $\frac{3}{4}$. What happens if we have $x=2$? Column A becomes $1-(\frac{1}{4})^2$. $\frac{1}{4}^2$ is $\frac{1}{4}\times\frac{1}{4}$ or $1-\frac{1}{16}$ is $\frac{15}{16}$. So what's bigger, $\frac{15}{16}$ or $\frac{19}{20}$? Still $\frac{19}{20}$, but as $x$ gets larger and we multiply $\frac{1}{4}$ times itself more times, the amount that we're taking away from 1 is going to get smaller and we'll be taking less than $\frac{1}{20}$ away from 1 as soon as we get to $x=3$. $\frac{1}{4}$ to the third power is $\frac{1}{64}$ and at that point Column A

# SECTION 6

becomes $\frac{63}{64}$. What is bigger, $\frac{19}{20}$ or $\frac{63}{64}$? Well, $\frac{63}{64}$ is bigger, it is closer to 1 and there are two possible relationships here. If $x$ is 1 or 2, Column B is greater. If $x$ is 3 or larger, Column A is greater. The answer is choice (D).

**14** A- If you draw in some diameters in the circles, you will see that $PS$ is equal to one diameter, and $PQ$ is equal to two diameters. Let one diameter be $d$. The perimeter of $PQRS$ is then $PS + PQ + SR + QR = 60$. The circumference of a circle is $\pi d$, where $d$ is a diameter. Since we have two circles, the combined circumferences is $2 \times \pi d = 2\pi d$. Since $\pi$ is greater than 3 (it's about 3.14), the value in Column A is greater than $6d$ in Column B.

**15** B- I hope you didn't try to figure out the exact values of each of these. Instead, if you look at Column B and Column A, they look sort of alike because they both have 3 in terms of a power. What is $3^{20}$? It's $3 \times 3^{19}$ right? So we can have $3^{19} + 3^{19} + 3^{19}$ in Column B. In Column A we have $3^{17} + 3^{18} + 3^{19}$. We can subtract $3^{19}$ from both sides and we're left with $3^{17} + 3^{18}$ in Column A and $3^{19} + 3^{19}$ in Column B. We know that $3^{19}$ is bigger than $3^{17}$ or $3^{18}$ so we know that $3^{19} + 3^{19}$ is bigger than $3^{17} + 3^{18}$. The answer is (B), the quantity in Column B is greater.

**16** E- We have $4 + y = 14 - 4y$ and we want to solve for $y$. We can isolate the $y$'s on one side of the equal sign by adding 4y to both sides, giving us $4 + 5y = 14$. Subtracting the 4 from both sides we get $5y = 10$. Divide both sides by 5 and get $y = 2$, (E).

**17** D- Let's go the quickest, most obvious route and use the common denominator method. With $\frac{4}{5}$ and $\frac{5}{4}$, the denominator that we will use, is easy to find; just use $5 \times 4$ or 20. $\frac{4}{5}$ is $\frac{16}{20}$ and $\frac{5}{4}$ is $\frac{25}{20}$, $\frac{16}{20} + \frac{25}{20}$ is $\frac{41}{20}$ which is (D).

**18** E- First we need to find $m$. We are told that $3^m$ is 81. Well, 81 is $9 \times 9$. 9 is $3^2$. So we have $3^2 \times 3^2 = 81$ or $3 \times 3 \times 3 \times 3 = 81$. How many factors of 3 are there in 81? There are 4, so $m$ has the value 4. Now what's $4^3$? 4 $\times$ 4 is 16. 16 $\times$ 4 is 64. So (E) is correct, 64 is $m^3$.

**19** B- We are looking for the area in square meters of square $C$. Now notice we have one side of square $B$ butted up against one side of square $A$—they're not the same length, but the difference in their lengths is made up by the length of a side of square $C$. One side of square $B$ + one side of square $C$ = one side of square $A$. We can figure out the length of the side of $A$ and length of the side of $B$, which will let us figure out the length of side of $C$. That is what we need to figure out the area of square $C$. The area of a square is its side squared. The area of square $A$ is 81, so it has a side of $\sqrt{81} = 9$. The area of square $B$ is 49, so it has sides of length $\sqrt{49} = 7$. So $9 = 7 + C$, so $C$ must have length 2. So we have 2 as the length of the side of square $C$, $2^2$ is 4, there are 4 square meters in gardening area $C$, and the answer is (B).

**20** E- We can figure out how many students scored exactly 85, 23 scored 85 or over, 18 were over 85. So 23 – 18 or 5 students scored exactly 85 on the exam, but that's no help. How many students scored less than 85? We don't know—we can't answer this question. It's (E), it can't be determined.

**21** C- In Question 21 we're asked in which year the energy use in country $Y$ was closest to 650 million kilowatt hours, so we just have to follow the jagged line which represents energy use from left to right until we encounter a vertical line representing a year where we're close to 650 million—the one year where this is true is 1970. In no other year are we as close, so (C), 1970, is our answer.

**22** C- In order to find how many categories had energy use greater than 150 million kilowatts, you have to find out how many total kilowatts were used in that year using the line graph. You see that there were 600 million kilowatts used in 1965. What is the relationship of 150 million kilowatts to 600 million kilowatts? It's 25% of 600 million kilowatts, so we're looking for categories with more than 25% of the energy use for 1965. How many categories exceeded 25%? Just 2, government and industrial. So 2 is our answer, (C).

**23** D- We can estimate quite a bit from our graph–if we look at our line chart, we can see that as time goes on, energy use goes up pretty steadily. It went up sharply between 1960 and 1965, then more gradually from 1965 to 1980. Now, because in more recent years the overall use was much larger, if the percent of industrial use was about the same over all the years, then as the overall use gets bigger, the amount used for industrial purposes will get larger also. Let's take a quick look at the bar graph and see if that is the case. Was the percent being used for industrial use about the same? Well, it didn't fluctuate much from 1960 to 1970, but in 1975 industrial use jumped significantly as a percent of the total, then shrank significantly going to 1980. 1975 is the most likely answer and if you find 40% of 690 million, your amount for 1975, you get 276 million kilowatt hours. Then if you find 20% of 710 million, your amount for 1980, you only get 142 million kilowatt hours, so (D), 1975, is the correct answer.

**24** D- What we are going to do for 1960 and 1965 is find the per capita personal use, then find the percent decrease from 1960 to 1965. To do that, we have to plug in a value for the population of this country for 1960. Let's use 100 million for the '60s population. The per capita use in 1960 is the total personal use, which is 30% of 500 million, that's 150 million. We know that 150 million, the total personal use, equals 100 million, the population × the per capita use. The per capita use is $\frac{3}{2}$ or 1.5. Going on to 1965, we are told the population increased by 20%, so in 1965 the population was 120 million people. What was the total personal use of energy? It was a little bit less than 20% of our total 600 million so we'll call it 20% of 600 million, or 120 million. Now if total personal use is 120 million and we have 120 million people, that's one kilowatt hour per person. What's the percent decrease? It's a decrease of $\frac{1}{3}$, $33\frac{1}{3}$%. But remember, in 1965, they were using a little more energy for personal use than we figured. So the correct answer must be a little greater than $33\frac{1}{3}$%, so 40%, (D), is the correct answer.

**25** A- Statement I says farm use of energy increased between 1960 and 1980. How many total kilowatt hours were used in 1960? 500 million. In 1980, 710 million. What was the percent of farm use in 1960? It was 30% of the total in 1960 and a little bit less than 30%, around 28%, in 1980. The percent is very close together while the whole has become much larger from 1960 to 1980, so 30% of 500 million is less than 28% of 710 million. Farm use of energy did go up in that 20 year period and numeral I is going to be part of our answer. That eliminates two answer choices, (B) and (D). How about Statement II? This one is harder. It says that in 1980, industrial use of energy was greater than industrial use of energy in 1965. But what was it in 1965? Industrial use of energy in 1965 was 30% of 600 million. We got the percent from the bar graph, the total from the line chart. Okay, 30% of 600 million is 180 million. But what about 1980? In 1980 industrial use of energy was 20% of a larger whole, 710 million kilowatt hours. Well, 20% of 710 is 142 million. That's less than 180 million, isn't it? In fact, industrial use of energy went down from 1965 to 1980, so this can't be inferred from the graph and it's not part of our answer. That cuts out (C) and (E), leaving choice (A), I only. Roman numeral III is another easy one to eliminate because it says

more people were employed by the government of country $Y$ in 1980 than in 1960. These graphs deal only with energy use, not with employment, so it's irrelevant and we can eliminate it. Only Statement I can be inferred, and (A) is correct.

**26** E- The average is $\frac{\text{The sum of terms}}{\text{The number of terms}}$. Here we have two terms, $y - z$, and the other number which we will call $x$. The average of $x$ and $y - z$ is $3y$ so $3y = \frac{x + y - z}{z}$. Multiplying both sides by 2 gives $6y = x + y - z$. Subtracting $y - z$ from both sides gives $5y + z = x$. So the other number, $x$, is $5y + z$, answer choice (E).

**27** B- We're told that the area of triangle $ABC$ is 35 and in our diagram we're given a height for triangle $ABC$. If we use $AC$ as the base of the triangle, the perpendicular distance from segment $AC$ up to point $B$ is 7 units, so we can find the length of $AC$. When we find the length $AC$, the base of triangle $ABC$, what do we have? We have the hypotenuse of right triangle $ABC$. Given the hypotenuse and the length of leg $AD$ which is given in the diagram as length 6, we'll be able to find the third leg of the triangle, side $DC$, which is what we're looking for. Okay, going back to triangle $ABC$ where we started, the area is 35 and the height is 7. The area of a triangle is $\frac{1}{2}$ base × height so $\frac{1}{2}$ base × height is 35, $\frac{1}{2}$ × 7 × length $AC$ is 35. That means 7 × length $AC$ is 70, so $AC$ must have length 10. Now we can look at right triangle $ADC$. Here is a right triangle with one leg length 6, the hypotenuse length 10 and the third side unknown; what we have is a 6, blank, 10 right triangle. That's one of our famous Pythagorean ratios, it's a 6, 8, 10 triangle. So $DC$ must have length 2 × 4, or 8, (B).

**28** A- We're trying to find the shortest distance in meters a person would have to walk to go from point $A$ to a point on side $BC$ of the triangular field represented in our diagram. In order to get the shortest distance from side $BC$ up to point $A$, we want to draw a perpendicular line from point $A$ down to side $BC$. That will divide up the triangular field into right triangles. Let's draw in the path from point $A$ down to segment $BC$ and call the new vertex we make point $D$. We just created two smaller right triangles, $ADC$ and $ADB$. Now our diagram tells us that length $BC$ is 160 meters and $AB$ is 100 meters—$AC$ is also 100 meters. Now each of these two right triangles has 100 meters as the length of its hypotenuse. What does that tell you about triangle $ABC$? $AB$ and $AC$ have the same lengths—this is an isosceles triangle and that means that when you drew in the perpendicular distance from $A$ down to $D$ you split that isosceles triangle into two identical right triangles. Length $BD$ is the same as length $BC$. So each of them is half of 160 meters, that means

80 meters each. We have right triangles with hypotenuses length 100 meters each and one leg of each these right triangles is 80 meters. This is a 3-4-5 right triangle, with each member of the ratio multiplied by 80. So $AD$ must have length 60, and the minimum distance is 60 meters, (A).

**29** D- We're told the ratio of $2a$ to $b$ is 8 times the ratio of $b$ to $a$. That's awkward to keep track of in English—it's a little easier to write fractions. The ratio of $2a$:$b$ is $2\frac{a}{b}$ ("is" means equals). So $2\frac{a}{b} = 8(\frac{b}{a})$. We're asked to find what $\frac{b}{a}$ could be; that may tell you there's more than one possible value for $\frac{b}{a}$, but let's start with the equation we just put together using translation and isolate $\frac{b}{a}$. To do that, we'll divide both sides of the equation by 8 which is the same as multiplying by $\frac{1}{8}$. So now we have $\frac{1}{8} \times 2\frac{a}{b} = \frac{b}{a}$. Well, what is $\frac{1}{8} \times 2\frac{a}{b}$? It's $\frac{a}{4b}$. So $\frac{a}{4b} = \frac{b}{a}$. We need to multiply both sides of the equation right now on both sides by $\frac{b}{a}$. It'll be more complicated on the right side but simpler on the left because the $a$'s and $b$'s on the left side will cancel out, and you'll be left with $\frac{1}{4}$. On the right you have

$\dfrac{b}{a} \times \dfrac{b}{a} = \dfrac{b^2}{a^2}$. So we have $\dfrac{1}{4} = \dfrac{b^2}{a^2}$. So $\dfrac{b}{a}$ could represent positive or negative $\dfrac{1}{2}$.

**30** D- A dentist earns $n$ dollars for each filling plus $x$ dollars for every 15 minutes. So the money is figured in two different ways; dollars for each filling and dollars per hour, represented in terms of 15 minutes. Our result will be a two part answer choice. If you can figure out one part, it will let you eliminate some choices. She put in 21 fillings. She makes $n$ dollars for each so she gets 21n dollars for fillings. You can eliminate (B) and (E) because (B) has only $14n$ in it, and (E) has $\dfrac{21}{4}n$ dollars in it. That narrows our choices to (A), (C) and (D). How about the hourly rate? The dentist works 14 hours in a week. Does that mean she makes $14x$ dollars? No, because the rate is dollars for every 15 minutes. Now if she makes $x$ dollars for every 15 minutes and 15 minutes is $\dfrac{1}{4}$ of an hour, then we have to multiply that rate by 4 to get the rate per hour, it's $4x$ dollars per hour. Well, $4x$ times 14 hours is $56x$, so (D), $56x + 21n$ is correct for Question 30.

# LAST-MINUTE
# TIPS

*Early tests proved that the #1 pencil would have to be abandoned.*

# LAST MINUTE TIPS

Is it starting to feel as if your whole life is a buildup to the GRE? You've known about it for years, worried about it for months, and now spent at least a few weeks in solid preparation for it. As the test gets closer, you may find that your anxiety is on the rise. You shouldn't worry. Armed with the preparation strategies that you've learned from this book, you're in good shape for test day.

To calm any pre-test jitters that you may have, though, let's go over a few strategies for the couple of days before and after the test.

## THE WEEK BEFORE TEST DAY

In the week or so leading up to test day, you should do the following:

- Recheck your admission ticket for accuracy; call ETS if corrections are necessary.

- Visit the testing center, if you can. Sometimes seeing the actual room where your test will be administered and taking notice of little things—such as the kind of desk you'll be working on, whether the room is likely to be hot or cold, and so forth—may help to calm your nerves. And if you've never been to the campus or building where your test will take place, this is a good way to ensure that you don't get lost. Remember: You must be on time; the proctors won't wait for you.

- Practice getting up early and working on test material, preferably a full-length test, as if it were the real test day.

- Time yourself accurately, with the same device and in the same manner in which you plan to keep track of time on test day.

- Evaluate thoroughly where you stand. Use the time remaining before test day to shore up your weak points, rereading the appropriate sections of this book. But make sure not to neglect your strong areas—after all, this is where you'll rack up most of your points.

### THE FINAL DAYS FOR YOUR PREPARATION ARE KEY

The tendency among students is to study too hard during the last few days before the test and then to forget the important, practical matters until the last minute. Part of taking control means avoiding this last-minute crush.

### PREPARATION, NOT DESPERATION

Don't try to cram lots of studying into the last day before the test. It probably won't do you much good, and it could bring on a case of test burnout.

## D-DAY MINUS ONE

Try to avoid doing intensive studying the day before the test. There's little you can do to help yourself at this late date, and you may just wind up exhausting yourself. Our advice is to review a few key concepts, get together everything that you'll need for test day, and then take the night off entirely. Go to see an early movie or watch some TV. Try not to think too much about the test.

## TEST DAY!!!

Let's now discuss what you can expect on test day itself. It should start with a moderate, high energy breakfast. Cereal, fruit, bagels, or eggs are good. Avoid donuts, danishes, or anything else with lots of sugar in it. Also, unless you are utterly catatonic without it, it's a good idea to stay away from coffee. Yeah, yeah, you drink two cups every morning and don't even notice it. But it's different on test day. Coffee won't make you alert (your adrenaline will do that much more effectively); it will just give you the jitters. Kaplan has done experiments in which test takers go into one exam having drunk various amounts of coffee and another exam without having drunk coffee. The results indicate that even the most caffeine-addicted test takers will lose their focus midway through section two if they've drunk coffee, but they report no alertness problems without it.

Taking the GRE, as we said early on, makes for a fairly long day. The total testing time is three and a half hours. When you add the administrative paperwork before and after, and the 10 to 15 minute break in the middle, you're looking at an experience of between four and six hours, depending on the efficiency of the proctors (better assume six).

After the test booklets are handed out, and you've filled out all of the requisite information, the test will begin. Your proctor should write the starting and ending time of each section on a blackboard in front of the room, and he or she will usually announce the time remaining at specified intervals, such as when there's ten minutes remaining, five minutes remaining, and one minute remaining.

Most test centers have a clock on the wall, which the proctor will use to time the test. But don't take anything for granted; your test center may not (stranger things have been known to happen). You should definitely bring along your own timing device, such as a watch or a stopwatch, so long as it doesn't make any noise (devices that beep on the hour or sound an alarm at specified times are prohibited from the testing site).

It's also best to practice using a timing routine that you'll follow during the real test. For example, some students find it helpful to set their watch at half past the hour, 11:30, for example. This way, they know that the section will end exactly when their watch says 12:00. Others reset their watches exactly on the hour at the beginning of each section and know that every section they take will end at 30 minutes after the hour. It doesn't matter which one of the these procedures you adopt, or even if you come up with one of your own that you're comfortable with, just as long as you use it consistently, so that keeping track of time on test day is second nature.

In between sections, the proctor will say "Time's up on this section . . . Go on to the next section." Except for the midpoint break, you won't have more than a few seconds between sections. You must go immediately from one section to the next. Use this time to shake out your wrist and hand, to take a deep breath, and to refocus your concentration. Also, if you finish a section early, you're not allowed to move on to another section. They're pretty strict about this one. If you have extra time, spend it looking back over your work.

Finally, here are some last-minute reminders to help guide your work on test day:

- To make sure that your answer sheet is gridded accurately, say the question number and choice to yourself (silently, of course) as you grid.

- Give all five answer choices a fair shot in Verbal (especially, Reading Comp) and in Logical Reasoning, time permitting. For Math and Logic Games, go with the objectively-correct answer as soon as you find it and blow off the rest.

- Remember, all the item types in Math and Short Verbal are presented in ascending order of difficulty. Make sure you get the easy ones right and don't spend too much time on the hard ones. Also, be careful to avoid trick choices in the hard questions.

- In Reading Comp and throughout the Analytical Sections, don't be alarmed if you run across extra-tough questions at the beginning. It happens. Skip past tough ones and come back to them later, making sure to circle them in the test booklet so you can find them fast.

- Preview the Logic Games and Reading Comprehension sections before you launch into them. The third or fourth game or the second reading passage could be the easiest one for you.

## LEAVE 'EM AT HOME

The following items are not allowed in the test room:
- ear plugs (People would cheat and keep working after the proctors call "Time.")
- highlighting pens (If you're one of those people who transforms your textbooks into an ocean of pink ink, think about doing reading passages by circling key text instead.)
- calculators or any printed reference material
- matches (The temptation would be too great.)

## SELF-TIMER

Don't rely on proctors to do the timekeeping. Be your own timer.

- Don't bother trying to figure out which section is unscored. It can't help you, and you might very well be wrong. Instead, just determine to do your best on every section.

- Pay no attention to people's nervous chatter during the break between Sections 3 and 4. They *should* be nervous. They're not as well prepared as you are.

- Dress in layers for maximum comfort. This way, you can adjust to the room's temperature accordingly.

- Take a few minutes now to look back over your preparation and give yourself credit for how far you've come. Confidence is key. *Accentuate the positives and don't dwell on the negatives!* Your attitude and outlook are crucial to your performance on test day.

- During the exam, try not to think about how you're scoring. It's like a baseball player who's thinking about the crowd's cheers, the sportswriters, and his contract as he steps up to the plate: There's no surer way to a strikeout. Instead, focus on the question-by-question task of picking (A), (B), (C), (D), or (E). The correct answer is there: You don't have to come up with it; it's sitting right there in front of you! Concentrate on each question, each passage, each game—on the mechanics, in other words—and you'll be much more likely to hit a home run.

## AFTER THE TEST

### Cancellation and Multiple Scores Policy

Unlike many things in life, the GRE allows you a second chance. If you walk out of the test feeling that you've really not done as well as you can, you always have the option to cancel your score—up to five business days after test day. Canceling a test means that it won't be scored. It will just appear on your score report as a canceled test. No one will know how well or poorly you really did—not even you.

Two legitimate reasons to cancel your test are illness and personal circumstances that cause you to perform unusually poorly on that particular day. Also, if you feel that you didn't prepare sufficiently, then it may be acceptable to cancel your score and approach your test preparation a little more seriously the next time.

But keep in mind that test takers historically underestimate their performance, especially immediately following the test. They tend to forget about all of the things that went right and focus on everything that went wrong. So unless your performance is terribly marred by unforeseen circumstances, don't cancel your test immediately—at least sleep on the decision for one or two nights. If you still feel that you want to do it again, then send in the form. Just remember, cancellations are permanent. Once the form is sent, you can't change your mind.

If you do cancel your test and then take it again for a score, your score report will indicate that you've canceled a previous score. Because it won't be scored, you don't have to worry about this score showing up on any subsequent score report. If you take more than one test without canceling, then all the scores will show up on each score report, so the graduate schools will see them all. Most grad schools average GRE scores, although there are a few exceptions. Check with individual schools for their policy on multiple scores.

## POST-GRE FESTIVITIES

After all the hard work that you've put in preparing for and taking the GRE, you want to make sure you take time to celebrate afterwards. Plan to get together with friends the evening after the test. Relax, have fun, let loose. After all, you've got lots to celebrate: You prepared for the test ahead of time. You did your best. You're going to get a good score.

### DO YOU *REALLY* WANT TO CANCEL?

The key question to ask yourself when deciding whether to cancel is this: Will I really do significantly better next time?

### ABOUT CANCELING

Although we hope you won't find it necessary to cancel your GRE score, here are a few points to keep in mind:
• Students sometimes underestimate their performance immediately after the test and think that they should cancel their scores. Doing poorly on one piece of the test does not necessarily mean that they've bombed. Scores should be canceled only after you've given the issue careful thought and decided that your overall performance was poorer than usual.
• Scores can be canceled within five working days after the test date.
• Use a mailgram, telegram, fax, or overnight letter.
• Use the form that is provided at the test site or write your own letter with name, address, social security number, signature, test date, test center name, and test center code number.

# ROOT LIST

The Kaplan Root List can boost your knowledge of GRE-level words, and that can help you get more questions right. No one can predict exactly which words will show up on your test, but there are certain words that the test makers favor. The Root List gives you the component parts of many typical GRE words. Knowing these words can help you because you may run across them on your GRE. Also, becoming comfortable with the types of words that pop up will reduce your anxiety about the test.

Knowing roots can help you in two more ways. First, instead of learning one word at a time, you can learn a whole group of words which contain a certain root. They'll be related in meaning, so if you remember one, it will be easier for you to remember others. Second, roots can often help you decode an unknown GRE word. If you recognize a familiar root, you could get a good enough idea of the word to answer the question.

## THE KAPLAN ROOT LIST

❑ **A, AN**—not, without
amoral, atrophy, asymmetrical, anarchy, anesthetic, anonymity, anomaly

❑ **AB, A**—from, away, apart
abnormal, abdicate, aberration, abhor, abject, abjure, ablution, abnegate, abortive, abrogate, abscond, absolve, abstemious, abstruse, annul, avert, aversion

❑ **AC, ACR**—sharp, sour
acid, acerbic, exacerbate, acute, acuity, acumen, acrid, acrimony

❑ **AD, A**—to, toward
adhere, adjacent, adjunct, admonish, adroit, adumbrate, advent, abeyance, abet, accede, accretion, acquiesce, affluent, aggrandize, aggregate, alleviate, alliteration, allude, allure, ascribe, aspersion, aspire, assail, assonance, attest

❑ **ALI, ALTR**—another
alias, alienate, inalienable, altruism

❑ **AM, AMI**—love
amorous, amicable, amiable, amity

❑ **AMBI, AMPHI**—both
ambiguous, ambivalent, ambidextrous, amphibious

❑ **AMBL, AMBUL**—walk
amble, ambulatory, perambulator, somnambulist

❑ **ANIM**—mind, spirit, breath
animal, animosity, unanimous, magnanimous

❑ **ANN, ENN**—year
annual, annuity, superannuated, biennial, perennial

❑ **ANTE, ANT**—before
antecedent, antediluvian, antebellum, antepenultimate, anterior, antiquity, antiquated, anticipate

❑ **ANTHROP**—human
anthropology, anthropomorphic, misanthrope, philanthropy

❑ **ANTI, ANT**—against, opposite
antidote, antipathy, antithesis, antacid, antagonist, antonym

❑ **AUD**—hear
audio, audience, audition, auditory, audible

❏ AUTO—self
autobiography, autocrat, autonomous

❏ BELLI, BELL—war
belligerent, bellicose, antebellum, rebellion

❏ BENE, BEN—good
benevolent, benefactor, beneficent, benign

❏ BI—two
bicycle, bisect, bilateral, bilingual, biped

❏ BIBLIO—book
Bible, bibliography, bibliophile

❏ BIO—life
biography, biology, amphibious, symbiotic, macrobiotics

❏ BURS—money, purse
reimburse, disburse, bursar

❏ CAD, CAS, CID—happen, fall
accident, cadence, cascade, deciduous

❏ CAP, CIP—head
captain, decapitate, capitulate, precipitous, precipitate

❏ CARN—flesh
carnal, carnage, carnival, carnivorous, incarnate

❏ CAP, CAPT, CEPT, CIP—take, hold, seize
capable, capacious, recapitulate, captivate, deception, intercept, precept, inception, anticipate, emancipation, incipient, percipient, cede, precede, accede, recede, antecedent, intercede, secede, cession

❏ CED, CESS—yield, go
cease, cessation, incessant, cede

❏ CHROM—color
chrome, chromatic, monochrome

❏ CHRON—time
chronology, chronic, anachronism

❏ CIDE—murder
suicide, homicide, regicide, patricide

❑ CIRCUM—around
circumference, circumlocution, circumnavigate, circumscribe, circumspect, circumvent

❑ CLIN, CLIV—slope
incline, declivity, proclivity

❑ CLUD, CLUS, CLAUS, CLOIS—shut, close
conclude, reclusive, claustrophobia, cloister, preclude, occlude

❑ CO, COM, CON—with, together
coeducation, coagulate, coalesce, coerce, cogent, cognate, collateral, colloquial, colloquy, commensurate, commodious, compassion, compatriot, complacent, compliant, complicity, compunction, concerto, conciliatory, concord, concur, condone, conflagration, congeal, congenial, congenital, conglomerate, conjure, conjugal, conscientious, consecrate, consensus, consonant, constrained, contentious, contrite, contusion, convalescence, convene, convivial, convoke, convoluted, congress

❑ COGN, GNO—know
recognize, cognition, cognizance, incognito, diagnosis, agnostic, prognosis, gnostic, ignorant

❑ CONTRA—against
controversy, incontrovertible, contravene

❑ CORP —body
corpse, corporeal, corpulence

❑ COSMO, COSM—world
cosmopolitan, cosmos, microcosm, macrocosm

❑ CRAC, CRAT—rule, power
democracy, bureaucracy, theocracy, autocrat, aristocrat, technocrat

❑ CRED—trust, believe
incredible, credulous, credence

❑ CRESC, CRET—grow
crescent, crescendo, accretion

❑ CULP—blame, fault
culprit, culpable, inculpate, exculpate

❑ CURR, CURS—run
current, concur, cursory, precursor, incursion

❑ DE—down, out, apart
depart, debase, debilitate, declivity, decry, deface, defamatory, defunct, delegate, demarcation, demean, demur, deplete, deplore, depravity, deprecate, deride, derivative, desist, detest, devoid

- ❏ DEC—ten, tenth
  decade, decimal, decathlon, decimate

- ❏ DEMO, DEM—people
  democrat, demographics, demagogue, epidemic, pandemic, endemic

- ❏ DI, DIURN—day
  diary, diurnal, quotidian

- ❏ DIA—across
  diagonal, diatribe, diaphanous

- ❏ DIC, DICT—speak
  diction, interdict, predict, abdicate, indict, verdict

- ❏ DIS, DIF, DI—not, apart, away
  disaffected, disband, disbar, disburse, discern, discordant, discredit, discursive, disheveled, disparage, disparate, dispassionate, dispirit, dissemble, disseminate, dissension, dissipate, dissonant, dissuade, distend, differentiate, diffidence, diffuse, digress, divert

- ❏ DOC, DOCT—teach
  doctrine, docile, doctrinaire

- ❏ DOL—pain
  condolence, doleful, dolorous, indolent

- ❏ DUC, DUCT—lead
  seduce, induce, conduct, viaduct, induct

- ❏ EGO—self
  ego, egoist, egocentric

- ❏ EN, EM—in, into
  enter, entice, encumber, endemic, ensconce, enthrall, entreat, embellish, embezzle, embroil, empathy

- ❏ ERR—wander
  erratic, aberration, errant

- ❏ EU—well, good
  eulogy, euphemism, euphony, euphoria, eurythmics, euthanasia

- ❏ EX, E—out, out of
  exit, exacerbate, excerpt, excommunicate, exculpate, execrable, exhume, exonerate, exorbitant, exorcise, expatriate, expedient, expiate, expunge, expurgate, extenuate, extort, extremity, extricate, extrinsic, exult, evoke, evict, evince, elicit, egress, egregious

❑ FAC, FIC, FECT, FY, FEA—make, do
factory, facility, benefactor, malefactor, fiction, fictive, beneficent, affect, confection, refectory, magnify, unify, rectify, vilify, feasible

❑ FAL, FALS—deceive
false, infallible, fallacious

❑ FERV—boil
fervent, fervid, effervescent

❑ FID—faith, trust
confident, diffidence, perfidious, fidelity

❑ FLU, FLUX—flow
fluent, flux, affluent, confluence, effluvia, superfluous

❑ FORE—before
forecast, foreboding, forestall

❑ FRAG, FRAC—break
fragment, fracture, diffract, fractious, refract

❑ FUS—pour
profuse, infusion, effusive, diffuse

❑ GEN—birth, class, kin
generation, congenital, homogeneous, heterogeneous, ingenious, engender, progenitor, progeny

❑ GRAD, GRESS—step
graduate, gradual, retrograde, centigrade, degrade, gradation, gradient, progress, congress, digress, transgress, ingress, egress

❑ GRAPH, GRAM—writing
biography, bibliography, epigraph, grammar, epigram

❑ GRAT—pleasing
grateful, gratitude, gratis, ingrate, congratulate, gratuitous, gratuity

❑ GRAV, GRIEV—heavy
grave, gravity, aggravate, grieve, aggrieve, grievous

❑ GREG—crowd, flock
segregate, gregarious, egregious, congregate, aggregate

❑ HABIT, HIBIT—have, hold
habit, inhibit, cohabit, habitat

- ❑ HAP—by chance
  happen, haphazard, hapless, mishap

- ❑ HELIO, HELI—sun
  heliocentric, helium, heliotrope, aphelion, perihelion

- ❑ HETERO—other
  heterosexual, heterogeneous, heterodox

- ❑ HOL—whole
  holocaust, catholic, holistic

- ❑ HOMO—same
  homosexual, homogenize, homogeneous, homonym

- ❑ HOMO—man
  homo sapiens, homicide, bonhomie

- ❑ HYDR—water
  hydrant, hydrate, dehydration

- ❑ HYPER—too much, excess
  hyperactive, hyperbole, hyperventilate

- ❑ HYPO—too little, under
  hypodermic, hypothermia, hypochondria, hypothesis, hypothetical

- ❑ IN, IG, IL, IM, IR—not
  incorrigible, indefatigable, indelible, indubitable, inept, inert, inexorable, insatiable, insentient, insolvent, insomnia, interminable, intractable, incessant, inextricable, infallible, infamy, innumerable, inoperable, insipid, intemperate, intrepid, inviolable, ignorant, ignominious, ignoble, illicit, illimitable, immaculate, immutable, impasse, impeccable, impecunious, impertinent, implacable, impotent, impregnable, improvident, impassioned, impervious, irregular, invade, inaugurate, incandescent, incarcerate, incense, indenture, induct, ingratiate, introvert, incarnate, inception, incisive, infer

- ❑ IN, IL, IM, IR—in, on, into
  infusion, ingress, innate, inquest, inscribe, insinuate, inter, illustrate, imbue, immerse, implicate, irrigate, irritate

- ❑ INTER—between, among
  intercede, intercept, interdiction, interject, interlocutor, interloper, intermediary, intermittent, interpolate, interpose, interregnum, interrogate, intersect, intervene

- ❑ INTRA, INTR—within
  intrastate, intravenous, intramural, intrinsic

- ❑ IT, ITER—between, among
  transit, itinerant, reiterate, transitory

❑ JECT, JET—throw
eject, interject, abject, trajectory, jettison

❑ JOUR—day
journal, adjourn, sojourn

❑ JUD—judge
judge, judicious, prejudice, adjudicate

❑ JUNCT, JUG—join
junction, adjunct, injunction, conjugal, subjugate

❑ JUR—swear, law
jury, abjure, adjure, conjure, perjure, jurisprudence

❑ LAT—side
lateral, collateral, unilateral, bilateral, quadrilateral

❑ LAV, LAU, LU—wash
lavatory, laundry, ablution, antediluvian

❑ LEG, LEC, LEX—read, speak
legible, lecture, lexicon

❑ LEV—light
elevate, levitate, levity, alleviate

❑ LIBER—free
liberty, liberal, libertarian, libertine

❑ LIG, LECT—choose, gather
eligible, elect, select

❑ LIG, LI, LY—bind
ligament, oblige, religion, liable, liaison, lien, ally

❑ LING, LANG—tongue
lingo, language, linguistics, bilingual

❑ LITER—letter
literate, alliteration, literal

❑ LITH—stone
monolith, lithograph, megalith

❑ LOQU, LOC, LOG—speech, thought
eloquent, loquacious, colloquial, colloquy, soliloquy, circumlocution, interlocutor, monologue, dialogue, eulogy, philology, neologism

❏ LUC, LUM—light
lucid, illuminate, elucidate, pellucid, translucent

❏ LUD, LUS—play
ludicrous, allude, delusion, allusion, illusory

❏ MACRO—great
macrocosm, macrobiotics

❏ MAG, MAJ, MAS, MAX—great
magnify, majesty, master, maximum, magnanimous, magnate, magnitude

❏ MAL—bad
malady, maladroit, malevolent, malodorous

❏ MAN—hand
manual, manuscript, emancipate, manifest

❏ MAR—sea
submarine, marine, maritime

❏ MATER, MATR—mother
maternal, matron, matrilineal

❏ MEDI—middle
intermediary, medieval, mediate

❏ MEGA—great
megaphone, megalomania, megaton, megalith

❏ MEM, MEN—remember
memory, memento, memorabilia, reminisce

❏ METER, METR, MENS—measure
meter, thermometer, perimeter, metronome, commensurate

❏ MICRO—small
microscope, microorganism, microcosm, microbe

❏ MIS—wrong, bad, hate
misunderstand, misanthrope, misapprehension, misconstrue, misnomer, mishap

❏ MIT, MISS—send
transmit, emit, missive

❏ MOLL—soft
mollify, emollient, mollusk

❑ MON, MONIT—warn
admonish, monitor, premonition

❑ MONO—one
monologue, monotonous, monogamy, monolith, monochrome

❑ MOR—custom, manner
moral, mores, morose

❑ MOR, MORT—dead
morbid, moribund, mortal, amortize

❑ MORPH—shape
amorphous, anthropomorphic, metamorphosis, morphology

❑ MOV, MOT, MOB, MOM—move
remove, motion, mobile, momentum, momentous

❑ MUT—change
mutate, mutability, immutable, commute

❑ NAT, NASC—born
native, nativity, natal, neonate, innate, cognate, nascent, renascent, renaissance

❑ NAU, NAV—ship, sailor
nautical, nauseous, navy, circumnavigate

❑ NEG—not, deny
negative, abnegate, renege

❑ NEO—new
neoclassical, neophyte, neologism, neonate

❑ NIHIL—none, nothing
annihilation, nihilism

❑ NOM, NYM—name
nominate, nomenclature, nominal, cognomen, misnomer, ignominious, antonym, homonym, pseudonym, synonym, anonymity

❑ NOX, NIC, NEC, NOC—harm
obnoxious, noxious, pernicious, internecine, innocuous

❑ NOV—new
novelty, innovation, novitiate

❑ NUMER—number
numeral, numerous, innumerable, enumerate

# ROOT APPENDIX

❏ OB—against
obstruct, obdurate, obfuscate, obnoxious, obsequious, obstinate, obstreperous, obtrusive

❏ OMNI—all
omnipresent, omnipotent, omniscient, omnivorous

❏ ONER—burden
onerous, onus, exonerate

❏ OPER—work
operate, cooperate, inoperable

❏ PAC—peace
pacify, pacifist, pacific

❏ PALP—feel
palpable, palpitation

❏ PAN—all
panorama, panacea, panegyric, pandemic, panoply

❏ PATER, PATR—father
paternal, paternity, patriot, compatriot, expatriate, patrimony, patricide, patrician

❏ PATH, PASS—feel, suffer
sympathy, antipathy, empathy, apathy, pathos, impassioned

❏ PEC—money
pecuniary, impecunious, peculation

❏ PED, POD—foot
pedestrian, pediment, expedient, biped, quadruped, tripod

❏ PEL, PULS—drive
compel, compelling, expel, propel, compulsion

❏ PEN—almost
peninsula, penultimate, penumbra

❏ PEND, PENS—hang
pendant, pendulous, compendium, suspense, propensity

❏ PER—through, by, for, throughout
perambulator, percipient, perfunctory, permeable, perspicacious, pertinacious, perturbation, perusal, perennial, peregrinate

❏ PER—against, destruction
perfidious, pernicious, perjure

❑ PERI—around
perimeter, periphery, perihelion, peripatetic

❑ PET—seek, go toward
petition, impetus, impetuous, petulant, centripetal

❑ PHIL—love
philosopher, philanderer, philanthropy, bibliophile, philology

❑ PHOB—fear
phobia, claustrophobia, xenophobia

❑ PHON—sound
phonograph, megaphone, euphony, phonetics, phonics

❑ PLAC—calm, please
placate, implacable, placid, complacent

❑ PON, POS—put, place
postpone, proponent, exponent, preposition, posit, interpose, juxtaposition, depose

❑ PORT—carry
portable, deportment, rapport

❑ POT—drink
potion, potable

❑ POT—power
potential, potent, impotent, potentate, omnipotence

❑ PRE—before
precede, precipitate, preclude, precocious, precursor, predilection, predisposition, preponderance, prepossessing, presage, prescient, prejudice, predict, premonition, preposition

❑ PRIM, PRI—first
prime, primary, primal, primeval, primordial, pristine

❑ PRO—ahead, forth
proceed, proclivity, procrastinator, profane, profuse, progenitor, progeny, prognosis, prologue, promontory, propel, proponent, propose, proscribe, protestation, provoke

❑ PROTO—first
prototype, protagonist, protocol

❑ PROX, PROP—near
approximate, propinquity, proximity

# Root Appendix

- [ ] PSEUDO—false
pseudoscientific, pseudonym

- [ ] PYR—fire
pyre, pyrotechnics, pyromania

- [ ] QUAD, QUAR, QUAT—four
quadrilateral, quadrant, quadruped, quarter, quarantine, quaternary

- [ ] QUES, QUER, QUIS, QUIR—question
quest, inquest, query, querulous, inquisitive, inquiry

- [ ] QUIE—quiet
disquiet, acquiesce, quiescent, requiem

- [ ] QUINT, QUIN—five
quintuplets, quintessence

- [ ] RADI, RAMI—branch
radius, radiate, radiant, eradicate, ramification

- [ ] RECT, REG—straight, rule
rectangle, rectitude, rectify, regular

- [ ] REG —king, rule
regal, regent, interregnum

- [ ] RETRO—backward
retrospective, retroactive, retrograde

- [ ] RID, RIS—laugh
ridiculous, deride, derision

- [ ] ROG—ask
interrogate, derogatory, abrogate, arrogate, arrogant

- [ ] RUD—rough, crude
rude, erudite, rudimentary

- [ ] RUPT—break
disrupt, interrupt, rupture

- [ ] SACR, SANCT—holy
sacred, sacrilege, consecrate, sanctify, sanction, sacrosanct

- [ ] SCRIB, SCRIPT, SCRIV—write
scribe, ascribe, circumscribe, inscribe, proscribe, script, manuscript, scrivener

❑ SE—apart, away
separate, segregate, secede, sedition

❑ SEC, SECT, SEG—cut
sector, dissect, bisect, intersect, segment, secant

❑ SED, SID—sit
sedate, sedentary, supersede, reside, residence, assiduous, insidious

❑ SEM—seed, sow
seminar, seminal, disseminate

❑ SEN—old
senior, senile, senescent

❑ SENT, SENS—feel, think
sentiment, nonsense, assent, sentient, consensus, sensual

❑ SEQU, SECU—follow
sequence, sequel, subsequent, obsequious, obsequy, non sequitur, consecutive

❑ SIM, SEM—similar, same
similar, semblance, dissemble, verisimilitude

❑ SIGN—mark, sign
signal, designation, assignation

❑ SIN—curve
sine curve, sinuous, insinuate

❑ SOL—sun
solar, parasol, solarium, solstice

❑ SOL—alone
solo, solitude, soliloquy, solipsism

❑ SOMN—sleep
insomnia, somnolent, somnambulist

❑ SON—sound
sonic, consonance, dissonance, assonance, sonorous, resonate

❑ SOPH—wisdom
philosopher, sophistry, sophisticated, sophomoric

❑ SPEC, SPIC—see, look
spectator, circumspect, retrospective, perspective, perspicacious

□ SPER—hope
prosper, prosperous, despair, desperate

□ SPERS, SPAR—scatter
disperse, sparse, aspersion, disparate

□ SPIR—breathe
respire, inspire, spiritual, aspire, transpire

□ STRICT, STRING—bind
strict, stricture, constrict, stringent, astringent

□ STRUCT, STRU—build
structure, construe, obstruct

□ SUB—under
subconscious, subjugate, subliminal, subpoena, subsequent, subterranean, subvert

□ SUMM—highest
summit, summary, consummate

□ SUPER, SUR—above
supervise, supercilious, supersede, superannuated, superfluous, insurmountable, surfeit

□ SURGE, SURRECT—rise
surge, resurgent, insurgent, insurrection

□ SYN, SYM—together
synthesis, sympathy, synonym, syncopation, synopsis, symposium, symbiosis

□ TACIT, TIC—silent
tacit, taciturn, reticent

□ TACT, TAG, TANG—touch
tact, tactile, contagious, tangent, tangential, tangible

□ TEN, TIN, TAIN—hold, twist
detention, tenable, tenacious, pertinacious, retinue, retain

□ TEND, TENS, TENT—stretch
intend, distend, tension, tensile, ostensible, contentious

□ TERM—end
terminal, terminus, terminate, interminable

□ TERR—earth, land
terrain, terrestrial, extraterrestrial, subterranean

❑ TEST—witness
testify, attest, testimonial, testament, detest, protestation

❑ THE—god
atheist, theology, apotheosis, theocracy

❑ THERM—heat
thermometer, thermal, thermonuclear, hypothermia

❑ TIM—fear, frightened
timid, intimidate, timorous

❑ TOP—place
topic, topography, utopia

❑ TORT—twist
distort, extort, tortuous

❑ TORP—stiff, numb
torpedo, torpid, torpor

❑ TOX—poison
toxic, toxin, intoxication

❑ TRACT—draw
tractor, intractable, protract

❑ TRANS—across, over, through, beyond
transport, transgress, transient, transitory, translucent, transmutation

❑ TREM, TREP—shake
tremble, tremor, tremulous, trepidation, intrepid

❑ TURB—shake
disturb, turbulent, perturbation

❑ UMBR—shadow
umbrella, umbrage, adumbrate, penumbra

❑ UNI, UN—one
unify, unilateral, unanimous

❑ URB—city
urban, suburban, urbane

❑ VAC—empty
vacant, evacuate, vacuous

❑ VAL, VAIL—value, strength
valid, valor, ambivalent, convalescence, avail, prevail, countervail

❑ VEN, VENT—come
convene, contravene, intervene, venue, convention, circumvent, advent, adventitious

❑ VER—true
verify, verity, verisimilitude, veracious, aver, verdict

❑ VERB—word
verbal, verbose, verbiage, verbatim

❑ VERT, VERS—turn
avert, convert, pervert, revert, incontrovertible, divert, subvert, versatile, aversion

❑ VICT, VINC—conquer
victory, conviction, evict, evince, invincible

❑ VID, VIS—see
evident, vision, visage, supervise

❑ VIL—base, mean
vile, vilify, revile

❑ VIV, VIT—life
vivid, vital, convivial, vivacious

❑ VOC, VOK, VOW—call, word
vocal, equivocate, vociferous, convoke, evoke, invoke, avow

❑ VOL—wish
voluntary, malevolent, benevolent, volition

❑ VOLV, VOLUT—turn, roll
revolve, evolve, convoluted

❑ VOR—eat
devour, carnivore, omnivorous, voracious

# MATH REFERENCE

The math on the GRE covers a lot of ground—from basic algebra to symbol problems to geometry.

Don't let yourself be intimidated. We've highlighted the 75 most important concepts that you need for GRE Math and listed them in this appendix.

Although you probably learned most of this stuff in high school, this list is a great way to refresh your memory.

# GRE MATH REFERENCE
## A CATALOG OF THE MATH YOU NEED TO KNOW

GRE Math tests your understanding of a relatively limited number of mathematical concepts. It is possible to learn all the math you need to know for the GRE in a short time. In fact, you've seen it all before. Listed on the following pages are **75 Things You Need to Know for the GRE**, divided into 3 levels.

**Level 1** is the most basic. You couldn't answer any GRE Math questions if you didn't know Level 1 Math. Most people preparing to take the GRE are already pretty good at Level 1 Math. Look over the Level 1 list below just to make sure you're comfortable with the basics.

**Level 2** is the place for most people to start their review of GRE Math. These skills and formulas come into play quite frequently on the GRE, especially in the medium and hard questions. If you're like a lot of students, your Level 2 Math is probably rusty.

**Level 3** is the hardest math you'll find on the GRE. These are skills and formulas that you might find difficult. Don't spend a lot of time on Level 3 if you still have gaps in Level 2. But once you've about mastered Level 2, then tackling Level 3 can put you over the top.

## LEVEL 1 *(Math you probably already know)*

1. How to add, subtract, multiply, and divide WHOLE NUMBERS

2. How to add, subtract, multiply, and divide FRACTIONS

3. How to add, subtract, multiply, and divide DECIMALS

4. How to convert FRACTIONS TO DECIMALS and DECIMALS TO FRACTIONS

5. How to add, subtract, multiply, and divide POSITIVE AND NEGATIVE NUMBERS

6. How to plot points on the NUMBER LINE

7. How to plug a number into an ALGEBRAIC EXPRESSION

8. How to SOLVE a simple EQUATION

9. How to add and subtract LINE SEGMENTS

10. How to find the THIRD ANGLE of a TRIANGLE, given the other two angles

## LEVEL 2 *(Math you might need to review)*

### 11. How to use the PERCENT FORMULA

Identify the part, the percent, and the whole.

$$Part = percent \times whole$$

> ☞ HINT—You'll usually find the Part near the word "is" and the Whole near the word "of."

**Example:** (Find the part):

What is 12 percent of 25 ?

**Set-up:** Part = $\dfrac{12}{100} \times 25 = 3$

**Example:** (Find the percent):

45 is what percent of 9?

**Set-up:** 45 = Percent $\times$ 9 = 5 $\times$ 9

Percent = 5 $\times$ 100% = 500%

**Example:** (Find the whole): 15 is $\dfrac{3}{5}$ percent of what number?

**Set-up:** $\dfrac{3}{5}$ percent = $\dfrac{3}{500}$

15 = $\dfrac{3}{500} \times$ whole

Whole = 2,500

## 12. How to use the PERCENT INCREASE/ DECREASE FORMULAS

Identify the Original Whole and the Amount of Increase/Decrease.

*Percent increase* = $\dfrac{amount\ of\ increase}{original\ whole} \times 100\%$

*Percent decrease* = $\dfrac{amount\ of\ decrease}{original\ whole} \times 100\%$

**Example:** The price goes up from $80 to $100. What is the percent increase?

**Set-up:** Percent increase = $\dfrac{20}{80} \times 100\% = 25\%$

☞ HINT—Be sure to use the original Whole— not the new whole—for the base.

## 13. How to predict whether a sum, difference, or product will be ODD or EVEN

Don't bother memorizing the rules. Just take simple numbers like 1 and 2 and see what happens.

**Example:** If $m$ is even and $n$ is odd, is the product $mn$ odd or even?

**Set-up:** Say $m = 2$ and $n = 1$.

$2 \times 1$ is even, so $mn$ is even.

## 14. How to recognize MULTIPLES of 2, 3, 4, 5, 6, 9, and 10

2: Last digit is even.
3: Sum of digits is multiple of 3.
4: Last two digits are a multiple of 4.
5: Last digit is 5 or 0.
6: Sum of digits is multiple of 3 AND last digit is even.
9: Sum of digits is multiple of 9.
10: Last digit is 0.

## 15. How to find a COMMON FACTOR

Break both numbers down to their prime factors to see what they have in common.

**Example:** What factors greater than 1 do 135 and 225 have in common?

**Set-up:** $135 = 3 \times 3 \times 3 \times 5$, and $225 = 3 \times 3 \times 5 \times 5$. They share two 3's and a 5. The common factors, then, are 3, 5, $3 \times 3 = 9$, $3 \times 5 = 15$, and $3 \times 3 \times 5 = 45$.

## 16. How to Find a COMMON MULTIPLE

The product is the easiest common multiple to find. If the two numbers have any factors in common, you can divide them out of the product to get a lower common multiple.

**Example:** What is the least common multiple of 28 and 42 ?

**Set-up:** The product $28 \times 42 = 1176$ is a common multiple, but not the least. $28 = 2 \times 2 \times 7$, and $42 = 2 \times 3 \times 7$. They share a 2 and a 7, so divide the product by 2 and then by 7. $1176 \div 2 = 588$. $588 \div 7 = 84$. The least common multiple is 84.

## 17. How to find the AVERAGE

$Average = \dfrac{sum\ of\ terms}{number\ of\ terms}$

## 18. How to use the AVERAGE to find the SUM

*Sum = (average)* $\times$ *(number of terms)*

**Example:** The average (arithmetic mean) of 24 numbers is 17.5. What is the sum?

**Set-up:** Sum = $17.5 \times 24 = 420$

## 19. How to find the AVERAGE of CONSECUTIVE NUMBERS

The average of evenly spaced numbers is simply the average of the smallest number and the largest number.

## 20. How to COUNT CONSECUTIVE NUMBERS

The number of integers from $A$ to $B$ inclusive is $B - A + 1$

**Example:** How many integers are there from 73 through 419, inclusive?

**Set-up:** 419 − 73 + 1 = 347

☞ HINT—Don't forget to add 1.

### 21. How to find the SUM of CONSECUTIVE NUMBERS

*Sum = (average) × (number of terms)*

**Example:** What is the sum of the integers from 10 through 50 inclusive?

**Set-up:** Average = (10 + 50) ÷ 2 = 30; number of terms = 50 − 10 + 1 = 41

Sum = 30 × 41 = 1,230

### 22. How to find the MEDIAN

Put the numbers in numerical order and take the middle number. (If there's an even number of numbers, take the average of the two numbers in the middle.)

### 23. How to find the MODE

Take the number that appears most often. (If there's a tie for most often, then there's more than one mode.)

### 24. How to use actual numbers to determine a RATIO

Identify the quantities to be compared. Either two parts, or a part and a whole.

$$Ratio = \frac{"of"}{"to"}$$

### 25. How to use a ratio to determine an ACTUAL NUMBER

Set up a proportion.

**Example:** The ratio of boys to girls is 3 to 4. If there are 135 boys, how many girls are there?

**Set-up:** $\frac{3}{4} = \frac{135}{x}$

$3 \times x = 4 \times 135$

$x = 180$

### 26. How to use actual numbers to determine a RATE

Identify the quantities and the units to be compared. Keep the units straight.

**Example:** Anders typed 9,450 words in $3\frac{1}{2}$ hours. What was his rate in words per minute?

**Set-up:** First convert $3\frac{1}{2}$ hours to 210 minutes. Then set up the rate with "words" on top and "minutes" on bottom:

$$\frac{9,450 \text{ words}}{210 \text{ minutes}} = 45 \text{ words per minute}$$

☞ HINT—The unit before "per" goes on top, and the unit after "per" goes on the bottom.

### 27. How to deal with TABLES, GRAPHS, and CHARTS

Read the question and all labels extra carefully. Ignore extraneous information and zero in on what's asked for.

### 28. How to count the NUMBER OF POSSIBILITIES

Forget about combinations and permutations formulas. You won't need them on the GRE The number of possibilities is generally so small that the best approach is just to write them out systematically and count them.

**Example:** How many 3-digit numbers can be formed with the digits 1, 3, and 5?

**Set-up:** Write them out. Be systematic so you don't miss any: 135, 153, 315, 351, 513, 531. Count 'em: 6 possibilities.

## 29. How to calculate a simple PROBABILITY

$$Probability = \frac{number\ of\ favorable\ outcomes}{total\ number\ of\ possible\ outcomes}$$

## 30. How to work with new SYMBOLS

If you see a symbol you've never seen before, don't freak out: It's a made-up symbol. Everything you need to know is in the question stem. Just follow the instructions.

## 31. How to SIMPLIFY POLYNOMIALS

First multiply to eliminate all parentheses. Then combine like terms.

## 32. How to FACTOR certain POLYNOMIALS

Learn to spot these classic factorables:

$$ab + ac = a(b + c)$$
$$a^2 + 2ab + b^2 = (a + b)^2$$
$$a^2 - 2ab + b^2 = (a - b)^2$$
$$a^2 - b^2 = (a - b)(a + b)$$

## 33. How to solve for one variable IN TERMS OF another

To find $x$ "in terms of" $y$: isolate $x$ on one side, leaving $y$ as the only variable on the other.

## 34. How to solve an INEQUALITY

Treat it much like an equation — adding, subtracting, multiplying, and dividing both sides by the same thing. Just remember to reverse the inequality sign if you multiply or divide by a negative.

## 35. How to TRANSLATE English into algebra

Look for the key words and systematically turn phrases into algebraic expressions and sentences into equations.

> ☞ HINT—Be extra careful of order when subtraction is called for.

## 36. How to find an ANGLE formed by INTERSECTING LINES

Vertical angles are equal. Adjacent angles add up to 180°.

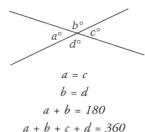

$$a = c$$
$$b = d$$
$$a + b = 180$$
$$a + b + c + d = 360$$

## 37. How to find an angle formed by a TRANSVERSAL across PARALLEL LINES

All the acute angles are equal. All the obtuse angles are equal. An acute plus an obtuse equals 180°. **Example:**

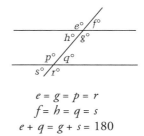

$$e = g = p = r$$
$$f = h = q = s$$
$$e + q = g + s = 180$$

> ☞ HINT — Forget about the terms "alternate interior," "alternate exterior," and "corresponding" angles. The GRE never uses them.

## 38. How to find the AREA of a TRIANGLE

$Area = \frac{1}{2} (base)(height)$

**Example:**

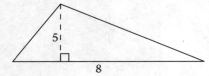

**Set-up:**

$Area = \frac{1}{2} (5)(8) = 20$

☞ **HINT** — You may have to construct an altitude.

## 39. How to work with ISOSCELES TRIANGLES

Isosceles triangles have two equal sides and two equal angles.

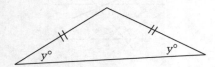

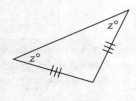

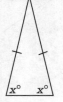

## 40. How to work with EQUILATERAL TRIANGLES

Equilateral triangles have three equal sides and three 60° angles.

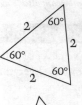

## 41. How to work with SIMILAR TRIANGLES

Corresponding sides are proportional.
Corresponding angles are equal.

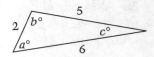

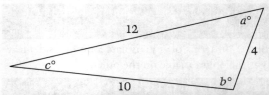

## 42. How to find the HYPOTENUSE or a LEG of a RIGHT TRIANGLE

*Pythagorean theorem:*
$a^2 + b^2 = c^2$

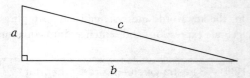

☞ HINT—Most right triangles on the GRE are "special" right triangles (see below), so you can often bypass the Pythagorean theorem.

## 43. How to spot SPECIAL RIGHT TRIANGLES

3-4-5
5-12-13
30-60-90
45-45-90

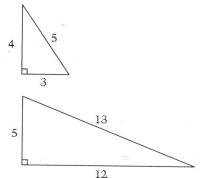

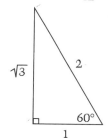

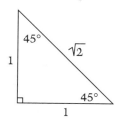

## 44. How to find the PERIMETER of a RECTANGLE

$Perimeter = 2(length + width)$

**Example:**

**Set-up:** Perimeter = 2(2 + 5) = 14

## 45. How to find the AREA of a RECTANGLE

$Area = (length)(width)$

**Example:**

**Set-up:** Area = 2 × 5 = 10

## 46. How to find the AREA of a SQUARE

$Area = (side)^2$

**Example:**

**Set-up:** Area = $3^2$ = 9

## 47. How to find the CIRCUMFERENCE of a CIRCLE

$Circumference = 2\pi r$

**Example:**

**Set-up:** $Circumference = 2\pi(5) = 10\pi$

## 48. How to find the AREA of a CIRCLE

$Area = \pi r^2$

**Example:**

**Set-up:** $Area = \pi \times 5^2 = 25\pi$

## 49. How to find the DISTANCE BETWEEN POINTS on the coordinate plane

If two points have the same $x$'s or the same $y$'s —that is, they make a line segment that is parallel to an axis—all you have to do is subtract the numbers that are different.

**Example:** What is the distance from (2, 3) to (–7, 3) ?

**Set-up:** The $y$'s are the same, so just subtract the $x$'s.

$2 -(-7) = 9.$

If the points have different $x$'s and different $y$'s, make a right triangle and use the Pythagorean theorem.

**Example:** What is the distance from (2, 3) to (–1, –1)?

**Set-up:**

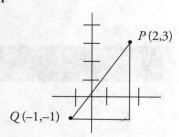

It's a 3-4-5 triangle!

$PQ = 5$

☞ HINT — Look for "special" right triangles.

## 50. How to find the SLOPE of a LINE

$Slope = \dfrac{rise}{run} = \dfrac{change\ in\ y}{change\ in\ x}$

**Example:** What is the slope of the line that contains the points (1, 2) and (4, –5) ?

**Set-up:** $Slope = \dfrac{2-(-5)}{1-4} = -\dfrac{7}{3}$

## LEVEL 3 *(Math you might find difficult)*

## 51. How to determine COMBINED PERCENT INCREASE/DECREASE

Start with 100 and see what happens.

**Example:** A price rises by 10 percent one year and by 20 percent the next. What's the combined percent increase?

**Set-up:** Say the original price is $100.

First year: $100 + (10% of 100)

= 100 + 10 = 110.

Second year: 110 + (20% of 110)

= 110 + 22 = 132.

From 100 to 132 — That's a 32 percent increase.

Think of a 15% increase over $x$ as $1.15x$ and set up an equation.

## 52. How to find the ORIGINAL WHOLE before percent increase/decrease

**Example:** After decreasing by 5 percent, the population is now 57,000. What was the original population?

**Set-up:** $.95 \times$ (Original Population) = 57,000

Original Population = 57,000 ÷ .95 = 60,000

### 53. How to solve a REMAINDERS problem

Pick a number that fits the given conditions and see what happens.

**Example:** When $n$ is divided by 7, the remainder is 5. What is the remainder when $2n$ is divided by 7 ?

**Set-up:** Find a number that leaves a remainder of 5 when divided by 7. A good choice would be 12. If $n = 12$, then $2n = 24$, which when divided by 7 leaves a remainder of 3.

### 54. How to solve a DIGITS problem

Use a little logic — and some trial and error.

**Example:** If $A$, $B$, $C$, and $D$ represent distinct digits in the addition problem below, what is the value of $D$ ?

$$
\begin{array}{r}
AB \\
+ BA \\
\hline
CDC
\end{array}
$$

**Set-up:** Two 2-digit numbers will add up to at most something in the 100's, so $C = 1$. $B$ plus $A$ in the units' column gives a 1, and since it can't simply be that $B + A = 1$, it must be that $B + A = 11$, and a 1 gets carried. In fact, $A$ and $B$ can be just about any pair of digits that add up to 11 (3 and 8, 4 and 7, etc.), but it doesn't matter what they are, they always give you the same thing for $D$:

$$
\begin{array}{cc}
47 & 83 \\
+74 & +38 \\
\hline
121 & 121
\end{array}
$$

### 55. How to find a WEIGHTED AVERAGE

Give each term the appropriate "weight."

**Example:** The girls' average score is 30. The boys' average score is 24. If there are twice as many boys as girls, what is the overall average?

**Set-up:**

$$
\text{Weighted Avg.} = \frac{1 \times 30 + 2 \times 24}{3} = \frac{78}{3} = 26
$$

☞ HINT—Don't just average the averages.

### 56. How to find the NEW AVERAGE when a number is added or deleted

Use the sum.

**Example:** Michael's average score after 4 tests is 80. If he scores 100 on the fifth test, what is his new average?

**Set-up:** Find the original sum from the original average:
Original sum $= 4 \times 80 = 320$
Add the fifth score to make the New Sum:
New sum $= 320 + 100 = 420$
Find the new average from the new sum:

$$
\text{New average} = \frac{420}{5} = 84
$$

### 57. How to use the ORIGINAL AVERAGE and NEW AVERAGE to figure out WHAT WAS ADDED OR DELETED

Use the sums.

*Number added = (new sum) − (original sum)*
*Number deleted = (original sum) − (new sum)*

**Example:** The average of 5 numbers is 2. After 1 number is deleted, the new average is −3. What number was deleted?

**Set-up:** Find the original sum from the original average:

Original sum $= 5 \times 2 = 10$

Find the new sum from the new average:

New sum $= 4 \times (-3) = -12$

The difference is the answer.

Number deleted $= 10 - (-12) = 22$

# Math Reference Appendix

## 58. How to find an AVERAGE RATE

Convert to totals.

$$Average\ A\ per\ B = \frac{Total\ A}{Total\ B}$$

**Example:** If the first 500 pages have an average of 150 words per page, and the remaining 100 pages have an average of 450 words per page, what is the average number of words per page for the entire 600 pages?

**Set-up:** Total pages = 500 + 100 = 600

Total words = 500 × 150 + 100 × 450

= 120,000

Average words per page = $\frac{120,000}{600}$ = 200

$$Average\ speed = \frac{total\ distance}{total\ time}$$

**Example:** Rosa drove 120 miles one way at an average speed of 40 miles per hour and returned by the same 120-mile route at an average speed of 60 miles per hour. What was Rosa's average speed for the entire 240-mile round trip?

**Set-up:** To drive 120 miles at 40 mph takes 3 hours. To return at 60 mph takes 2 hours. The total time, then, is 5 hours.

Average speed = $\frac{240\ miles}{5\ hours}$ = 48 mph

☞ HINT—Don't just average the rates.

## 59. How to determine a COMBINED RATIO

Multiply one or both ratios by whatever you need to in order to get the terms they have in common to match.

**Example:** The ratio of $a$ to $b$ is 7:3 . The ratio of $b$ to $c$ is 2:5. What is the ratio of $a$ to $c$?

**Set-up:** Multiply each member of $a$:$b$ by 2 and multiply each member of $b:c$ by 3 and you get $a$:$b$ = 14:6 and $b$:$c$ = 6:15. Now that the $b$'s match, you can just take $a$ and $c$ and say $a$:$c$ = 14:15.

## 60. How to MULTIPLY/DIVIDE POWERS

Add/subtract the exponents.

$$x^a \times x^b = x^{(a+b)} \qquad 2^3 \times 2^4 = 2^7$$

$$\frac{x^c}{x^d} = x^{(c-d)} \qquad \frac{5^6}{5^2} = 5^4$$

## 61. How to RAISE A POWER TO A POWER

Multiply the exponents.

$$(x^a)^b = x^{ab} \qquad (3^4)^5 = 3^{20}$$

## 62. How to ADD, SUBTRACT, MULTIPLY, and DIVIDE ROOTS

You can add/subtract roots only when the parts inside the $\sqrt{\phantom{x}}$ are identical.

**Example:.** $\sqrt{2} + 3\sqrt{2} = 4\sqrt{2}$

$\sqrt{2} - 3\sqrt{2} = -2\sqrt{2}$

$\sqrt{2} + \sqrt{3}$ — cannot be combined.

To multiply/divide, deal with what's inside the $\sqrt{\phantom{x}}$ and outside the $\sqrt{\phantom{x}}$ separately.

**Example:**

$$(2\sqrt{3})(7\sqrt{5}) = (2 \times 7)(\sqrt{3 \times 5}) = 14\sqrt{15}$$

$$\frac{10\sqrt{21}}{5\sqrt{3}} = \frac{10}{5}\sqrt{\frac{21}{3}} = 2\sqrt{7}$$

## 63. How to SIMPLIFY A SQUARE ROOT

Look for perfect squares (4, 9, 16, 25, 36,...) inside the $\sqrt{\phantom{x}}$ . Factor them out and "unsquare" them.

**Example:**

$$\sqrt{48} = \sqrt{16} \times \sqrt{3} = 4\sqrt{3}$$

$$\sqrt{180} = \sqrt{36} \times \sqrt{5} = 6\sqrt{5}$$

## 64. How to solve certain QUADRATIC EQUATIONS

Forget the quadratic formula. Manipulate the equation (if necessary) into the "_____ = 0" form, factor the left side, and break the quadratic into two simple equations.

> Example: $x^2 + 6 = 5x$
> $x^2 - 5x + 6 = 0$
> $(x - 2)(x - 3) = 0$
> $x - 2 = 0$ or $x - 3 = 0$
> $x = 2$ or $3$

> Example: $x^2 = 9$
>
> $x = 3$ or $-3$

☞ HINT—Watch out for $x^2$. There can be two solutions.

## 65. How to solve MULTIPLE EQUATIONS

When you see two equations with two variables on the GRE, they're probably easy to combine in such a way that you get something closer to what you're looking for.

> Example: If $5x - 2y = -9$ and $3y - 4x = 6$, what is the value of $x + y$?

> Set-up: The question doesn't ask for $x$ and $y$ separately, so don't solve for them separately if you don't have to. Look what happens if you just rearrange a little and "add" the equations:

> $5x - 2y = -9$
>
> $-4x + 3y = 6$
> _____
> $x + y = -3$

☞ HINT—Don't do more work than you have to. Look for the shortcut.

## 66. How to find the MAXIMUM and MINIMUM lengths for a SIDE of a TRIANGLE

If you know two sides of a triangle, then you know that the third side is somewhere between the difference and the sum.

> Example: The length of one side of a triangle is 7. The length of another side is 3. What is the range of possible lengths for the third side?

> Set-up: The third side is greater than the difference ($7 - 3 = 4$) and less than the sum ($7 + 3 = 10$).

## 67. How to find one angle or the sum of all the ANGLES of a REGULAR POLYGON

> *Sum of the interior angles in a polygon with $n$ sides =*
> $(n - 2) \times 180$

> *Degree measure of one angle in a Regular Polygon with $n$ sides =*
> $$\frac{(n - 2) \times 180}{n}$$

> Example: What is the measure of one angle of a regular pentagon?

> Set-up: Plug $n = 5$ into the formula:

> Degree measure of One Angle =
> $$\frac{(5 - 2) \times 180}{5} = \frac{540}{5} = 108$$

## 68. How to find the LENGTH of an ARC

Think of an arc as a fraction of the circle's circumference.

> *Length of arc $= \dfrac{n}{360} \times 2\pi r$*

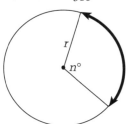

### 69. How to find the AREA of a SECTOR

Think of a sector as a fraction of the circle's area.

$$Area\ of\ sector = \frac{n}{360} \times \pi r^2$$

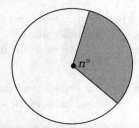

### 70. How to find the dimensions or area of an INSCRIBED or CIRCUMSCRIBED FIGURE

Look for the connection. Is the diameter the same as a side or a diagonal?

**Example:** If the area of the square is 36, what is the circumference of the circle?

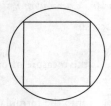

**Set-up:** To get the circumference, you need the diameter or radius. The circle's diameter is also the square's diagonal, which (it's a 45-45-90 triangle!) is $6\sqrt{2}$

Circumference = $\pi$(diameter) = $6\pi\sqrt{2}$

### 71. How to find the VOLUME of a RECTANGULAR SOLID

$$Volume = length \times width \times height$$

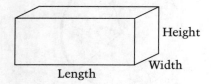

### 72. How to find the SURFACE AREA of a RECTANGULAR SOLID

$$Surface\ area =$$
$$2(length \times width + length \times height + width \times height)$$

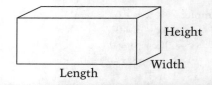

### 73. How to find the DIAGONAL of a RECTANGULAR SOLID

Use the Pythagorean theorem twice.

**Example:** What is the length of $AG$?

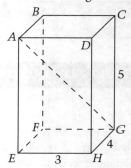

**Set-up:** Draw diagonal $AC$.

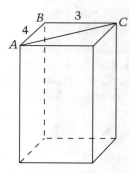

$ABC$ is a 3-4-5 triangle, so $AC = 5$. Now look at triangle $ACG$:

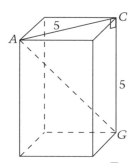

It's a 45-45-90, so $AG = 5\sqrt{2}$

## 74. How to find the VOLUME of a CYLINDER

$Volume = \pi r^2 h$

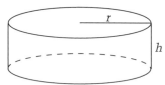

## 75. How to find the VOLUME of a SPHERE

$Volume = \dfrac{4}{3} \pi r^3$

# ABOUT THE AUTHORS

**Jose Ferreira** was formerly Kaplan's National GRE Product Director. In 1993, he invented a GRE test strategy so powerful that ETS had to remove the question-type—pattern identifications—from the test.

**Gretchen VanEsselstyn** has been a writer and editor for Kaplan for four years and she is currently Associate Director of Product Technology. Gretchen is also a writer of fiction and her plans include starting a magazine and maybe someday getting that @*%^# doctorate.

# ABOUT KAPLAN

## Kaplan: Looking Forward to Your Future

There are points in life when you need to reach an important goal. Whether your goal is a high score on a critical test, admission to a competitive school, or applying for funding for education, Kaplan will help you get there. Kaplan is the largest test preparation company and one of the largest private education companies in the nation. We're a wholly-owned subsidiary of The Washington Post Company, which also owns *Newsweek*. Through our legendary courses and expanding catalog of products and services, we've already helped more than 2 million students get ahead. We can help you and your family, too.

## Test Prep

The world leader in test preparation, Kaplan will help you get a higher score on standardized tests such as the PSAT, SAT, and ACT for college, the LSAT, MCAT, GMAT, and GRE for graduate school, professional licensing exams for medicine, nursing, dentistry, and accounting, and specialized exams for international students and professionals.

## School Selection and Admissions

Kaplan offers expert advice on how to find the college, graduate school, or professional school that's right for you. We also reveal how to maximize your chances of getting into that school, by showing you step-by-step how to conduct an effective admissions campaign.

## Financial Aid

With the price of higher education skyrocketing, it's essential that you get your share of financial aid and figure out how you're going to pay your share of the total cost. Kaplan's financial aid experts walk you through this often-bewildering application process and show you how you can afford college or graduate school.

## Kaplan: Tools for Real Life

Kaplan provides information via the latest interactive technologies, for every stage of your life and for every level of commitment. Here's a glimpse of the resources Kaplan puts at your disposal:

## Live Courses

Kaplan's founder started coaching students for tests over 55 years ago, bucking a system that didn't believe—or didn't want you to know—that you can drastically improve your scores on standardized tests. Now, with 160 permanent centers and approximately 750 satellite classrooms nationwide, we're the acknowledged leader in test prep. Kaplan enrolls more than 150,000 students annually in our live courses, which offer the most comprehensive preparation available.

## Books

Kaplan offers the best-written, easiest-to-use books for students headed to college and graduate school. Our growing library of titles includes guides for test preparation, selection, admissions, and financial aid.

## Software

With innovative products for college and graduate school preparation, Kaplan sets the standard for educational software. Our groundbreaking RoadTrip™ test-prep software, available on disk and CD-ROM, offers timed tests and performance analysis at new levels of sophistication and thoroughness. Our On Campus™ CD-ROM set is the ultimate multimedia college guide, offering all the facts you need on more than 1,700 schools, exciting animation, and video tours.

## Online Services

Kaplan's top-ranked site on the Internet's World Wide Web, innovative site on America Online, and our newest site on the MSN™ online service offer test and admissions advice, chat areas, conferences, links to relevant sites, and plenty of downloadable text files, games, and software. It's the best academic information available by modem.

## Student Loans

Through KapLoan, The Kaplan Student Information Program, we can help students get information and advice about educational loans for college and graduate school. Through an affiliation with one of the nation's largest student loan providers, you can access valuable information and guidance on federally-insured parent and student loans. Kaplan directs you to the financing you need to reach your educational goals.

## Kaplan: Here

Want more information about any of our services and products or about the nearest Kaplan Center?

## By Telephone

Call our nationwide toll-free numbers:
1–800–KAP–TEST (for information on our live courses)
1–800–KAP–ITEM (for information on our products)
1–800–KAP–1057 (for information on student loans)

## By Modem

Connect with us in cyberspace:
On AOL, keyword "Kaplan"
On the Internet's World Wide Web, open "http://www.kaplan.com"
On The MSN™ online service, Go Word "KAPLAN"
Via e-mail, "info@kaplan.com"

## By Snail Mail

Write to: Kaplan Educational Centers,
810 Seventh Avenue,
New York, NY 10019.

*RoadTrip™ is a trademark of Stanley H. Kaplan Educational Center Ltd. All rights reserved. On Campus™ is a trademark of Meetinghouse Technologies. All rights reserved.*

FOR SOFTWARE HELP, CALL
THE KAPLAN TECH SUPPORT
LINE AT 1-800-591-8400

## Software Installation Instructions

**\*Windows™ Version**
1. Insert diskette in your floppy disk drive.
2. Start Windows™ and select Run from the Program Manager File menu.
3. Type a:\install.exe in the Command Line text box that appears.
4. Click OK.
5. Follow the directions on the screen.

At one point in the installation, the program will go to DOS to expand some files, and will return to Windows™ when finished. It will set up a Program Manager group with a KAPLAN icon in it.

**\*\*Macintosh® Version**
1. Insert diskette in your floppy disk drive.
2. Double click on the application icon.
3. A dialogue will appear with the message "Select Destination Folder... ." Select the volume (and folder) where you want to install the application, then select "Extract."
4. A progress dialogue will show you the progress of the install. After the install is completed, remove the floppy disk from the drive.

### System Requirements

*Requirements for Macintosh® Version:*
- 68020 CPU or higher
- 4 MB of RAM or greater
- 3.5" high density floppy drive
- Hard disk with 3.0 MB of available space
- Display:
  640 x 400 screen or higher
  16 colors (or gray scale) or higher
- System 7.01 or higher

*Requirements for Windows™ Version:*
- 386SX CPU or higher
- 4 MB of RAM or greater
- 3.5" high density floppy drive
- Hard disk with 6.5 MB of available space
- VGA or better display:
  640 x 480 screen or higher
  16 colors (or gray scale) or higher
- Windows™ 3.1 in 386 Enhanced mode or higher

\*Windows™ is a trademark of Microsoft Corporation
\*\*Macintosh® is a trademark of Apple Computer, Inc.